BIG BLUE DAYS

BIG BLUE DAYS

**The Story of a Small-Town Football Dynasty
in Swampscott, Massachusetts**

By Robert E. Jauron

Peter E. Randall Publisher
Portsmouth, NH
2018

ISBN13: 978-1-937721-55-8
Library of Congress Control Number: 2018930418

Published by
Peter E. Randall Publisher
PO Box 4726
Portsmouth NH 03802

Photo credits are based on reasonably available source information. Photographs for which such information was unavailable or incomplete were likely produced by some of the people or publications recognized in the Acknowledgments.

Dust cover and frontispiece images: Coach Bondelevitch and Bill Adams. 1968 *Seagull*; Dick Jauron running against Marblehead. 1967 *Seagull*; Mike Lynch kicking winning field goal against Marblehead in 1969. Donald T. Young photo, courtesy *Boston Herald*. Back of dust cover: Blocksidge Field. 2016 author photo; George Blais eluding opponent. 1959 *Seagull*.

Book design by Tim Holtz

In memory of my parents, Robert and Katherine Jauron, who, in addition to giving us so much else, made it possible for my siblings and me to experience many Big Blue days.

Contents

Acknowledgments   ix

Preface   xiii

The '50s

Time for a Change   1

A Breath of Fresh Air   7

1953   Giant Killers   16

1954   Sculpins No More   26

1955   You Couldn't Hit Him with a Handful of Raisins   40

1956   A Cure for Fumbleitis   48

1957   The Fairytale Season   59

1958   Anything You Can Do, We Can Do Better   77

1959   Tough as Nails   89

The '60s

1960   The Woburn "World Series"   109

1961   The Sad Season   119

1962   Our Tiny Country School   131

1963   The Gritty Champs   150

1964   Harvard and Yale can move over—this is THE GAME!   164

Contents

1965 The Aberrant Season   173

1966 The Bandito Resurgence   187

1967 Dickie, Speed, and the Harpooned Whale   211

1968 Juggernaut   235

1969 Determined to Do Well   255

The '70s

1970 Homegrown Heartbreaker   275

1971 I Wonder Who Will Beat This Team   292

1972 Super Champs   304

1973 End of the Reign   322

Epilogue   337

Appendix A—The Record   353

Appendix B—Undefeated Teams   354

Appendix C—All-Stars (1953–1973)   362

Notes   363

Index   377

Acknowledgments

This is a work of nonfiction. The people and events are real. Statistical information is derived from published reports and articles. However, this book also contains some stories that can be fairly described as anecdotal. While I have made an effort to be accurate in the re-telling; memories, especially of matters from the distant past, are necessarily imperfect and individuals will often have differing and sometimes conflicting recollections of the same event. Factual errors, to the extent they exist, are regretted and unintended.

Thanks to all who consented to interviews or otherwise offered recollections, materials and/or assistance. They include Bill Adams, Lloyd Benson, David Bondelevitch, Steve Bulpett, Bill Bush, Don Cahoon, Bob Carlin, Frank Challant, Keith Chevalier, Roger Coe, Marv Cohen, Jeff Collier, Janet Juel Cook, David Corcoran, Ron Corcoran, Gary Cordette, Walter Costello, Sally Bondelevitch DeCost, Richard Dedrick, Frank DeFelice, Mickey DePaolo, Ray DiPietro, Mike DiPrisco, John Flanagan, Richard Fuller, Louis Gallo, Barry Gallup, Tom Gorman, Dick Gowen, Ted Grant, Doug Haley, Woody Harper, Bob Hopkins, Jim Hughes, Norman Jacobs, Mike Janvrin, Dick Jauron, Kacy Jauron, Michael Jauron, Susan Jauron, Nancy Bondelevitch Joy, Carl Kester, Al King, Michael Kramer, Steve Kruger, Ed Loveday, Mike Lynch, Jack Milo, Jim Morash, Arthur Palleschi, Mike Powers, Andy Rose, Bruce Savatsky, Gary Savatsky, Winslow Shaw, David Shribman, Peter Shribman, Bill Sjogren, John Squires, Mark Stevenson, Myron Stone, Jack Taymore, Sandy Tennant, Randy Werner, Dick Winick, Nelson Woodfork, Jai Wurfbain, Fran York, and Barbara Segel Yozell.

Several gentlemen merit special recognition for going above and beyond with volunteered time and help. Thank you, Coach Richard Lynch, for multiple interview sessions and a zillion entertaining and/or illuminating tales from what you deem "the golden era." Thanks, Dr. Jack Resch, for your generous, thorough review, many questions, and highly valuable and detailed editorial assistance.

Shortly after I embarked on this project, I approached then-Swampscott High School coach Steve Dembowski and asked if he knew the identity of the author of "The Fairytale of 1957," an entertaining and informative short summary of the 1957 football season anonymously posted on the Swampscott football website. The coach recalled that the piece had been written by Jim Gorman and gave me his phone number. One of the best things that I did to make this book a reality was pick up my phone in May of 2015, dial that number, and introduce myself to Mr. Gorman. Jim offered more help than I could have reasonably expected and pulled in his good friend, former SHS basketball captain and publishing professional, Bob "Gump" Gormley. Together they served as a sounding board during the many months that I worked on this project—always there with encouragement, humor and countless shared recollections, reviews of drafts and suggestions. Thank you, guys!

In performing necessary research, I spent many hours scanning microfilm of old issues of the *Daily Evening Item* newspaper in the Lynn Public Library. I also spent time tracking down information in the Swampscott, Acton, Hudson, Maynard, Salem, and Newburyport public libraries, the Swampscott High School Library, the Saint Anselm College Library, and the Marblehead Historical Society Archives. I am grateful to those institutions and the librarians and archivists who offered assistance.

Thanks to the *Swampscott Reporter*, the *Danvers Herald*, the *Salem News*, the *Boston Globe*, and the *Boston Herald* for portions of articles and/or photographs reproduced or referenced herein. Thanks also to Swampscott Superintendent of Schools Pamela Angelakis and Swampscott High School Principal Robert Murphy for their cooperation and assistance in allowing me free access to, and use of, photographs and other materials contained in the high school yearbooks ("*Seagulls*") and magazines ("*Swampscottas*").

I am especially grateful to the *Daily Item,* formerly the *Daily Evening Item* (the "*Item*"), for having so extensively covered and reported on the Swampscott High School and North Shore sports scene over the years and for permitting me to reproduce in this book some of the results of such coverage. In addition to quoting from numerous *Item* articles, and reproducing photographs and/or illustrations, I have relied on the newspaper as the primary source for statistics and many of the other details of high school football games described in this book. This story could not exist had it not been for the preserved writing and work product of sports writers of the past. In a very real sense, the book also serves as a tribute to those individuals who, through their work, recorded sports history.

I much appreciate all of the help provided by the professionals with Peter E. Randall Publisher.

Thanks to my wife Sally, daughters Kathy, Laurie, and Caroline, and the rest of the family for helping me find the time and space necessary to complete this undertaking and for your constant understanding and support.

Finally, the people written about in this book represent a small percentage of the thousands of players, students, coaches, parents, teachers, and Boosters who collectively helped to make the 1953–1973 period in Swampscott a special time in a special place. Whether or not individually mentioned, every person who played on, or supported, any of the high school teams during that era contributed to *Big Blue Days*.

Preface

Thanksgiving morning, 1966. I ran the hook pattern, turned, and caught the pass. Immediately someone hit me from behind. As I started to go down, my brother Dick sprinted into view. As planned, I tossed the ball back toward him before hitting the ground. Commonly referred to as a "hook and lateral," in our offense the play was the "Happy Jack Pass," dubbed such by our coach, Stan Bondelevitch.

The gimmicky play was designed for a desperate situation. We faced one, trailing Marblehead 22–21, with the ball not even over midfield and time running out. Hopefully, the defensive backs would converge on me and not react in time as I pitched it to Dick. Though only a sophomore, he was our most explosive player, capable of going the distance if given the slightest opening. But it failed. Perhaps our timing was off or our opponents simply did a great job defending. In any case, we were finished. I heard a whistle, looked up and saw the "Headers" celebrating.

The game ended. Knowing that I would never again have the chance to beat Marblehead on Thanksgiving, I sensed that this would be the game I'd recall most bitterly in future years. And I was regretting that a special time was coming to a close. Twelve days earlier, our dreams of an unbeaten season and championship had been shattered by powerhouse Newburyport. Now we had also lost the traditional season-ending game to our archrivals.

As of that time, Bondy, as he was often called, had a splendid record as Swampscott High School's coach. Thirteen of his fourteen teams had finished with winning seasons. Three had been undefeated and won state championships. But we were a senior-laden squad. Swampscott's fans had to be wondering when their school might again contend for a title. In fact, it did not take long.

In the seven seasons immediately following that disappointing Thanksgiving morning, the high school team from the little town of Swampscott, Massachusetts, clinched seven conference titles, finished unbeaten five times, and won four Eastern Massachusetts Class B championships and the first Eastern Massachusetts High School Super Bowl game. Over a 16-year span from 1957 through 1972, the teams coached by Stan Bondelevitch and key assistant Dick Lynch finished with perfect records eight times. Three of the boys on the 1967 roster eventually went on to multi-year careers as NFL players. At one point, Swampscott's Big Blue owned a record of 59–1. In 1976, one local newspaper reported that Bondy's announced retirement brought to an end "the greatest coaching era in the history of New England schoolboy football."

He inevitably became "legendary coach" Stan Bondelevitch. Sports writers will deem a coach legendary based on an extraordinary career record of wins and championships. Yet, even without such a remarkable record, Bondy would have been a legend in Swampscott. He was more than a coach. In some respects, he was a consummate salesman. His genius lay not so much in command of the intricacies of football strategy and the so-called "x's & o's" as in an uncanny ability to promote, persuade, and motivate individuals, groups, and, ultimately, an entire community.

He was far from perfect. But any shortcomings were eclipsed by his positives. Colorful and entertaining, he inspired a generation of kids, hundreds of whom he helped in numerous ways. *Reader's Digest* magazine had run a longstanding regular feature titled "The Most Unforgettable Character I Ever Met." For me, and I suspect many others in Swampscott, that was Stanley W. Bondelevitch.

As incredible as Swampscott's records were during the Bondelevitch era, there have been high school programs with longer winning streaks. Yet in some respects, it is hard to imagine anything quite like what was experienced in Swampscott. This was not Texas, western Pennsylvania, or some other long-established football hotbed known for its development of dominating players and teams. It was a quiet little seaside town on Boston's North Shore. After Bondy arrived, interest and involvement in the high school football program grew to the point that it played a central role in the life of the community.

While playing football can be physically and emotionally challenging, Bondy often found ways to make even practices enjoyable. He liked to say that playing the game was fun, but playing and winning was much more fun. At times, Big Blue football almost seemed like a three-ring circus, with the smiling, wise-cracking, gregarious coach acting as both ring-master and featured attraction. And through it all, hundreds of teenagers learned lessons that served them well in later life.

The educational value of secondary school athletics is too often over-looked or trivialized. Sports and other so-called "extra-curricular activities" are treated as superfluous luxuries that can be pared down or jettisoned in an age of tight budgets and waning interests. However, for numerous adolescents, their most valuable, enduring learning experiences were, and should continue to be, those associated with such activities. Their most memorable teachers were, and should continue to be, some of the men and women devoted to coaching young people. That was clearly the case for many of the boys who played football in Swampscott during the period between 1953 and 1973. They look back now and recall it as a special time in a special place. This is a story about that special place and about the players and the men who coached them in those bygone days.

The '50s

The 1957 undefeated Big Blue team at Miami's Sorrento Hotel.
Courtesy Richard Winick

Time for a Change

The cupola with its green spire, now faded and crumbling, still marks the highest point in the small seaside town. It rests precariously atop a sad old brick building that sits vacant and neglected on a hill high above Swampscott Harbor. The abandoned edifice is silent and still. But it was not always so. Once it was alive with hundreds of youthful voices. A bell would ring, triggering an eruption of noise and activity as seas of teenage boys and girls poured out of classrooms and flooded the corridors. Hallway lockers were opened and closed and shouts and laughter reverberated. Then a second bell rang, the youthful flood receded, teachers shut the doors, and the only sounds heard in the empty halls were faint, muffled voices from within the classrooms. The old relic was once the home of Swampscott High School. It witnessed the hopes and dreams, joys and sorrows, and triumphs and failures of generations of students and their teachers.

In the fall when the final bell signaled the end of another school day, the high school's athletes hustled off to Phillips Park for practice with their respective teams. The majority, lacking cars or rides, trooped down Greenwood Avenue to Humphrey Street where they could gaze across the blue waters of Nahant Bay to the Boston skyline, some 15 miles distant. Turning left, they continued past Fisherman's Beach, the Surf Theatre, and the historic Fish House, the community's most famous landmark. They then passed the well-worn executive golf course behind the once grand New Ocean House Hotel before arriving at the Veterans Memorial Fieldhouse and Phillips Park.

The Fieldhouse still stands today, just beyond a short road called Bondelevitch Way. That road leads to the parking lot behind Blocksidge Field, home of Swampscott's Big Blue football team. But the road was not

1

always Bondelevitch Way, and Blocksidge Field was not always the home of the Big Blue. Back in 1952, it was the home of the Sculpins.

Sculpins are inactive, bottom-dwelling fish. They have little value to humans, except that some have been used to bait lobster traps. They are also strikingly unattractive. In the early 1950s, the high school football team seemed to be living down to the lowly image of those creatures. The Swampscott Sculpins suffered one ugly defeat after another, and they slunk along at the bottom of the Northeastern Conference standings.

Popular longtime head coach Harold Martin had thrown in the towel after the 1950 season. Martin was replaced by a man named Harry Lehman. Harry had previously coached at several schools in New Hampshire. Coach Lehman's Swampscott teams were spectacularly unsuccessful. The 1951 squad failed to win a single game, was outscored 267 to 55, and was humiliated by powerhouse Amesbury, 54–0. The misery continued through 1952. The Sculpins managed to win just one game, against what the local newspaper, Lynn's *Daily Evening Item* (the "*Item*"), described as "a crippled Methuen team that most any school could have defeated over the telephone." Prior to the Methuen win, Swampscott had lost 22 consecutive games. During one particularly ugly five-game stretch, the Sculpins were outscored 109 to 0. The record for the two-year period was 1–18.

After the abysmal 1952 season, the *Item* reported that a reluctant school committee had announced that Harry Lehman, "the former wizard of the New Hampshire sticks of Plymouth," would be retired from the town payroll. A search was undertaken for a new coach who might be able to at least restore some level of respectability to the football program. It was time for a change.

While the Swampscott football team had been struggling through a miserable season, a man in a town some 30 miles away was coaching another high school squad to an unblemished, 10–0 record. His given name was Stanley Walter Bandalewicz. He had been born in Boston on March 29, 1918, the third and final child of immigrants from Eastern Europe. His parents were Walter Bandalewicz and Mary Kasparowicz Bandalewicz. Walter was of Polish descent and had reportedly been a decorated veteran of the Russian army, having fought in the Russo-Japanese War of 1904–05. Mary Kasparowicz was Lithuanian. Family lore was that she had broken off an engagement to a count or some other high personage and run off with Walter to America. Whatever their motives for leaving, the couple eventually arrived in the United States where, like millions of other European immigrants, they struggled to build a new life.

They settled in a poor section of Boston where Walter worked for a time as a laborer, possibly in a rubber factory. Then, while Stanley was still quite young, his parents moved the family to a farm in Acton, Massachusetts. Thereafter, for the remainder of his life, Walter Bandalewicz operated the farm, which was productive enough to provide a reasonable living for the family.

Stanley's parents had little formal education. Both were essentially illiterate. Polish and a smattering of Russian, Lithuanian, and Yiddish were spoken in the Bandalewicz home. Walter and Mary would never be able to speak or understand much English. Prior to commencement of formal schooling in Acton, young Stanley's exposure to spoken English was therefore limited to what he was able to pick up from his older siblings and playmates. Perhaps due to some public record-keeping error, the family name was transformed into Bondelevitch well before Stanley's high school years.

As a youth in Acton, Stanley Bondelevitch discovered athletics and ultimately excelled as a running back on the high school football team. His gridiron exploits eventually earned him a chance for a scholarship to attend Saint Anselm College in Manchester, New Hampshire. But Walter strongly resisted the plan. He urged the boy to remain in Acton and follow in his footsteps as a farmer. Perhaps recognizing that further formal education would be essential in providing him with greater opportunities in life, Stanley defied his father and enrolled at Saint Anselm in 1937.

By that point, he had developed a husky build. At six feet and weighing around 180 pounds, he seemed to fit the profile of an end and was moved to that position during his first season with the Saint Anselm football team. The dispute with Walter had been sufficiently serious that, for a period of time, father and son did not speak with one another. That changed after his parents attended one of his college football games. When Walter heard the roar of approval from the large crowd after his son made a good play, he apparently decided that the boy's choice of college and football over farming might not have been such a bad decision. Father and son reconciled.

At Saint Anselm, Stan was frequently referred to as "the Count," possibly as a result of the tale of his mother's broken engagement. At some point an additional nickname, spelled both "Bondy" and "Bondi," surfaced. In 1938, he played on an undefeated squad led by future Chicago Bears star Ray "Scooter" McLean. The Count played well enough during his senior season to earn recognition on an All-New England team. According to the November 23, 1940, Saint Anselm v. American International College game program, "Playing at end, Bondi has shown his ability on the defense by smashing up end sweeps and getting down under punts. The team clown, he can be counted on for a laugh to relieve tension in tight spots."

In addition to football, Stan participated in a number of other activities, particularly those relating to the performing arts. The history major was not only a member of the college glee club and choir; he directed and performed in a well-received musical revue during his senior year. Recognized as "best natured" by his senior classmates, the profile of Stan Bondelevitch from his college days matched that of the coach and mentor that hundreds of high school boys would come to recognize in future years. Bondy was rugged but good-natured, funny and entertaining. He loved to perform and seemed to enjoy, if not crave, attention. He knew how to lead and direct. Throughout his life, Stan Bondelevitch would remain grateful for his Saint Anselm education.

Following his 1941 graduation, and amidst growing concern that America could be drawn into the war that was raging in Europe, Stan enlisted in the naval reserve. In November, he accepted appointment as an aviation cadet and commenced training to become a pilot. His dream of becoming a flyboy ended when he crashed a plane during a training mission, destroying the aircraft and seriously injuring himself. He was hospitalized for a lengthy period and then discharged in March of 1942 for failure to qualify as physically fit for further flight training. In later years, Stan suggested that the dual cause of the crash was a mechanical problem and his own "hot-dogging."

He recovered from his injuries and was able to play some semi-professional football with the Providence Steamrollers before resuming military service, entering the army in April of 1943. He remained stateside throughout his 33-month stint, assigned as an armorer and athletic instructor. During that period, among other duties, he played two seasons of army football, while also coaching the line. In addition, he briefly taught history and English.

After his honorable discharge in January of 1946, Stan returned to the Acton area and managed to secure a position teaching history and coaching high school football in nearby Maynard. He expected that the job would be temporary because he planned to attend law school. A legal career, particularly as a trial lawyer, seemed to make sense. He had a logical mind, a great sense of humor, and a flair for the dramatic. He was a gifted speaker who could use his strong voice to maximum persuasive effect. He was also someone who relished an audience. And Stan was personable, competitive, and ambitious. He was driven to become one of life's winners. With such qualities, he appeared to be well-suited for a career in trial practice, sales, or even theatre.

However, by the end of his first year in Maynard he had decided to stay with coaching. The work gave him an opportunity to make use of all of the traits and skills, and pursue all of the interests, that would have made him successful in many fields. Moreover, it afforded a chance to remain connected with a sport that he loved while teaching young people valuable lessons. Through coaching, he could influence the lives of hundreds of boys in a way that his high school and college coaches and teachers had influenced his. Stan had found his calling.

In 1946 Stan took over a Maynard High School team that had won only two games the year before. In his first season as coach, the team won five times. Coaching seemed natural. In fact, he thought it was almost too easy. "Why should I work for a living when I can coach?" he asked himself. In 1948, he enjoyed his most successful season with Maynard, losing only twice, to powerhouses Natick and Concord.

One day, Stan got into an argument about use of the practice field with Maynard's field hockey coach, a young Irish-American woman named Dorothy "Dot" Tierney. They were able to resolve their differences and discovered that they shared some interests, including sports, education, music, and theatre. Dot was a teacher who played the violin and piano and served as director of the drama club. She was also an accomplished coach. In the December 1947 Maynard *Screech Owl* yearbook, one of her players wrote, "Miss Tierney has the ability to make a winning team from any kind of material she has to work with and M.H.S. should be grateful to her."

Stan and Dot married in 1949. For the rest of her life, Dot Bondelevitch was subjected to her husband's never-ending collection of Irish jokes. After three seasons in Maynard, Stan accepted a position teaching science and coaching football at neighboring Hudson High School. Dot also changed jobs and became the Sudbury director of physical education for girls, and head coach of the girls' high school basketball, field hockey, and cheerleading squads.

In his first season at Hudson, Stan's team won only three games. In 1950, it again won three but tied two others. And one of the wins was an upset victory over archrival Marlboro on Thanksgiving Day—the first in five years. In 1951, he posted a winning record, finishing 5–4. Then, in his fourth season as Hudson's head coach, Stan's team finished with a perfect 10–0 record. Along the way, his Night Hawks shut out seven opponents, including powerful Concord, thereby ending that team's famous 59-game unbeaten streak. Over the course of 10 games, Hudson scored 275 points while surrendering only 30. It was the most successful football season in school history. Meanwhile, Dot met with similar success at Sudbury, where both her field hockey and basketball teams completed undefeated seasons.

In early 1953, Stan enrolled in some graduate-level education courses at Boston University. There he befriended a Lynn, Massachusetts, resident named Elmo Benedetto. The two outgoing, energetic men shared a passion for high school football. One day, Stan noticed an advertisement in a Boston newspaper concerning an opening for a high school football coach. Perhaps it was time for another challenge. "Where the hell is Swampscott, Benny?" he asked.

A Breath of Fresh Air

In answer to Stan's question, Elmo could have said that the small town hugs a piece of coastline 15 miles north of Boston, nestled between the old manufacturing city of Lynn to the southwest and the affluent harbor town of Marblehead to the northeast. Salem, "the Witch City," also forms part of its northwesterly border. Swampscott occupies just over three square miles of land adjacent to Nahant Bay and is part of what is generally known as the North Shore.

To the Naumkeag Indians, who visited to hunt and fish, the area was "M'sqiompsk" (red rock) or "M'squompskut" (at the Red Rock). After Deputy Governor of Massachusetts Bay Colony John Humphrey was granted 500 acres and the earliest settlers arrived, the name morphed into "Swampscott" (pronounced "swamp-skutt"). Thereafter, for more than two centuries it remained part of the larger municipality of Lynn. But while Lynn grew as a manufacturing center Swampscott remained a fishing village. In the pre-dawn, men would exit their seaside shacks on Blaney Beach Reservation (generally known now as Fisherman's Beach) and trawl the waters of Nahant Bay. In 1852, the villagers successfully petitioned the Massachusetts legislature for approval to split from Lynn and incorporate Swampscott as a town.

With its seaside location, numerous beaches and close proximity to Boston, Swampscott developed as one of New England's first summer resort communities. By the early twentieth century, hotels and inns dotted the town's shoreline. The largest was the Ocean House, located on land fronting Whales and Eisman's beaches. After the resort underwent renovations in 1902 it became the New Ocean House Hotel, eventually covering 22 acres, offering more than 500 guest rooms, and featuring a large beachfront swimming pool, bath house, cottages, tennis courts, and an executive golf course.

In total, at one time or another, the town boasted in excess of 20 hotels, inns, and boarding houses. Among the other better-known establishments were the Preston Beach Inn, the Lincoln House Hotel, the Hotel Bellevue, the Willey House, and Cap'n Jack's Seaside Resort.

Affluent families from Boston and inland areas saw Swampscott as an ideal location for summer vacation homes. Stately dwellings were built in seaside locations east of Blaney Beach in spots such as Galloupe's Point, Lincoln House Point, and Little's Point, which was named for the family of acclaimed Boston architect Arthur Little. He designed and built some of the mansions, including White Court, which served as the summer White House for President and Mrs. Calvin Coolidge in 1925.

Irish and Italian immigrants and other newcomers arrived, seeking employment in fishing, the growing resort economy, or public services. Some commuted to commercial or manufacturing jobs in Lynn or other North Shore communities. By the 1950s, Swampscott also was home to a sizable and growing Jewish population that was contributing in a major way to the town's cultural, educational, and economic well-being. Swampscott had developed a more suburban, middle-class character, although there continued to be a fair number of wealthy families among its roughly 12,000 inhabitants. Town residents were, like those of all other small towns on Boston's North Shore, primarily of western European descent. There was sufficient religious diversity to support a number of Protestant churches, a Catholic church, and several synagogues.

While the town maintained four public grammar schools, known as Hadley, Stanley, Clarke, and Machon, many youngsters from Roman Catholic families attended Saint John the Evangelist Elementary School (grades one–nine), adjacent to the Catholic church in the middle of town on Humphrey Street. Typical of the era, sports activities for grammar school kids were generally limited to informal games played in the town's parks. There were also some town-sponsored youth recreational programs offered at those locations on weekday mornings during the summer.

Many Swampscott children identified closely with the parks where they spent most of their free time. In the winter, they could skate and play hockey in some small rinks set up at the parks or on frozen ponds. Like parents in numerous other small American communities, Swampscotters believed their children were safe to roam the community and engage in unsupervised play and games wherever they could find the open space. For the majority of youngsters, the town afforded an ideal environment.

The smallest of the three parks was Abbott, adjacent to the Clarke School in a central location off of Paradise Road. Its basketball court, some swings, slides, a jungle gym, and a couple of miniature baseball fields made Abbott a magnet for kids in surrounding neighborhoods who regularly gathered to compete in an assortment of games. The larger Jackson Park, located off Essex Street, was in the northern section of town and abutted the Machon School. Abbott and Jackson had at different times both been the site of the home football field for the high school team.

Phillips Park was (and remains) the town's largest. Located off Humphrey Street and just a short distance from the New Ocean House Hotel and the beach, the spacious park included an outdoor basketball court, tennis courts, a playground, and field hockey, baseball, and football fields. In 1936, it replaced Jackson Park as the site of the high school's home football games when a new playing field, with bleachers, was completed near the park's southwest border.

It was christened Blocksidge Field in honor of Corporal John Enos Blocksidge, a young Swampscott man who was killed in action during World War I only 39 days before the Armistice was signed. The red brick Veterans Memorial Fieldhouse was added in 1948, dedicated to the memory of the 52 Swampscott men who lost their lives in World War II.

The town's high school sat at the crest of steep Greenwood Avenue and overlooked Swampscott Harbor. It was built in 1894 and was originally christened Phillips High School in recognition of the affluent, public-spirited family that had donated the land. However, after a substantial town-financed renovation and addition was completed in 1936, the building's name was changed to Swampscott High School, educating students from grades nine through twelve.

The high school teams participated in the Northeastern Conference. As suggested by its name, the conference was made up of communities located along the rocky Atlantic coastline that stretches unevenly from Boston to New Hampshire. At the time that Stan Bondelevitch was asking Elmo Benedetto about Swampscott, the other member schools in the conference were Amesbury, Danvers, Marblehead, Winthrop, and Woburn. Swampscott's football team had experienced some good seasons under Coach Harold Martin, the best being 1943 when the boys lost just one game by one point and claimed a Class C championship. But Martin had stepped down in 1950 after consecutive losing seasons. By the time Stan became interested in the program in 1953, it had hit rock bottom.

After learning more about Swampscott, Stan decided to further explore the opportunity. On a Saturday morning in late February of 1953, he met with town officials for an interview, following which he was offered the job. He beat out some stiff competition, including Moody Sarno, destined to become a legendary coach in Everett, Massachusetts.

While the offer exceeded what he had been making in Hudson, Stan had reportedly passed up other more lucrative opportunities, including collegiate positions. But there were additional things about the Swampscott job that must have appealed to him. The seaside community seemed a good place for Stan and Dot to work, live, and raise a family. And its proximity to Lynn, Salem, and Boston offered a chance for broader media coverage. The football team had been a doormat in the Northeastern Conference for several years. Having succeeded in twice turning around losing programs elsewhere, Stan no doubt relished the challenge of doing so again, this time on the North Shore under a brighter spotlight.

He accepted the offer and gave Hudson his resignation notice on Saint Patrick's Day, March 17, 1953. While Dot was also leaving her Sudbury positions, she was not looking for coaching jobs. She and Stan were expecting their first child. During the spring, Stan traveled continuously between Hudson, where he continued to teach, and Swampscott, where he worked to familiarize himself with all aspects of the town's physical education and sports programs and oversaw spring football practice.

Swampscott High School freshman Robert "Bobby" Carlin was blessed with an athletic pedigree. His father Bill, a town patrolman who would eventually become police chief, had captained the 1936 Sculpins, while two of Bobby's uncles on his mother's side had also played football in Swampscott. One of them, Robert Friberg, helped lead Harold Martin's 1943 team to a conference and state championship and in the process starred in a 32–0 shellacking of archrival Marblehead on Thanksgiving Day. Both uncles played football at Springfield College and thereafter became coaches. Moreover, Carlin's grandfather, Bernie Friberg, was one of the most famous athletes ever to have come out of neighboring Lynn.

Bernie had been a standout at Lynn English High School and ultimately enjoyed a solid major league baseball career with the Chicago Cubs, Philadelphia Phillies, and Boston Red Sox. In sum, there was little doubt that Virginia Friberg Carlin's only son would be playing ball.

Bobby was fast, athletic, and played sports from an early age. However, he did not believe that he was very good at football and was not enthusiastic about continuing. He also had little interest in school. By the time he reached his freshman year, Bobby was drifting along, without much focus or motivation. Then, one day in early 1953, he was called into a classroom where he was met by a husky, close-cropped, broad-faced, smiling man who introduced himself as the new football coach.

Stan Bondelevitch assured Carlin that he and his teammates were going to be winners. His enthusiasm was contagious. Suddenly, there was this energetic, charismatic man overseeing youth sports in Swampscott. Bobby was mesmerized and left their first meeting motivated and excited. He could hardly wait to put on pads and play for the man whom many in Swampscott would soon be calling "Bondy." Carlin was one of the first boys to have met the new coach and started spreading the word.

Tom Gorman was excited to hear the news. The Gorman family had moved into town from upstate New York in 1937. As a youngster, Tom greatly enjoyed playing sports in neighbors' backyards and at the town's parks. His father and two older brothers had all played football and baseball and Tom, who served as a waterboy for the Sculpins when he was in the sixth grade, looked forward to eventually playing for the high school team.

However, in 1947 when Tom was 12 years old and younger brother Jimmy was eight, Mr. Gorman's work took him back to New York and the family moved to Albany. The boys missed Swampscott so badly that they secretly packed their bags one day and made it all the way to an Albany bus stop before they got cold feet and trudged home. Fortunately, their father's job situation changed and the family returned to the town in 1949. The boys were able to resume their unsupervised baseball and football games in the parks.

Like many of the Swampscott kids from Roman Catholic families, the Gorman children attended the Saint John the Evangelist grammar school. From there, Tom's two older brothers went on to high school at Saint John's Prep in Danvers. Mrs. Gorman had the same plan for Tom.

But her son resisted. His dream was to play for Swampscott High School ("SHS") alongside his childhood buddies. His parents capitulated.

As a freshman, Tom made the varsity football roster and then became a three-sport starter as a sophomore. By the time that Bondy arrived, Tom had developed into an outstanding two-way back and one of the team's leaders. Yet the squads on which he excelled lost almost every game. He was not sure how that might change in his senior season, but he wanted to win.

The football experience for the players that the new coach greeted at their first team meeting had been less than uplifting. They felt like losers and lacked confidence that the future would be different. That all began to change the moment they heard Bondy speak. Stan Bondelevitch was like a breath of fresh air. He explained that his teams had been winners in Maynard and Hudson and confidently promised that they were also going to be winners in Swampscott. "I know how to win and I'll teach you," he told them. "We'll do it together."

The squad that showed up for spring practice in early March was led by a small nucleus of veteran players who would be seniors in the fall, including Tom Gorman, Peter "Hopalong" Cassidy, Bob "Bun" Mansfield, Dick Jeffers, and co-captains Jim Ryan and George Stinson. These boys had stuck with it through the depressing losing seasons and hoped to experience something else in their final year at SHS.

The team responded well to the new coach who frequently offered praise and encouragement. At one point, he told Bobby Carlin, "I can't believe that I'll have you on my team for the next three years. I'm a lucky man!" Stan liked to say that playing football was fun, but winning was a lot more fun. He had arrived in Swampscott like a pied piper and the boys gravitated to him.

Bondy was outgoing, optimistic, proactive, and passionate. He was all about inspiring boys to play. He charmed the players with his broad smile, booming voice, and hearty laugh. It seemed that he always had something to chuckle about, even if it was occasionally at the expense of a player. He usually had a gleam in his eye and was often both amused and amusing. He loved the job. He could not recall ever having told his wife that he was leaving for work because he had never looked at coaching as *work*.

From the first days of spring practice, Bondy was a "big picture" coach. Most of the individual drilling and teaching of fundamentals was performed by his assistants. Yet the players were always aware of the head man's presence. Bondy possessed the perfect coach's voice and had no problem being heard on the practice field. A baritone, he was blessed with the ability to easily change his tone to immediately impart the intended mood or emotion.

When he saw something that he either liked or did not like, everyone at Phillips Park usually heard about it. He might loudly praise one player for a great block or tackle and shortly thereafter berate another for being "slower than my grandmother with a piano on her back." Bondy could be critical but rarely sounded angry. He was a yeller, not a screamer. And more often than not, his tool was humor and positive reinforcement, rather than negative attack. The players were discovering that high school football under the new boss, though challenging and tough, could be something else. At times it was actually *fun*.

In his first year, Bondy's varsity assistants were Dick Stevenson, who handled the linemen, and Hal Foster, who coached the backfield. These were the men who would be working together to try to put the kids in a position to succeed.

Stevenson was a teacher and ultimately became an administrator in the Swampscott school system. At one time or another, he taught history, business law, economics, and civics. The tall, lean, athletic, and chain-smoking Winthrop native was a Dartmouth graduate and had played football for the Big Green. He also held a master's degree from Boston University. He was a bright, capable line coach who had worked briefly with the junior varsity prior to Bondy's arrival. He also became the school's new varsity baseball coach. While he could be critical at times, Stevenson was more often complimentary. Like his new boss, Dick Stevenson used positive feedback as one of his primary coaching tools. Also, like Bondy, Stevenson was a high-energy guy with a great smile. In fact, his toothy grin earned him a secret nickname with the players. He was "the chipmunk."

Harold "Hal" Foster, a Lynn English and Penn graduate, lived in Lynn where he worked in the insurance business. A serious, thoughtful, likable, and fairly quiet man, Hal was not as outgoing or flamboyant as Stevenson, let alone Bondelevitch. But he was a solid coach who knew his stuff. He was particularly adept at teaching fundamentals to the running backs, focusing on things such as balance, change of pace, staying low, and dropping the shoulder to take on, and break through, tacklers.

Bondy's approach, which would never change over the next 20 years, was to keep things simple and emphasize execution. He implemented the wing-T offense, replacing the single-wing and T-formation attacks that had been used by his predecessors. It was a smart move. Swampscott was a small town and almost every opponent fielded bigger players. Bondy's wing-T emphasized timing and quickness over size. It was heavily run-oriented and featured only a handful of plays, such as dives, traps, and sweeps run out of closed alignments.

The quarterback took the snap from directly behind the center, with the fullback positioned behind the quarterback. One halfback set up parallel to the fullback while the other was on the opposite side, but farther out behind the end and closer to the line of scrimmage, thereby becoming the so-called wingback. Thus in the "wing right" formation, the left halfback lined up left of, and parallel to, the fullback while the right halfback positioned about a yard behind the right end.

Play terminology was elementary. Even numbers designated areas to the center's right. The "2" hole was located between the center and right guard, the "4" hole between the right guard and tackle, and so forth. Odd numbers would similarly designate the corresponding points of attack to the center's left. The left halfback was the "3" back, the right halfback was the "2" back, and the fullback was the "4" back. Thus, for example, the 33-dive involved a hand-off to the left halfback who ran straight into the line between the left guard and tackle.

While Bondy's offense focused heavily on running the football, there were a handful of pass plays. In some, the quarterback immediately dropped back to throw the ball, while other so-called "play-action passes" were preceded by faked hand-offs to running backs. Defensive alignments were also straightforward, typically utilizing five down linemen. The scheme was usually a "5–2" (five linemen and two linebackers) or "5–3" (five linemen and three linebackers). There were no complicated stunts and blitzes.

The coaches drilled the boys in fundamentals before having them endlessly execute the plays, insisting that they "run out" each one by sprinting a considerable distance downfield. This improved their fitness and stamina and got them into position to assist with downfield blocking. Bondy preached that if each player performed his assignment, every play would result in a touchdown.

Bondy worked at developing relationships with players that went beyond the football field. Never cold or remote, he encouraged them to stop by his office or house, where they were always welcomed. On weekends, it was not uncommon for groups of players to spend hours at the Bondelevitch home, with Dot typically providing sandwiches or other food. Players also frequently traipsed down to Bondy's high school office where he regaled them with stories. This became a tradition that continued throughout his long tenure as athletic director and head coach.

While Bondy could be entertaining, there was more to it than fun and games. His goal was to win the boys over to the program. Nonetheless, he clearly enjoyed working with and helping them. He'd spend considerable time trying to learn more about what was going on in their lives and encourage many to focus on school and developing the skills that would help them further their educations and become successful.

In his first year in Swampscott, Stan learned that one of his players had a difficult home life. The boy's irresponsible parents provided little support or guidance and he struggled to get passing grades. But Bondy saw potential and encouraged him to think about college. On occasion, he took the kid into his home where he could enjoy a decent meal and good night's sleep. The coach continued to offer help long after that player's SHS football days ended and the young man ultimately graduated from college and earned an advanced degree before pursuing a successful career. He was one of hundreds whom Bondy assisted in various ways during his years in Swampscott.

The players discovered that the coach cared about their futures. Speaking many decades after he starred on Bondy's first Swampscott team, Tom Gorman had this to say: "With great pride, he followed his players in their lives—how they did in school, or in their jobs, or in their marriages. For football was not the end to Stan—it was just the beginning."

Giant Killers

During the summer of 1953, Stan continued to prepare for his first season as Swampscott's new coach, while also working at Camp Columbus, a youth day camp in Danvers, Massachusetts. As the 1953–54 school year approached, so did preseason football practice. The new coach put his players through some grueling sessions, yet had an instinctive sense of when to ratchet things down.

One of the first practices was held on a brutally hot day, and Bondy announced that he was cutting it short, explaining to an *Item* reporter, "You could float a toy duck on any one of those kids out there." He concluded, "It's weather like this that might stunt the enthusiasm." Bondy was all about enthusiasm. Instead of an extended practice in the extreme heat, the coaches oversaw a "skull practice," i.e., using a blackboard to explain or review assignments.

While blackboard sessions were fine, Bondy hated the sight of clipboards and papers on the field. He felt strongly that coaches communicated most effectively when engaged face to face with players. It was not possible to look a boy in the eye while staring at materials attached to a clipboard.

Recognizing that building a winning football culture required more than simply coaching the players, Stan worked to generate new spirit and pride in the wider community. At the high school, he consistently praised and credited the student body, particularly the cheerleaders, drill team, and band members. He recognized that they all were part of a successful football program. For example, in speaking years later about the role of the high school band he said, "You've got to have music. We have music in church, at funerals, at weddings. Music inspires. It has a place in football."

He encouraged younger boys to aspire to become SHS football players. He consistently urged Swampscott citizens to support the team. He reached out to local and Greater Boston media representatives, feeding them information that would result in favorable publicity. Knowing that it was all important to the long-term success of his program, particularly in a small town like Swampscott, he worked nonstop to build excitement and support, successfully employing his unique blend of energy, enthusiasm, and humor.

His team prepared for the opener against Lynn Trade High School at Blocksidge Field. Trade, as the name implied, was a vocational school for students interested in technical training that prepared them for careers as machinists, plumbers, electricians, carpenters, mechanics, and the like. Lynn's other high schools, Classical and English, as their names also implied, offered the more traditional academic curricula. Trade was somewhat smaller than the other two Lynn schools and its sports teams played in a lower-ranked division. With this match-up, Swampscott had a golden opportunity to start on the right foot.

By any objective measure, the Sculpins exceeded expectations, destroying Trade, 34–0. It was the widest margin of victory for an SHS team in over a decade. Senior Tom Gorman scored twice, including on a 65-yard punt return, and the offense rushed for a total of 325 yards. The *Item* observed, "For Swampscott grid followers it was an entirely new script." While the one-sided win was gratifying, elation was tempered by recognition that the Sculpins had triumphed over a relatively weak team. Such would not be the case with Swampscott's next opponent.

Class B Reading was bigger than Swampscott, with a solid, well-established program. Yet the Sculpins won again by a score of 12–0. The highlight was Gorman's interception on his own 5-yard line, which he returned 95 yards for the team's first touchdown. Peter Cassidy was another standout, picking off a pass to kill a Reading drive, and then throwing to junior end Norman Walker for another score.

After two games, the Sculpins had doubled the victories achieved over the past two seasons and had outscored the opposition 46–0. In the face of this success, and with Bondy's support and encouragement, the Swampscott Boosters Club sprang to life, making arrangements to provide transportation for those interested in attending away games.

The next game was at Gloucester, one of the strongest teams on the North Shore. Hindered by multiple fumbles, the Sculpins lost, 24–14. However, it was encouraging that Class C Swampscott was competitive against the larger, highly regarded Class B team.

Even more encouraging was the team's subsequent 33–0 pasting of conference foe Winthrop in what many expected would be a close contest. SHS had posted shutouts in three of its first four games while outscoring the opposition by a combined 93–24. Some fans were so excited about the early successes that they carried Bondy off the field following the Winthrop victory.

The squad next faced its biggest challenge. The Amesbury Indians were the top-ranked Class C football team in Massachusetts, unbeaten in 31 consecutive games. Also known as the Carriagemakers because the town was once a center for carriage construction, they had outscored their first four 1953 opponents 134–12. The veteran squad, described as "big, powerful and dangerous," featured talented halfback Willard Gamble, the leading scorer in Essex County.

Assessing what would "undoubtedly prove Swampscott's crucial game of the season," local pundits saw little chance for the Sculpins. Ed Cahill, the sports editor for the *Item*, wrote:

> There's small consolation for Swampscott in Coach Tony Tassinari's record as coach at Amesbury. Tassinari, whose boys entertain the Sculpins at Amesbury tomorrow, has sent the Indians into exactly 100 games, including last Saturday's tilt. Of these he has won 67 while losing 29 and tying four. No team in its Class (Class C) has ever beaten a Tassinari team by more than six points. In fact, over the past 10 seasons he has lost only six games to Class C rivals. All of which indicates Swampscott is in for no picnic.

But Cahill failed to mention Bondy's recent record. Since the beginning of the 1952 season, Bondelevitch-coached teams were 13–1. Perhaps even more telling was that one year earlier his Hudson squad had ended Concord's record 59-game unbeaten streak. In hindsight, the Amesbury match seemed the perfect scenario for Stan Bondelevitch.

Yet if the coach was looking forward to the contest, some of his players were less enthusiastic. The Sculpins had been outscored in their last four games against the Indians, 123–6, and were humiliated, 54–0, during their most recent visit. Bondy kept working at building a winning attitude, assuring the boys that they were ready.

The coaches devised a game plan with some new wrinkles. Bondy emphasized the need to slow the pace of play, thereby limiting the opportunities for Amesbury's explosive offense. Quarterback Cassidy was told to first count to 15 in the huddle before any play was called.

Another change was something that the coaches dubbed the "hurricane offense." It involved some plays run from an unbalanced line, with four linemen set to one side of the center. The backfield also aligned more toward the strong side. From such formations, the team planned to run its fleet halfbacks in quick-hitting sweeps. Hopefully, the Indians would be slow to adjust and react. If the defense started to aggressively pursue and perhaps overplay the sweeps to the strong side, Swampscott could take advantage and strike with a series of "counter" plays. The most oft-used of these was the 22-trap, in which the wingback (the "2" back in the right-wing formation) followed the right tackle and ran against the flow of play into the middle of the line, where he received the hand-off and cut behind the tackle's trap block through the 2-hole.

A third element of the plan was designed to eliminate, or at least minimize, the big plays by Gamble. Leon "Doc" Marden, Swampscott's affable freshman coach, was the assistant primarily responsible for scouting opponents. As part of his report on Amesbury, Doc explained that the Indians liked to send Gamble in motion toward the sideline and then throw to him in the flat where he could turn such short passes into long gains. In hope of disrupting such plays, Bondy told his defensive backs that if Gamble ran in motion toward their side of the field they should close quickly and make contact, i.e., run into him, as soon as possible, regardless of whether he had the ball.

Bondy impressed upon his players that if they executed the plan they could win. By the time the boys boarded the bus on a sparkling October Saturday to travel up I-95 to Amesbury they were starting to believe.

However, despite all of the planning and preparation, the team got off to a shaky start when Gamble broke open, caught a 25-yard pass, and took it the remaining 20 yards to the end zone. Prior to 1958, post-touchdown conversions, all attempted from the three-yard line, counted for a single point, whether accomplished by running, passing, or kicking. Gamble converted the point-after-touchdown ("PAT") and the Indians held a 7–0 lead.

Swampscott junior Roger Coe, a 5-foot, 8-inch, 160-pound defensive back, was an offensive reserve, playing behind starter Bobby Carlin. Now, in the biggest game of the year, Carlin went down with an injury and Coe was called upon. As a freshman baseball player, Roger had been brought up to the varsity and inserted into a big game. The nervous freshman struggled and the team lost. After the game, the varsity coach dismissively sent Roger back to the freshman team, saying the promotion had been a mistake. His implied message was that Coe had let everyone down and was not good enough to play at a higher level. That incident continued to nag at Roger's confidence.

This time, however, the coach was Stan Bondelevitch. Before having him take Carlin's place Bondy said, "Don't worry. Just do what you know how to do. I *know* that you can do it!" While still jittery as he entered the offensive backfield, Roger was buoyed by the knowledge that his coach believed in him.

The offense focused on executing the game plan. Once in the huddle Cassidy literally carried out Bondy's order, slowly counting to 15 before the play was called. While the strategy resulted in some penalties for delay of game, it reduced the number of Amesbury's possessions. Once at the line, the Sculpins attacked with the hurricane sweeps. Surprisingly, the Indians did not adjust. Gorman, Coe, and Bun Mansfield picked up big chunks of yardage.

As the second quarter wore on, the Sculpins methodically drove to the Amesbury 3-yard line. From that point, Coe carried for the touchdown. The conversion attempt failed and the half ended with the Carriagemakers leading 7–6. The players were realizing that Bondy had been right—they could compete with Amesbury. Roger Coe was also realizing that Bondy had been right in trusting that he could do the job and help the team.

One of the remarkable things about Stan Bondelevitch was his motivational skill. While former players agree that his locker room talks were masterful, few, if any, can recall much of what was said. There were, of course, themes that he would return to year-after-year. These included emotional, and sometimes tearful, assurances that the team he was then addressing was made up of the finest group of boys he had ever coached. Former players were sometimes shocked when they visited the locker room before the start of the Thanksgiving Day game and heard what sounded like a recording of Bondy's oration delivered to them years earlier. One such alum, on hearing the head man speak to the team, whispered to an assistant, "But I thought that *we* were the finest boys!"

Bondy followed a standard pregame routine. First, the assistant coaches talked to the boys, individually and/or collectively, addressing assignments and focusing on details. When the time came for the big man to speak it was always quite a performance. He sometimes first removed his jacket and/or hitched-up his trousers.

He usually started slowly, often impressing upon the boys how hard they had worked and how ready they were to take on and meet the challenge. At some point, he recited the name of each starter, a form of recognition the players appreciated. Starters often felt a special responsibility to perform well after hearing their names spoken by the coach. Others, particularly reserve underclassmen, yearned for the day when their names might be included in those mentioned by Bondy in his pregame talk.

As he moved toward the end of his speech he grew more animated, increasing his tempo and raising his voice until it became a shout. He spoke of toughness and the need to hit harder than the opponents throughout the entire game. He emphasized total commitment. "Just remember and repeat to yourself, 'I *can* and I *will*,'" he might tell them. "I *can* and I *will* make the block! I *can* and I *will* make the tackle! I *can* and I *will* make the catch!" He often touched upon matters such as disrespect from opponents or the media, avenging past injustices, his love for his boys, and always his belief in them. Typically, it ended with an explosive demand that they go out and *do it*. The players then stampeded out of the locker room and charged on to the field.

Before his players took the field at Amesbury, Bondy told them that while many folks were picking Swampscott to make a good showing "nobody but ourselves really thinks we're going to win. I know you can do it." In short, it was the old "nobody believes in us but us" theme.

Trailing 7–6 at the end of the first half, he said nothing for most of the time that they were in the locker room; instead letting his assistants review adjustments with the players. Then, just before it was time to return to the field, Bondy told the boys that he found it strange that the better team was trailing. While he surely must have said more, Stan's genius was not so much in what he said, but in how and when he said it. He could bring a level of intensity to his delivery that could fire up the troops even if the topic was the weather. He must have done so then, as his players reportedly almost tore the door off its hinges in their desire to return to the field and prove that they were the better team.

However, early in the third quarter Gamble broke free for another reception and touchdown. With the PAT Amesbury's lead increased to 14–6. The Sculpins soon struck back, piecing together a five-play scoring drive, capped by Bun Mansfield's 23-yard run. The conversion attempt failed and Amesbury led by two points.

Swampscott's defense had stifled the home team's running attack but was still struggling in its attempt to stop the big pass play. The passes to Gamble were not a surprise, and Roger Coe was trying to follow Bondy's order to hit Amesbury's star every time he ventured toward Coe's side of the field. On one play, Coe did run into Gamble and disrupt the planned pass. But on a later occasion, he made contact while the pass was in the air, drawing a penalty which gave Amesbury a first down.

When Roger came off the field and saw Bondy approaching he expected a tongue-lashing. Instead, the coach told him not to worry about the penalty. "We wanted to take that play away from them and I'll take 15 yards versus a touchdown," he said. He encouraged Roger to keep playing hard, and Coe's confidence soared.

In the fourth quarter, the Sculpins launched a final scoring drive, with Coe running the ball into the end zone to put Swampscott ahead. Amesbury never crossed the goal line again. The boys had pulled off the upset of the season, beating the Carriagemakers, 18–14. The win was no fluke. Showing remarkable resilience, they had scored after both of Amesbury's tallies, before finally seizing the lead with Coe's second touchdown. Swampscott destroyed the Indians on the ground, rushing for a total of 265 yards while holding Amesbury's offense to a mere 35. In short, they had been the more physical squad and out-played the top-ranked team in Class C.

The only bad news was that Bobby Carlin was lost for the remainder of the season with a broken wrist. While his teammates celebrated on the bus ride home, Carlin was in tears. When Bondy attempted to console him, the sophomore explained that his distress was not due to wrist pain but to the realization that he would not be able to play in the upcoming games.

There is something uniquely captivating in the kind of spontaneous small-town celebration that erupted following the conclusion of the Amesbury game. Hundreds of exuberant students and joyous Boosters gathered with most of the high school's marching band near the foot of Redington Street, not far from the Lynn/Swampscott border. They then ambled in a noisy impromptu victory parade down Humphrey Street, through the center of town, to Blocksidge Field where they wildly cheered the returning heroes. The jubilant crowd blocked part of the street, thereby preventing the team bus from making it to the Fieldhouse and forcing the coaches and players to exit and wade through the party.

If Swampscott's fans had been elated after the Winthrop win, they were now "agog," according to the *Item*, after defeating mighty Amesbury. Headlines in the October 26, 1953, *Item* raved, "Bondelevitch Boys Spoil State's Longest Streak" and "Sculpins Come From Behind Twice To Amaze Schoolboy Grid World." They'd slain the Amesbury giant. For Bondy, there was an element of déjà vu. One year earlier he had witnessed something similar when his Hudson Night Hawks had ended Concord's 59-game unbeaten streak.

On the following Saturday, a crowd of supporters took to the road to cheer their team against Danvers, sometimes also referred to as the "Oniontowners." The nickname took hold because Danvers farmers had once developed a new breed of vegetable known as the Danvers onion. The resurgent Sculpins had no difficulty slicing up the Oniontowners 28–7. By this point, some folks in Swampscott were seized by football hysteria. The *Item's* Cahill wrote:

> They're touting Stan Bondelevitch, Swampscott High coach, as the greatest thing since penicillin. The more hysterical Sculpin fans have had to be restrained in their efforts to erect a monument to the youthful football Moses, who has led the Swampscott football forces out of the morass of defeatism to the shores of victory. One disciple has suggested that the name of Humphrey Street be changed to Bondelevitch Boulevard.

The next contest against a weak Methuen team was rained out. With only two games remaining, the 5–1 Sculpins were undefeated in Class C and looking at the possibility of a conference championship.

In their eighth game, they faced potent, non-conference Stoughton, led by Danny Gonsalves, one of the top scorers in the state. Stoughton had clobbered most of its foes, losing only once. It did not help that speedy Bobby Carlin was not available. As well as the boys had been playing, they fell hard at Stoughton, losing 33–6. Gonsalves lived up to his reputation, scoring three touchdowns and an extra point.

The season's final contest was with Marblehead High School, Swampscott's neighbor, and traditional rival. Swampscott v. Marblehead was one of the oldest continuous high school rivalries in Massachusetts, dating back to 1909. Dressed in black and red and formally known as the Magicians, the Marblehead players were also sometimes referred to as the Yachtsmen because of the harbor town's seafaring history and wealthy sportsmen. But in Swampscott, they were known as "Headers" (pronounced "Headas") or "Whips." While the reason for use of the latter term is not completely clear, one source asserts that it was understood by every true Marbleheader as "a profoundly indecent swear word."

School spirit always peaked during the week leading up to the Marblehead game, with posters and signs covering the gym walls and rousing pep rallies where "Whip the Whips" was the main theme. Played annually on Thanksgiving morning before standing-room-only crowds, the game marked not only the season's final contest but the last time that most of the seniors would play organized football. For many, it would be the game they would most often recall in later years, with either warm satisfaction or forlorn regret.

While the Sculpins had not managed to whip the Whips since 1946, it seemed that this might finally be the year, as the suddenly resurgent Swampscott program was generating much-excited community support and the team had knocked off powerful Amesbury. Moreover, Marblehead seemed vulnerable, coming into the game with a losing record.

However, playing at home on a poor field, the Magicians used an eight-man defensive front to shut down the Sculpins' rushing attack. The two teams hammered at one another without much offensive success. Swampscott, playing without the injured Carlin, was further hampered by the unavailability of quarterback Peter Cassidy, who had broken his leg during the preceding week. Ultimately the Headers managed to push the ball over the goal line for a late fourth-quarter touchdown and the Sculpins suffered their first shutout loss of the season, falling by a 6–0 score.

Losing to Marblehead was a huge disappointment, particularly for the seniors. But the team had still finished with a solid 5–3 winning record. There were a number of factors contributing to the quick turnaround from the past several years. While the squad was hardly lacking in talent, Bondy knew that spirit, teamwork, and confidence were essential components of a winning program. He had worked constantly to foster all of these in his players.

The coach befriended and entertained the boys and boosted their interest in playing. He tried to avoid things that would, as he phrased it, "stunt the enthusiasm." He also focused on generating excitement about the team within the school and town. He assured that there was good coverage in the newspapers, and established close relations with the Boosters and other organizations within the community that might throw their support behind the team. The players grew even more enthused knowing that they had such support and interest within the town.

Stan also took on highly capable assistants in Foster, Stevenson, and Marden, and he and his staff worked together to assure that the players were prepared through a combination of conditioning, good fundamentals, and understanding of assignments. Then he supported and/or organized events such as weekly chalk talks and pregame house parties that brought his players closer together. Finally, he drew on the force and intensity of his own unique personality to motivate the boys and build their confidence. All of these factors would continue to be part of his blueprint for success in the years to come.

Peter "Hopalong" Cassidy ultimately became Swampscott's police chief. Thirty-four years after he quarterbacked Bondy's first SHS team, he offered the following comments as he reminisced about the coach's impact:

> When Stan came around in my senior year he turned the team and the community around. It was a rebirth of football in Swampscott. His magic was that he made you believe in yourself…. I love him.

SHS football had come a long way in just one season under Stan Bondelevitch. But more would be required to build a program that consistently produced not just winning seasons but championships.

Sculpins No More

The most positive development for SHS sports in 1954 was the arrival of a lean, feisty new gym teacher and coach named Richard Lynch. He had grown up in neighboring Lynn during the depression. Despite hard economic times, Lynn had offered very good youth sports programs. Young Dick Lynch had taken full advantage, spending countless hours playing organized football, baseball, and basketball in the city's parks. Though he was slightly built and lacked height, Dick had gone on to excel in sports at Lynn English High School.

After graduation, he enlisted in the navy. In early August of 1945, Seaman Lynch was assigned to the naval facility at San Francisco's Treasure Island to become part of the mammoth military force assembled for the planned invasion of Japan. But several days after his California arrival the atomic bomb was dropped on Hiroshima. Following a second detonation over Nagasaki, Japan surrendered and the war was over. Lynch never left the shores of the United States, quipping that he had served on the USS *Neversail*, and seen plenty of action during the war—in places like Milwaukee and Chicago.

After his discharge, he attended Boston University on a basketball scholarship. As a starting guard, he competed against players like future Boston Celtics legend Bob Cousy, then starring at Holy Cross. By the time he finished college, Lynch knew that he wanted to coach. He landed a job teaching physical education and coaching baseball and basketball at Milford High School in New Hampshire. He had made the right career choice. Dick Lynch was an outstanding coach, focusing considerable energy on drilling fundamentals. His style was tough, aggressive, and passionate. He was a clear communicator, with a quick Irish wit. He was honest with players so they always knew where they stood. Coach Lynch commanded respect.

During the summer of 1953, Lynch worked as a waterfront counselor at Camp Columbus where he met another summer employee, Stan Bondelevitch. He returned to his Milford job in the fall but at some point was contacted by Stan's friend Elmo Benedetto, the well-connected athletic director of the Lynn public schools. Elmo mentioned that there would soon be an opening for a physical education teacher and assistant coach at an unidentified school in the Greater Lynn area and asked whether Lynch might be interested.

Dick's wife Joanne was also a Lynn native, and their roots remained planted in Boston's North Shore where family and friends resided. For the Lynches, Milford, New Hampshire, might just as well have been a remote town in the middle of Kansas. They wanted to go home. Lynch told Elmo that he was indeed interested. Shortly thereafter, Bondy contacted him and explained that the job opening was at Swampscott High School. An interview was arranged and lasted about five minutes, after which Dick accepted Stan's offer.

Back in the 1950s, many coaches employed a direct, "hands-on" method of assuring a player's undivided attention. The contact could range from a hand merely touching a player's arm while a coach explained something, to a vice-like grip as he chewed out an unruly kid. Most athletes would never have considered complaining to their parents, knowing that the likely response would have been an accusatory inquiry about the misconduct that had prompted the coach's action. Parents generally seemed more interested in assuring that their children behaved respectfully than in complaining that coaches had harshly scolded their disobedient youngsters.

However, James Dunn, the popular longtime SHS principal, had at least one occasion to address a complaint about abusive treatment and it involved new gym teacher Dick Lynch. During Lynch's first year in Swampscott, one of the biggest kids in the school visited the principal's office and reported that during gym class Mr. Lynch had grabbed him, held him against a wall, threatened him, and then hit him. With the complaining boy still present in his office, Dunn summoned Lynch and asked whether the story was true. Lynch, after detailing the continuous misconduct that had led to the disciplinary action, confirmed that he had indeed grabbed and held the boy while announcing that he was not going to put up with any more crap. "But," said Lynch, "I never hit him."

The principal had heard enough. He rose from his desk and limped to a spot several inches from the boy's face. Dunn limped because he had an artificial leg, having lost the real one in a mill accident many years earlier. Looking the boy square in the eye, Mr. Dunn told him, "I don't believe that Mr. Lynch hit you, but if he did you certainly deserved it. And I'll tell you something else. If you ever behave like that again in this school I may hit you myself. Now get out of here!" Richard Lynch was very fond of James Dunn.

Coach Lynch continued in Swampscott until 1973. Over those 19 years his responsibilities varied. In addition to teaching physical education classes, in the earlier years he coached track, baseball, freshman basketball, and junior varsity football. Today he is most famously recognized in town as Bondy's key assistant and backfield coach during an unprecedented run of football championships, and as perhaps the best boys' basketball coach in the school's history. But back in 1954, he was just the new young gym teacher and football assistant.

Having completed the Lynch hiring, Bondy moved to further reshape the high school sports scene. From the time he had arrived, Stan disliked the Sculpin nickname. Bondy reported that he had consulted a dictionary and learned that a sculpin was a large-headed, broad-mouthed, bottom-dwelling, worthless fish, and was also known as a mud hake. He was appalled. "It's fortunate for us that our rivals over the years haven't uncovered the true meaning of the word or we would have been heckled off the field," he said. "It's pretty difficult to inspire fear in the opposition with the announcement that the Mud-Hakes are coming."

He met with his assistants, explaining that he wanted to drop the nickname. They all felt that the school's proximity to the sea should still be reflected in any new name for its athletic teams. Coach Lynch suggested "The Blue Wave." Coach Stevenson countered with "The Big Blue." Both men had in mind the blue expanse of the Atlantic Ocean, only a stone's throw from Blocksidge Field and visible from the high school's hilltop location. Stevenson's suggestion may also have been influenced by his having played for Dartmouth's "Big Green."

Initially, Dick Lynch was not keen on "Big Blue," feeling that it seemed a bit over-the-top for a small-town team. But that majestic image was exactly what appealed to Bondy. He would expect his players, regardless of their sizes, to live up to the name—to play up to the name.

Despite opposition from some of the old-timers who had proudly played on past Sculpin teams, the fish was returned to the ocean floor. Henceforth it would be The Big Blue. New royal blue uniforms replaced the dark blue colors that had been worn by the Sculpins. Stan Bondelevitch wanted change and folks in Swampscott were learning that he usually got what he wanted.

Getting more boys to join, and stick with, Big Blue football would be critical to the program's success. With a large number of players on the roster, the coaches would be better able to substitute and platoon between offense, defense, and special teams, and to have qualified reserves ready to step in and take the place of starters who were injured or otherwise unavailable. It also assured that there would be sufficient players for practice sessions where it was frequently helpful to have multiple squads of 11 facing off against one another. Finally, increasing the number of players had the ripple effect of automatically increasing the number of other people involved with the program, such as parents, siblings, and friends of those boys.

Intent on increasing participation, Bondy enthusiastically preached that every red-blooded American lad should have the wonderful experience of playing the great game of football. Yet, while the numbers had already risen since Stan's arrival, he sensed that there were many parents, particularly mothers, who were fearful that their boys risked serious injury by participating in such a rough sport. As part of his attempt to assuage their fears, on Saturday, September 18, 1954, he conducted the team's first Parents Clinic at Blocksidge Field.

He was clear about his motive, telling Ed Cahill,

With this program we hope to wipe out all traces of parental objection to football for their boys.... At least every parent will know exactly what we ask of their youngsters. In that way much misunderstanding that sometimes makes for prejudice against football may be dissipated.

He sent letters to parents of players urging them to attend. The event was widely publicized, with the hope that many others who were reluctant to have their sons participate would come, watch, listen, and change their minds. In announcing the Clinic, Stan said,

> We want the parents of every boy on the Swampscott squad to see just what we're doing with their youngster.... Mothers, especially, are apt to get the wrong impression of what their boys go through as candidates for the high school football team. I'm afraid some of them think of it as little less than organized murder, with their own beloved son as the particular target of the others. We want to prove to these parents, if we can, that football is fun, and, properly supervised, is not much more dangerous than a fast set of tennis.

Other coaches and players must have wondered just what brand of "fast tennis" Bondy had in mind. Yet, by all accounts, the first Parents Clinic was a smashing success, with a large number of adults in attendance. After a tour of the Fieldhouse, they were led to the Blocksidge Field stands where Bondy outlined the plan for the rest of the morning. His team of fully equipped players then took the field wearing their new Big Blue uniforms.

A little show-and-tell followed. Bondy and Bill Driscoll of Brine Sporting Goods explained each piece of equipment. The presentation began when a player stepped forward and removed his helmet. Its cost, design, and purpose were discussed, with emphasis on safety features. The player then removed and displayed another piece of equipment, with Bondy and Driscoll providing similar details. Shoulder pads, elbow pads, hip pads, thigh pads, knee pads, and cleats were all successively addressed. By the time the presentation ended some parents may have been convinced that almost nothing could harm their sons given the magnificent suits of armor that they would be wearing into battle.

The coaches next ran the players through the normal drills that were part of a practice session, while explaining the purpose of each. Assistants discussed matters within their areas of expertise, and the junior varsity ("JV") coach described the developmental aspects of that program. Fundamentals were explained and demonstrated. According to the *Item*,

> Brush blocks, body blocks, cross blocks, double-teaming, and other "'inside" football were shown in detail to the open-mouthed parents. An eight-man, a seven-man, and a six-man line were all explained. Pass defenses were outlined.

Dick Lynch, whose many duties included serving as the team's trainer, demonstrated how, and explained why, ankles and other joints were taped.

After Coach Stevenson suffered a charley horse during one demonstration, Bondy quipped that he was thankful it had not been a player who was injured, noting that while "[w]e can always spare a coach for a day or two,… we sure want those players in top shape." He must have loved all the favorable publicity, such as one mother's quoted comment that she had never realized how much she was missing while watching a game and was certain that she would "enjoy the game 10 times as much in the future."

The Clinic was followed on the next weekend by the Boosters' annual fund-raising drive. Dubbed "dollar day," it involved door-to-door canvassing by about 150 volunteers with the goal of enrolling at least 3,000 Boosters through donations of one dollar each. The Boosters had always been active in backing SHS athletics. With Bondy's promotional efforts and the successful prior season, the organization was offering even greater financial assistance and support.

There was, however, at least one occasion when a Boosters gift proved problematic. There was a whirlpool tub at the Fieldhouse that had been supplied by the Boosters. Early in his tenure Bondy came downstairs from the coaches' offices and noticed a line of players waiting to use the tub. When he inquired, he was told of various bumps and bruises that the boys were hoping to soak in its soothing waters.

He immediately located Fieldhouse manager Vinny Easterbrooks, and told him to grab a wrench and disconnect the contraption. He then ordered several players to carry the tub outside and dispose of it. The boys would not be relaxing in any whirlpool tubs. They were expected to ignore and play through minor injuries. This, however, was one message that was not included in Bondy's presentations to the Boosters or the moms and dads at the Parents Clinic.

Every year the Joyce Jamboree served as the curtain raiser for North Shore high school football. Named after longtime Lynn Classical coach Bill Joyce, and held under the lights at Lynn's venerable Manning Bowl, the well-attended event featured a number of brief exhibition games between local squads. It was typically held in September one week before the opening games of the regular season. Each contest lasted 12 minutes.

For some reason, SHS had not participated in 1953, but Bondy made sure that the Big Blue was included in 1954. The team came away with a solid 14–0 victory over Revere High School. According to the *Item*, the Blue "showed all the spark and dash that marked their successful season a year ago." Junior left halfback Bobby Carlin was a particular standout, breaking off long runs and scoring both a touchdown and conversion.

Carlin was joined in the backfield by senior running backs Roger Coe and Mike Farren and junior quarterback Billy Nelson. Carlin and Coe were both fast and shifty while fullback Farren was a good blocker and solid football player. Coe was often positioned as the wingback, lining-up directly behind his friend, 6-foot, 2-inch, 200-pound right end Winslow Shaw. In that spot, it could be hard for opposing defenses to see him, especially when he turned and followed big tackle Al Owens into the line on the 22-trap. Roger loved the play because of the deception that typically had the defenders running away from the point of attack.

The team's starting ends, Winslow Shaw and Norman Walker, were not only strong football players but outstanding all-around athletes and leaders. They came from different backgrounds. Shaw was born and raised in Swampscott. His parents were both members of well-established Swampscott families that had resided in town for generations. By contrast, Walker was a newcomer. His father had been a member of the 1948 U.S. Olympic hockey team. After moving into town from Scituate, Massachusetts, in 1953, Norman joined the high school team as a junior and soon established himself as a solid player. Both Shaw and Walker also played basketball and baseball. Walker was elected Junior Class treasurer and then Senior Class president. Shaw, in addition to being co-captain of the football team, served as captain of the basketball team. The two seniors were the line's sturdy bookends.

The squad boasted a valuable addition to the coaching staff, a new nickname and uniforms, supportive and well-informed parents, strong financial backing from the Boosters, a number of good returning players, and an impressive winning performance in the Jamboree. The stage was set for a strong and successful start to the second season under the coach whom some were now calling "Stan the Man." But it did not happen.

The high expectations were dashed when the boys first fell to Woburn, 20–7, and then lost to Reading, 24–13, in a frustrating game in which the offense failed to score five different times from inside the 20-yard line. In the third game at home against Gloucester, the Big Blue lost again, 26–7, with its only score coming off a Nelson-Coe pass.

At halftime of the Gloucester game, Coach Foster had been called away due to a family emergency. After the game, the team learned that Foster's five-year-old son had been killed in a freak accident. The boy was at home in Lynn playing with friends when the Fosters' new electronic overhead garage door somehow engaged and closed down on him. He was rushed by his mother to Lynn Hospital where he died about one hour later, minutes after his distraught father arrived.

Many players struggled to express their sadness and sympathy to the low-key backfield coach. Unlike Bondy, Stevenson, Lynch, or Marden, Hal Foster did not work within the Swampscott School System. He, therefore, had fewer interactions with the players than did the other coaches. While he continued as Swampscott's backfield coach for another three years, he seemed understandably more withdrawn after the tragic loss of his young son.

Six games remained and people were beginning to wonder what had become of the new, winning, Bondelevitch era. A future that had looked so bright after his inaugural season seemed much darker with the team's 0–3 start. Was 1953, with its winning record and dramatic upset of Amesbury, a flash in the pan? Was Swampscott reverting to the losing ways that had characterized the teams in 1951 and 1952? Suddenly, there was not much that seemed big about the Big Blue. Were they mud hakes after all?

In fact, things were not as dire as they appeared. The schedule had been front-loaded with strong teams that made getting off to a good start next to impossible. Woburn was an established conference power with one of the best backs in Massachusetts in rugged junior Joe Castiglione. After beating Swampscott, the Tanners went on to win not only the conference championship but the Eastern Massachusetts Class C title. Reading was also a strong squad with a fullback whom Bondy considered to be among the best in New England and a halfback who was nearly as good. Class B Gloucester literally outclassed Class C Swampscott and was one of the area's top teams. Swampscott had not beaten the Fishermen, as they were known, in 12 years.

Compared to the players on those teams, the boys on the Big Blue were hardly *big*. Only a couple weighed more than 180 pounds. Also, despite fleet-footed backs like Carlin and Coe, the team needed more speed. Yet there had been positive signs. Although too often failing to find the end zone, the boys had managed to move the ball and create a number of scoring opportunities against Reading. And they had missed Carlin, again often hampered by illness or injury. When able to take the field, he continued to make big plays, as did his backfield mate Coe. Thus, despite the 0–3 start, there was cause for some optimism.

Carlin was still on crutches as the team prepared for conference rival Winthrop. Unlike Swampscott's first three opponents, winless Winthrop did not have a size advantage. Playing without Carlin, the Blue exploded for 39 points, while shutting out the hosts. A number of players participated in the scoring, including Roger Coe with two touchdowns. In an emotional postgame locker room, the boys presented the game ball to Hal Foster. In the aftermath of the tragedy, the players had pulled closer together.

Next was defending conference champion Amesbury, a team seeking revenge for Swampscott's historic 1953 victory. Carlin, however, was finally able to play and SHS again defeated the Carriagemakers, 26–14. Amesbury's fans could no longer claim that Coach Tassinari's teams had never lost to another Class C school by more than six points. Carlin, while "still sporting a limp and used only in spots," scored on runs of 11 and 40 yards. Coe also scored twice, including by an 80-yard kick return. There was little question that this team could generate offense, having scored a total of 65 points in its last two games.

The Big Blue followed the Amesbury win with a decisive 35–13 victory at Danvers. Linemen Al Owens, Joe Massidda, and Norman Walker all turned in strong performances, as did Winslow Shaw who broke through the line and tackled the Danvers fullback in the end zone for a safety. Bobby Carlin, now fully recovered, scored four touchdowns. Despite having missed the better part of four games, he was the leading scorer in Essex County. The boys had managed to rebound from their 0–3 start with three consecutive wins, all against conference opponents.

Misfortune, however, attacked in the form of illnesses and injuries that decimated the roster and threatened to reverse, or at least stall, the winning momentum. Bondy announced that Mike Farren suffered an infected spleen and was lost for the remainder of the season. Lineman

Fred Burk underwent surgery for an arm injury. Three other regulars were sidelined with a virus. Then a potentially more serious risk appeared. "Swampscott Grid Star Is Stricken With Polio" read the front page headline of the November 5, 1954, *Item*.

Left tackle Tommy "Mash" Lyons had been hospitalized and released for what was thought a virus. He was then re-admitted after his condition worsened and he spiked a fever. While the *Item* revealed that his polio was non-paralytic, mention of the dreaded disease gave rise to considerable fear. But after consultation, Bondy and the town health officer agreed that the team could continue to play. Travelling to take on weak Methuen, and missing five of its regulars, Swampscott still managed a 27–13 victory. Roger Coe scored three touchdowns on runs of 41, 70, and 90 yards.

The Big Blue's next opponent was Class C leader Stoughton, a team that had crushed the 1953 Sculpins and was riding an 11-game winning streak. Stoughton presented a huge challenge. The 1954 team may have been even stronger than its predecessor. While Gonsalves was gone he had been replaced by another star in Frank Jardine, the state's leading scorer. This game seemed a perfect opportunity for Bondy to build on his reputation as a miracle worker.

However, there was understandable concern in Swampscott about a virus that attacked players who had been sharing the locker room with Mash Lyons. Amidst these worries, Bondy and his assistants awaited a scouting report from Doc Marden, who had been sent to observe Stoughton's last game. The coaches must have been stunned by what they heard. When asked by Bondy for the briefing on Stoughton, Marden delivered perhaps the shortest scouting report in football history. "Don't play them!" he said. The clear message was that there was no way that the weakened squad could contend with Stoughton.

Marden's bleak assessment coincided with more discouraging news. While not diagnosed as polio, the virus that had sidelined three regulars for the Methuen game attacked a greater number of team members. Bondy likely asked himself whether it was wise to require his decimated squad to face Stoughton. The Marblehead game was always of paramount importance in Swampscott. Temporarily suspending football activities was the best way to assure that the players would be in condition to play on Thanksgiving.

On Tuesday, November 9, Bondy announced the cancellation of the Stoughton game and suspension of football practice until further notice, explaining:

> This step was taken upon the advice of the team physician in consultation with the school doctors. Seventeen members of the squad are ill or have recently returned to school after being ill … Suspension of all football is necessary to stop the spread of this illness, which is at the point of interfering with school studies.

Although cancellation seemed reasonable, a number of players were disappointed. They had become believers under Bondy and wanted a chance to pull off another upset win. Many regretted what they saw as a lost opportunity. They were even more anxious about the possibility that the Thanksgiving Day game might be canceled. For the seniors, it would be their last shot at the Headers. A few days later they were relieved to hear that the Marblehead game would be played. The team resumed practices.

Among the starters who had recovered were Bobby Carlin and co-captains Bill McGinn and Winslow Shaw. Then even Mash Lyons returned to practice, having recovered from his polio bout. While technically polio, the non-paralytic variety, also sometimes called abortive polio, was actually not considered a serious illness as it did not attack the central nervous system and more closely resembled the flu in its symptoms and duration. Mike Farren also suited up despite having been earlier described as lost for the season with an infected spleen.

All of this caused some folks to question the severity of the mini-epidemic that had allegedly led to the cancellation of the game against the team's strongest opponent. Three years later, when a seemingly confident Saugus coach was asked about his upcoming match against the undefeated Big Blue, he replied that he was just praying that flu did not break out in the Swampscott camp before the game.

The seniors had been through an up-and-down football experience. During their first two high school years, Swampscott had managed just one win. Then as juniors, they had responded to their new coach and discovered a winning formula. In the process, they had pulled off the upset of the season, if not the decade, ending Amesbury's record winning streak. As seniors, they had struggled through three successive early season losses and, far worse, seen Coach Foster suffer the tragic, senseless death of his young son. However, they managed to pull together, bounce back, and win four consecutive games before their scheduled contest with the top-ranked team in the division was canceled.

Now it would all be coming to an end against the Headers. Since 1946, no Swampscott team had beaten Marblehead. The seniors had been fourth graders when Swampscott last managed a Thanksgiving Day win. They could end their roller-coaster ride on the most positive of notes with a final victory in the game that they would most likely remember for the rest of their lives.

Roger Coe had scored multiple touchdowns on long runs throughout the season and was enjoying a highly productive start in his final high school game on Thanksgiving morning. In fact, he ran for almost 100 yards in the first quarter alone. He appeared headed for a career day and was in the midst of returning a punt when he was tripped and crashed headfirst into an opponent's knee. Roger's helmet cracked during the collision and the front edge cut into his forehead, slicing a nasty gash in his scalp.

By the time Roger reached the sideline and removed the helmet blood was streaming down his face and had pooled in one of his eye sockets. As Coach Lynch examined the wound, Bondy quickly approached and threw a hood over Coe's head, thus hiding the gruesome sight from onlookers in the stands. He suggested that Lynch take Coe into the locker room for treatment, noting that seeing the kid in that condition could unduly frighten the spectators. After receiving multiple stitches from the team doctor Roger returned to the sideline but was not allowed to re-enter the game. His Swampscott playing days were over.

While disappointed that he could not finish the final game of his senior year, Roger was not disappointed by what he witnessed from the sideline. Swampscott's seven-year drought ended at Blocksidge Field on a chilly, drizzly Thanksgiving morning in 1954. The Big Blue won 13–6. Headers could no longer boast that Coach Herm Hussey's teams had never lost to their Swampscott rivals.

The Big Blue finished with the same 5–3 record as had the prior year's squad, but this time the boys had beaten archrival Marblehead. With that victory and a second solid winning season, Swampscott's football program took another step forward.

Roger Coe had enjoyed an exciting, productive final season, scoring 10 touchdowns, none of them covering less than 17 yards. Winslow Shaw and Norman Walker had also played their final high school game. Coe, Shaw, and Walker were multi-sport standouts, class leaders and fine role models. They would be missed, but all moved on to bright futures.

Coe attended Bowdoin and was a starting sophomore halfback before suffering a career-ending torn ACL. Following graduation, Roger obtained an MBA from Dartmouth's Tuck School. After serving as a U.S. Army officer, he pursued a career in business, including 27 years with Samsonite where he held numerous executive positions. Now retired, he splits his time between homes in California and Colorado. Winslow Shaw played football at Norwich University and thereafter embarked on a distinguished military career, ultimately retiring as a highly decorated colonel before enjoying a second career as an executive with Gulfstream.

Shaw's fellow end Norman Walker graduated from Williams College where he played football and, after receiving a Master's in Education from Harvard, became a remarkable teacher and coach, with his high school and prep school teams capturing numerous championships and compiling a total of 276 victories and few losses. At one point, his Holderness School football squads had built a cumulative regular season record of 83–1. He credited his outstanding high school coaches with having influenced his own career choice.

As the 1954–55 school year wound down, Bondy firmed up his summer plans. His previous experience working at Camp Columbus gave him the idea of operating his own day camp for youngsters. This allowed him to supplement his income, employ a few players and become better acquainted with some of the younger kids in town. He located a vacant seaside tract in the Lanesville area of Gloucester and announced the opening of "Camp Fun." Ever the consummate salesman, he proclaimed that every child should enjoy the wonderful experience of attending summer camp, convincing a number of parents to sign up their youngsters.

Bondy only operated the camp for a few years, but then became director of Swampscott's summer parks program where he made it a practice to hire student-athletes as supervisors. The boys were typically players on his football team, while the girls were also actively involved as SHS athletes. As had been the case with Camp Fun, he was able to maintain closer contact with some of his players through the summer while also supplying paying jobs that enabled them to gain experience supervising youngsters and assuming responsibility. An added bonus was the opportunity to meet impressionable youngsters at the parks and encourage their dreams of an exciting future with the Big Blue.

You Couldn't Hit Him
with a Handful of Raisins

The shocking North Shore story in the summer of 1955 was the sudden, tragic death of Aristotle George "Harry" Agganis. The news hit Dick Lynch hard. He and Harry had been good friends. They had grown up in Lynn, attended Boston University, and been occasional basketball teammates. Known as "the Golden Greek," Agganis is still considered the greatest athlete ever produced in Lynn, Massachusetts. He had been a spectacular football and baseball player at Classical High School and then at Boston University. As a quarterback, he became BU's first All-American.

Harry passed up an opportunity to play professional football and instead remained close to home, signing a baseball contract with the Boston Red Sox. In his second season as the team's first baseman, he became ill. Undergoing treatment in a Cambridge hospital for pneumonia and phlebitis, he suffered a fatal pulmonary embolism.

Harry was only 26 years old when he died. It was estimated that 20,000 to 30,000 people paid their respects at Saint George's Greek Orthodox Church in Lynn during the one and a half days that his body lay in state. By all accounts, Harry Agganis was not only a remarkable athlete but a charismatic, admirable human being. He is revered to this day on Boston's North Shore.

Soon after the start of preseason practices, Bondy conducted another Parents Clinic. As a new feature, he had the four teams in the Big Blue program (eighth grade, ninth grade, JV, and varsity) consecutively run the same series of plays so as to demonstrate how expertise and execution improved as players advanced through the system. The varsity players must have looked like the New York Giants compared to the eighth-grade neophytes.

He further wooed Swampscott parents by mentioning numerous past players who had earned college scholarships and then pursued successful careers. Bondy had a genuine interest in helping players further their educations after high school. He took boys like Bobby Carlin on trips to various colleges. He was particularly high on Dartmouth. In 1952, Dartmouth's head coach, Tuss McLaughry, had been the featured speaker at Hudson's postseason banquet honoring Stan's undefeated Night Hawks.

Bondy frequently reached out to such coaches, encouraging them to consider his players for admission and scholarships. And he could be very persuasive. Elmo Benedetto also established contacts with folks in positions of authority at numerous schools, and he and Bondy sometimes joined forces to help players gain admission. The schools, depending upon the particular player, could run the gamut from elite Ivy League institutions to distant junior colleges with names that few, if any, North Shore residents recognized. It is doubtful that any other local high school coach had as much long-term success helping boys move on to prep schools and colleges.

The Joyce Jamboree, played in memory of Harry Agganis, drew 12,000 fans. A "smart-looking, aggressive Swampscott team" bested Salem 6–0. Bobby Carlin, now a 5-foot, 11-inch, 165-pound senior, was a standout. One of his new backfield mates was a rugged, hard-running sophomore named Charles "Billy" Carlyn. Billy's father, Bud, had been an accomplished athlete at Lynn English High School. After moving to Swampscott, he became a major supporter of the football program.

Billy Carlyn weighed close to 180 pounds as a sophomore and made good use of his size and ability, whether as a runner, blocker, or tackler. He was initially utilized as a right halfback and linebacker. For the rest of the season, and thereafter, fans and reporters frequently garbled the homophonic names of Carlin and Carlyn. Players identified as "Billy Carlin" and "Bobby Carlyn" were often credited with great performances. While Ray "Buzzy" Mansfield, Bun's younger brother, was slotted as the starting fullback, Carlyn would also be spending time in that spot, with juniors David Bartram and Freddy Marino seeing action at right halfback.

Heading into the regular season, Bondy seemed pleased with his squad, singling out Carlin and senior quarterback Billy Nelson for particular praise. They, along with tackle Bob Hurley, served as tri-captains. Other regulars in the interior line included juniors Fred Burk, Bill Hayden, and Ralph Francis, and seniors Joe Massidda and Jim Rothwell, who at about 200 pounds was the largest offensive lineman and was starting his third consecutive season at left tackle.

While the boys were poised for a successful start, they fell again to Woburn in the opener, this time losing 26–7 to the reigning Class C champs. Standout fullback Joe Castiglione, having scored 127 points as a junior, returned to torment the Big Blue. Castiglione (not the famous present-day Red Sox radio announcer) was an outstanding athlete, excelling as an All-Scholastic baseball catcher as well as a star running back. With his aggressive style and closely shaved, if not bald, head, Castiglione seemed a man among boys. Some thought he must have been at least 25 years old; he was that intimidating. Solidly built and weighing in the neighborhood of 200 pounds, he was tough to bring down. Stopping him was like trying to bring down a large, speeding bowling ball. Playing in the rain, he rolled over a number of Big Blue defenders, scoring three of the Tanners' four touchdowns.

Nonconference Reading was no longer on the Blue's schedule, and there was an open date on the Saturday following the Woburn loss. The ever-resourceful Swampscott coach filled the opening with a last-minute booking of Matignon High School. The Blue managed to scrape by with a 7–6 win. Prior to the season's third game, Bondy moved Billy Nelson to left end, replacing him at quarterback with sophomore Pete MacConachie, a decision likely influenced by the team's meager point production. The offense came to life, crushing Danvers, 45–13. As he had in 1954, Bobby Carlin scored four touchdowns. The Oniontowners must have been thankful that Carlin was a senior.

Next on the agenda was Winthrop. Bondy scheduled the game for Saturday morning. He promoted the early start as a convenience for football fans, who could watch another game in the afternoon. He further explained his reasoning with ice cream and medical metaphors:

> If I were running an ice cream parlor, I wouldn't feature vanilla every week. You might find that chocolate is a more popular flavor. A few schools have tried Saturday morning games with

varying degrees of success. It may be just what the doctor ordered for Swampscott. If not, we'll be back on an afternoon schedule. There's only one way to find out and that's to play one.

Bondy never found out whether it was "just what the doctor ordered" because the game was postponed to Monday due to rain. It seemed to make little difference to the SHS players, as they easily took down Winthrop, 34–13. Carlin, described in the local paper as a "twisting, squirming, hard-running, 165-pound halfback," again tallied four times.

In his two most recent games, the talented senior had scored eight touchdowns. He had been a very good running back since his sophomore season but had struggled at times with injuries and illness. Now he was healthy and benefiting from over two years of coaching by the SHS staff. Dick Lynch, in particular, had pushed Carlin to improve. Bobby had been quick and shifty as a junior but sometimes danced around a bit. When Coach Lynch thought that Bobby was weaving or juking too much he forcefully got the halfback's undivided attention, pointing toward the end zone, and shouting, "Carlin, knock it off. The *dance* isn't until Saturday night. The *goal line* is over there!"

As coaches, Stan Bondelevitch and Dick Lynch used different skills to mold high school players. Bondy generally left instruction in football fundamentals to Lynch and the other assistants. He was much more about inspiring kids to play and building support in the community. Stan *built* Carlin up while Dick *coached* him up. They would do the same for hundreds of other boys over the years. In Bobby's case, the coaching and his own hard work had paid off. By the midpoint of the 1955 season, Carlin was the leading scorer in Essex County.

Swampscott's next game was against perennial powerhouse Amesbury. Prior to Stan's arrival, losing to the Carriagemakers had become a bad habit. Since his arrival in 1953, Bondy's teams had beaten Amesbury twice. However, the Carriagemakers were a strong, well coached club, and the visiting Big Blue fell short, losing by a touchdown, 25–19. Sadly, the game was the last coached by Amesbury's Tony Tassinari against Swampscott. One month later, and only hours after his Amesbury team defeated Newburyport in the annual Thanksgiving Day game, Coach Tassinari suffered a fatal heart attack.

The Gloucester Fishermen had easily beaten Swampscott in 1953 and 1954 but would not have a chance to do it again in 1955, as they had been replaced on the schedule with Lynn's Saint Mary's High School. The change likely benefited the Big Blue, as the Fishermen won the Class B title in 1955 and 1956, while SHS got by Saint Mary's, 7–6.

A third one-point victory followed as the boys took down Methuen, 14–13. They then crushed Stoneham, 31–6, with yet another four-touchdown performance by Carlin. He scored on runs of 65, 31, 25 and 3 yards. It was the third time in the season that Carlin tallied four touchdowns. An *Item* sportswriter started to refer to the Swampscott star as "the Comet" but it did not catch on. To everyone else, he remained simply Bobby Carlin.

The Big Blue prepared for its Thanksgiving date with the Headers. Prior to 1954, Coach Hussey's team had never fallen to Swampscott. While he and his players were undoubtedly focused on avoiding a second consecutive loss, the Swampscott boys, having experienced what a victory over their rivals felt like, were intent on winning again. As an added incentive, Swampscott merchants "[i]n a spontaneous, unprecedented move, indicative of the widespread interest in the Big Blue football successes" were offering over 25 awards to players in the form of gift certificates, products, or services for notable accomplishments on Thanksgiving.

The game was a classic. As reported by the *Item*:

> In a ding-dong battle that left nearly 5000 fans limp and breathless, the Big Blue of Swampscott squeezed out a 19 to 18 victory over Marblehead yesterday forenoon at Veterans Stadium, Marblehead, in one of the most thrilling clashes ever staged by the ancient and traditional foes.

Early in the contest Bondy reinserted Billy Nelson at quarterback. Respected by his teammates, the senior tri-captain helped spark the offense. The well-matched rivals slugged it out, with the lead changing hands five times. Late in the third quarter, the Blue regained the edge, 13–12, on a Billy Carlyn conversion following Bobby Carlin's 40-yard touchdown sprint.

The Headers were talented and dangerous; with athletic sophomore quarterback Ronnie Conn and strong junior halfback Dick Mezquita. One of their most effective plays was a quarterback read-option, with Conn rolling to his left while reading the defensive end, and Mezquita running behind him toward the sideline. If Conn saw the defensive end closing on him, he would toss the ball out to Mezquita. But if the end instead drifted away from Conn toward Mezquita, the quarterback would keep the ball and turn upfield. The Blue defense had seen the play repeatedly in practice for over a week, run by the JV offense as it had tried to mimic the Marblehead attack.

By early in the fourth quarter, Conn and his teammates had driven almost to the SHS goal line and appeared on the verge of re-taking the lead. Junior Doug Haley was Swampscott's right outside linebacker. Big Blue hockey star Dick Massey was the right defensive end. When Conn rolled to his left and Dick Mezquita sprinted behind him toward the sideline, Haley recognized the option play. His job was to cover Mezquita while Massey closed on Conn. When Massey drove toward Conn, the Header quarterback flipped a high toss toward Mezquita. Haley, anticipating beautifully, leaped and was just able to reach the ball and snatch it out of the air before it could sail over his head to Mezquita.

Ninety-five yards of open space lay between Doug and the end zone. Years later, Dick Lynch enjoyed describing the play whenever Haley was within earshot. It was, Lynch recounted, "the longest run in Big Blue history, lasting over a minute." He'd sometimes add that the referee *walked* alongside Haley all the way to the goal line. Joking aside, it was a huge play, allowing the Big Blue to extend its lead to 19–12. Yet, the game was not over.

The Headers responded quickly with halfback Charlie Gilligan returning the kickoff all the way to the visitors' 5-yard line. Ronnie Conn ran it in on second down to make the score 19–18. The Headers could have tied the game with a successful conversion, but the defense stopped Gilligan short of the end zone. A final bid by Marblehead was then snuffed out when Haley again picked off Conn. Swampscott held on for the thrilling one-point victory. Doug Haley collected quite a few of the prizes offered by local merchants, including the most outstanding player award.

In addition to numerous lead changes, Haley's heroics, and the razor-thin margin of victory, the exciting game had featured the most bizarre tackle ever made in the rivalry's long history. It happened following Conn's touchdown. A Big Blue player, inactive due to injury and standing on the sideline in his street clothes, was so incensed when he saw Conn score that he raced onto the field and tackled the Header quarterback in the end zone. Police officers quickly apprehended Swampscott's self-appointed 12th man and hauled him away.

It had been a very good year for SHS football. The team defeated the Headers for the second straight season, the first time that Swampscott had done so in 40 years. And it had posted the best record (7–2) in more than a decade. The only losses were to a strong Amesbury squad and defending Class C champion Woburn. Looking back on that long-ago season, Bob Carlin now marvels that the team was able to garner seven victories. "We really were not very good," he confesses. Recalling that the 1954 squad had been bigger, faster, and more experienced, he notes that not having to face Gloucester and Reading likely helped the 1955 team post a better record. But even with a less difficult schedule, Carlin maintains that the boys were able to win so many games simply because the coaches convinced them that they could.

After the season Bondy confided to Carlin that he was considering becoming the football coach at Colby College and asked whether Bobby would be interested in attending that school. Bondy had been a mentor to Carlin for three years, encouraging him to focus on his studies and take an active leadership role in school activities. Following examples set by predecessors like Tom Gorman and Winslow Shaw, Bobby had done just that. He enthusiastically assured his coach that he would love to join him at Colby. He would have gone anywhere to play for Stan Bondelevitch. But Carlin had played his final game for Bondy. Stan remained in Swampscott.

Bobby capped off his high school career by being named co-winner of the prestigious Thom McAn Shoe Trophy, a bronzed football shoe and plaque awarded annually to the high school senior deemed the top student-football player on Boston's North Shore. The accolade was well-deserved. A role model for younger players, he was a leader on and off the football field. He served as tri-captain of the 1955 team, and also lettered in basketball and baseball. He was elected a class officer in three consecutive years, including class president. He was an honor student.

While he scored four offensive touchdowns in four separate games and ran away with the 1955 Essex County scoring title, his coach described him as "the best defensive man on our team." His combination of speed and athleticism made him one of the most exciting players in Swampscott's history. As Coach Lynch put it, "You couldn't hit him with a handful of raisins." Bondy praised him as, "The finest boy I've ever coached."

Bobby Carlin was elected football captain at Brown University, and then, like his mentor Bondy, spent time playing for the semi-pro Providence Steamrollers. Returning to the North Shore, he became an insurance executive while volunteering as a coach of various youth sports teams in Swampscott. Today he resides in Marblehead, where he follows the athletic exploits of his grandchildren. He has never forgotten that spring day in 1953 when he first met Stan Bondelevitch; a day that he is convinced changed his life.

A Cure for Fumbleitis

As the summer of 1956 neared its conclusion, there was cause for optimism about the upcoming Big Blue football season. Most of the team's seniors had been in Bondy's program since they were freshmen. Despite Carlin's graduation, the squad had good backfield depth, including seniors Freddy Marino, Tony Savino, and Ray "Buzzy" Mansfield, junior Billy Carlyn, and sophomores George Blais and Jackie Milo. The backfield was so crowded that senior Dave Bartram, who had played regularly as a halfback in 1955, was moved to right end.

Billy Carlyn was the kind of player who could put a smile on a coach's face. He had good speed and hit like a locomotive. As a lead blocker, he frequently knocked down defensive ends and other opponents. As a linebacker, he dropped running backs with punishing tackles. And as a ball carrier, he powered through or ran around most defenders. His playing style had earned him the nickname, "Bull." He could also kick the ball when called upon. In short, Carlyn was the complete package. He was also a popular kid who could light up a room with his beaming grin, easy manner, and outgoing personality.

Buzzy Mansfield, the younger brother of Bob "Bun" Mansfield, was a strong, rugged, and good-sized fullback. Left halfback Savino, a sturdy, six-foot, two-inch, 200-pound converted end, was one of the hardest runners ever to play for Swampscott. Nicknamed "the Hairy Wonder," Tony was also occasionally referred to as "Knees" due to his unique running style. He pumped his knees up like firing pistons as he charged forward. This could be punishing on prospective tacklers. During one scrimmage Savino's knee hit a teammate's helmet with such force that the kid was knocked unconscious. Thereafter the coaches sometimes barred him from running with the ball during contact drills out of concern for the safety of the defensive players.

Savino also had a unique way of finishing touchdowns. After crossing the goal line, he touched the goal post with the football before handing it to an official. He was coached to perform the ritual following the 1955 Stoneham game, during which he hauled in a pass on his own 40-yard line and raced toward the end zone 60 yards away. However, when he reached the 5-yard line, he mistakenly believed he had scored. Slowing almost a stop, he was about to hand the ball to the referee and celebrate when a pursuing Stoneham player managed to knock him into the end zone for the touchdown. To prevent future premature Savino touchdown celebrations, the coaches ordered him to touch the goal post with the football immediately after each score.

In addition to his football talents, the Hairy Wonder was an outstanding high school baseball player. Aware that Dick Lynch served as a part-time scout for the Philadelphia Phillies, he told the coach that he wanted to play in the major leagues. "Yeh, so do I!" snapped Lynch. But Savino ultimately did attract some interest from several professional teams. With Knees Savino, Bull Carlyn, and Buzzy Mansfield, Swampscott had a trio of good-sized, hard-running backs, also capable of leading the way as blockers.

Another senior who would be playing a major role was right half-back, Freddy Marino. Standing about 5-foot, 8-inches, Freddy had good speed and weighed a solid 165 pounds. Jackie Milo and George Blais, two promising, athletic sophomore speedsters, were also making their presence felt. Milo may have been the fastest player on the squad, while Blais could have been more aptly named "Blaze" because of his ability to torch defenses with super-quick blasts through the line and fantastic acceleration. Like Marino, Blais was also left-handed and assigned to the right halfback position, while Milo backed up Savino on the other side.

The co-captains were end Doug Haley and guard Fred Burk, son of the school nurse. Joining them in the front line were veteran seniors Bill Hayden, Ralph Francis, Terry Lyons, and Dave Bartram, and junior center Dave Frary.

Doug Haley's parents divorced when he was young and his father moved to another state. His mother was the person primarily responsible for raising him and his younger sister. Mrs. Haley encouraged her son to participate in sports, believing that the experience would be socially and emotionally beneficial.

Doug started out, as did most kids in Swampscott, by joining other boys for informal games in the town parks. On Saturday afternoons, he and his friends gathered outside the fence behind the stands at Blocksidge Field, waiting for the band to play the national anthem. When it did and the police officers were at attention with their eyes fixed on the flag, the boys crawled through a hole under the fence. It seemed that the public works department never got around to filling the hole and the town's police officers always managed to look the other way as, year after year, Swampscott kids *snuck* into the Saturday games.

Once inside, Doug and his pals, while occasionally watching the action on the field, spent most of their time engaged in what they called "tackle-fumble football" in the grassy area behind the south end zone. This game, which Swampscott boys seemed to have played from the beginning of time, was quite simple. A kid grabbed a football and ran. The other boys gave chase, with each trying to tackle the ball carrier, rip the football loose, and then similarly run with it until also being knocked down and forced to give up the ball. It was essentially a rough free-for-all with no scoring involved.

Haley entered the ninth grade in 1953 and signed up for the freshman team. It was Bondy's first year in town, so Doug, his teammates, and the head coach started off together. Freshman coach Doc Marden taught the boys how to put on and wear the equipment, explained various positions, and taught fundamentals such as blocking and tackling. After that they began to learn the plays. Doug performed well enough as an end and linebacker to be selected as one of the several ninth graders allowed to dress with the varsity on Thanksgiving. While he did not get a chance to play, it was a thrill to run onto the field in a varsity uniform.

Haley viewed Bondy as almost a second father because the coach took a genuine interest in his life and encouraged him to focus on school work as well as sports. At one point, Doug suffered a serious arm injury when he was cleated during practice. After infection and blood poisoning set in he was kept at home on bed rest for a lengthy period. Bondy showed up at the Haley house every day to check on his condition and talk with Doug and his mother.

After Doug was elected co-captain of the 1956 squad, Bondy made sure to credit Doug's mother for her son's development and achievements, writing her a letter that included the following:

Doug is loyal, a high character, respectful, and most important an example to the younger boys.… Most of the credit goes to one person; a boy does not grow up that way. At times he must be pushed into the right path. In my opinion Doug's mother deserves the credit. Congratulations Mrs. Haley for the wonderful job you are doing on a wonderful boy.

By the start of his senior year, Haley had already played a considerable amount of varsity football. At around 150 pounds, he had absorbed his share of punishment, including being run over or knocked down by stronger, older opponents like Woburn's human bowling ball, Joe Castiglione. But Doug had also made a number of impact plays, including two that he labeled "the pick-off" and "the pinch."

It seemed that everyone remembered the pick-off, and thousands saw it happen. It was the most exciting moment in the 19–18 victory over the Headers at the 1955 Thanksgiving game. Haley's interception and 95-yard return of a Ronnie Conn lateral was one of the most memorable plays in the long history of the fabled rivalry. By contrast, "the pinch," which also took place during Haley's junior year, was seen by no one and never lauded in the newspapers nor celebrated by Swampscott's fans. Yet, in Doug's mind, it had played perhaps as big a role in the Blue's win over Methuen as had "the pick-off" in the victory over the Headers.

The 1955 Methuen game was played at Blocksidge Field in rain and mud. Both teams struggled to generate offense, and SHS was trailing 7–6 late in the fourth quarter. The team held the ball on its own 45-yard line, facing fourth down with the first down marker three yards distant. With the little time remaining, Bondy decided to try for the first down by running Bull Carlyn on a play in which Doug blocked down on the defensive tackle. But the play failed, as Methuen defenders broke through the line and stopped Carlyn in the backfield.

There was a pileup near the line of scrimmage, with Haley lying in the mud beneath Methuen's mammoth tackle whose jersey had rolled up to his chest. Doug was staring at a big, exposed belly. Whether out of frustration, anger, or both, he grabbed a roll of uncovered flesh, twisted and squeezed. The tackle screamed and then wound up and delivered a hard punch to Haley's face. It was Doug's, and Swampscott's, lucky day. Protective translucent bars had been affixed to the players' helmets about a month earlier. The punch smashed harmlessly into Doug's face guard. But while the pinch had been hidden from view, the Methuen player's retaliatory punch was seen by many, including the referee who assessed an unsportsmanlike conduct penalty against Methuen. The Big Blue was awarded a first down on the visitor's 40. From that point, the offense drove to the Methuen end zone for the winning touchdown.

Following the game, Doug told the coaches about the pinch. But they dismissed the story as a figment of his imagination, telling him to forget about it. Yet he always remembered that the tackle's loss of control hurt his team and bailed out Doug for his own foolish action. If the big kid had refrained from retaliating Methuen would have taken possession in Swampscott territory with the lead and an excellent chance of winning.

Bondy continued to promote his program with the support and assistance of local sports writers like the *Item's* Ed Cahill, who wrote in glowing terms about the Swampscott Boosters. Cahill pointed out that while the Boosters had always been supportive, enthusiasm mounted with the return of winning football. He wrote that few, if any, organizations in New England contributed so heavily to support youth sports, mentioning that the latest achievement was an all-electric scoreboard at Blocksidge. Other contributions included refreshments for both the home and visiting teams at half-time, game films, an annual sports night awards banquet, some of the team uniforms, and scholarships. Cahill urged all Swampscott residents to support the Boosters, declaring, "Every buck is a boost!"

The support from Cahill and other writers was not surprising. With an engaging and commanding personality, Stan was a master of public and media relations. He managed to befriend most of those in the local sports media, including writers and editors at the *Item*, *Salem News*, and Boston newspapers. He worked at it constantly. There were regular Sunday night gatherings at his house where assistant coaches and at least one invited sports reporter or other media representative socialized. Bondy made certain that there was plenty to eat and drink. He would hold forth and often produce the 1953 Amesbury game film for viewing. Dick Lynch thought that he must have watched it 100 times.

If Bondy saw nothing positive in the newspapers over a period of time he contacted the reporters and columnists and encouraged them to write something. And he was not above reminding them that he had provided good material for stories in the past. He was seldom disappointed with the results.

The Blue again opened against Woburn, a team that had been the conference bully in recent years. Swampscott suffered one-sided losses in 1954 and 1955. In their last meeting, the boys were soundly beaten by a score of 26–7. The Tanners went on to win every game and were the defending conference champions. The good news was that the intimidating Castiglione was finally gone and SHS had the depth and talent to compete. In the week leading up to the game line coach Stevenson told his players that, given Swampscott's talented backs, the offense could put plenty of points on the board if the linemen did their jobs.

Everyone, it seemed, did their jobs in the opener. After Bondy concluded a locker room speech that would have been the envy of Knute Rockne, the boys stormed onto the field and thrashed the Tanners, 38–6. It was the best possible start. Knees Savino enjoyed a big day; galloping 35 yards for one touchdown and intercepting a pass and returning it 50 for another. The team next walloped Cambridge Latin, 32–6, and Danvers, 39–0. In the season's first three games, SHS outscored its opponents, 109–12. Moreover, the Blue had now won seven consecutive contests since its 1955 loss to Amesbury.

As the season progressed, Bondy continued to find ways to generate publicity. For example, on October 2, 1956, the *Item* printed a photo of the coach issuing wireless directives to his helmeted starting quarterback Chuck Lynch (not related to Dick Lynch). Under a subheading titled, "Swampscott Tinkers With Short-Wave Radio," Cahill wrote about Bondy's experimentation with a walkie-talkie developed by Tom Eickelberger, the head of the SHS Manual Arts Department. Cleveland Browns coach Paul Brown had apparently been the first to come up with the idea of inserting a small receiver inside the helmet that allowed him to directly communicate with his quarterback, thereby eliminating the need to shuffle players in and out of games to relay messages.

As Cahill explained,

Swampscott, quick to borrow any progressive innovation, wasn't long in coming up with the same type of gadget. Trouble is, unlike the pros, the schoolboys are prevented by the rules from receiving any coaching from the sidelines.

Stan complained that the rule had outlived its usefulness and that coaches of other sports were not prevented from coaching while the game was in progress. He argued that changing the rule "would take the pressure off of a 16-year-old quarterback who is now expected to function like a mature man when selecting his plays in a tough spot." However, Bondy was careful to qualify his criticism, noting that the team was "blessed with a smart little quarterback in Chuck Lynch" who was "calling the plays better than I could do, and perhaps it's been just as well we haven't been using the radio-phone."

Having routed three opponents, the unbeaten Big Blue next faced an away game against tough Winthrop. Swampscott was 3–0 against Winthrop since Bondy's arrival and during that time had outscored its southern neighbor 106–13. The one-sided affairs were particularly galling for many in Winthrop who believed that their players were tougher than the boys from the more affluent community to the north.

While Winthrop was smaller in area than even Swampscott, it had considerably more inhabitants. But the two communities were similar in a number of ways. Both were small, suburban, seaside locales featuring sandy beaches, fishermen, lobster boats, and water views of Boston and Nahant. And both towns were primarily populated by folks of English, Irish, and Italian ancestry. Also, like Swampscott, Winthrop was home to a significant Jewish population.

Winners of two of their first three games, the Winthrop players were anxious to avoid another loss to SHS. The game was scheduled for Monday morning—Columbus Day. Swampscott did not have the services of George Blais, down with a viral infection. Moreover, Billy Carlyn, still hampered by an ankle injury sustained against Woburn, could only be used sparingly.

It was a rainy, wet day and the home team, with a big defensive front, shut down Swampscott's running attack, holding the visitors to a single touchdown. Suffering from what the *Item* termed an epidemic of "fumbleitis," the Blue coughed up the ball five times. The last fumble occurred in the fourth quarter with Swampscott on Winthrop's 25-yard line and the game tied at 6–6. A 210-pound defensive tackle named Frank DeFelice recovered the ball and Winthrop then drove 75 yards in six plays to score, sealing a 12–6 victory. Much of the yardage was gained running behind DeFelice. The Frank DeFelice story was just beginning for Swampscott. A decade later he would be re-surfacing to play a more colorful, positive and enduring role in the Big Blue's athletic fortunes.

While Bondy was not pleased with the result of the Winthrop game, he managed to use it for an amusing story. The following short blurb, entitled "Bondelevitch Pup Gets New Name," appeared in the *Item* next to the report of the disappointing loss:

> Coach Stan Bondelevitch whose Swampscott High Team dropped its first decision in eight successive starts yesterday, may have lost a ball game but he hasn't lost his sense of humor. The Big Blue fumbled away its chances to an aggressive Winthrop High eleven at Winthrop, bowing 12–6. As a result the Bondelevitch family pooch has a new name. He was affectionately known up to yesterday as "Fumble." Today he was rechristened. "From now on," smiled Bondelevitch, "we're calling him 'Touchdown.'"

Bondy may have joked with the newspaper about "Fumble" but there was nothing funny in the message he delivered to his players following the game. The boys heard that they had lost a game that should have been won. There had been too much sloppy play, including the multiple fumbles.

During the regular season, the players were usually allowed to rest for a couple of days following a game. Bondy loaned the game films and projector to the boys so that they could gather at the home of one of their teammates and have a good time hooting and howling over their individual heroics and occasional screw-ups on the road to victory. Mondays were reserved for a more serious and occasionally critical film review with the coaches. During the remainder of the week, the team practiced but there was little, if any, contact. Such, however, was not the case in the wake of the Winthrop loss.

There were no "days off." The boys were told to prepare for a full-contact practice on the following afternoon and that all starting jobs were up for grabs. Stan Bondelevitch did not believe in maintaining the status quo after losing a winnable game. There was a price to be paid when his team failed to play up to its potential. The players on the 1956 squad do not have fond memories of the Winthrop game, nor of the long, grueling practice on the following day.

It was a particularly hot October Tuesday, and the intrasquad scrimmage felt like it would never end. Junior Jimmy Gorman, a reserve tackle, never left the playing field during that seemingly endless ordeal. Many decades later he joked that it was the football equivalent of the Bataan Death March. But following that endurance test Jimmy began to see regular duty in varsity games.

There may not have been any laughter on the practice field following the Winthrop loss, but Bondy usually found ways to lighten the mood. Humor was one of his most oft-used coaching tools. Gorman recalled a practice when Bondy made certain that everyone appreciated his exasperation over a particular miscue. As he wailed, he tore off his hat, threw it to the ground, and then jumped up and down repeatedly on the abused chapeau. Describing the silly spectacle many decades later, Gorman noted that "such an image has a tendency to stay with you."

On another occasion, Stan was looking away from the practice field when one of the reserve players ran him over while trying to catch a pass. "If you keep hitting like that," barked Bondy, "you'll be a star!" And when the coach was once knocked down on the sideline during a scrimmage he quickly managed to complete a rolling somersault and bounce back up on his feet, shouting, "You can't hurt a tough Polack!"

Having dropped its first game after seven consecutive victories, the team prepared to face visiting Amesbury. Bondy announced line-up changes that included inserting speedy Jackie Milo as a starting halfback. The boys rebounded from their sloppy Winthrop performance. Milo and Marino both scored as they shut out the Carriagemakers, 12–0. The Big Blue improved to 4–1 but then stumbled in the rain against Saint Mary's of Lynn, losing 22–20 despite Marino's three touchdowns. The two-point loss was particularly hard to accept. The winning points were scored late in the game when Jackie Milo's momentum after intercepting a pass carried him into his own end zone where he was tackled. The officials deemed it a safety and awarded Saint Mary's the crucial points.

While the losses against Winthrop and Saint Mary's were disappointing, the future looked bright. Now into his fourth season as athletic director and head coach, Bondy had implemented a highly organized, tightly controlled, and increasingly successful, youth sports program. His centerpiece was, of course, football. An article at the top of the *Item's* October 25, 1956, sports page reported that Swampscott's seventh-, eighth-, and ninth-grade teams had all won on the preceding day at Phillips Park. While noting that over 144 boys participated in the three football games, the writer added that more than 60 high school girls were also at the park preparing for their upcoming field hockey matches. He concluded by mentioning that Coach Bondelevitch was "well pleased with the results."

An efficient feeder system for his varsity was humming along. Seventh graders began learning the plays and progressed for the next few years with new coaches, but still operating under the same system. By the time they reported to the high school team most were fully familiar with the varsity's schemes, plays, terminologies and each other. And Bondy had good reason to be "well pleased". His ninth-grade squad went on to defeat every team on their schedule. Moreover, his sophomore players had likewise been unbeaten as freshmen. Now a few were seeing regular action with the varsity while the rest were playing on the JVs and they too would complete the season with an unblemished record. In doing so, the 8–0 JVs would post four shutouts.

On October 31, 1956, another unusual article about Swampscott football appeared atop the *Item's* sports page. This time it was an uplifting story about two sophomores who overcame disabilities to play for the varsity. Billy Sentner was diabetic and John Flanagan was missing the toes on his left foot. Bondy praised the two as an inspiration, noting that they were "proof that physical handicaps mean little to boys who have a real desire to play football." He concluded prophetically, "Give me 11 boys like these two and we'd win the State championship."

The team bounced back from the Saint Mary's loss by beating Revere, 20–13, and Rindge Tech, 34–13. Swampscott and Marblehead seemed evenly matched going into their annual Thanksgiving morning tilt. The

Big Blue sported a 6–2 record while Marblehead stood at 6–1–1. In addition to the usual bragging rights, the conference crown was up for grabs.

Unfortunately for Swampscott, quarterback Chuck Lynch missed the game with an infected foot. Tony Savino scored twice, including running back a kickoff 85 yards for a touchdown. However, Freddy Marino suffered a broken collarbone on the last play of the first half and missed the remainder of the game. The squad took a 12–7 lead into the locker room at halftime, but never scored again, losing 19–12.

After graduating from SHS, Doug Haley, master of "the pick-off" and "the pinch," spent a postgraduate year at Phillips Exeter Academy and then attended Williams College, followed by law school. He enjoyed success as both a real estate lawyer and developer. Recently he and his wife relocated to Marblehead, site of his 1955 Thanksgiving Day heroics.

Although Doug and his teammates finished the 1956 season with a solid 6–3 record, they and their fans were surely disappointed by the loss to Marblehead, which cost Swampscott the conference title. Bondy's team completed its fourth consecutive winning season. But by that point in Hudson his Night Hawks had finished with a perfect record and a title. Championships and perfect records still eluded the Big Blue. That was about to change.

The Fairytale Season

By 1957, Bondy had made SHS football a centerpiece of community involvement and interest. Increasing numbers of boys competed for positions on Big Blue teams, beginning in the seventh grade. Increasing numbers of students and residents actively supported the teams.

While good players had graduated, a core of highly capable seniors returned to lead the 1957 squad and a deep group of talented juniors joined them. Billy Carlyn and Jimmy Gorman were named co-captains. The two friends had followed different paths to their leadership positions. Carlyn was a recognized star. The fullback/linebacker had been playing regularly for the varsity from the day that he stepped onto the field as a sophomore. He was a remarkably gifted athlete for whom outstanding performance in football, or almost any sport, came naturally. He seemed to excel everywhere but in the classroom. His election as one of the team's captains was a foregone conclusion.

By contrast, Jimmy Gorman, who did excel in the classroom, had worked and sweated over the preceding several years to finally win a starting job as a varsity lineman. He, like so many Swampscott kids, had enjoyed playing tackle-fumble football while growing up. But in those pre-Bondy days, he had paid scant attention to the high school team, even when older brother Tom was playing.

Although Jimmy hailed from a football-playing family, his introduction to organized football came only after he entered high school. When he and his classmates reported for the first day of freshman practice, Coach Marden explained the different positions and then asked each boy to line up at the position he wished to play. One boy stepped into the center spot. Every other kid, including Jimmy, lined up as either a back or an end. Apparently, the idea of toiling as obscure linemen offered little appeal. Jimmy soon found himself assigned to play guard on offense and linebacker on defense, and he continued in those positions as a sophomore with the JVs.

Early in his first season with the varsity, Jimmy made the switch to offensive tackle. This change did not result from a coach's careful review of Gorman's abilities. Rather, it happened because he was the first player to respond to a request from the man the boys called the chipmunk. Coach Stevenson was working with his first-team defensive line. In attempting to assemble an opposing offense he shouted, "Give me a tackle right here," while pointing to a vacant spot. Gorman was standing nearby and when no one else stepped in he did.

As a second-stringer, Gorman saw almost no action during the first four games in 1956. It was only after the "Bataan Death March" scrimmage following the mid-season Winthrop loss that he managed to get onto the field more often. He finally broke into the starting line-up for the next-to-last game. However, he was then benched without explanation late in the first half of the Marblehead contest.

Thus, his 1957 election as co-captain came as a surprise, if not a shock. He even wondered whether it was a mistake or whether the coaches had for some reason rigged the election. His mother's reaction when she heard the news was not reassuring. "Why did they pick *you?*" she asked incredulously. But it was no fluke. There was much for his teammates to respect. He had developed into a solid varsity tackle by the end of his junior season. Bright and popular, he was active in other school activities. He was student council president and a member of the National Honor Society. And his older brother Tom had starred on Bondy's inaugural 1953 squad.

In addition to the 6-foot, 2-inch, 180-pound Gorman, seniors Dave "Bear" Frary, Billy Wood, Matt Faino, Frank Parsons, Dick Gowen, and Eliot Rothwell, and juniors Dick Maitland, Bob Andrews, and John Flanagan would be playing regularly up front. Frary had the most varsity experience. The quiet 190-pound center/linebacker had seen some action as a sophomore backing up starter Joe Massidda before starting throughout the 1956 campaign. He was one of the team's best linemen, a highly reliable center who also excelled as a long snapper.

Wood and Maitland were the starting guards while Gorman and Andrews filled the tackle slots. Flanagan was a fixture at left end. Gowen and Rothwell shared right end duties. While they were capable receivers both had earned less than complimentary nicknames from Coach Lynch while playing on his JV squad. He christened Gowen "Just out of Reach" while Rothwell became "Can't catch up." Starting defensive end Matt Faino backed up the guards on offense while middle guard Frank Parsons did the same for the offensive tackles. At over 200 pounds, he was the biggest player on the roster.

There was plenty of backfield depth. Bull Carlyn returned to start at fullback. By the first game, juniors George Blais and Jackie Milo had nailed down the two starting halfback spots. Others who were available to fill in as running backs included seniors Dick Winick, Ed Cohen, and Terry Cotton, and juniors Frank "Truck" Cahoon, Dick Coe, and Phil Cudmore.

Winick, who also served as the team's kicker, had suffered the humiliation of completely missing the football while kicking off in a JV game. During kickoffs, players on receiving teams frequently targeted the kickers, who sometimes did not take their eyes off the football in time to see oncoming blockers who would administer vicious hits. The coaches were constantly emphasizing the need for kickers to protect themselves by looking up quickly to avoid such attacks. Dick had tried to follow that advice but on one occasion actually looked up before striking the ball. His foot never made contact and the football remained motionless on the tee while his teammates charged downfield. Coach Lynch never lost an opportunity to needle Winick about his whiff.

While Chuck Lynch, who had quarterbacked the 1956 squad, was still available, a 6-foot, 175-pound junior named Eddie Loveday became the starting signal caller during preseason. Eddie, a three-sport athlete and cousin of 1954 co-captain Winslow Shaw, had led both the freshmen and JVs to undefeated seasons, and then played well for the varsity when he was inserted during spring practice. Chuck handled the situation gracefully, complimenting Loveday on his strong performance. When Eddie said, "I'm only keeping the seat warm for you, Chucky," Lynch had replied matter-of-factly, "I don't think so." But Chuck was a solid football player who would contribute to the defense throughout the 1957 campaign.

Though a bit light, the 1957 squad featured good depth, backfield speed, and some fine athletes. Many of the boys had been playing in the program for several years. As a result, they were adept at executing the wing-T, where timing, quickness, and agility were more critical to success than size. Most of the linemen were quick and agile and had run the plays so often they could probably perform their assignments blindfolded.

Spring practice in Swampscott was always an iffy proposition due to scheduling and weather. Many players and coaches were involved in other sports such as basketball, hockey, baseball, and track. As a result, spring football sessions were squeezed into a tight two-week window, typically beginning in early March when the Massachusetts weather is anything but "spring-like."

It is sometimes said that there are four seasons on the North Shore: summer, fall, winter, and *mud*. Players reporting for spring practice often found a field covered with snow, flooded, or otherwise unplayable. There were times when they would be required to tote shovels to Phillips Park and clear away enough snow to allow the team to practice. On other occasions, when the field was simply unplayable, Bondy took the boys down to one of the beaches for drills. Such events presented perfect opportunities for publicity, and media representatives were summoned to photograph and write about the seaside workouts.

Despite frequent poor conditions, there was considerable hitting and scrimmaging. Bondy knew that players who were banged up during spring drills had the entire summer to recover. The less-than-ideal conditions and the demanding nature of the drills may have explained the squad's languid performance during most of the practices in March of 1957. To use Bondy's phrase, such factors could have a tendency to "stunt the enthusiasm," particularly with no actual game on the immediate horizon.

Most of the boys were looking forward to the final day of spring drills until they learned that it would be spent in a full-contact scrimmage against Waltham High School. Waltham was an established Class A power. The scrimmage was held at Blocksidge Field on a raw, snowy afternoon. If, as seems likely, many Swampscott players approached the game with feelings akin to dread, those emotions changed dramatically as the scrimmage played out. The team surprised itself, dominating the larger Waltham squad. In retrospect, it was a watershed day because the boys realized that, playing together and supporting each other, they were very good. They had no reason to fear any opponent. Besting the Class A power had been more than gratifying—it had been downright fun.

Recalling their triumph over Waltham, the players were generally upbeat and optimistic about the upcoming season. Perhaps they could compete not only for a conference championship but for an Eastern Massachusetts Class C title. Since there were no playoffs, titles were determined solely by a team's ranking within its class at season's end. Rankings were influenced by strength of schedule, with more points awarded for victories over teams in higher classes. While Swampscott was in Class C, a few of the other conference teams, including Marblehead, were in Class B. Victories over such teams would help the Big Blue's rankings.

However, shortly before the start of the season, the governing body for interscholastic sports in Massachusetts, often referred to as "the Headmasters Association," rearranged secondary school classifications. Swampscott and the remaining Class C schools in the Northeastern Conference were elevated to Class B. If the Big Blue was going to win a state title it would have to do so in the higher class. The good news was that no Class C teams remained on the schedule and the team would play Saugus, a Class A opponent. If the boys could manage to run the table they might have a chance to win the Class B title.

Prior to the season's start, hundreds of parents were treated to another Parents Clinic at Blocksidge Field. It seemed that each year Bondy added new features to enliven the production and impress the parents. The 1957 Clinic included a presentation by team doctor Robert Bessom on "The Health of Your Boy." As an added feature, a certified football official explained football rules and officiating signals. By all accounts the Clinic was well-received, generating further community support for Bondy's program.

The Boosters' annual fundraiser soon followed. Since his arrival, Bondy had focused on keeping the group fully engaged. Among other things, he started a tradition of meeting with the Boosters on Sunday or Monday nights during the fall at different places in town like the Ionic Social Club or the Fire Station, where he would show and narrate the film of the team's most recent game. These and other efforts were returning huge dividends.

The *Item's* Ed Cahill wrote:

Booster Clubs are not exactly a new device, but few have developed the many refinements introduced by the Swampscott organization. The Boosters do everything but find Saturday night dates for the youngsters.... They've bought letters, sweaters, trophies, special equipment, special books, band uniforms, instruments— in fact everything from coffee and doughnuts to an electronic scoreboard for Blocksidge Field. They've dined as many as one third of the high school's total enrollments at the annual sports banquet.... That the investment is paying off is proved by the extensive participation in sports and other extra-curricular activities which has resulted in Swampscott. This season Swampscott has uniformed a total of 195 football players on Junior High and High School football squads. More than 165 girls have been equipped for field hockey.

Cahill did not exaggerate the role played by the Boosters. Due in large part to the club's largesse, the Big Blue took a backseat to no one when it came to uniforms and equipment. Face and mouth guards were something of a rarity for high school players in the 1950s, but by 1955 the SHS players' helmets were equipped with both. And the 1957 team could choose from four variations of uniform—blue jerseys with white pants, white jerseys with blue pants, all white, or all blue. The players were also issued long, dark-blue capes with hoods that fit over their helmets.

As the regular season approached Bondy told the *Item* that six starting positions were still being contested and that there was "first string talent two deep in each of the four backfield spots." At the Joyce Jamboree, Swampscott, one of the smallest schools with one of the physically smallest rosters in the event, was matched against mighty Class A Lawrence. The Lancers were a perennial power, drawing their players from an old mill city of roughly 80,000 residents. This was another opportunity for the boys to test themselves against what most believed was a much stronger opponent, albeit in an abbreviated scrimmage. While the team surrendered only six points to Lawrence, Bondy was sufficiently disappointed in his offense's inability to score that he made several more roster changes before the season opener.

As it had in 1956 the team opened against Woburn and came away with a victory, winning 25–6 as Blais tallied twice. The boys then routed Cambridge Latin, 44–7, and Danvers, 31–6. After three games, undefeated Swampscott had outscored its opposition 100–19.

A number of key players were injured or ill heading into the next game against visiting 2–1 Winthrop, including Carlyn, limited due to a sprained back. Dick Coe, Roger's younger brother, filled in at fullback. He was a sure-handed, 150-pound athletic junior who could capably perform in both the offensive and defensive backfields. Others stepping in for disabled starters included tackle Frank Parsons and center Tim Nevils. Speedy Jackie Milo, also less than full strength, would be used sparingly, but effectively, during the game. Fortunately, there was very good backfield depth. Dick Winick and Ed Cohen would see additional action.

Co-captains Carlyn and Gorman had worked out a routine for handling the traditional pregame meeting with opposing captains at midfield. The two amateur psychologists hoped to confuse and intimidate their counterparts by performing something of a "good cop-bad cop" act. Billy flashed his brightest nice guy smile and warmly shook hands with the opposing captains. By contrast, Gorman, adorned in his hooded, dark cape, glared sullenly and tried to give every impression that he hated the idea of shaking hands and wished to physically attack and destroy his adversaries then and there.

However, their pregame antics did not prevent the big, fast, visitors from striking first with a 72-yard touchdown run. While the conversion failed, the Big Blue trailed for the first time all season. Winthrop continued to dominate through most of a rain-soaked first half until Jackie Milo finally broke loose late in the second period, sprinting 51 yards to the four. George Blais ran it in from there to even the score. The PAT attempt failed and the teams ended the first half deadlocked at 6–6.

Heading into the Fieldhouse, Bondy was approached by Jim Hughes. Affectionately known to the players as "Hugga," Hughes was a Swampscott native and local insurance man who served as a volunteer assistant coach. Hugga and Doc Marden had observed that the players were struggling during the first half and lacked their usual energy. Mentioning this to Bondy as they entered the locker room, Hughes asked what might be done to ignite a spark. Bondy, with a gleam in his eye, whispered, "Watch this!"

The coach stood in front of his players, started to speak, and delivered an award-winning performance. Instead of beginning softly and slowly, as was his custom, he immediately blew up at the boys, shouting and gesturing wildly. He continued in that vein for some time until he appeared emotionally spent. With his voice reduced to a hoarse whisper; he fell to his knees and tearfully begged his lads to play their hearts out in the second half. Big lineman Frank Parsons led the squad out the door, which he threw open with such force that Fieldhouse manager Vinny Easterbrooks had to later perform a repair job.

The re-energized squad seized control. The defense, led by junior linebackers Truck Cahoon and Bob Browning, stymied the visitors for almost the entire second half while the Blue offense got untracked. Early in the fourth quarter, Milo returned a Winthrop punt to the visitors' 34-yard line and Loveday then threw to Blais who caught the ball on the 11 and ran it in. Blais struck again on the first play of Swampscott's next possession when he broke through the line on his own 37 and scampered 63 yards to pay dirt for his third touchdown. Winick's kick for the extra point was good. During the second half, Winthrop failed to gain a first down until just three minutes remained. The visitors managed to narrow Swampscott's winning margin by scoring on the game's last play. With its hard-fought 19–12 victory, the Big Blue remained unbeaten.

While Carlyn and Gorman were never sure whether the "good cop-bad cop" routine made a difference, they learned that their hooded blue capes, translucent face masks, and rubber mouth guards had. On the Monday following the game, they met one of Winthrop's varsity co-captains at the JV contest between the schools. He told them that when the SHS players had taken the field on Saturday in long dark capes and helmets with oddly shaped masks and mouth guards, they had looked like creatures from Mars. "At that point, we thought we were doomed," he confessed.

Bull Carlyn, who had missed most of the Winthrop game, did not play at all in the next outing against Amesbury. Frank Cahoon and Dick Coe filled in as SHS won easily, 27–0. By this point, roster depth was paying major dividends.

The 5–0 team next faced the visiting Saugus Sachems in what many expected might be its toughest test. Saugus had lost its opener by one point but had then run off three impressive wins, including recent victories over two previously unbeaten teams in Beverly and Marblehead. The Sachems had an opportunity to knock off yet another undefeated club in Swampscott. Their coach, former Boston College star lineman John Janusas, sounded confident when he told a reporter, "We're just praying that the flu bug doesn't break out in the Swampscott camp before tomorrow's game." Bondy made no public response to what seemed a thinly veiled ridicule of his 1954 cancellation of the Stoughton contest. But he, his staff, and the Big Blue players put in a solid week of hard work in preparation for the invasion of the Sachems.

It rained heavily all Saturday morning. While cancellation was considered, the teams decided to play. Saugus wanted to beat another undefeated team; while a win over the Class A visitors would boost Swampscott's hopes of seizing a Class B title. As game time approached, the field and surrounding area were practically flooded. Cheerleaders stood on the team bench to escape ankle deep water. Like so many of the big games played during the Bondelevitch era, the 1957 battle with Saugus was fought in miserable rain and mud.

The team warmed up briefly and then retreated to the shelter of the Fieldhouse. The locker room atmosphere prior to a high school football game is always tense. Some players pace, while others sit silently with eyes closed. Some bang pads and encourage teammates. A few vomit or otherwise deal with upset stomachs in the bathroom. When contests are considered "big games," emotions can typically run even higher. The smell in high school locker rooms before big football games is generally not pleasant. This match-up against Saugus was a very big game.

Bondy's fiery pregame oration prior to the start of the 1957 Saugus game is ranked by many as one of the coach's best. As Jimmy Gorman recalled it:

The locker room grew hush. Coach Bondelevitch began to speak, at first rather quietly and rather controlled. He began by offering his observation that he felt that we were ready, that we had worked hard for this moment, and that he knew we really did not need a "pep talk." But, after a pause, he went on, and as he did, his voice rose, both in pitch and fervor. And when he reached his final "… now, get out there and hit and hit hard!" exhortation, there was an absolute explosion of team emotion. Of primary importance is the fact that we never lost that emotional edge during the entire game.

The contestants slugged it out in the early going when neither club was able to generate points. Swampscott finally got on the board after Loveday faked a handoff to Blais and pitched to Milo who raced around right end. Aided by great blocks from Carlyn and several linemen, Milo sprinted 56 yards for a touchdown. The Blue went on to defeat Saugus 19–6 in what the *Item* described as "definitely a team victory." While Blais, Carlyn, Milo, Winick, and Loveday all played notable roles in scoring drives, Bondy singled out the play of the line, led by Frary and Gorman.

The players and coaches were ecstatic, recognizing that they had cleared a huge hurdle. With Winthrop and Saugus in the win column, it seemed more likely that the team could finish the season undefeated. Like everyone, Jimmy Gorman was excited about that possibility. He was also excited about the season that his brother Tom was having as the senior quarterback for unbeaten Amherst College. Recognizing that his brother's team was, like SHS, on a quest for a perfect season, Jimmy became as invested in Amherst's fortunes as he was in Swampscott's. His secret hope was that on Thanksgiving he and his older brother would be able to join in a special celebration of their mutual unblemished records.

With the team's continued success, Swampscotters started to talk about finding a special way to reward the boys for their efforts. Some were interested in the possibility of sending the team south to play a postseason game against a Florida powerhouse. There were precedents for such a junket, including a game played in Miami by Class B champion Gloucester during the preceding December. The Lions Club took the lead to raise $5,000 to send the team to Miami or "as far as the money lasted out, even if they only get a trip to New York." Many other civic organizations joined in a community-wide effort to raise money.

The initial plan was to turn the funds over to the team for use in an educational trip, with the possibility that if the boys finished the season undefeated they might play a game against a high school team in Florida. Discussion eventually centered on Miami Edison Senior High School as the potential opponent. Edison was one of the strongest teams in Florida with a well-established winning tradition.

Yet the season was only two-thirds completed. Three games remained, including the Thanksgiving contest against a strong Marblehead squad. There was no guarantee that the boys would finish undefeated or even best the 6–3 record posted by the 1956 squad. The next opponent, much larger Revere High School, was hardly a pushover. In fact, the Patriots, as they were known, had surrendered a total of just two touchdowns over their last four games. As the coaches tried to keep the boys focused, they must have been concerned with the distractions generated by all of the talk about postseason awards and games in Florida.

As it turned out there was no need for worry. The Blue steamrolled Revere, 32–0. When the Patriots tried stacking the defensive line, Loveday took to the air, completing scoring passes to Rothwell and Blais. And the stacked defense could not stop Carlyn, who ran for three touchdowns. Meanwhile, the freshman team was also chugging along unbeaten. In fact, with its 33–0 demolition of Saugus, the Baby Blues won their 28th consecutive game. In reporting on that contest, the *Item* mentioned that spectator Stan Bondelevitch had "smiled with approval."

Now an interesting secondary story was developing. The *Item* always devoted coverage to Essex County's individual scoring leaders. The county encompassed almost all of the towns in the conference as well as cities like Lynn, Salem, Beverly, Peabody, and Lawrence. In 1955, Bobby Carlin had run away with the scoring title, tallying more than twice as many points as the next highest scorer. However, the race in 1957 was very tight, and it was between two Big Blue teammates. At the conclusion of the Revere game, George Blais was the leading scorer in Essex County. Billy Carlyn was one point behind.

Like most great backs, both players liked to run with the football. There was, however, a sense among the boys that when a particular player was largely responsible for getting the team into scoring position that player should have the chance to complete the job. In one game, George Blais made a brilliant run to bring the Blue very close to the goal line. When the team next huddled Eddie Loveday called a 44-dive, which meant that fullback Carlyn would carry the ball, running behind his friend, classmate, and fellow co-captain, Jimmy Gorman. But Gorman vetoed the call, insisting that since Blais had made a great run to put them into scoring position, he be given the opportunity to score. The play was changed to a 24-dive and Blais carried for the touchdown. This was not the only occasion when the boys changed a call as a means of recognizing a teammate's contribution.

With only two games remaining, planning for a postseason trip shifted into high gear. The team would be sent to Miami where the players would attend the Orange Bowl Game on New Year's Day. The idea of a football game with Miami Edison had been shelved. Edison had a much higher enrollment than little SHS. Moreover, Edison players were, on average, one to two years older than the Swampscott boys. Town authorities likely concluded that sending their lads to Florida to play against such an opponent would not amount to much of a *reward*.

The eighth game was against Rindge Tech of Cambridge. The Big Blue had not lost a game, while Rindge Tech had lost every game. If keeping the team focused had been a challenge in preparing for Revere, it must have been next to impossible with respect to the winless Cambridge squad. While the Blue won, 27–6, the *Item* observed that the team was "lacking the drive exhibited in previous games." The Rindge Tech coach felt that his boys had played their best game of the season. It seems that Swampscott may have played its worst, but it was good enough. Blais and Carlyn each scored six points, so Blais remained one point ahead in the Essex County scoring race.

Shortly after the players returned to the Fieldhouse from Cambridge, Jimmy Gorman slipped into a small storage room and closed the door behind him. For the first time since he had been a young child, he cried. Jimmy had just learned that previously-unbeaten Amherst had been upset that afternoon in its season-ending game against rival Williams College, dashing his dream. He and his brother Tom would not jointly celebrate their teams' perfect seasons. That realization hit him hard. His happiness over the Big Blue's victory was replaced by sadness and extreme disappointment over the Amherst loss. While teammates laughed and shouted on the other side of the door Gorman sat with his head in his hands, shedding tears over the special celebration with his brother that would never happen.

It was finally time to prepare for Marblehead. The Headers were good. Athletic and talented senior quarterback Ronnie Conn had led the offense since his sophomore year. Among the Magicians' other weapons were two big, capable ends in Ed Carey and Bill "Spider" Healey, and an exceptional two-way halfback in Jack Robarts. The squad had been undefeated prior to its loss to Saugus. During the remainder of the season, the Headers had struggled with injuries and illness that had caused the cancellation of one game. They held a 4–3 record but had only lost once in the conference.

There was no chance that Swampscott would overlook its arch-rival. Conference and Class B titles were on the line, as well as an undefeated season. And for the seniors, it would be a chance to avenge their 1956 Thanksgiving loss. But even without those motivating factors, this was an opportunity to beat the neighboring team in what was always a special game. Swampscott v. Marblehead typically generated the greatest amount of pregame media attention, the most excitement in the two communities, and the largest over-flow crowds.

The Lions Club feted the team at its annual pre-Thanksgiving banquet. The Baby Blues did their part, running their unbeaten streak to 29 games by routing the Marblehead Freshmen 35–0. Frank Coletti, Swampscott's Athletic Manager, announced that tickets for the Thanksgiving game were sold out. For the first time in Essex County football history, two teammates would be competing for the county scoring crown during the last game of the season.

Perhaps as a way of further accentuating how special the season had been and how important the final game was, team members were excused from attending classes on Wednesday. Instead, they met with the coaches at Blocksidge Field in the morning for their final practice session. They then returned to the high school gym where they were greeted by the cheerleaders, band, faculty, and the rest of the student body for the "Beat Marblehead Pep Rally." Among other things, each senior on the team spoke at the event.

If the players needed even more motivation, it came when Bondy addressed them in the locker room at Marblehead on Thanksgiving morning. An article in the game program concluded with the assertion that the Headers should be able to take down the undefeated Big Blue, noting that the opponent was, after all, "only Swampscott." Bondy must have felt like kissing the author. While the statement had likely been written tongue-in-cheek, Stan highlighted it as an example of the disrespect being shown his boys. By the time he finished speaking the players were sky-high and charged onto the field intent on redressing the insult.

The team played well through the first two quarters, scoring a couple of touchdowns while shutting out the Headers. In the locker room at halftime, the coaches concentrated on keeping the boys focused. As the start of the second half neared it was time to again fire up the squad.

Coach Lynch approached the seated Gorman and, bending down so that they were face to face, shouted in his most challenging voice, "What's the score, Jimmy Gorman?" Lynch expected that the senior would enthusiastically confirm that the score was 0–0, demonstrating that he and his teammates recognized that their first-half lead meant nothing and that they needed to take the field and play as if it was the start of a new game. This is a message that millions of players on sports teams have received from their coaches during halftime intermissions since the onset of formal athletic competitions. Gorman, Lynch believed, would be the reassuring voice of a squad that was determined to outplay the Headers through the second half.

But the 16-year-old was caught off-guard by Dick Lynch's question, which he interpreted literally. Why, he wondered, was Coach Lynch asking him to recite the score? Didn't Lynch know? He sheepishly and unsuccessfully looked around for support from nearby teammates before replying, "Gee, I think it's 13–0, right coach?" Young lawyers are taught that during a trial they should never ask a witness a question if they do not already know what the answer will be. Coach Lynch should have applied the same rule in his questioning of Gorman. But it did not matter. Lynch set the record straight, emphasizing that it was a new game and the score was 0–0. The boys needed to redouble their efforts in the second half.

They did just that. The 1957 Big Blue ended its perfect season in perfect fashion, shutting out the Headers 27–0. One play that preserved the momentum came early in the fourth quarter when SHS was forced to punt from inside its own territory. A rare imperfect long snap sailed high and it seemed might fly over punter Eddie Loveday's head toward the goal line. But Loveday leaped and managed to knock the ball down. Scooping it up, he took off, dodging tacklers, passing the first-down marker, and covering perhaps another 30 yards before being caught.

Later in the quarter, the Blue offense mounted another drive. On fourth down with the ball on the Headers' 3-yard line, Loveday called Carlyn's number. Billy vetoed the play, telling Eddie to keep the ball and follow him into the end zone. It was a classy move by the senior full-back, recognizing that his quarterback had earlier made a big play on the botched punt and deserved a chance to score. Carlyn and his teammates cleared the way as Loveday ran around end for the final touchdown of the championship season.

The boys completed the first perfect full season in the 49-year history of SHS football. Nearly 1,000 supporters awaited the team bus when it returned to Blocksidge Field. The Fieldhouse was adorned with a large sign that read, "Welcome Home, Champs." Billy Carlyn, having scored 14 points in the final game, won the county scoring title, edging his teammate George Blais. Blais was a junior and would have another year to contend for that title.

Bondy was named head coach of the North Shore All-Star team that would play in the first Agganis Memorial All-Star game at Manning Bowl on December 8. Joe Zeno headed up the opposing All-Star team comprised of players from other greater Boston communities. Zeno was the coach of the Waltham club that Swampscott had scrimmaged on that watershed day back in March. Zeno's team lived up to its reputation as a Class A power, finishing the 1957 season with just one loss.

Bondy named six of his seniors—Carlyn, Gorman, Rothwell, Parsons, Frary, and Faino—to the North All-Star squad. Carlyn left the game in the first quarter with a concussion. Before suffering his injury, Bull had scored twice, helping to put the North All-Stars in front, 13–0. Once he left the game they never scored again, losing 25–13. Despite playing less than a quarter of the contest, Billy was awarded the Agganis trophy as the game's outstanding player.

As in past years, the football squad and members of other teams and support groups such as the cheerleaders, drill team, and band, were feted at the Boosters' postseason awards banquet. In addition to the Florida trip, team members were awarded jackets and other gifts, as well as numerous trophies. The varsity football squad was not the only SHS team to finish with an unblemished record. The freshmen and JVs also concluded perfect seasons, as did Coach Flora McLearn's girl's field hockey team. This, however, was nothing new. The girls had not lost since 1952.

In late December, the players, managers, coaches, and a couple of school administrators boarded their own dedicated rail car at Boston's South Station for the 30-hour trip to Miami. Bondy, abandoning his no-smoking rule, announced that if people wanted to smoke inside the car he had no objection. This was, of course, long before any published warnings from the Surgeon General about the dangers of tobacco. Cigarette and cigar smoke soon filled the air and conditions only worsened over the ensuing hours. The only escape from the foul, acrid atmosphere occurred during mealtimes when the group traipsed to the dining car.

The travelers arrived in Miami and were transferred to their lodgings at the Sorrento Hotel. Bondy announced that he knew the players were not excited about spending much time with him and the other adults, and assured them that the feeling was mutual. He proclaimed that, aside from attendance at several planned functions, they were free to do as they pleased. His message was "have a good time but don't get into trouble." Thereafter, Stan Bondelevitch was rarely seen at the Sorrento.

Left to their own devices, the boys enjoyed themselves. At least one of them reportedly met some girls, climbed into their car, and disappeared for several days. A few others, having little or no available cash, were strolling the grounds of the nearby luxurious Fontainebleau Hotel when they noticed a shallow wishing well where the resort's well-heeled guests had thrown hundreds of quarters and fifty cent pieces. Later that night the boys revisited the well and returned to the Sorrento—their pockets bulging with wet coins. Their wishes for replenished cash reserves had been answered.

One evening, Dick Lynch was confronted by the distraught hotel manager who complained that "all hell" had broken loose. It seems that some of the more rambunctious Swampscott teenagers had thought it a good idea to throw pieces of furniture, coconuts, and other items off the hotel roof. Lynch managed to gain control before revelry turned into full-scale riot.

On New Year's Day, prior to the Orange Bowl game, the group attended a morning church service. While some sat in the pews or knelt, several others suffered the effects of their New Year's Eve celebrations and worshipped from prone positions sprawled across the benches. While it had been an educational trip, the *education* for a few may have differed from that envisioned by the sponsors. But the players, with the help of Coach Lynch and others, had managed to avoid any serious trouble.

Predictably, Bondy had nothing but public praise for his beloved champions, telling the *Item's* Ed Cahill, "So well behaved were our youngsters that they were mistaken at various times for both the Oklahoma University squad and West Point cadets…. We couldn't have been prouder of them."

Dick Lynch, having found himself in the unenviable position of chaperone by default was happy to get back home. After the train rolled into Boston's South Station, he delivered his own message. "Stan," he said, "if you ever want to do this again count me out!"

The boys had enjoyed their Miami trip but a few regretted not playing Edison, especially after Class A champion Lawrence played the postseason game against the Miami school and lost by a single point. The SHS players had met Lawrence in the Jamboree and felt that they were at least as good as the Lancers. They had longed for a chance to test themselves against a team widely recognized as one of Florida's strongest. Having never seen Edison, they were nonetheless confident that they would have been competitive against that squad or any other high school team. They may have been right.

In retrospect, it is not surprising that Swampscott won the Class B crown. Bondy had been working to develop a championship team since he had arrived in town. Many of the starters, having played with their teammates in the Big Blue program for at least several years, had become highly proficient in executing their assignments on both sides of the line. There were a number of solid players on the roster, as well as several truly exceptional athletes. From the moment that they had come together in the scrimmage on the final day of spring practice to take down a powerful Waltham squad, it seemed that these guys would be special. The 1957 team raised Big Blue football to new heights, and the players forever carried with them the memories of that golden season.

Following high school, Jim Gorman attended the United States Military Academy. He denies that the decision was influenced by Bondy's comment about him and his teammates being mistaken for West Point

Cadets during their Miami trip. After graduating, Jim accepted a commission in the United States Marine Corps and served four years, including 10 months in Vietnam. After leaving the service and working in the government and corporate worlds for several years, Jim attended law school. Admitted to the California Bar in 1977, he practiced law in San Diego until 2017 when he retired. Not long ago, brief summaries of past football seasons were sought for posting on the Swampscott football website and Jim responded with a delightfully entertaining narrative titled "The Fairytale of 1957."

Anything You Can Do,
We Can Do Better

P rior to 1958, post-touchdown conversions counted for one point, regardless of how accomplished. But under a new rule, PATs scored by running or passing would now be worth two points. Bondy was critical of the change, maintaining that a kicked conversion should have counted for more points, not less, since it required great effort "on the part of the line to hold off the opposition, the center who has to snap the ball a longer distance, the holder and of course the kicker." He also observed that while successful conversion kicks in the NFL might seem almost automatic, such was typically not the case with high school kickers.

In late August, some of the former SHS seniors who had competed in the December 1957 Agganis game participated in another All-Star event. In the second annual Polio Bowl Game, the North Shore All-Stars met the Merrimack Valley All-Stars at the Manning Bowl. Bondy again coached the North Shore team. His counterpart was Lawrence High School coach Ed Buckley. Nine of Buckley's players from the Class A Champion Lawrence Lancers started for the Merrimack Valley team, which was rated a three-touchdown favorite.

Bondy's underdog North Shore squad pulled off the upset, winning 16–14. His criticism of the new conversion rule did not prevent him from using it to his team's advantage. After each touchdown, Bull Carlyn ran the ball in for two-point conversions that provided the winning margin. He played both ways and was praised by Bondy for his outstanding blocking and defensive performance. Charles "Billy" Carlyn was, without doubt, one of the best football players Stan Bondelevitch ever coached.

Shortly after the game's conclusion, he departed for Indiana University where he joined the freshman squad.

Bondy took further steps to expand the town's youth football program. Prior to his arrival, participation in organized football was limited to high school students. He added an eighth-grade squad in 1954 and a seventh-grade team in 1956. Now the Boosters announced the creation of a Pop Warner team for boys as young as nine, the first of its kind on the North Shore. Alfie Cerone was the coach of the new "Little Blue," assisted by Al Duratti. Both were familiar to Swampscott kids as little league baseball coaches. Bondy was of course involved. It was the latest addition to his developmental program. The resulting extensive community of players, parents, and sports enthusiasts fueled an ever-increasing pride, spirit, and cohesiveness in the town.

Pop Warner football afforded an opportunity to train boys within the same system, playing together, using the same schemes, and running the same plays for five or six continuous years before doing so on Stan's varsity. He would have a chance to become better acquainted with younger prospects and help shape their attitudes toward football and the Big Blue. More than perhaps anything else, Stan Bondelevitch was a master at instilling "want to" in youngsters.

The 1958 roster was full of seasoned veterans, including three-fourths of the backfield from the prior year's championship squad. Milo, Blais, and Loveday returned. Speedy Jackie Milo was capable of pulling away from most defenders and of running down most receivers and ball carriers. George Blais, though hardly big at 5-foot, 9-inches, and 160 pounds, could do it all. He was a phenomenal athlete. Ambidextrous and acrobatic, George performed amazing feats off diving boards, on basketball courts, baseball diamonds, and football fields. He was lightning quick, physically tough, and a gifted, instinctive runner. He was also a sure-handed receiver and a strong-armed, accurate passer, enabling the offense to sting opponents with the halfback-option pass. And George took particular pride in his defensive prowess where he seemed equally effective as ball hawk or tackler.

With Carlyn gone, senior Frank "Truck" Cahoon took over as the hard-charging, 190-pound fullback, while also again starting as an outstanding linebacker. Truck proved a reliable short-yardage option as well as a strong lead blocker for the speedsters in the backfield. Ed Loveday, back to direct the offense, had been a steady presence throughout the 1957 campaign. With Hal Foster having accepted the head coaching job at Saint Mary's High School in Lynn, Dick Lynch took over as backfield coach.

Two-way end John Flanagan had been one of the two sophomores featured in the 1956 article about players with disabilities. Bondy had said that if he had 11 kids like Flanagan and classmate Bill Sentner, he could win the state championship. He must have found those other players because the 1957 team won the championship. John was a good athlete and tough customer. By his senior year, he was up to about 210 pounds and stood 6-foot, 2-inches. After high school, he played football at Boston College, where his missing toes earned him the nickname "The Hoof."

Left tackle Bob Andrews and right guard Dick Maitland were the other returning offensive starters. They were joined by center Tim Nevils, tackle Ken Stein, guard Bob Browning, and converted back Dick Coe, starting at left end. All were seniors. The quick 5-foot, 9-inch, 175-pound Browning had moved into town from Florida a year earlier and was expected to be one of the better linemen and linebackers on the North Shore. Andrews, Blais, and Cahoon were elected tri-captains.

Richard Maitland, who had been a solid contributor during 1957, was a Dick Lynch recruit. Lynch had been teaching wrestling to his gym class and was impressed with Maitland, who was quick, strong, and athletic. In response to Lynch's query as to why Maitland had not come out for football, the boy explained that he had watched some practices and it looked like hard work. Lynch assured Maitland that he would love it, and had the kid equipped and playing in no time. Maitland was not the only good player discovered by the gym teacher. Even with Bondy's youth football program and non-stop promotion of the great American game, some prospects still escaped notice until they were spotted by Lynch during gym classes and encouraged to join the team.

The coaches relied on a trio of rugged juniors to fill spots on the defensive side. Mike Powers and Bruce Jordan were defensive tackles, while Jimmy Lyons was inserted as a linebacker. Powers and Lyons each weighed about 185 pounds, while Jordan was over 200. Bruce was somewhat unique in that he played football and also performed in the high school band. He was a soft-spoken, well-mannered kid whose father was the popular principal of the junior high school. Off the field, he might have been mistaken for an almost passive boy, incapable of hurting a fly. He seemed a gentle giant until he put on the pads and helmet and turned into an intimidating dynamo.

But there was nothing gentle about Jimmy Lyons. Unlike Jordan, he was an aggressive, combative kid who tended to get into fights off the field. Nicknamed "Gangsta," he welcomed, and perhaps occasionally instigated, physical challenges. Mike Powers resembled Jordan in that he wore glasses. Otherwise, he seemed a bit more like his good friend Lyons. In any case, Powers, Lyons, and Jordan were all tough customers on the football field. Defensive end Phil Janvrin was the only other junior to secure a starting spot. Seniors Andrews, Flanagan, Cahoon, Browning, Blais, Milo, and Coe were all two-way starters.

There was one notable difference between the 1957 and 1958 teams that had nothing to do with size or speed. In 1957, the confidence level had generally increased as the year wore on, commencing with the surprise win over Waltham in the spring scrimmage and growing throughout the fall with each successive victory. But many players had not realized how good the team was until the one-sided, season-ending win over strong Marblehead. By contrast, the core players in 1958 were supremely confident from the outset. Undefeated as freshmen, JVs, and members of the 1957 varsity, they expected to dominate every team on their schedule. These guys believed they could not be beaten.

The boys gave early notice that they would again contend for conference and state titles, outplaying defending Class A champ Lawrence at the Jamboree. Reporting on the Blue's 16–0 win, the *Item* wrote that "Swampscott again looked like the class of the party, tearing through and round Lawrence in a one-sided match." The opener against new conference foe Andover was rained out. As a result, the Big Blue's first game was at Woburn. The *Item* predicted:

> The football setup at Swampscott with its big squad of eager beavers, its pulchritudinous cheer leaders and drill team and its 90-piece band under Conductor Don Hammond will be there in full force.

Woburn seemed a worthy challenger. After losing to Swampscott in the first game of the prior season, the Tanners ran the table, finishing on Thanksgiving with a 32–7 drubbing of archrival Winchester. They then opened the new season by destroying Newburyport 20–0. Playing at home, Woburn had the chance to avenge its only loss of 1957 and keep its own winning streak alive. "All we need is a dry day and some sunshine and the luck that goes with the game," said Bondy.

The home team started off strong, scoring first and then scoring again in the second quarter after Swampscott had gone ahead. However, that was Woburn's last lead and last score as the Big Blue cruised in a 46–12 rout. Blais and Milo each scored twice, while Coe and Cahoon also tallied. Truck Cahoon, Mike Powers, and the Brownings, Bob and younger brother Randy, stood out defensively. Contrary to Bondy's pregame comment, the Blue did not need luck to dismantle Woburn.

Having dominated Lawrence in the Jamboree and crushed a strong Woburn team, this squad looked every bit the equal of the '57 champions. Interest was already building over the Blue's game with potent Saugus on November 1. While each club faced another three opponents before that date, Swampscott's impressive win at Woburn and the Sachems' 54–20 bashing of Lynn Classical had local fans salivating over a potential match between unbeaten teams. Should their records remain perfect, Swampscott v. Saugus would be a huge attraction.

The *Item* raised the possibility of shifting the Saugus game from relatively small Stackpole Field to Lynn's Manning Bowl, which was the only local venue capable of holding more than 10,000 fans. Bondy, always looking for advantages and greater exposure for the Big Blue, must have loved the suggestion. Surprisingly, Saugus coach John Janusas confidently stated that if his team remained undefeated, "[Y]ou can quote me … we'll play Swampscott anywhere." While he clarified that he meant anywhere but in Swampscott, it is hard to understand why he would have considered giving up his team's home-field advantage.

In their next games, both teams romped, with Saugus clobbering Marblehead, 30–0, and the Big Blue annihilating Danvers, 41–0. In the Danvers contest, Blais again scored twice and added a two-point conversion. A sophomore named George Pleau also kicked an extra point.

Like Winthrop's Frank DeFelice, Pleau would ultimately re-emerge in the Swampscott story years after his playing days ended.

Going into the team's next game at long-time adversary Winthrop, Bondy sounded pessimistic saying, "We'll be lucky to survive." The Blue Devils, as they had recently taken to calling themselves, were a veteran group but the Big Blue rolled on, shutting them out, 22–0. Blais scored 16 points.

As Swampscott prepared for its home opener against Amesbury, Bondy sounded more confident, saying that it would take "a real good football team" to defeat his club. The 2–2 Carriagemakers were not that team. Blais tallied 18 more while leading the Blue to a decisive 38–6 win.

Finally, it was time to face Saugus. While the Sachems were no longer perfect, having fallen to undefeated Beverly, they were seen as Swampscott's greatest challenge. The Class A team had won four of five games. The only loss had been to a squad many considered one of the state's best. However, talk of playing at Manning Bowl had ceased, either because of the loss to Beverly or because Coach Janusas had realized that he would need the home-field advantage and every other bit of good luck he could find if his team was going to have any chance of beating the Big Blue.

Bondy sounded pessimistic again, telling the *Item*, "The honeymoon is over." Playing before 7,000 fans in packed Stackpole Field, the Blue fell behind 12–0 but roared back, posting 38 consecutive points. Blais again played a prominent role, running, receiving, and passing for scores. After Saugus took the two-touchdown lead early in the contest, a distraught cheerleader expressed her concern to Eddie Loveday on the sideline. Loveday calmly assured her that Swampscott would win. The early Saugus scores had been set up by turnovers. Loveday expected that once things settled down the Blue would play most of the game in the Saugus end of the field. It did. Swampscott was so dominant that it never punted during the contest. The "honeymoon" continued.

SHS had three games remaining. The first was against non-conference (2–3) Malden Catholic. Speedster Phil Cudmore started in place of Blais, who was sidelined with a shoulder injury. Bondy, no doubt concerned about a possible let-down following the Saugus win, tried to keep his team focused, claiming that he was "scared to death" of Malden Catholic. Noting that it was the biggest squad that his boys would face, he groused that the school had three times the male enrollment of little SHS. He also complained that his players were not keyed up enough for the game.

While Bondy was ahead of his time in many respects, when it came to his 1958 offensive philosophy he was somewhat "old school." Like Ohio State's Woody Hayes, he believed that three things could happen when the quarterback passed and two were bad, i.e., incompletions and interceptions. Malden Catholic was aware of the Big Blue's offensive tendencies and used eight- and nine-man defensive fronts in hopes of bottling up the running backs. The few remaining defenders lined up only several yards behind the front line. That strategy, combined with Blais' absence, seemed to be working and the vaunted Swampscott ground attack met with little success in the early going. Dick Lynch urged Bondy to change the game plan by attempting a few passes.

Given the team's potent running attack, senior quarterback Eddie Loveday had not been required to pass much during his varsity career. Yet he was capable of airing it out if necessary and tough enough to withstand punishment from defensive linemen after he did. His coaches had seen to that. Many high school coaches, realizing that they could not easily replace talented signal callers, put red vests on their quarterbacks during practices and issued orders that they were not to be touched. But during the 1957 preseason, the Swampscott coaches had taken the opposite approach with Loveday as a means of assuring that he would be able to handle pressure and absorb hard hits.

Full-contact drills were conducted, during which Loveday took the snap from center and dropped back to pass. An outnumbered offensive line attempted to block an overloaded pass rush. For example, a dozen defensive players might line up and rush against only five or six pass blockers. Loveday was expected to drop back and attempt to complete passes. He never had a chance. Typically, he was hit and buried by several players before or while throwing the ball.

During one such punishing drill, Loveday was clobbered and taken down repeatedly. Finally, he was flattened and buried under a massive pass rush. After the defensive players got to their feet, Loveday remained on the ground. Coach Lynch raced over, leaned down, and enthusiastically shouted to his prone quarterback, "Nice job Eddie. Way to hang in there! Are you ready to try it again?" Loveday remained down, with a wide-eyed, vacant look on his face. Then, in a somewhat shaky and hesitant voice, he mumbled, "I don't … know." But Eddie eventually got up and returned to the fray.

Now the veteran quarterback was at the helm in a pressure situation which required him to pass against an aggressive rush. The coaches knew that he was plenty tough and could hurt opponents with his arm, something he had demonstrated in the 1957 Revere game.

In reality, while Swampscott relied heavily on its rushing offense, it had a highly capable passer in Loveday and solid receivers in ends Flanagan and Coe, and backs Blais and Milo. Flanagan, also a starter on Swampscott's basketball team, was big, rugged, and rangy. Like his older brother Roger, athletic Dick Coe played three varsity sports. He had grown up only a few doors from the Loveday family and had spent many evenings catching passes from Eddie underneath the street light. Loveday could not recall Coe ever having dropped one. Yet on November 8, 1958, the team kept trying to run through Malden Catholic's stacked defense.

The first quarter ended with neither team having scored. Finally, Bondy agreed with Lynch's suggestion and allowed Loveday to attempt a pass. The result was a completion to Flanagan for a touchdown. Another pass, this time to Coe, yielded another touchdown. The offense was demonstrating that it was hardly one-dimensional. Eddie Loveday believes that he threw only six passes during the Malden Catholic game. Five of them were good for touchdowns, while the sixth found its target for a successful post-touchdown conversion. His six passes were good for 32 points.

Sparked by the successful passing attack, which caused Malden Catholic to loosen up its run defense, the Big Blue rolled to what was likely its most one-sided victory in school history, decimating its opponent, 58–0. Bondy was no longer "scared to death" of Malden Catholic.

The boys next traveled to Newburyport. Playing again without Blais, but also with Milo hampered by a leg injury, they relied heavily on Truck Cahoon's running and solid defense to control the game. They managed only 16 points. But the defense kept the Clippers out of the end zone as Swampscott secured its 16th straight win, out-rushing the home squad 287 yards to 106, and posting 17 first downs to Newburyport's five. The contest ended with the Blue offense on the Clippers' 4-yard line.

Meanwhile, as the varsity rolled along toward what seemed another championship, the freshmen actually managed to lose a game but bounced back and ended their season by thrashing Marblehead, 46–6. The freshman fullback, a well-built, red-headed boy named David Coughlin, scored four touchdowns in that game.

As the season wound down, rumors began to swirl about Bondy's possible departure. Word was that he was exploring opportunities, including becoming the head coach at Bowdoin College, or taking over the programs in Beverly or even Marblehead. Acknowledging that he'd received some feelers, the coach stated that it would take "an awfully good offer to get me out of Swampscott." For Big Blue fans, it would have been tough to see Bondy leave to take the helm at Bowdoin, but it would have been unbearable should he become coach at Marblehead. Stan could feel confident that the school committee would do everything within its power to retain him.

Thanksgiving approached with the chance to conclude a second consecutive undefeated season and repeat as conference and Class B champion. Only Marblehead stood in the way, which meant that there would be the added satisfaction of winning the title by whipping the Whips. This was the 50th anniversary game between the traditional rivals and would be played in Swampscott. While the undefeated Big Blue had outscored its first eight opponents 259 to 30, Marblehead suffered through a disastrous season. The Magicians were winless, had been shut out five times, and outscored 206 to 24.

Although it seemed that Marblehead would not be able to challenge Swampscott, it was still Thanksgiving and the final game. Bondy's pregame Thanksgiving talk was always emotional and it was no different in 1958. Roger Coe returned to watch younger brother Dick's final game and was allowed inside the locker room prior to the opening kickoff. Although he had not been a member of the team for four years, Roger was sufficiently moved by Bondy's speech that his eyes welled up and tears ran down his face. This did not escape Stan's notice and he thereafter teased Roger about it at every opportunity.

Marblehead, hoping to confuse their clearly superior rivals, set up early in a bizarre offensive formation, with most of the linemen and backs spread some distance from the center and quarterback. But the strategy had little impact on the outcome. The Big Blue walloped Marblehead, 41–6. Even without the injured Milo, SHS had no problem destroying the Headers.

John Flanagan had a chance to run with the football and score a two-point conversion as the coaches moved him from end to Milo's left half-back spot. However, George Blais was the main attraction. He concluded his stellar SHS career by running over, through, and around the Headers, scoring four touchdowns while throwing for another. The Blue led 35–0 as the third quarter ended. Bondy cleared his bench and Swampscott's regulars spent much of the second half enjoying the game from the sidelines.

While Swampscott repeated as undefeated Class B champion, there was no return trip to Miami. Instead, the boys received watches. Bondy was chosen to coach the Harry Agganis Memorial All-Star Scholarship Football Game at Manning Bowl on December 7, 1958, which pitted the Greater Lynn/Swampscott All-Stars against the Greater Salem/Beverly All-Stars. There were 13 Big Blue seniors on Bondy's roster, while the opposing All-Star squad included 17 players from unbeaten Class A champion Beverly, complemented by 9 from Salem, another strong Class A team. The Salem/Beverly contingent was heavily favored, with some suggesting that it was "potentially one of the greatest All-Star squads in history."

On a bitterly cold December Sunday, another Bondelevitch-coached team staged an upset, winning 14–6. The Salem/Beverly squad included a number of "all-everything" players, including halfback Mike Tomeo, who was the leading scorer in the county and regarded by some as the best back in New England. Nevertheless, George Blais was named the game's outstanding player. He ran 33 yards for one score, combined with quarterback Eddie Loveday on a 67-yard pass for a second touchdown, completed a 41-yard pass of his own to teammate Dick Coe that almost resulted in a third touchdown, and sealed the victory with a late-game interception that he returned 39 yards.

In late August 1959, All-Star teams with essentially the same rosters that had played in the 1958 Agganis Game met again at the Polio Bowl Game played at Manning Bowl before a large crowd. Bondy's club defeated the Greater Salem/Beverly All-Stars, coached by Salem's Walter Sheridan, by a score of 26–16. With the winning margin even wider in this rematch, it seemed clear that the 1958 Big Blue had been the best high school team on the North Shore, if not the entire state.

John Flanagan, Bob Browning, and Jackie Milo joined George Blais on the first team of the Lynn *Item* All-Stars. Milo, although having missed considerable playing time due to injury, was named a co-winner of the Thom McAn Shoe Award as the outstanding senior student/football player on the North Shore. He went on to star at Bowdoin. In 2016, he became the fourth and final member of the 1957 backfield inducted into the SHS Hall of Fame. As part of his speech at the induction ceremony, he said that there were only several players at Bowdoin who might have been able to start on his Big Blue teams and that the coaching he received at SHS was better than anything he ever experienced in college.

Eddie Loveday, Dick Coe, and a number of other seniors finished their SHS football careers having won every game they played. Their freshman team was undefeated. As sophomores, they played on the undefeated JV squad. As juniors and seniors, they were members of two successive unbeaten Big Blue varsity teams. In his two seasons as starting quarterback, Eddie Loveday was never sacked. Bondy typically glanced at Loveday after each contest, smiled and muttered, "No need to send your uniform to the cleaners this week."

Playing in only six games during his senior year, George Blais scored 106 points, for an average of almost 18 per game. That exceeded the per-game averages of Bobby Carlin and Billy Carlyn, both of whom had won county scoring titles. George received numerous postseason awards and was named to the rosters of various all-state teams.

Blais took his dazzling football talents to Northeastern Oklahoma A&M College. One year later, his 1957 backfield mate Billy Carlyn, having left Indiana, joined him on the Oklahoma team as they won the junior college championship game, known as the Little Rose Bowl. Blais went on to play at Western State College of Colorado (now Western State Colorado University), where he was reunited with another former Big Blue player, Bob "Bun" Mansfield. After his playing days ended, George pursued a business career and returned to the North Shore where he stays in touch with Eddie Loveday and some of his other high school teammates. George Blais was surely one of the most gifted and exciting athletes in Big Blue football history.

Statistically, the 1958 squad was even more dominant than its predecessor. While the 1957 team's average margin of victory was an impressive

23 points, the 1958 club won its games by an incredible average of 38. Swampscott and Stan Bondelevitch stood atop the Massachusetts high school football world, but the coach sounded an ominous note. All of the offensive starters as well as most of the defensive regulars were graduating. He predicted that "whoever will be coaching in Swampscott next year will have a real tough job."

Tough as Nails

Whatever had been required in the off-season to assure Bondy's return had been accomplished. His Big Blue was riding a 17-game winning streak, but the roster was full of new names. There were just a few returning boys who had seen action in 1958. Of the 75 players who participated in preseason practice, only 11 were seniors and most had little varsity experience. Blais, Milo, Loveday, and Cahoon had all graduated. Up front, Flanagan, Coe, Maitland, Andrews, Browning, Stein and Nevils, among others, were gone. Another defensive starter from the prior year, senior Phil Janvrin, was ineligible due to his age and would serve as a student-coach.

With so many neophytes, Bondy went to work building the boys' confidence, promising that they would be a very good defensive team and that it would take "a well-coached, well-drilled football team to beat this stubborn and spirited group." As part of his motivational strategy, Bondy frequently used absolutes like *ever* and *never* when describing his new squad. For example, he mentioned that, with all due respect to his championship teams, the 1959 bunch was "the best I've ever coached." He further asserted that "never" in his 14 years of coaching had he "seen a better attitude toward the game by the players."

Bondy was addicted to superlatives. He regularly used adjectives like "best," "greatest," and "finest" to describe numerous players and teams throughout his coaching career. Such terms adorned his speeches at pep rallies, Booster Club meetings, media sessions, and in the locker rooms before games. Perhaps the 1959 team was in some way "the best" he'd ever coached, but if there was such a thing as a re-building year in high school football this looked to be one in Swampscott.

One of the best athletes in the senior class was not allowed to play football. Her name was Barbara Segel. Growing up, Barb was an unabashed tomboy, spending every free moment in sports competitions with other Abbott Parkers like Dick Gowen, Jackie Milo, and John Flanagan. She practically lived at the park. In the winter, she laced up her girl's figure skates and joined the boys in ice hockey. Baseball was one of her favorite sports. When she was old enough, youth baseball coaches Al Cerone and Andy Holmes approached the board of the Swampscott Little League seeking special permission for Barbara to participate. She desperately wanted to play and knew that she was good enough to hold her own. But it was the '50s and the board was not going to permit a girl to play organized baseball with the boys. Barbara was disappointed and frustrated.

Barb's talent and interest in sports was something of a mystery. Neither of her parents had athletic backgrounds, and her twin sister Linda was a top student who was more interested in academic pursuits. While Linda focused on homework assignments, Barb occupied herself with sports-related matters, even if it involved re-reading the latest edition of *Sports Illustrated*.

In 1956, Barb entered SHS where she could play on sports teams coached by Mrs. Flora McLearn. Finally, Barb had a chance to play regularly in formal athletic competition. Tutored by McLearn, she flourished, starring on the field hockey, basketball, and softball teams. She also fell in love with golf. Barb was a natural athlete, excelling at everything she tried. In early spring of her junior year, she asked Walter Henshaw, the high school golf coach, about possibly playing with the team. Henshaw told Mrs. McLearn. Flora was all about winning and was not going to lose her star softball player to the golf team. She summoned Barb to her office and sternly warned the girl that if she persisted with her efforts to play on the golf team she would not be allowed to serve as field hockey captain in the fall. Frustrated again, Barb surrendered.

While Barb wasn't able to join Mr. Henshaw's high school golf team, she made up for it in later years, becoming a highly accomplished, award-winning golfer. Barb Segel did not have the sports opportunities that are available for girls today. But she enthusiastically played with the hand she was dealt and played it very well. Today Barbara Segel Yozell resides in Swampscott and works as a real estate broker. While she no longer runs off to Abbott Park to play baseball or hockey with the boys, she seizes every opportunity for a quick round of golf. □

The 1959 football team co-captains were two senior linemen, guard Mike Powers and center Bruce Jordan. These two, along with Jimmy Lyons and Paul Langevin, may have been the only players with much varsity experience. Powers and Lyons were great pals. To say that both had a pugnacious disposition would be an understatement.

Powers grew up in Lynn where he attended Saint Joseph's School with his older brother Billy. Mike wore black-rimmed glasses that always seemed to be held together with white tape, as they were continually broken in scuffles of one sort or another. Prior to the start of the 1955 school year, Mike's family moved into Swampscott. He enrolled as a Hadley eighth-grader. When classes ended on the first day of school, Mike walked to Blocksidge Field and joined the eighth-grade football team. Like a number of others who had never before worn a football uniform, he was confused by some of the equipment, including thigh pads which he inserted backwards. If any boys laughed at him, they likely never did again. Powers was a tough kid who could take care of himself. He soon got his equipment straightened out and enjoyed playing football with his classmates.

In 1956, Powers joined the freshman squad and met Lyons. Jimmy was the younger brother of Tommy "Mash" Lyons, who had been the subject of the *Item's* 1954 polio story, and Terry "T-Butts" Lyons, an all-star tackle on the 1956 varsity. Mash got his nickname because the mess of light-colored hair sitting atop his head reminded some of mashed potatoes, and Terry had been "T-Butts" since Bondy caught him smoking cigarettes.

Jimmy's nickname "Gangsta" was the easiest to understand. He knew how to use his fists and was not reluctant to do so. He'd been in a number of fights and many at SHS gave him a wide berth. Powers did not. The two young Irish-Americans liked one another immediately and became fast friends. They seemed to be practically joined at the hip. In addition to a tendency to become involved in physical altercations, they had a few other things in common, not the least of which was a love of football. Naturally, Bondy took notice.

Dick Lynch first encountered the pair as freshman basketball coach. Bondy asked him to keep an eye on the boys, as they had a tendency to get into troubles of one sort or another. They were rugged and determined, but neither had much basketball ability. However, Lynch wanted to help keep them out of trouble; not only because of Bondy's request but also as a result of a visit he received from Jimmy's mother. Speaking with a heavy Irish brogue, Mrs. Lyons informed Lynch that she was at her wits' end and he had her permission to do whatever he felt necessary to keep her boy in line. So Lynch, hopeful of keeping the boys out of trouble, carried Powers and Lyons on the freshman squad and gave them some playing time, usually in the second half of games.

The plan, however, was not foolproof. During an away game in Lynn against the Saint Mary's freshmen, four older kids constantly heckled the Swampscott players from the stands, particularly Lyons and Powers. The contest ended in some controversy and an unhappy Coach Lynch ordered his players to exit the gym and board the bus, while he remained and discussed matters with game officials.

When Lynch later left the building, he came upon a bizarre scene. The four boys who had been taunting his players were strewn about the area. One was lying facedown, seemingly unconscious. Another was also on the ground, bleeding, while a third was leaning against a fence, nursing a large gash on his forehead. The fourth held his hand against his head as he staggered about, looking dazed.

The coach made his way through the carnage to the team bus where, he recalled, it was "as quiet as church." Lyons and Powers were sitting together, staring straight ahead. Lyons had a small bruise under his eye. Blood trailed from Powers' nose and his eyeglasses were broken. Pointing to the scene outside the bus, Lynch asked the driver if he knew what had happened. The man nodded and told Lynch that he could not believe what he had seen.

Lyons and Powers had been on the bus when someone yelled that their teammate, Billy Bufalino, was being attacked by some Lynn kids. Jimmy and Mike flew off the bus and found their teammate surrounded by the four older, bigger guys. Words were exchanged and someone pushed either Lyons or Powers. A quick, bloody and decisive brawl ensued. The driver was not sure who had done what to whom. But one of the antagonists had been quickly decked with a haymaker. A second had been grabbed around the neck and run into a fence. The other two had also been quickly dispatched. According to the driver, after all four had been beaten into submission, the Swampscott boys quietly re-boarded. Coach Lynch realized that he would have to be even more vigilant in efforts to help the dynamic duo avoid future trouble.

The boys did not limit themselves to battles against third parties. They also enjoyed facing off outside the Paradise Dairy Bar near Vinnin Square. It was the local hang-out for the town's teenagers, particularly on weekend nights. There Lyons and Powers would pace a number of steps in opposite directions before turning and facing one another. On an agreed signal, they would charge forward as fast and hard as they could and collide, each trying to knock the other down. It was their idea of great fun. Now the two were seniors and leaders on the football team. Along with Bruce Jordan, they were the backbone of the defense, supplying skill, strength, experience, and tenacity. But even these veterans had not been regular offensive starters in 1958.

Reduced expectations in 1959 did not mean reduced publicity. In early September, the *Item* carried an article titled "Stan Bondelevitch Tells Why Big Blue Succeeds." It included typical Bondy quotes, including that he would not have fatheads or cocky kids on his teams and that his players had to be "tough, stable, punctual always at the practice sessions, keep their school marks up, and behave on the street." Asserting that "the most important thing to the boys is schooling," he added that, "Fundamentally, we go to school to learn and let our parents and church teach us our morals." He explained that he limited practice sessions to 90 minutes to prevent players from getting bored or tired. Once again, he praised his 1959 team as "the best bunch I have ever coached."

The published programs for Big Blue home games included a short column that, over the years, was written under various headings, including "Gridiron Grits," "Big Blue Bulletin," and "Big Blue Notes" The style and content were unmistakably Bondy, with articles praising not only the players, but the entire support structure for SHS sports, including the band, drill team, cheerleaders, and spirit squad. Parents, teachers, and administrators were also frequently lauded and school work emphasized. The message invariably centered on spirit, pride, and teamwork. An example can be found in the following from the 1958 Big Blue Bulletin:

> The most important part of life in our high school is the Academic. School work comes before any other phase of our school life—our boys are told day after day to study hard and to report back to the teachers for extra help. Our high school faculty is the best. We have high standards and fine people who are dedicated to teach us.... The term "Big Blue" stands for spirit, pride and loyalty. People working together, and boys and girls who want to be the Big Blue help to make Swampscott High School.

The unseasoned 1959 club opened at Andover and managed to keep the winning streak alive, grinding out a 12–6 victory. While Jimmy Lyons had seen action as a guard in 1958, he was converted to fullback for the 1959 opener. Lyons was not as fast or flashy as some of the great running backs from the recent past, but he was a very tough, good-sized player who hit and ran hard and loved to play. Against Andover, he tallied both touchdowns.

The Blue won again in its home opener, beating Woburn 20–6. Lyons supplied much of the firepower with two more touchdowns. Swampscott owned the state's longest winning streak.

While Big Blue fans watched their team win its 19th consecutive game, they experienced something new. The home team sideline and stands had always faced westward. When games ran late into the afternoon, Swampscott's coaches and fans had sometimes struggled to see the action due to the sun's glare. Prior to the start of the 1959 season, Bondy solved that problem. The stands on the west side of the field (the side facing east toward Marblehead) were improved and expanded and became the home team side for future games. Sun glare would henceforth be the visitors' problem.

At this point, another human-interest story about the Big Blue found its way into the *Item* in an article entitled "Swampscott Has Three Blind Mice." The reference was to three of the team's starting linemen who ordinarily wore glasses in the classroom but managed to play without them. The players were Mike Powers, Bruce Jordan, and junior guard Mike Janvrin. The secret was that, compliments of the Boosters, they wore contact lenses. It was another example of Bondy finding ways to manufacture positive news about the football program.

The boys next faced Danvers. According to Bondy, the Oniontowners had their best team in seven years. Could this be the "well-coached, well-drilled" squad that Bondy feared might bring down the Big Blue? Danvers teams had often been humiliated by Swampscott. For example, Bobby Carlin had run for eight touchdowns against them during his final two seasons. In fact, Danvers had not come close to beating any Bondelevitch-coached team. In six prior meetings, the Oniontowners had lost by an average margin of 30 points, and the closest had been Swampscott's 28–7 victory in 1953.

But 1959 was different. While Lyons and new halfback Tom Santanello each scored, the team failed on both conversion attempts. That proved to be the difference. Danvers won 14–12. Intent on recognizing his players' efforts and inspiring further commitment and spirit, Bondy praised them after the game, with yet another "ever" speech:

> No coach ever worked with a finer or more loyal bunch of boys than I have at Swampscott this year.... We were bound to reach the end of the string someday. They gave it all they had, and nobody could ask more than that.

With the Danvers loss, it seemed that the players could now just focus on football without the pressure of the streak. However, there was a different kind of distraction the following week. As the team practiced in preparation for its game against Winthrop, a Swampscott police officer rode his motorcycle onto the field and approached the head coach. After a brief conversation, an irate Bondy yelled for Lyons and Powers. It seemed that the two had once again gotten into trouble, partly as a result of the *Item's* "Three Blind Mice" story.

Some Danvers players had been aware of the story and had mocked Powers and his near-sighted teammates during the game with chants of "three blind mice." When the Blue lost, resentment over the taunting festered and Powers and Lyons had visited Danvers and located several of their opponents from Saturday's game. Their conversation ended when Mike took offense at a comment by one of the Oniontowners and decked the kid with a hard punch.

Any hope that Bondy would not learn of this latest transgression evaporated when Mike and Jimmy saw the police officer at practice. Bondy hotly berated the boys for their foolish conduct and sent them home. Mike realized that he had made a bad mistake and may have jeopardized his senior season. While he and Jimmy were two of the best players on the team, they needed Swampscott football much more than it needed them. They had derived so much from the program, including feelings of loyalty, pride, accomplishment, and camaraderie. Participating in football also provided structure and discipline.

Mike felt sick over the possibility that he might lose his position as co-captain or even be thrown off the team. His involvement with Big Blue football had become one of the most important things in his world. He respected the coaches and valued his relationship with teammates. The last thing that he wanted was to let them down.

At school on the following day, Lyons and Powers were summoned to Bondy's office. The coach, still upset, again blasted the boys, suggesting at one point that they should perhaps leave school and enlist in military service. As he put it, "If you like to fight so much, join the army so you can at least fight against our country's enemies." Finally, Bondy told them to get out of his office, adding that he would see them at practice that afternoon. They had survived.

While Bondy and Lynch could be driven to exasperation by the two young Irish-Americans, there were certain things about them that their coaches loved. They were as tough as nails and neither would ever back down from a physical challenge. Each would try his best to run through a wall if asked to do so. Finally, the coaches knew that the boys very much needed Big Blue football. Participation offered a positive outlet for their aggressive energies, and provided essential lessons about things like commitment and teamwork. The program afforded kids like Lyons and Powers a constructive path away from what otherwise may have been a self-destructive road to nowhere.

The rebuilding team lost to Winthrop, 12–6. Bondy juggled the line-up. Lyons, whose hand was in a cast due to a fracture sustained in the Winthrop game, was returned to his former position at guard. Tom Santanello replaced him at fullback and sophomore Ronny Corcoran took over the right halfback position. New faces also appeared in several spots in the line.

Going into the next game at Amesbury, the offensive starters included five juniors and two sophomores. Playing in the mud and rain the Big Blue escaped with a 12–8 victory. Sophomore David "Red" Coughlin, the boy who had scored four touchdowns in a 1958 freshman game, caught a short pass from quarterback Dick Leger and ran it in with only minutes remaining to notch the decisive points.

The 3–2 team prepared to host 4–1 Saugus. On paper, the Blue was overmatched. Saugus head coach Janusas had spoken confidently about facing Swampscott's undefeated teams in 1957 and 1958 before losing both games. Now, with his team the clear favorite, he was cautiously non-committal about the likely outcome. Bondy, of course, had nothing but praise for the Sachems, describing them as one of the better teams with two of the best quarterbacks in the area, and as being "very well drilled and well coached."

Stan and his staff were particularly adept at preparing teams for con-tests against superior opponents. Playing in the mud, wind and rain, the boys battled Saugus to a 0–0 tie—a victory of sorts for the underdogs. In fact, this may have been their best overall effort of the season, as they managed to hold the highly regarded Sachems scoreless. Coach Janusas was once more frustrated by Bondy and the Big Blue.

As SHS prepared to visit Manning Bowl to take on Lynn Classical, Bondy, always intent on motivating the younger players, praised the recent play of four sophomores: tackle Ted Rafter, linebacker Richie Fuller, and running backs Red Coughlin and Ronny Corcoran.

Ronny was another who had grown up with Big Blue football. He was a Swampscott native. The Corcoran family lived near Phillips Park and Ronny's mother worked in the high school cafeteria. As a youngster, Ronny had liked hanging around the varsity players whenever he could. He was in awe of stars like Tom Gorman, Roger Coe, and Bobby Carlin. He attended Camp Fun and then had an opportunity to serve as a water-boy. It was the start of his long relationship with Stan Bondelevitch and Big Blue football. He was destined to spend many years with the program, first as a player and then as a coach.

In one of his first opportunities to play with the varsity, Ronny discov-ered that Jim Lyons and Mike Powers employed their own unique moti-vational skills. The offense needed several yards for a critical first down and quarterback Dick Leger told the huddled players that they would be running a dive with Corcoran carrying the ball. Lyons immediately yelled, "Run it right over my ass!" He also warned the sophomore that he'd better make the first down. But then Powers chimed in, shouting, "No, you run it right behind me! I'll clear it out for you!"

Lyons and Powers continued to shout conflicting orders at Ronny while everyone else remained silent. Finally, Leger yelled that they needed to hurry to the line and snap the ball. By this point, Corcoran was almost paralyzed with fears that had nothing to do with the opposition. The only thing that he knew was that he had better make the first down. When he was handed the ball, he ran forward as fast and hard as he could. He was not sure whether he hit the line behind Lyons, Powers, or center Bruce Jordan, but he somehow picked up enough yardage to secure the first down and avoid possible retribution from one or both of the senior guards.

On a brutally cold day, the Big Blue traveled to Manning Bowl to take on Classical. Playing in a practically deserted stadium, the team managed to fumble the ball away five times and lose, 8–0. The anemic offense had failed to score a point in two consecutive games. Several days later, Mike Powers sat in Bondy's office as the two watched the game film and the coach lamented that they were unable to consistently run, or protect, the football. Powers was quick to volunteer his services as a running back, assuring Bondy that he would get the job done. Powers, like Lyons, lacked the speed and athleticism of some of the stellar backs of the past. But, also like Lyons, Powers was as tough and competitive as they came.

Bondy took Powers at his word, moving him from guard to fullback for the Newburyport game. When Vinny Easterbrooks learned that Powers would be playing fullback he asked whether Mike would like to wear Billy Carlyn's #33 jersey. Mike thanked the ever-helpful Vinny but replied that he would stick with his own #74 so that "all of my fans will recognize me." He added, "All two of them—my mom and dad!"

Once the game got underway, Mike, like his pal Jimmy, rose to the challenge, scoring three times while leading the Blue to a 20–12 win. Billy Bufalino, the classmate whom Lyons and Powers had rescued three years earlier after the freshman basketball game, played a key role. With the score knotted at 12–12 late in the fourth quarter, Bufalino picked off a

Clipper pass and returned it deep into Newburyport territory. Leger then connected with end Pete Gnaedinger, who was brought down just short of the goal line. From there Powers plunged into the end zone for the game-winner. Leger connected again with Gnaedinger for the two-point conversion, raising the final score to 20–12.

When Mike Powers, still aglow after his three touchdowns, arrived home following the game, he asked his mother what she thought of his performance. Perhaps in hope of preventing her son from getting a swollen head, she replied, "I don't think that I have ever seen a slower running back!"

The 4–3–1 squad started preparing for Thanksgiving. The 3–5 Headers were playing under new coach Noel Reebenacker, who had replaced long-time mentor Herm Hussey after the winless 1958 campaign. At the annual Lions Club pre-Thanksgiving banquet, Bondy bestowed another accolade on his club, calling it "the best-conditioned group" he had ever coached.

While the annual "Beat Marblehead" pep rally, held in the high school gym, was always a season highlight, it was especially memorable in 1959. One of Swampscott's most famous natives, actor Walter Brennan, was back in town. The three-time Oscar winner, who had been a member of the 1912 and 1913 Sculpin football teams, attended the rally and spoke. He then conducted the band as it played the Swampscott fight song. Set to the tune *On Wisconsin*, the song was played by the band and sung by cheerleaders, drill team and spirit squad members, and other students on countless occasions over the years, including at pep rallies, half-time performances, and after every Swampscott score, always concluding with:

> *Swampscott High School, Swampscott High School*
> *Show your loyalty*
> *On, Big Blue*
> *March right on to victory*

The SHS kids had a chance to play and sing the song a number of times on Thanksgiving morning 1959 as the visiting Big Blue concluded its seventh consecutive winning season with an 18–0 win over Marblehead. Backs Dave Corbett and Bob Arnold joined converted guard Mike Powers in running for touchdowns. Walter Brennan traveled to Marblehead for the game, sat in the stands, and cheered the boys to victory.

Jim Lyons, Mike Powers, Bruce Jordan, and their senior teammates had played their last game for the Big Blue. The three tough guys received some well-deserved postseason recognition. But unlike some seniors on past squads, they would not be competing in any December All-Star games. Earlier in 1959, the Headmasters Association had banned such events from being held during the school year.

Another senior who celebrated the Thanksgiving victory was 175-pound reserve end, Arthur Palleschi. Arthur's maternal grandparents had emigrated from Italy to the United States. They and Arthur's parents lived behind Jackson Park in a hilly area characterized by apartment houses and heavily populated by folks of Italian descent, many of whom were first-generation Americans. In those politically incorrect days, the place was referred to by many, including those living there, as "Guinea Hill."

As a young child, Arthur resided with his mother and her parents while his father was away, serving in the army during World War II. Like many of the older folks in that section of town, Arthur's grandparents spoke only Italian. As a result, Arthur and most of his friends and neighbors grew up bilingual. It was an extremely close-knit neighborhood.

Palleschi attended nearby Machon School where the majority of his classmates were also Italian-American. It was not until he reached the seventh grade and entered Hadley that he encountered many kids from other areas of town who did not share his ethnic background, and who had grown up in different, more financially privileged circumstances. It was an eye-opener for Arthur, who started to realize that there was a much wider world beyond his insulated neighborhood.

Arthur liked football and also thought that playing would afford an opportunity to become better acquainted with some of the kids from that wider world. He, therefore, signed up for the eighth-grade squad. Palleschi was never a starter but he stuck with football throughout high school. One reason was the coach. Bondy frequently visited the J. M. Fields Department Store in Vinnin Square where Mrs. Palleschi worked and always sought her out to talk about Arthur. He told her repeatedly that Arthur was a fine boy and doing well, but that the squad was so deep that it was hard to find him much playing time. Nonetheless, he said, Arthur was highly valued, contributing in a major way to the Big Blue's success, and that she had every reason to feel proud. Mrs. Palleschi of course then repeated the coach's nice words to her son.

Practices could be difficult for the reserve end because he had to battle hard-hitting, tough players like John Flanagan, Jim Lyons, and Mike Powers. During one intrasquad scrimmage in 1958, the bar across the front of Arthur's helmet was not enough to protect his face from a hard forearm. By the time Bondy and other coaches reached him he was covered in blood. He was taken to the team doctor. Later that evening, Coach Bondelevitch visited the Palleschi home. After checking on Arthur's condition, he spent time chatting with the boy and his parents.

For Arthur and others who did not see much playing time, the personal attention from the head coach kept them motivated. This was one reason that boys like Palleschi stayed with the program, continuing to report to practice without much hope of seeing regular action in the games on Saturday. Arthur emerged from his high school football experience with a sense of accomplishment and pride over his role as a valued member of the Big Blue.

Following graduation, Palleschi attended Nichols College, together with teammates Bill Bufalino and Stu Bass. Bondy had written strong letters of recommendation for all three. Arthur went on to law school. He continued to live in Swampscott. Eventually, at the urging of friends from the old neighborhood, he ran for selectman. He spent many cold winter evenings knocking on doors but fell short. Palleschi did not give up and won his second race with the highest vote total, which made him chairman of the Board of Selectmen. He served for 10 years, and then as town counsel for another 15. Arthur recognized that lessons about perseverance learned on the practice fields at Phillips Park were critical to his success in later life.

Whether players were reserves or stars, they received some of the same messages from the head coach. There was the time when Bondy called the entire team together at the Fieldhouse and announced that one of the players had skipped practice and then lied to both his mother and his coach. Bondy said that such conduct would not be tolerated. Without naming the offending player he stated that he wanted the kid to clean out his locker, go home, and not bother to show up for the game that

Saturday. Many of the boys were stunned when one of the top players on the squad quickly cleaned out his locker and exited the building. That left an impression.

On another occasion, Bondy heard one of his biggest linemen shout out *motherfucker*, an obscenity that Stan found highly offensive, particularly when uttered by a teenager. Bondy held women, especially mothers, in high esteem. He frequently lectured the players about the need to respect their mothers and sometimes spoke about his own mother and the sacrifices that she had made. When he heard the coarse expletive, he blew up. The big kid spent most of the remainder of that practice running laps around the field. It is unlikely that he soon used the word again, at least in any setting where Coach Bondelevitch might have overheard.

Despite the end of the streak, 1959 was a successful season. The boys overcame inexperience and lack of team speed to post a 5–3–1 record and soundly defeat the Headers. They scored just 100 points but held their opponents to a mere 59. Bondy had been right. This was a very good defensive team. The three losses were by a total of 16 points. The team had hung tough and battled in every game.

Jim Lyons secured a football scholarship to Northeastern University where he served as captain of the 1964 Huskies. After college, he played semi-professional football and coached. Jim eventually also worked providing rehabilitation help for alcoholics. He and his brother Terry, having struggled with alcohol abuse, counseled and assisted many others afflicted with addiction. In so doing, they undoubtedly salvaged lives.

Having served as football co-captain, class president, student council president, Boys State Representative, and participated in hockey, track, and the high school band, Bruce Jordan took his diverse talents to the University of Massachusetts where he played football and served as defensive captain. He thereafter became a highly respected teacher and football coach at rival Marblehead. Those who played with or for Jordan have nothing but praise for the gentle giant. Mike Janvrin, who succeeded Bruce as an SHS co-captain, summed it up nicely, describing him as a great leader and "a wonderful guy with a heart of gold."

In March of 1960, Mike Powers and a couple of other seniors visited Phillips Park to watch spring football practice. But as Mike walked past the Blocksidge Field stands, he felt oddly out of place, recognizing that he was no longer part of the team. He could not bear the thought of standing on the sidelines in street clothes watching the players engaged in the activity that had meant so much to him. He turned around, left, and never returned.

Decades later, Dick Lynch was attending a function when he was approached by a man who identified himself as Mike Powers and asked if they might speak privately. When they were alone Mike told Lynch about his job, his wife of many years, and his college-educated children, explaining that he had built a good life and felt blessed in many ways. He then thanked Coach Lynch, stating that if it had not been for the guidance and discipline that Lynch provided, his life would never have turned out so well. "I owe it all to you, Coach Lynch," he said. The hard-nosed Lynch struggled to hold back tears.

From that day Powers maintained regular contact, offering help, particularly during a time when Lynch was battling illness. Reflecting back on the days when he and Gangsta Lyons roamed the halls of SHS, Powers says, "Fortunately we had coaches, teachers, and a principal who saw good in the two of us and gave us opportunities to correct our behavior and contribute to the school." In the words of former teammate Jim Gorman, "You'd have to go a long way to find a nicer guy than Mike Powers. He is really into serving the needs of his fellow man and if you asked him for his shirt, he would only ask if you first wanted it laundered."

2017—The silent old high school building on Greenwood Avenue. Photo by author

"Count" Bondelevitch. Courtesy Saint Anselm College

Drawing by SHS student George Rousseau depicting demise of the Sculpins and emergence of the Big Blue. *Swampscotta, Fall 1954*

Bondy's first SHS coaching staff: (l-r) Dick Stevenson, Hal Foster, Leon "Doc" Marden, Stan Bondelevitch. *Swampscotta, Fall 1953*

1954 SHS Band and Drill Team. 1955 *Seagull*

Bobby Carlin (20) and Billy Carlyn (33) in action in 1955. 1956 *Seagull*

1957 co-captains Jimmy Gorman (l)
and Billy Carlyn (r). 1958 *Seagull*

Doug Haley wearing translucent
faceguard that protected him
from "the punch" following "the
pinch." 1957 *Seagull*

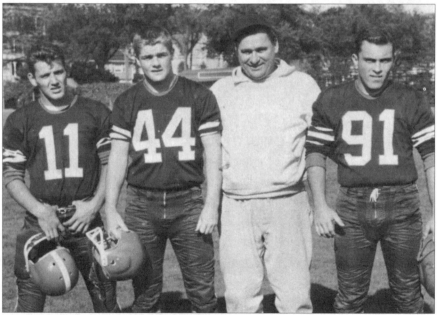

Bondy with 1958 tri-captains George Blais (11), Frank Cahoon (44) and Bob
Andrews (91). 1959 *Seagull*

George Blais eludes a frustrated opponent. 1959 *Seagull*

Bondy with 1959 co-captains Mike
Powers (l) and Bruce Jordan (r).
1960 *Seagull*

Bondy with his "three blind mice,"
(l-r) Mike Janvrin, Bruce Jordan, and
Mike Powers. Courtesy Mike Powers
and *Daily Item*

The '60s

Excitement in 1966 at Blocksidge Field. 1967 *Seagull*

The Woburn
"World Series"

Heading into the 1960 season, Swampscott boasted the area's best win-loss record over the preceding five years, having won 35 games while losing only eight. And there was cause for optimism as a number of starters returned and many others had varsity experience. While this team would be hard-pressed to match the 1958 champions in backfield talent, it finally had good front line size, including two big, veteran, two-way tackles in Jim Randell and Dave Landry. Randell was 6-foot, 4-inches, and all of 220 pounds, while the 6-foot, 2-inch Landry tipped in at around 210.

Prior to his junior year, Landry had been a member of the band and had not played football. His classmate Mike Janvrin kept urging him to join the team and Dave finally did, quitting the band, but neglecting to inform his parents. They only learned the truth when their son failed to appear for a band concert. While Mrs. Landry was understandably upset, she overcame her disappointment and fully supported her son's athletic endeavors, attending all his games.

In addition to the two tackles, the starting offensive line featured juniors Ted Rafter, Richard Fuller, and George Forbes, at center, guard, and end, respectively. The 200-pound Rafter had played regularly in the varsity line as a sophomore while Forbes and Fuller had seen action on defense; Forbes as a 6-foot, 2-inch, 190-pound end, and Fuller as a linebacker. Tobey Moore, a 165-pound senior, would be starting as the other offensive end, while also playing in the defensive backfield. Co-captain Mike Janvrin returned to his position as the team's right guard. The line was solid.

The Janvrin family moved into town in 1955, after spending four years in Jamaica where Mr. Janvrin had worked in bauxite mining. Mike and older brother Phil quickly embraced football. Phil played on Swampscott's freshman squad but there was no football program at Saint John where Mike was enrolled. He and classmates Dave Corbett and Dick Leger therefore launched a campaign for permission to play on the Hadley eighth-grade team. Eventually they were allowed early release so they could participate. Stan Bondelevitch was more than happy to welcome the boys into the program, offering words of praise and encouragement.

Mike played with the JVs in 1958 and then broke into the starting line-up early in his junior year after battling against tough veterans like Lyons and Powers. While initially anxious about facing them in one-on-one drills, Janvrin met the challenge, earning a spot at right guard. Although he was not big, weighing just over 160 pounds, Mike performed well enough as a junior to win election as a co-captain of the 1960 squad.

Despite halfback Bobby Arnold's general unavailability due to injury, there was more experience, depth, and speed at running back than in the prior season. Senior John DiLisio was a strong runner, able receiver, and good defensive back. He was joined by classmates Dave Corbett and Tom Santanello, who competed with juniors Dana and David Coughlin and Ronny Corcoran for playing time. All had some varsity experience.

Dick Leger departed for private school, leaving senior Billy Loveday to battle junior Danny Goodwin for the starting quarterback job. The 6-foot, 170-pound Loveday, younger brother of Eddie, had good size and was a strong, accurate passer. Goodwin, shorter and tipping in at no more than 140 pounds, was christened "Mumbles" by Bondy due to his almost inaudible signal calling. Dan did not have great arm strength and the coaches generally barred him from throwing anything other than what Bondy coined "the dinky pass," executed by tossing a short jump-pass over the line to one of the ends. But Bondy loved the boy's tough, competitive spirit, and ability to smoothly run the offense and protect the football, rarely turning it over. Loveday and Goodwin would both be seeing considerable action throughout the season, often spelling one another during the same game.

Bondy again conducted his highly publicized Parents Clinic at Blocksidge Field, adding a new wrinkle by including players and coaches from Beverly High School and concluding with a controlled scrimmage against the Class A squad. As the *Item's* Cahill observed:

Promoting football interest at Swampscott High is a full-time job. And if there's a switch or a gimmick which will add to that interest, count on Stan Bondelevitch, the athletic director and head coach of the Big Blue, to come up with it.

The 17th Annual Football Jamboree followed the Clinic, with SHS playing Lawrence in the featured game. Event organizer Elmo Benedetto had obviously concluded that this match-up generated interest and sold tickets since the teams were typically contenders in their respective classes.

Adding to the preseason buzz, Bondy announced that his team would unveil a new "Hi-Fi" offense, described as a variant of the "Maryland I." His much-hyped new scheme received plenty of attention, including these words in the Jamboree Program:

Coach Bondelevitch and his new Hi-Fi offense are the talk of the North Shore, and everyone is waiting to see the new "Slant-I" Bondy has devised for Northeastern Conference opponents.

The team emerged from its 12-minute mini-game with a 6–0 win. DiLisio, Corcoran, and Dana Coughlin ran the ball effectively in a sustained scoring drive. However, despite the much ballyhooed "Hi-Fi," the offense on display at the Jamboree bore a striking resemblance to Bondy's tried-and-true wing-T.

The happiest boy on the team following the event was probably Dana Coughlin. While SHS players were typically issued high-top football cleats, many, particularly the backs, longed to wear low-cuts, which they thought were sleek and cool-looking. Bondy, always searching for new motivational tactics, announced prior to the Jamboree that any boy scoring a touchdown would receive a pair of new low-cut cleats. Dana registered the only touchdown and claimed his prize.

The Big Blue continued to impress in its opener, crushing Andover, 38–8. A number of players contributed to the scoring, including DiLisio, Corcoran, Corbett, and Billy Loveday, who threw two touchdown passes. However, Bondy reserved his highest praise for Jim Randell, telling the *Boston Globe's* Ernie Dalton that Randell was "the best tackle in the country, in North America, from both sides of the Iron Curtain." The Swampscott coach was not known for understatement.

The boys had little time to celebrate the opening victory because they had to prepare for the next game against powerful Woburn. After losing to Swampscott in 1959, Woburn had rebounded to win the conference championship. With seven returning starters, the Tanners were expected to contend again. Coach Walter White accurately predicted that his junior quarterback, Ed Foley, would be one of the finest passers in school history. In its first game, Woburn rolled over Newburyport, 30–0. Swampscott v. Woburn was seen as a battle between perhaps the conference's two strongest teams. The Tanners were favored.

Having in mind that major league baseball's World Series was about to commence, Stan suggested that the *real* world series would not begin in Pittsburgh but rather in Woburn on the upcoming Saturday afternoon, promising:

> It will be a one-game affair played in four innings.… We'll throw our best pitchers at 'em, and you can be sure our good hitters will be in there hitting.

He emphasized that his linemen would need to win the battles up front and slow down Woburn's potent offense.

As often happened when a Bondelevitch team was the underdog, his players found a way to win, upsetting the Tanners, 22–16. Dana Coughlin, resplendent in his new low-cuts, scored twice. And Billy Loveday connected with John DiLisio on a long TD pass. Ronny Corcoran rushed twice for conversions. The line performed as the coach had hoped, blocking well, while holding Woburn to just two touchdowns. Even so, the game came down to the final seconds, with Woburn just inches from the Swampscott goal line when time ran out. With the win, the Blue became the early front-runner for the conference crown.

The *Item* predicted, "With Saturday's 22–16 win over Woburn safely on the record books, the locals should have no trouble with Danvers, whose showing has only been fair this season." Not even the publicity-hungry Bondelevitch wanted this kind of media attention. With his boys having marshaled the intensity and focus required to meet the Woburn challenge, the last thing they needed was a suggestion that they could coast to victory over the Oniontowners. Danvers had beaten Swampscott in 1959, ending the Big Blue's winning streak. This would be a tough opponent.

It is unknown how many players were aware of the *Item's* prediction, but the team played miserably, losing 34–6. In one of the most lopsided defeats of the Bondelevitch era, anything that could go wrong did. The low point was a fourth-down play, with Swampscott punting. Mike Janvrin and Richard Fuller were in the backfield providing protection. As soon as they heard the sound of the football being kicked they sprinted downfield to cover the punt. As they ran they noticed that the Danvers return man made no effort to position himself to catch the ball. They glanced back toward the line of scrimmage and then stopped and stared at each other in wonderment.

The football lay on the ground, *behind* punter Ronny Corcoran. Knowing that no defender had been in a position to block the kick, Mike and Richie were perplexed until they later viewed the game film and saw one of their teammates step in front of Corcoran just as he was kicking. The ball careened off that teammate's butt and over Corcoran's head.

Reporting on the Danvers results, the *Item* observed that the Big Blue had not seemed nearly as motivated as it had against Woburn. Bondy may have been tempted to pen a sarcastic note, thanking the newspaper for its role in bringing about that change when it implied that SHS would have no difficulty in beating the Oniontowners. Instead, he offered no excuses, simply stating, "We were outplayed completely." Danvers went on to defeat several other strong teams, including Woburn and Marblehead.

Swampscott, having started its season on such a promising note, had stumbled badly and needed to find a way to quickly rebound against Winthrop. For some time, Winthrop had been searching for the right nickname for its high school teams. Most recently they had played as "the Blue Devils." But that changed in 1960. The former Blue Devils became "the Vikings," a name that the school's sports teams would continue to use. Not only had Winthrop beaten Bondy's team in 1959, the Vikings were 3–0 in 1960, having put away Methuen, Amesbury, and Newburyport. In short, SHS faced another big test. The loss to Danvers had been a setback, but a second defeat at Winthrop would seem like a derailment for a team that had appeared on track for a championship.

The players were informed that poor play cost them their day off. There would be an intrasquad scrimmage on Monday reminiscent of the infamous "Bataan Death March" practice following the 1956 "fumbleitis" defeat. The head coach was not pleased with the team's Danvers performance and the boys caught an earful.

One of his cutting assessments was particularly embarrassing for junior Richard Fuller, a starting linebacker/left guard. Bondy growled, "We haven't had a left guard since the second half of the Woburn game." Richie silently vowed that his coach would never again have cause to single him out for criticism, which was exactly the response Bondy had hoped to elicit. As he typically did after a bad loss, Bondy tried some players at new positions, including inserting Fuller as a fullback during the scrimmage.

Richard "Bronco" Fuller grew up with Bondy's Big Blue football program. His family had moved into town from urban Somerville when he was an infant, settling in a house near Abbott Park. He eventually started his formal education at Clarke School. Like other active youngsters in the modest, middle-class neighborhood, Fuller spent his non-classroom time playing games at the park. There was baseball and, of course, tackle-fumble football. In the winter, the town flooded a section of the park and kids played hockey or figure-skated. Richie loved hockey, baseball, and football.

When Bondy took charge of youth sports, Fuller was about 10 years old. Shortly thereafter as summer vacation approached, Richie's mother informed him that he would be attending Coach Bondelevitch's Camp Fun in Lanesville. Wearing tee shirts bearing the camp's name, Richie and some of his fellow-campers were driven to and from Lanesville by counselor and SHS star Bobby Carlin.

One day at camp Richie was running across a field when he stepped on the sharp end of a root which cut deeply into his heel. He tried to hold back tears as Bondy treated the wound. Turning to his distressed camper, the big man mused, "I guess we are going to find out whether Richard Fuller is tough enough to play for the Big Blue." Clenching his teeth, Richie was determined not to cry or whimper, regardless of the pain.

Soon he, like fellow camper Ronny Corcoran, was serving as a Big Blue waterboy. Fuller loved spending time with the varsity players and coaches. There was no formal Pop Warner program back then, but older kids were soon explaining some of the Big Blue's plays to him and his friends. Well before they joined the supervised seventh-grade football program, the youngsters were running plays like the 38-power and 22-trap in their sandlot games.

Richie had his first opportunity to play in the football program as a Hadley seventh grader and he took to heart and never forgot Coach Fran Chiary's message during their initial practice. "Always give 100% and hit the other player faster and harder than he can hit you," Chiary told them. "And never let up, because if you do, you are going to get hurt."

As an eighth and ninth grader, Fuller watched the varsity claim consecutive championships as it won 17 straight games. His heroes included stars like George Blais, Jackie Milo, and Billy Carlyn, who had been one of his Abbott Park playground counselors. In 1959, Richie entered the tenth grade. Tough-guy seniors Mike Powers and Jimmy Lyons befriended the sophomore, showing him the ropes. Although not a particularly big kid, Fuller was rugged enough to play for the varsity, seeing regular duty, especially as a linebacker.

As a junior, he was starting as both linebacker and left guard prior to being tried as a fullback during the scrimmage following the Danvers loss. He performed well in that position. In 1959 Bondy had, at different times, moved both Lyons and Powers from the offensive line to the starting backfield. Now he did the same with Fuller, naming him starting fullback for the Winthrop game. Bondy liked rugged players who ran hard. Richard Fuller was such a player.

While Winthrop always seemed to get up for the Big Blue, Swampscott's players were not lacking in motivation. They needed to rebound from the Danvers fiasco and earn back their free Mondays. They also had Coach Stevenson, a Winthrop native, telling them how much it would mean to him if they could defeat his alma mater. The boys did not want to disappoint the chipmunk.

In a hard-fought, low-scoring affair, defensive end George Forbes made the play of the game near the end of the third quarter when he ripped the ball out of the grip of a Winthrop running back on the Vikings' 15-yard line. Ultimately Dana Coughlin ran in for the touchdown, giving the Blue a 6–0 lead. Billy Loveday connected with Forbes for the two-point conversion. The defense continued to shut out the Vikings and Swampscott had its 8–0 victory.

Next up was Amesbury. Bondy did more juggling, including permanently moving David Coughlin from the backfield to the offensive line. The muscular, red-headed junior had the size, strength, and passion to excel as a lineman. At around 190 pounds, he may have been the best-built player on the team. Former teammates describe him as "chiseled." In any case, David's size and complexion had earned him the nicknames "Red" and "Big Red." Now Bondy told him, "You are no longer Big Red. You are Huge Red!" In a sloppy Blocksidge Field battle, the Blue rallied in the second half from a 6-point deficit to beat the Carriagemakers, 16–8. Dana Coughlin and Ronny Corcoran each ran for a touchdown.

The Saugus Sachems, after starting the season well, had failed to tally a single point in their last three contests. But Coach Janusas told the *Item* that his boys had fallen to inferior teams, asserting that the losses had resulted from "goofing off, slipping, bobbling the ball, and outright fumbling." His assessment may have been accurate. His players apparently stopped "goofing off" and emerged with a surprising 14–6 victory over the Big Blue. It was the Saugus coach's first and only win over Bondy and Swampscott.

The 1960 season had thus far been unpredictable, with the boys performing in yo-yo fashion. They posted impressive wins over strong opponents like Woburn and Winthrop, only to stumble against Danvers and Saugus. Now 4–2, they entertained Lynn Classical. Bondy was no Janusas. Instead of boasting that his team was better than the opponent, he implied that there was little hope of victory, pleading, "Just imagine us taking on this big Class A power year after year…. Why, we're lucky we can be on the same field with Classical."

Classical's coach George Moriarty, unwilling to build up Swampscott, commented, "We certainly don't intend to be taken on two successive weekends by Class B teams…. We respect Swampscott as a good team but I think we can win this one." Moriarty was wrong. Classical lost to the Blue, 14–12. Converted guard Fuller scored twice, while Corcoran tallied the critical two-point conversion.

On the following Saturday, SHS surprisingly transformed into a passing machine and destroyed Newburyport, 32–0. Billy Loveday, flashing the skills he would use to become a record-setting quarterback at Colby College, completed touchdown passes to Ronny Corcoran and Dana

Coughlin. Halfback John DiLisio also connected on an option pass with Tobey Moore for another score. And Mumbles Goodwin contributed by running the ball in from a short distance and then hitting Forbes with the "dinky pass" for the two-point conversion. Corcoran also intercepted passes on two consecutive plays, picking off a second after his first interception was nullified by a penalty.

The 6–2 squad prepared to face 7–1 Marblehead. The Headers' only blemish was a one-point loss to Danvers. They were averaging 33 points a game while Swampscott was averaging fewer than 18. Marblehead's passing offense featured strong-armed quarterback Tom "Bucket" Manning and rangy receiver Bob Radcliffe. At 6-foot, 5-inches, and about 200 pounds, Radcliffe was a great target.

While Manning was a talented quarterback, his nickname had nothing to do with his passing prowess. He had earned the name as a youngster at Marblehead's Star of the Sea elementary school. One of the nuns, apparently exasperated by Manning's classroom conduct, had exclaimed, "Empty buckets make a barrel of noise and you have an empty bucket, you bucket head!" The classroom erupted in laughter and from that time forward Tom was "Bucket" Manning.

While Swampscott entered the Thanksgiving game as an underdog, both teams were highly ranked and would be competing for the conference crown. It was the last game of the season. It was Thanksgiving. It was Swampscott v. Marblehead. No one could ask for more.

Marblehead coach Noel Reebenacker praised the Big Blue, telling the *Item*,

Swampscott is the toughest opponent we will face this season. They have the best coach on the North Shore and I have the deepest respect for both the staff and the team.

Bucket Manning had reportedly injured his back in a fall at home and word from the Headers was that he might not play in the big game. Bondy, however, predicted that Bucket would be there on Turkey Day, flinging the ball all over Blocksidge Field.

Excepting possibly Danvers, Swampscott did prove to be the Headers' toughest opponent. And, as predicted by Stan, Manning did show up on

Thanksgiving and fling the ball around Blocksidge Field. In an effort to keep Marblehead's high-octane offense off the field, Bondy employed the slow-down strategy that had worked so well in the 1953 upset of Amesbury. The quarterback made sure to take his time in the huddle before calling each play, thereby eating up clock and keeping the ball out of Bucket's hands.

That strategy, along with an outstanding defensive performance, limited the explosive Magicians to just 12 points, both on touchdown passes from Manning to Radcliffe, completed because Bucket put the ball up where only his tall receiver could grab it. While this represented Marblehead's lowest point total of the season, it was still enough to give the Headers a 12–6 lead going into the second half. Swampscott's only touchdown had been registered by Fuller on a short plunge at the end of a long drive.

Late in the game, SHS drove inside the Marblehead 10-yard line and then ran the 38-power, a sweep to the right side. When Mike Janvrin pulled from his guard position and led around the end looking for someone to block, there was no defender in sight. Mike was elated, believing the halfback would be able to waltz into the end zone for the tying touchdown. A good PAT would then put the Blue ahead. But when he glanced over his shoulder his spirits sank. The ball carrier was lying on the ground in the backfield, having somehow tripped and fallen during the quarterback exchange. Mike is haunted by that disheartening sight whenever he thinks about his team's 12–6 loss to Marblehead.

The game was characterized by an unusually large number of penalties assessed against Swampscott, including some critical calls late in the fourth quarter. According to the *Item*, "But for numerous penalties against the Big Blue on its last series of plays, the outcome may have been a tie or a victory for Swampscott." Perhaps not coincidentally, less than a week later Coach Bondelevitch told the *Item's* Cahill, "We need a commissioner to weed out incompetent officials."

Dartmouth-bound Jim Randell claimed the Thom McAn trophy. He was the third of Bondy's players, and the first Big Blue lineman, to receive the award. But the Headers took the team honors as conference champions. It was the third time that Marblehead had prevented a Bondelevitch team from winning the title by beating SHS on Thanksgiving. There were plenty of tears in the locker room when the seniors removed their jerseys for the final time.

The Sad Season

Prior to the start of the 1961 season, Bondy was prominently featured in an *Item* story about Swampscott's new youth fitness program. As the town's athletic director, he announced that intramural touch football, volleyball, and kickball would be offered in the parks for boys in the third through sixth grades, while a similar program would be available for seventh, eighth, and ninth graders at the Alice Shaw Junior High School. That facility had opened in 1959. With ninth graders attending Shaw, SHS had changed to a three-year high school. Confirming that there would also be a girls' fitness program, Bondy assured the *Item*, "This is just the beginning and we're hopeful that eventually it will be the most successful on the North Shore."

However, Bondy did not expect his 1961 football team to be "the most successful on the North Shore," as he offered the following:

> We haven't a championship team, but we'll be okay. We hope to stand up against all opponents. Our trouble will come against boys who already shave. We need speed and I hope to develop it.

In short, he was saying that the team lacked experience and speed.

Despite his less-than-glowing assessment, the cupboard was not bare. Danny Goodwin returned at quarterback, joined by a couple of veteran running backs in co-captains Ronny Corcoran and Dana Coughlin. Corcoran was also a defensive standout, with Dick Lynch judging him one of the top three safeties he ever coached. Dana Coughlin's cousin, David "Red" Coughlin, was another seasoned veteran. After scoring four touchdowns in one freshman game, Red played regularly with the varsity over the next two seasons, notching the game-winner against Amesbury in 1959, but then moving to guard mid-way through the 1960 season. Now a senior, David was a two-way starting tackle.

George Forbes and Ted Rafter were two more veterans starting their senior seasons at new positions. Forbes, whom Bondy would one day recall as the most tenacious, but possibly slowest, end he ever coached, was moved to center. Rafter switched from center to tackle. Senior Henry Legere started the season at offensive guard and defensive end. Co-captain Richie Fuller, a very strong player, returned as a linebacker/fullback.

The seniors were joined by a number of promising younger players, including juniors Billy Hinch, Billy Sjogren, and Steven Santanello, and sophomore Barry Gallup. Hinch was a good-sized, aggressive, and hard-hitting end. Santanello was a stocky, hard-charging running back, with decent speed. Sjogren was a very good two-way player, manning positions as an offensive guard and defensive halfback.

Barry Gallup's father Earl, a highly respected Swampscott native and SHS Hall-of-Famer, had captained the school's football and basketball teams and played varsity baseball. At well over six feet and weighing approximately 200 pounds, Barry took after his father. He was an outstanding all-around athlete, excelling in football, basketball, and baseball. Barry was also fiercely competitive, with a burning desire to win. He loved everything about Big Blue sports.

Bondy typically scheduled preseason scrimmages against powerful opponents, no doubt believing that his team benefited from testing itself against the best. Beverly was that kind of team. Coach Roy Norden's Panthers were always tough. His outstanding 1961 squad thoroughly outplayed Swampscott, with Panther backs frequently exploding for long gains and touchdowns. The SHS players felt embarrassed by their poor performance. The good news was that they did not have long to wait for a chance at redemption as they faced Lynn's highly regarded Saint Mary's team in the Jamboree.

Hal Foster, Bondy's former assistant, coached Saint Mary's. He could not have enjoyed the reunion. Gallup scored the first touchdown, catching a halfback option pass thrown by Santanello. The defense then took over, shutting out Saint Mary's while registering two touchdowns. Future Boston Red Sox star Tony Conigliaro, making his debut as Saint Mary's

quarterback, did not have a good night. Conigliaro's first pass was intercepted by Sjogren, who took it all the way to the end zone. Tony tried
again during his team's next possession and was picked off by Fuller, who
also ran it back for a touchdown. Swampscott came away from the exhibition with a 20–0 victory. Saint Mary's went on to win all but one of its
games. Perhaps this SHS team might be better than just "okay."

While the team opened at Andover, more media attention was focused
on the following week's game against Woburn. The Tanners, with senior
quarterback Ed Foley, were generally considered the preseason conference
favorite. Neither Swampscott nor Woburn were expected to struggle in
their openers and, as in 1960, many believed that the winner of their
match-up would have the inside track to the title.

On September 23, 1961, the team traveled to Andover and, playing
on a hazy, humid afternoon, managed to win in a surprisingly close game.
In fact, the hosts held a late 8–6 lead and probably would have come
away with a win had it not been for Barry Gallup. When Andover was
forced to punt on fourth down from deep in its territory, Gallup broke
through and blocked the kick. The offense then found the end zone on
a Goodwin quarterback sneak. The Blue escaped with a 14–8 victory.
However, a tragedy followed that cast a pall over the team and the entire
Swampscott community.

As the boys prepared to board the bus for the trip home, one of them
informed the coaches that there was something wrong with David Coughlin. When the coaches checked with Red he said he was feeling okay. He
seemed tired but coherent. Playing both ways for most of the game, he
had come out early in the fourth quarter with a leg cramp but apparently
recovered and returned during the final minutes. If the boys had played
at home he would have been seen by team doctor Robert Bessom, but the
doctor did not accompany them on road games. The coaches had David
drink some water and munch on an apple.

Once the bus arrived back at the Fieldhouse the players headed into
the locker room and the coaches convened in the second-floor office.
The assistants were chatting and Bondy was on the phone when a player
informed them that Red Coughlin was having a problem. Dick Lynch,
who continued to serve as the team's de facto trainer, hurried downstairs
and observed that the boy was confused and unsteady. He walked David

up to the office and had him sit down. Coach Lynch was about to ask a question when David's eyes suddenly rolled back, his head fell to the side and he slumped over, unconscious. Lynch shouted to Bondy to call an ambulance.

David never regained consciousness. He died in Lynn Hospital on Monday afternoon, September 25, 1961. Cause of death was heat stroke. The term "heat stroke" is a misnomer, since it does not involve a blockage of blood flow to the brain. Instead, it is a lethal, often irreversible, condition of hyperthermia characterized by body temperatures in excess of 104 degrees Fahrenheit and resulting unconsciousness, organ failure, and death. Healthy young people can experience heat stroke after engaging in strenuous physical activity in hot, muggy weather. While David's leg cramp might have been a symptom of his body overheating, muscle spasms experienced after physical exertion in humid conditions are not unusual and rarely signify a serious health problem.

People have varying recollections of the weather on that fateful September Saturday, with many maintaining that it had been brutally hot—with temperatures in the 90s or even over 100 degrees. In actuality, the recorded high temperature in the area was 79 degrees Fahrenheit, while the mean was 75. In Swampscott that morning, conditions were crisp, dry, and almost cool, ideal for football. The players dressed in their heavier game jerseys before boarding the bus for the trip to Andover, approximately 22 miles to the northwest. However, as the bus traveled away from the coast the weather grew increasingly hazy and the humidity grew oppressive. By the time the game started it was so muggy that Richard Fuller's legs felt as heavy as tree trunks when he ran with the football. The teams battled through the afternoon in an energy-draining, fatigue-inducing swelter.

News of David's death caused a range of emotional reactions. One of the teachers unfairly vilified the coaches as murderers. The Big Blue coaches were not doctors trained to identify potentially fatal heat stroke. And even if Dr. Bessom had traveled with the team, the result may have been no different. Combating the lethal effects of heat stroke required quick diagnosis and immediate steps to try to bring about a decrease in body temperature. Sometimes it worked and sometimes it did not.

Dr. Bessom stated that it was hard to explain why heat stroke became irreversible in some cases and not others.

David had been vice president of the Junior Class, president of the student council, a Boys' State representative, and an active member of his church's youth group. He was also a champion dory sailor. Bondy had known him since he had been a fifth grader. David loved football, had played on organized teams since junior high school and had been a water-boy. Shortly before his death, he completed an English class assignment by writing an essay on the virtues of football titled, "The Man-Maker." He had recently told Bondy that he hoped to attend a small college and then become a teacher and coach.

His tragic death touched virtually everyone in town, many in a highly personal way. David had been as much a part of the fabric of the close-knit community as a 17-year-old could have been. The Coughlins were a well-established Swampscott family. David's father, Oliver, a co-captain of the 1933 SHS football team, served for many years as town clerk and treasurer. David's uncle, Richard Coughlin, was town counsel. One of David's aunts was married to John Ingalls, among the community's most publicly active and influential citizens and a descendant of Swampscott's earliest resident. Another was married to Ozzie Keiver Jr. He and his brother Bobby, members of a well-known Swampscott family, had both been outstanding SHS football players. And David's cousin Dana was, of course, his teammate.

Shortly after David died, Bondy told the *Item's* Ed Cahill:

It's a shattering thing. I'll see that boy's face in front of me as long as I live. Why should a boy like that, a model youngster, be taken at 17? Only God knows the answer.... He was everything I'd want in a son.

While one of the high school's teachers had been quick to blame the coaches, David's parents never did. They continued to support Big Blue football for the rest of that season and many years thereafter. The Boosters Club added the David Coughlin Memorial Trophy to the awards distributed at each season-ending banquet. It was given to a player who exhibited the positive qualities that had so characterized David.

In a commendable act of respect and sympathy, Woburn coach Walter White appeared at David's wake, accompanied by many of his players. In the aftermath of the Coughlin tragedy, people wondered if the Woburn game should be canceled or postponed out of respect for the Coughlins. While the family had no objection to it being played as scheduled, the *Item* reported on Wednesday, September 27 that the game was off. On the following day, officials released students and teachers from school to attend David's funeral.

When asked whether the Woburn game might be rescheduled to later in the year, perhaps on the Saturday before Thanksgiving, Bondy responded that he did not want to play then, because Marblehead was always of paramount importance. However, he added that if Swampscott and Woburn tied for the conference title he would personally recommend at the league meeting that Woburn be officially designated champion. "It's hard for us to think of football at a time like this," he said. "We'll play football because we need it. But winning and rivalries are farthest from our minds right now."

The team resumed practice for the October 7 Danvers game. The Oniontowners were undefeated, having most recently beaten Andover 32–0. They were heavier up-front than Swampscott and at least as fast in the backfield. Under normal circumstances, the Big Blue would have been hard-pressed to find a way to win. The wild card was the Coughlin tragedy.

Sadly, it was not the first time that the seniors on the squad had experienced the death of a classmate. Two years earlier they had lost George Sentner to diabetes. Then, shortly after the end of the 1960 football season, a second member of the class, Elizabeth "Betsy" Loveday, was killed in a tragic and senseless automobile crash. Betsy, the younger sister of quarterbacks Ed and Billy, had been a popular student, an exceptional swimmer and tennis player, and the captain-elect of the SHS field hockey team. Now they had lost a third classmate. Many of the boys had grown up with David and been his friend and teammate for years. He had died as a result of playing the same game that they all played. It was impossible to predict how his loss might affect the team's performance.

Bondy made some position moves. Richie Fuller left the backfield and was once again a guard. Ronny Corcoran moved to fullback. The other offensive starters were quarterback Goodwin, halfbacks Dana Coughlin and Steven Santanello, ends Tom Bufalino and Billy Hinch, tackles Ted Rafter and Andy Repetto, guard Bill Sjogren, and center George Forbes. Oliver Coughlin spoke to the team before it took the field, telling the boys that his son would have wanted them to play their best. They responded with an inspired effort, upsetting Danvers, 20–6.

The boys next faced unbeaten Winthrop, another bigger team. As was usually the case when Winthrop met Swampscott, it was a hard-hitting contest. SHS prevailed, 16–6. Ronny Corcoran rushed for a touchdown and a two-point conversion. Fuller scored the other touchdown off a blocked punt and Gallup caught a Goodwin pass for a conversion.

Woburn, like Swampscott, continued to win its conference games and questions resurfaced about a possible title-deciding contest between them. Bondy contradicted his earlier comment, telling the *Item* his team would play on the Saturday before Thanksgiving if necessary to decide the championship. Over the next couple of weeks, he restated that position several times, including in the following published statement:

> We are not eager to play a game the Saturday before Thanksgiving Day. But we feel an obligation to reschedule this date with Woburn, if the outcome will affect the final Conference standing.

Having beaten two highly regarded opponents on successive Saturdays, the 3–0 Blue prepared for Amesbury. The coach's preseason assessment had not changed. "This isn't a great football team," he told the *Item's* Cahill. "We're not talking in terms of an undefeated season." He felt that Danvers and Winthrop had been physically superior and that his boys had won through spirit and determination. David Coughlin was never far from their minds. A photograph of their deceased teammate hung in the Fieldhouse and the flag flew at half-staff at all home games. Mr. and Mrs. Coughlin remained close to the players. They attended the games and some of the boys regularly stopped by the Coughlin home to chat. They were, as Bondy put it, "playing better football than we, or they, thought they could."

Swampscott rolled over Amesbury, 41–14. Ronny Corcoran scored three touchdowns in the one-sided affair. Dana Coughlin also ran well, breaking off a 64-yard touchdown run, and setting up Corcoran's first score with another 42-yard ramble. The *Item* reported that this was Stan's 100th high school coaching victory.

Next up for the unbeaten Blue was winless Saugus at Blocksidge Field. Not surprisingly, Swampscott won easily, 41–20. Corcoran, who was by now near the top of the list of Essex County's leading scorers, repeated his three-touchdown performance of the previous week.

Woburn also continued to win. On October 27, 1961, *Item* columnist J. F. Williams wrote:

> As for the present it appears that Swampscott High School and Woburn High School will have to play their postponed game to decide the Northeastern Conference Football championship. Coach Stanley Bondelevitch had often mentioned that if the game will decide a title, he will play it.

In addition to all of the speculation about a possible game between Swampscott and Woburn, Bondy was frequently mentioned in the sports pages for other reasons. On October 23, the paper reported that the conference approved his proposal to suspend spring football. School-boys anxious to focus on baseball or other sports or who found the typically punishing sessions less than pleasurable undoubtedly welcomed the decision.

In the November 1 *Item*, Bondy was mentioned in connection with three different matters. He was recognized as a member of a committee voicing concern about player safety and the need for improvement in football equipment. Second, the *Item* reported that Bondy had signed a contract with his senior players agreeing to dismiss them each day from practice no later than 4:15 p.m. Finally, Bondy was reportedly confident that two of his players, Santanello and Corcoran, could kick field goals from 30 yards. In that era, it was unusual for high school teams to attempt field goals. In fact, many did not even kick for points after touchdown, particularly after the rule change that allowed more points for rushing or passing conversions.

In a single newspaper article, Bondy had been credited for addressing issues of player safety, treating his players like adults by entering into contracts to assure fair treatment, and developing specialists (field goal kickers) who might score the decisive points in close games. On the following day, he was on the sports page again, this time in an article about his having reached the 100-win milestone. He reminisced about his greatest wins and biggest disappointments. It almost read like a testimonial, as if he were about to retire. Noting that he did not expect to be around long enough to ever hit the 200-win mark, Bondy concluded:

> If I had my life to live over again I wouldn't have lived it any other way. I can't think of any career more rewarding than working with young boys in the world of sports, and realizing that you have played an important part in molding their lives.

Stan may have won 100 games, but he was hardly finished coaching. Going into the first weekend of November, his idle team was in a three-way tie in the Class B title race with Archbishop Williams (5–0) and New Bedford (4–0–1). SHS had a chance to repeat the trifecta it had achieved in 1957 and 1958—namely, beating Marblehead, winning the conference championship, and winning the Class B title. The *Item* now assumed that Swampscott would definitely play Woburn, noting that if the Big Blue could beat its three remaining opponents, Newburyport, Woburn, and Marblehead, it would clinch the Class B crown. The article correctly noted that even if the other Class B contenders won their remaining games, the Blue could claim the title outright by finishing unbeaten.

The other frontrunners won that weekend, yet fell behind idle Swampscott. This illogical result was dictated by the state's schoolboy football team ranking system. Rankings were determined by dividing total awarded "points" by the number of games played. Wins over Class A teams were worth 10 points; Class B teams, 8 points; and Class C teams, 6 points. Assuming that Swampscott won its remaining scheduled games, and played and beat Woburn, it would finish the season 8–0 but with a higher point rating than Archbishop Williams, even if that team finished 9–0. The even more bizarre result was that Swampscott could forego playing Woburn, win its final two games, and, with a 7–0 record, still claim the Class B title. In fact, the differential would be greater. While it hardly seemed fair, that was the result under the applicable formula.

Woburn had beaten Danvers over the weekend to remain tied with Swampscott atop the conference standings. It seemed the two teams were on a collision course and that their much-discussed game would be played on the Saturday before Thanksgiving. However, Swampscott announced that there would be no game with Woburn. Bondy cited the importance of the Marblehead game as the reason for not playing on the Saturday before the traditional Thursday morning contest. This had been his original position when he said that rather than play a game to decide whether Woburn or Swampscott won the conference title, he would request that it be given to Woburn.

Only Newburyport and Marblehead stood in the way of an undefeated season and Class B crown. Playing at Blocksidge Field, the Big Blue had little trouble dispatching the weak Clippers, winning 34–6. Once again Ronny Corcoran and Dana Coughlin scored most of the points. Santanello and Hinch also intercepted passes to help thwart the visitors.

Just the Thanksgiving game at Marblehead remained. The Headers were a strong team despite their 3–3–2 record. Two of their three losses had been to Gloucester and unbeaten Woburn, neither of whom Swampscott had played. The other loss had come against Danvers in a close game that could have gone either way. Led by powerful running back Dan "Jake" Healey, the Headers were capable of putting up points. And they could shut down an opponent's ground game. If they had an Achilles heel it was pass defense.

Bondy described Marblehead as "a generally improved ball club" over the one that had beaten his team a year earlier. Coach Reebenacker stated that his boys were "up and ready" and he expected they would give Swampscott "a real run for the money." It snowed during the week prior to the game which made outdoor practice impossible. The SHS players were limited to walking through plays and formations in the high school's pocket-size gymnasium. When they took the field in Marblehead on Thanksgiving morning, they found it in deplorable condition. In plowing away the snow someone had apparently also managed to scrape off the topsoil. They would be playing on dirt and mud, instead of grass.

Ronny Corcoran sparkled in his final game, picking off a pass on the third play from scrimmage and returning it 60 yards for the game's first score. After the hosts tied things up, Corcoran put the Blue ahead again, this time hauling in a Goodwin pass at the Whips' 35-yard line and racing to the end zone.

But the efforts of Corcoran and his teammates fell short. When the final whistle blew on Thanksgiving Day the cancellation of the Woburn game and the cockamamie Class B rating system ceased to matter. The Headers upended Swampscott, 35–14. Jake Healey could not be stopped, scorching the defense with four touchdowns. Meanwhile, the Headers shut down Swampscott's running game. With the exception of the one touchdown pass from Goodwin to Corcoran, the Big Blue had no answers.

Many fans were shocked by the result. Perhaps they should not have been. Bondy had said repeatedly that this was not a championship squad. The wins over Danvers and Winthrop had not altered his expectation that at some point the team would falter. In speaking of the Thanksgiving loss years later he said, "We were going into the game undefeated; how, I don't know." But he lauded the 1961 team's spirit and persistence and remained fascinated by the character and great loyalty to each other displayed by the boys.

Among the stalwarts who had played their final game for the Big Blue were Richard Fuller and Ronny Corcoran. The former Camp Fun boys were named to various postseason All-Star rosters. Fuller went on to star as a Boston College hockey player before embarking on a business career in telecommunications. Like Bob Carlin, he now lives in Marblehead and the two former stars regularly get together for a round of golf. As for Ronny Corcoran, SHS players and fans had not seen the last of him. In a few years, he would be returning to play a different role in the Big Blue story.

In the 1961 Swampscott Town Report, Acting School Superintendent Philip A. Jenkin concluded his summary of the school year with the following:

> I would be remiss indeed if I brought this report to a close without mention of David Coughlin, whose death on Monday, September 25th, left us stunned and grieved. Here was a boy who symbolized the very finest qualities in all phases of his well-rounded character. He was a splendid young citizen, athlete, and gentleman.
>
> This was a sudden and sobering experience in the daily round of our school. That we came through it without complete shattering

of morale is due in large part to the innate strength and great
natural dignity and decency of the student body. It is due, also,
to the deep humanity and firm leadership displayed in that very
sad hour by Principal John I. McLaughlin and Athletic Director
Stan Bondelevitch. It is due also, and in very large measure, to the
heartening example of fortitude set by David's parents, Mr. and
Mrs. Oliver Coughlin. There could never be two more devoted
friends of the boys and girls of Swampscott High School.

Losing to Marblehead cost the boys an undefeated season and the Class
B Championship. However, the greatest, saddest loss by far had occurred
in September with the tragic death of their beloved teammate.

Our Tiny Country School

ondy acknowledged in 1961 that David Coughlin's death had taken a terrific emotional toll. For a while, he contemplated giving up coaching. "But do you know what changed my mind?" he asked the *Boston Globe's* Will McDonough. "Smiles. There's nothing like a boy's smile. There weren't any around here for a while, but when they came back I knew I would always have to be a coach."

Dick Stevenson, David's line coach, was badly shaken by the tragedy. When the boy died, much of Stevenson's passion for coaching football seemed to die as well. Following the 1961 season, he informed Bondy that he would not be returning. Coach Stevenson had been with Stan since 1953 and would be missed. He became a highly valued school administrator, first in Swampscott and then with several other school systems.

Billy Gillis, a former Marblehead co-captain and all-scholastic guard with a pleasant, low-key personality joined the staff and worked with the linemen. JV coach Doc Marden also pitched in to assist at all levels. From the time that Bondy first arrived in Swampscott, Doc had served in various roles, including as a scout and freshman or JV coach. Marden was an even-tempered straight shooter, popular with the players, as was his pal Jim "Hugga" Hughes, who helped with the JVs.

The coaches looked for boys who could fill the holes left by players who had graduated, such as Ronny Corcoran, Richard Fuller, George Forbes, Henry Legere, Ted Rafter, Dana Coughlin, Danny Goodwin, and Andy Repetto. All had been key contributors to the team's success. The small core of returning lettermen included seniors Bill Sjogren, Tom Bufalino, Billy Hinch, and Steven Santanello, and junior Barry Gallup.

Sjogren had arrived from Lynn in 1959 and enrolled in the new Shaw Junior High School. It was actually a homecoming because his family had lived in Swampscott until they moved to Lynn after Bill finished first grade. Mrs. Sjogren had always yearned to return and they did so in time for her son to play a few games for the ninth-grade team. During the following summer, he played Legion baseball and was sent into a game as a relief pitcher with the bases loaded and no outs. Sjogren struck out the side, throwing nine straight strikes.

Bondy, observing the boy's athleticism and strong arm, began recruiting him as a potential quarterback. He enlisted Eddie Loveday, who spent hours working with Sjogren at Jackson Park. Bill's talent, however, lay in pitching baseballs, not passing footballs. Although he did not become a quarterback, Bill became an outstanding football player, first as a JV fullback and then as a junior starting guard and defensive halfback. He had the speed to play in the defensive backfield and the intelligence to call out the various alignments. Now Sjogren and Hinch served as co-captains of the 1962 squad.

Barry Gallup joined Hinch as a starting end while Tom Bufalino, who had spent time as an end during his junior year, moved to the interior line. While the team would be looking to its small core of experienced veterans for leadership, Stan announced that he'd be "going with the kids," meaning that he would, of necessity, be starting some younger but uniquely talented players.

Among those "kids" was 15-year-old, 130-pound Walter Costello Jr. Swampscott was a small town and not much escaped Bondy's notice, especially athletic boys with the potential to become standout players. Noticing that Costello was such a youngster, Bondy had asked him to serve as a waterboy. The coach loved to enlist promising young athletes to fill those positions. By serving as waterboys, many future players developed a close attachment to the Big Blue at an early age and became better acquainted with the coach. Walter jumped at the chance because he saw high school football as the biggest thing in town. Everyone seemed to be at the games on Saturday afternoons and the teams usually won, especially in 1957 and 1958 when they went undefeated.

Walter's future varsity teammates, Peter Smith and Norm DeRobertis, joined him as waterboys. Keeping track of the footballs or carrying the water buckets onto the field made them feel that they played an important role. Bondy reinforced that feeling by frequently recognizing and complimenting the youngsters.

Walter had started playing organized football in the seventh grade. He began as a halfback and remained one throughout his football-playing career. By the end of his first year in the system, he had already run the 22-trap and other standard plays hundreds of times. Bondy regularly stopped by the practices, often saying something to make the boys laugh, while also offering words of encouragement. As ninth graders, Walter and his teammates discovered that their games were written up in the *Item* and naturally loved to see their names in print. Bondy became even more visible, frequently taking time to chat with Costello, which made the boy feel special.

As a sophomore, Walter was finally able to join the high school team but needed to adjust to not being a starter. A number of upperclassmen filled the varsity backfield, including Ronny Corcoran, Dana Coughlin, and Steven Santanello. Walter played regularly with the JVs but also dressed for varsity games and had a chance to play in the Blue's one-sided victories. While typically only seeing action during "mop up" time, it was still a good experience.

Walter also enjoyed playing baseball and looked forward to trying out for the SHS team in the spring of 1962. However, Coach Lynch said that he wanted Costello to run track. Walter tried to explain that he preferred baseball but Lynch's message was clear: "We need you to work on your speed and you'll be running track in the spring." Just like that, the boy's Swampscott baseball career was over before it started. Walter's dad, who enjoyed watching his son play, did not take the news well, exclaiming, "You're not going to be one of those kids who run around in their underwear!" But his son knew that the die was cast. In the spring, he ran sprints and hurdles for the track team. He had been fast. He became faster.

As a junior, Costello was ready to back up talented senior halfback Steven Santanello on offense and to start in the defensive secondary. Walter was a very good defensive back. Though hardly big, he was smart, fast, sure-handed, and a solid tackler. Bondy knew how to motivate him, asking if he needed any special equipment. Walter replied that he would love a pair of KangaROOS football cleats, thinking that the cool-looking, low-cut, lightweight shoes would make him faster. Bondy gave him a slip of paper and sent him to Musinsky's Sporting Goods in Lynn. The happy teen returned with his new shoes. This was just one of many reasons that Costello loved playing for Coach Bondelevitch.

Another 15-year-old was a quiet 160-pound sophomore named Billy Conigliaro. Fast, with good moves and hands, he was talented enough to immediately step in as a starting halfback. Billy's family had recently moved into Swampscott from East Boston. His older brother Tony had starred in football and baseball at Lynn's Saint Mary's High School before embarking on a professional baseball career. Like Tony, Billy had exceptional athletic ability.

Though slated as the starter, junior quarterback Peter Smith was being pushed by Peter Cohen, another 15-year-old sophomore. Cohen was a smart kid with a strong arm. Rugged, 190-pound senior Bob Marino was named the starting fullback. Two other backs, senior Ernie "Butch" Bessette and junior Bill Herlihy, pushed for playing time. Linemen joining the veterans Sjogren and Bufalino included seniors Bill "Rocky" Rothwell, John Ladik, Bob Spediacci, and Frank Challant, and juniors Paul Legere and Steve Buswell. Legere, who weighed about 200 pounds, was the biggest of the group.

While Bondy lamented his team's youth and lack of size, he sounded unusually optimistic about the upcoming season, predicting that if the boys managed to win their first two games they would be tough to handle. One reason for his optimism may have been speed. This squad, he said, was faster than the 1961 edition.

As always, the coach found ways to generate a little extra publicity. A photo appeared in the *Item* showing Walter Costello in his Big Blue practice jersey being carried off the practice field by a couple of mammoth Denver Broncos linemen. The Broncos were staying in the area prior to their scheduled game against the Boston Patriots and Bondy offered them use of Phillips Park for practice. The photo of Costello appeared under the caption, "You're Not Ready, Sonny!" According to the fictitious story, Costello had been caught trying to sneak into the Denver backfield during the team's workout.

The *Item* predicted that there were quite a few legitimate contenders for the conference crown, mentioning favored Winthrop, Swampscott, Marblehead, Woburn, and dark horse Newburyport. The Big Blue previewed well in the Jamboree, besting Gloucester 6–0. The score came on a Santanello interception. In its opener against visiting Andover, the team struggled early but rallied in the second half for an 18–14 win, with most of the damage done on the ground by Santanello and Marino. The defense also registered a safety.

The team next faced Woburn. While Swampscott had not lost to the Tanners since 1955, the 1961 tilt had been canceled due to the Coughlin tragedy and Woburn had gone on to win the conference title. The 1962 Tanners featured good receivers and running backs and a number of experienced defensive players. They boasted the heaviest line in the conference, significantly outweighing Swampscott. Adding to the challenge was the fact that the game was played on Rosh Hashanah, a Jewish holiday. Seven Big Blue players were unavailable.

Meanwhile, the *Item* was engaged in a public dispute with Lynn officials concerning the use of mouth guards by high school teams. The newspaper questioned why the schools did not provide them. Some Lynn administrators bristled at what they felt was unfair publicity, with one claiming that most teams did not provide mouth guards. Ed Cahill responded that Bondy, who had been equipping his players with the devices since the '50s, believed they were essential. The Swampscott coach predicted that they would become mandatory for schoolboy players.

While the mouth guards may have prevented SHS players from losing some teeth at Woburn, they did not prevent the team from losing some footballs and the game. Swampscott fumbled the ball away three times. Those turnovers, combined with an interception, a bad snap from center, and an untimely penalty, were too much to overcome in the 12–8 loss. Woburn's touchdowns came at the end of short drives of nine and 28 yards, both set up by turnovers. Moreover, on one of those drives, the defense stopped the Tanners on fourth down, but was penalized for too many men on the field. With new life, the Tanners went on to score. The *Item* reported that sophomore Billy Conigliaro was outstanding in a losing cause. However, contrary to Bondy's hopes, the Big Blue had not managed to get by Woburn. Would future opponents still encounter a Swampscott team that was "hard to handle"?

As was often the case after a loss, Bondy made some roster changes. The most surprising was moving Barry Gallup from end to halfback, especially since the coach announced that the team would be passing the ball more frequently. Gallup was tall, strong, and athletic, with good size and speed, and excellent hands. He seemed the perfect end. Tom Bufalino moved from guard to fill the vacancy at end. Santanello moved to fullback because Bob Marino was ill and expected to see limited action. Bondy made further changes when the game was postponed to Monday due to rain. Monday was Yom Kippur and a number of boys would miss their second consecutive game, including center Frank Challant and quarterback Peter Cohen.

Bondy took his re-shuffled line-up to Oniontown to play what the *Item* claimed was a mediocre Danvers team. The Oniontowners had tied their first two games. Like Woburn, Danvers was bigger than Swampscott. Despite the roster shuffling, the Blue fell again, losing 6–0. The only scoring came off a Swampscott fumble. This was particularly troubling because in the prior game with Woburn both touchdown drives began with Swampscott turnovers. Another disturbing trend was the lack of point production, with 18 points in the first game, eight in the second, and none against Danvers.

The team was 1–2. Unless Swampscott could figure out a way to generate some points, Bondy might be looking at his first losing season. As the Blue prepared to travel to Winthrop, he lamented the anemic offense and mentioned that sophomore Cohen might break into the line-up, commenting that "he throws pretty good." Marino came off the injured list and Gallup returned to what seemed his natural position at left end. The good news was that SHS was not the only conference team struggling to score. In their only game of the season the Vikings had been shut out by Newburyport, losing 26–0.

The team traveled to Winthrop but did not bring much offense. For the second consecutive week, the boys failed to register a touchdown. Fortunately, the Vikings also failed to reach the Swampscott end zone. A combination of good defense and bad weather stalled both teams' offensive units. The game was played in near Nor'easter conditions, with heavy rains and strong winds blowing from one end of the field to the other. Swampscott managed to take a 2–0 lead with a safety in the first quarter.

The defense fought to keep Winthrop off the scoreboard. Among key plays were an interception by Costello deep in Swampscott territory and a Sjogren recovery of a Winthrop fumble near the SHS goal line. Perhaps the game's most memorable play was made by the punting squad in the second half. The Big Blue faced a fourth down on its own 2-yard line.

Punter Billy Hinch stood deep in the end zone with the howling wind at his back. Senior center Frank Challant was under more pressure than he had ever faced as a player. He needed to snap the ball back about 12 yards to Hinch. If he failed to make a perfect snap it was unlikely that Hinch would be able to kick the ball out of the end zone before being tackled or having the punt blocked. The result would be either a safety or Winthrop touchdown. While Hinch would be kicking with the gusting wind at his back, Challant would be snapping the ball directly into that same wind.

Frank Challant was another kid who had grown up with Big Blue football. His father, Nate, was one of Bondy's friends and an active Boosters Club member. As a young boy, Frank had attended Bondy's Camp Fun where he had been asked to play the center position during a game of touch football. Thereafter, he became a center on the seventh-grade team and remained one throughout his remaining school years. Though not blessed with great athleticism Frank worked to develop the necessary technique to assure consistent and accurate long snaps. His father helped by bringing home an old net from the Swampscott Fish House and placing it in the basement of their home where the boy spent many hours perfecting his technique.

Frank had been a backup center during the 1961 season but now held the starting job. By this point, he was confident in his abilities as a long snapper. Yet he had never faced anything like the conditions in Winthrop. The rain and a blustery wind made it next to impossible to gauge how hard he needed to propel the ball back to the punter. His normal snap would certainly fall short, but if he used too much force he risked sailing the ball over Hinch's head and out of the end zone. All he could do was make his best educated guess and use good technique.

Frank guessed correctly and the ball flew back into Hinch's hands. Bill got off a beauty that sailed a long distance with the benefit of the strong tailwind. Once it hit the ground, the ball continued to roll until it finally went out of bounds well inside the Winthrop 10-yard line. In total, the ball had traveled more than 100 yards. Challant breathed a sigh of relief and the team hung on for the 2–0 victory.

The Blue had evened its record at 2–2, but the offense had been shut out in consecutive games. It seemed inconceivable that, with talented playmakers like Santanello, Hinch, Gallup, Conigliaro, Costello, Sjogren, and Cohen, the team was having such trouble putting points on the board. Next up was once-beaten Amesbury. Continuation of the scoring drought would likely be fatal against the favored Carriagemakers, who were enjoying a good season. Their only blemish was a one-point loss to undefeated Classical. Most recently, Amesbury had pulverized Methuen 51–0.

While Peter Cohen had seen action at Winthrop and would be starting against visiting Amesbury, the team's most experienced running back, Steven Santanello, was out with a sprained ankle. Butch Bessette took Santanello's place while Billy Herlihy made his first start as fullback. The *Item* predicted that Amesbury would romp.

The Big Blue got off to a horrible start when Indians star Murray Johnson intercepted a Cohen pass and returned it 57 yards for a touchdown. However, Swampscott bounced back and upset Amesbury 20–14. Shaking off the early interception, Cohen turned in a solid performance, connecting with Hinch on two touchdown passes and Gallup on a conversion. Herlihy scored his first varsity touchdown on a 10-yard run that was set up by a Conigliaro interception return. The defense continued to play well. Costello picked off two passes.

After the offensive struggles of the preceding three weeks, the point production against Amesbury was a relief. With Saugus next, things seemed to be looking up. Bondy claimed that Saugus would be a strong opponent, but its record suggested otherwise. The Sachems had lost four straight. The team picked up at Saugus where it had left off with Amesbury, this time scoring 35 points while shutting out the Sachems. Despite playing without Santanello the boys exploded for 426 yards, including 350 on the ground. Marino, Hinch, and Bessette each scored a touchdown while Conigliaro tallied two. The other points came on a safety, courtesy of a Herlihy tackle, a conversion reception by Hinch, and a PAT kick by lineman Rocky Rothwell, younger brother of Jim and Eliot. Meanwhile, the defense held the Sachems to less than 100 yards total offense. The Big Blue was finally firing on all cylinders. And it had hit its stride at the right time because the next opponent was undefeated Lynn Classical.

The 1962 Classical team was coached by my father, Robert Thomas Jauron. Most everyone called him either Bob or Coach, but to his former teammates from Boston College he would always be "Jocko." He grew up in a dysfunctional household in Nashua, New Hampshire. He never knew his father. His mother was the daughter of Irish immigrant millworkers. She was apparently a sweet, well-intentioned woman but somewhat naïve and irresponsible. To the extent that my father received any "parenting," it mainly came from his mother's sister, Margaret. His aunt Margaret was a kind-hearted and earnest human being, but ill-equipped to act as her nephew's caregiver. A single, congenitally nervous woman, she struggled to make ends meet on a paltry income derived from work cleaning buildings and homes.

Sports offered an outlet and an opportunity for my dad to rise above his dreary family circumstances. He loved to play and he played well, excelling at football, baseball, basketball, and track. He became an all-state baseball and football player and set a New Hampshire record in the 100-yard dash. As had been the case for a great many athletic high school kids, sports gave young Bob Jauron a chance to escape the dismal environment of his childhood.

Pete Chesnulevich was his high school coach. Pete was a Boston College graduate and steered his young star in that direction. Chesnulevich made arrangements for my dad to visit the college and meet with the coaches in the hope of landing a scholarship. Chesnulevich, who was familiar with BC's dour football coach, the legendary "Gloomy Gil" Dobie, gave my dad one piece of advice. "If Coach Dobie asks how much you weigh tell him that you weigh 180 pounds," he said. "Dobie likes big running backs."

When my dad visited BC, Dobie had him run through some drills with other potential recruits. When they met later, Gloomy Gil asked, "Jauron, how much do you weigh?" As instructed, he answered that he weighed 180 pounds. Dobie's eyes narrowed as he grabbed and squeezed my dad's wrist. He shook his head and said, "Bullshit! You can't be more than 165." Dobie then told him, "But we've decided to give you a scholarship." Without a scholarship, Bob Jauron would not have been able to go to college.

In 1938 my dad enrolled at Boston College. The following year, Coach Dobie retired and was replaced by the great Frank Leahy. Under Leahy the Eagles made trips to the Sugar Bowl and Cotton Bowl. One day during my dad's senior year, he was trekking up Chestnut Hill to the campus when a car pulled alongside. Gloomy Gil Dobie offered him a ride. The two engaged in small talk during the drive up the hill. When they reached the campus and Jocko was about to exit the car Dobie stared at him intently for a moment and then announced, "Well, you might weigh 180 now!"

Like millions of other young men of his generation, after his 1942 graduation Bob Jauron entered military service. He wanted to become a pilot with the U.S. Army Air Corps but color blindness kept him out of the cockpit and he never left the country. He was soon promoted to staff sergeant and designated an athletic instructor. The job included playing and coaching football and baseball. At one point, he was assigned to an air base in Sioux Falls, South Dakota. While there he attended a USO dance where he met a Sioux Falls girl named Katherine Strain. They soon married and Kay Jauron ultimately became the wonderful mother of five lucky children, three of whom ended up playing football for Swampscott High School.

Following his honorable discharge from the army, Bob Jauron secured a teaching and coaching position at a high school in Miles City, Montana, becoming the head football coach of the Custer County Cowboys. As a young coach, he was even more successful than Stanley Bondelevitch. After a couple of years in Montana he successively coached high school teams in Peoria and Alton, Illinois, and Dayton, Ohio, and in each case quickly produced winners. Overall, his teams in Montana and the Midwest amassed a total record of 70–6–1, and at one point won 27 consecutive games.

During this period, the football program at a small Catholic college in Rensselaer, Indiana, was struggling. The teams frequently finished at or near the bottom of the Indiana Collegiate Conference (ICC). The Saint Joseph's College Pumas had posted one winning record over the preceding eight years and were a combined 2–14–1 through the 1952 and 1953 seasons. In 1954 the college searched for a new coach and chose Jauron. By the time he left five years later, he was destined for the Saint Joseph's College Hall of Fame.

He never suffered a losing season at Saint Joe's. His 1955 team was conference co-champion, while the 1956 and 1957 squads won ICC championships outright. Moreover, the 1956 team met high-scoring Montana State for the national little college championship in a game titled "the Aluminum Bowl Classic" in Little Rock, Arkansas. His Pumas battled in the mud and driving rain and came away with a 0–0 tie. As a result,

Saint Joe's won a share of the national championship and confirmed its rating as the nation's best little college defensive team. Jauron was named Little All-American Football Coach of the Year.

After several other coaching stints, Jauron came to the North Shore in 1961 to participate in a failed experiment. The authorities in Lynn concocted a plan which they felt would save money while improving performance of the high school teams. The athletic teams of the city's schools—Classical, English, and Trade—were replaced by one squad in each sport, comprised of athletes from all three schools. Expectations were that the merged team, to be known as the Lynn Lions, would be a powerhouse, since it would be made up of the best athletes in the entire city. There was a feeling that the Lynn schools were disadvantaged competing against city-wide teams like Lawrence, Lowell, and Peabody that could draw from a wider pool of potential players. The merger might at least put Lynn on an even footing. Essentially the city was now fielding All-Star teams.

However, the plan did not produce an immediate winner. There were several reasons. The new coach discovered that there were only a few lettermen among the boys reporting for the first day's practice. Classical and English had posted a combined record in 1960 of five wins and 12 loses. 1959 had been worse, with four wins and 13 losses. But there may have been a bigger obstacle to success. The school-based relationships and loyalties were not easily transferred to "merged" relationships and loyalties. The merger lacked an ingredient that Bondy knew was essential to a winning culture—community.

In Swampscott, the Big Blue community included boys who as sixth or seventh graders played football with their friends in the system devised by Bondy, while dreaming of one day performing for the varsity. The Big Blue community included the large supporting cast of the drill team, spirit squad, band members, and cheerleaders. It also included alumni, parents, and the ever-supportive Boosters; folks who genuinely cared about and took pride in the town's high school football program.

In time, with sustained effort and innovation, Lynn's new merged team may have enjoyed a comparable level of cohesion and community. But in the interim, lacking such infrastructure, the Lions struggled, finishing their inaugural season with a 2–7 record.

In 1962 the school committee wisely voted to restore the Classical, English, and Trade teams. With three teams instead of just one, many more kids would be able to participate in interscholastic athletics. Perhaps the worst thing about the merger was that it significantly reduced such opportunities for Lynn students. My dad's job as coach of the Lions disappeared. He accepted the head coaching position at Lynn Classical.

The 1962 Classical squad was inexperienced up front, but had talented veterans in the backfield, led by senior halfback Dave Giarla, the team's captain. Giarla may have been the best all-around back on the North Shore. He was quick, athletic, tough, and a fierce competitor. While no more than 165 pounds, he could run through, as well as around, defensive players. Quarterback Bobby Nash was a big, athletic kid who excelled in three sports and ultimately signed a professional baseball contract. He was about 6-foot, 2-inches and weighed close to 200 pounds. He had played fullback as a junior but was now one of the area's top quarterbacks. Nash had a strong arm and was dangerous when he ran with the ball. He was also a capable kicker. The Rams filled out the backfield with two other multi-sport athletes, junior speedster Joey Silvonic and 200-pound bruising senior fullback Sam Sapira.

The only real question for the Rams was the line. Classical's two biggest players may have been Nash and Sapira. But the linemen performed well enough on both sides of the ball to post a record of 6–0, with the potential of finishing unbeaten with just three games remaining. In their last outing, the Rams had demolished Newburyport by a score of 43–14, with Giarla and Nash each scoring three touchdowns.

Speaking with the *Item's* Ed Cahill after the Newburyport win, Coach Jauron expressed concern about the upcoming match with the Big Blue. He correctly noted that Swampscott was getting stronger as the season wore on. SHS had scored more points in its recent win over Saugus than it had against its first four opponents combined. And the defense had given up no points against the Sachems, its second shutout in six games. Swampscott's young but talented players were gaining experience and confidence and had rapidly improved. They were, of course, well coached. This would not be an easy game for Classical.

Meanwhile, Bondy was giving the local sports reporters other things to write about. In his October 13, 1962, column *Item* sports writer

J. F. Williams reported that Swampscott's coaching staff had begun handing out gold hawk emblems to defensive players for causing turnovers by recovering fumbles, intercepting passes, or blocking kicks. The emblems, which Bondy would frequently use in future years to recognize and motivate strong performances, were pasted on players' helmets. Prior to the Classical game, co-captain Billy Sjogren led the team with five hawk emblems, while junior Walter Costello was next in line with four.

As interest in the Swampscott-Classical tilt heated up, so did a battle of words between the teams' head coaches. Jauron predictably told the *Item* that Swampscott was a tough squad, that the teams' respective records did not mean anything, and that the game should be rated a tossup. "We're in for a battle," he said. Bondy was just as predictable, claiming that "We're facing a Class A power with our tiny country school. Classical is a very strong team and much bigger than the one we'll field." He failed to mention that his "tiny country school" had just annihilated another Class A team.

For Bondy, there was something about playing a Lynn school that always seemed to bring out some of his best "poor us" hyperbole. Two years earlier, he had laid it on thick, suggesting that it was remarkable that his little boys could be on the same field with the big Class A powerhouse, and expressing wonderment and mock fear that SHS would have to face the urban high school year-after-year. Swampscott then beat Classical at Blocksidge Field. There was no game in 1961 as a result of the merger, but Bondy had left the date open on Swampscott's schedule. Now the Big Blue would face Classical and Bondy returned to his David v. Goliath theme.

Speaking with the *Item's* Red Hoffman, he lamented the tender ages and diminutive sizes of a number of his players who would have to face seasoned, intimidating stars like Giarla, Nash, and Sapira. But Classical's coach would have none of it, telling the *Item's* Ed Cahill:

> He wanted this game with us. In fact, he kept the game open for Classical because he thought it was a soft touch, and I hope you'll quote me on that. Now he's crying about his little country team playing our big city boys.

Jauron went on to assert that the Big Blue was a more experienced team than Classical, with a bigger line. He even offered to have the players weighed in order to prove his point. He also asserted that the Rams would have at least as many underclassmen playing as would Swampscott. He concluded, "So any talk about this being a mismatch is strictly for the birds."

The only common opponent had been Amesbury where Classical had struggled before finally coming away with a 7–6 win, thanks to a Nash conversion kick. Swampscott defeated the Carriagemakers, 20–14, and did so after giving up a touchdown on the game's first play. Moreover, Peter Cohen, now firmly in place as the starting quarterback, had not played in either of Swampscott's losses. He was undefeated as the team's signal caller. Bondy brought the war of words to a halt, saying,

> We can't play the game in the newspapers. And Bob and I can't play it. The last time we faced one another was in 1940, when he was with Boston College and I was at St. Anselm's, but that was 100 pounds ago for both of us. The kids will have to play this one.

Bondy was only half-kidding about the added weight of the two coaches. He may have put on close to 100 pounds since his Saint Anselm days, while my dad had likely exceeded the number. In that game back in 1940, played at Boston's Fenway Park, a considerably leaner and faster Bob Jauron had run for two touchdowns and two conversions as the Eagles crushed Saint Anselm, 55–0. Classical's coach knew that the upcoming battle would not be such a one-sided affair.

As it had in past years when a Swampscott game attracted a large crowd, the *Item* raised the possibility of moving the event to a large stadium such as Lynn's Manning Bowl. Coach Jauron, of course, thought it a marvelous idea, noting that it would be more comfortable for the fans, many of whom might have to stand if they kept the game in Swampscott. Bondy's response was hardly surprising. He had fully supported the suggestion that the 1958 Saugus game be relocated from Stackpole Field to a site that could accommodate more fans, but now he had the home field advantage. Amused by the suggestion, he graciously responded that his club would be happy to play Classical at Manning Bowl, "next year when it's their home game."

The coaches had been having fun trading barbs through the media. Now it was time for their teams to meet. It seemed that Swampscott's biggest games were often played in bad weather. Such was definitely the case when the Big Blue met Classical at Blocksidge Field on Saturday, November 3, 1962. Conditions were miserable. Both teams struggled against the elements which severely hampered play. According to the *Item's* Red Hoffman:

> There weren't a thousand fans at Blocksidge Park because of the driving rains and high winds. But those who braved the elements were regaled with four of the most thrilling pigskin periods Blocksidge has ever seen.

Classical got off to a great start, taking the opening kick and reaching the Swampscott end zone after nine consecutive rushes. The key play was the last one, a 40-yard burst by Giarla. Rather than have Nash attempt to kick the extra point in the wind, rain, and mud, Classical went for two, running the big quarterback on a keeper off right tackle. It appeared momentarily that he had an opening and would score but Walter Costello closed quickly from his defensive backfield position. Costello, about 60 pounds lighter than Nash, managed to stop him just short of the goal line. The Rams held a 6–0 lead.

After receiving the kickoff and moving the ball some distance, the Big Blue was forced to punt. Classical next advanced to the 49-yard line where it faced fourth and one. Nash tried a quarterback sneak for the first down. There was a pileup near the line of scrimmage. Once the officials finally unraveled the players and spotted the ball, they declared that Nash had fallen short by just an inch or two. Swampscott took over.

Sophomore Peter Cohen then led the team on what may have been the most impressive scoring drive of his high school career. Throwing into near gale-force wind and rain, he connected with Hinch and Gallup on key completions. These, combined with runs by Marino, Santanello, and Conigliaro, brought the ball from midfield to the Classical 17-yard line. At that point, Marino carried on a draw play, powering up the middle into the end zone while bouncing off a defender or two along the way. Cohen then rolled out and connected with Hinch for the all-important two-point conversion and Swampscott led 8–6.

Both teams had other scoring opportunities, with the final Classical chance ending late in the fourth quarter when Silvonic was stopped just an inch short of a first down on fourth and one at the home team's 29. Swampscott then took over and ran out the clock, claiming a hard-fought 8–6 victory over the previously unbeaten Rams.

Billy Hinch, who had almost missed the game due to injury, was a huge contributor, recovering a fumble, intercepting a pass, making a key reception on the team's only touchdown drive, and scoring the winning conversion. The rivals ended the day in a statistical dead heat with each having amassed 133 yards of offense. Given the abysmal weather and strong defenses, the seemingly modest offensive production was understandable.

For the frustrated Rams, it was a miserable end to a miserable day. The dream of finishing undefeated ended on a wet, windy day at Block-sidge Field. As a 13-year-old Lynn junior high school student, I rode on the Classical team bus to the game with younger brother Dick, and we cheered for the Rams. Our older brother Wayne was a senior on the Classical team coached by our dad. Like everyone else on that gloomy ride back to Lynn, we felt no love for the Big Blue.

It was of course a memorable big-game victory for Bondy and SHS. They had beaten the team considered the best on the North Shore. It was the first and last time that Stan Bondelevitch and Bob Jauron would face one another as coaches of opposing teams. But Bondy had not seen the last of Coach Jauron. He would be re-surfacing in Swampscott in several years but as an ally rather than a foe.

In upending Classical, the Swampscott team went a long way toward turning around a season that had seemed bleak a few weeks earlier after the boys had lost consecutive games. Since then the Big Blue had won four straight and at 5–2 was assured a winning record. If the team could win its remaining two, especially the finale against the Headers, it could end the season on a high note, finishing with a strong 7–2 record.

On the following Saturday, the team traveled up Interstate 95 to Newburyport for its eighth game. The Clippers were still in contention for the conference title. They were a dangerous bunch and had easily taken down both Woburn and Winthrop. The *Item*, however, predicted the boys would find the game against the Clippers "much less of a test" than Classical. They did not.

On the first play from scrimmage Newburyport's speedster, Bill Johnson, ran 70 yards for a touchdown. Swampscott had beaten Amesbury after a similarly bad start, but this time the team could not overcome the early deficit. Instead, the offense gave up a second touchdown on an interception and the Clippers then scored a third time. Swampscott trailed 19–0 in the fourth quarter when Barry Gallup blocked a punt, giving the Blue good field position. Barry had been blocking punts regularly since the first game of his sophomore year. This one led to a 28-yard touchdown pass from Cohen to Hinch. But it was too little, too late. Swampscott failed its test in Newburyport, losing 19–6. A strong performance by the Clippers, combined perhaps with some lingering exhaustion from the Classical battle, had been too much to overcome.

Only Marblehead remained. The Headers relied heavily on two gifted junior quarterbacks in Don Jermyn and Daynor Prince. Coach Reebenacker had called on both throughout the season, replacing one with the other when he thought it made sense. Jermyn was also used at times as a receiver. Going into the season's next-to-last game, every conference team but Woburn had remained in the hunt for the championship. While Swampscott's chance had evaporated at Newburyport, the Headers (5–2–1) had clinched at least a share by beating Andover.

Marblehead's only conference loss had been to Danvers, while they had tied Amesbury. By winning on Thanksgiving, the Headers could finish in sole possession of first place. Thus, as often was the case, there was added incentive for both clubs. Marblehead could seize the conference crown by beating Swampscott, while the Big Blue could play the spoiler and also avenge the 1961 loss which had cost it the Class B championship and an undefeated season.

Conditions at Blocksidge Field on Thanksgiving morning were hardly ideal. Heavy rains caused postponement of a number of games in the area, but Bondy elected to play. Perhaps he was remembering his team's last outing in awful weather when the boys defeated the Classical Rams.

However, the Big Blue's offense sputtered against Marblehead and failed to produce a single point. The Headers' offense fared no better, also coming up empty. As had been the case at Winthrop, the impotence was likely caused by a combination of solid defensive play and bad weather. It had continued to rain throughout the contest, making for a muddy field and slippery football. According to the *Item*, "It would have taken the New York Giants to get a ground offensive going in the slop."

Both teams turned the ball over numerous times. There were multiple fumbles, interceptions, and blocked kicks. While Swampscott drove deep into Marblehead territory on several occasions, each drive halted as a result of penalties, other miscues, and/or the Header defense. Marblehead's offense had also been unable to cash in on some scoring opportunities. Ultimately, the only score, and the difference in the game, proved to be an 81-yard touchdown on a kickoff return by Marblehead's Ken Eldridge at the start of the second half. The Headers survived with a 6–0 victory.

The Big Blue finished with a winning, but somewhat disappointing, 5–4 record. It had been a season of peaks and valleys, with the big triumph over undefeated Classical as the high point. It was the Blue's fourth consecutive victory. But SHS never won again, losing to Newburyport and Marblehead.

Defense had clearly been its strength throughout the season, with nine opponents combining for only 77 points, many of which had come as a result of turnovers or kick returns. One of the unsung heroes for the Blue was senior defensive specialist Bob Spediacci, who made countless tackles and big plays throughout the season. Unfortunately, the offense had often sputtered, scoring no touchdowns in three games, and only a single touchdown in each of three more. For the first time since Bondy's arrival in Swampscott, his team had finished with a losing conference record.

Billy Sjogren was the fourth Big Blue player to win the Thom McAn Shoe Award. However, he had played on so many wet, muddy fields that neither of his football cleats was in any condition to be bronzed. A solution was found because of John Flanagan. His football shoes had been of no use to any future player since one of them had been re-configured to accommodate his foot disability. His other standard-design shoe was therefore bronzed and used for Sjogren's Thom McAn trophy. Bill Sjogren went on to an outstanding college career at Dartmouth where he starred as an All-Ivy League guard and also played baseball. After college, he pursued a number of business opportunities before ultimately returning to Dartmouth, accepting a position as a Grants Officer.

Center Frank Challant enrolled at Springfield College, attracted by its outstanding physical education program. He was back in Swampscott in less than two years, the result of too much partying and too little attention to his studies. However, with Bondy's help, he was then able to secure a scholarship to Parsons College in Iowa. Once there, he realized that he would not be able to play on the football team, given the size and talent of the Parsons players. He was able to hold on to his scholarship by becoming the school's assistant athletic trainer. That fortuitous circumstance set him on a career path that, among other things, resulted in his owning NBA championship rings after he accepted an offer to become the athletic trainer for the Boston Celtics. Frank served in that position for a number of years, during which the team won two league titles (1974 and 1976).

Rugged Billy Hinch had also played his final football game for Swampscott. While Hinch concentrated on hockey in college, excelling as a member of the Boston University team and serving as captain in his senior year, he and Barry Gallup may have been the most skillful and productive tandem of two-way ends in SHS history. The good news was that Gallup and a number of other experienced, talented players would be returning in 1963.

The Gritty Champs

S hortly after the end of the 1962 season, the Boosters held their annual awards banquet. In keeping with tradition, Bondy announced to the hundreds of assembled students, parents, administrators, and supporters, that Paul Legere and Bill Herlihy had been elected by their teammates as co-captains of the 1963 team.

The news came as a crushing blow to Barry Gallup. He was so emotionally staggered that he broke into tears. And once he started crying he could not stop. Bondy took him into a private room and tried to console him. Coach Lynch joined them. But it took the men a long time to help the devastated junior regain control.

Big Blue football was a huge part of Barry's life for as long as he could remember. As the only member of his class to start for the varsity as a sophomore, he had been one of the team's best playmakers over the past two years. His father Earl had been an SHS football captain and Barry dreamed of following in his dad's footsteps.

It was hard to understand why someone with such talent, character, and leadership skills would not have been elected captain. In later years, he wondered whether all the time spent with upperclassmen as a sophomore may have been a factor. He had even attended the senior prom. Perhaps classmates and underclassmen considered him more connected to those past players than to their group. Whatever the reason, it hurt.

1963 marked a new phase in Bondy's life. In early January, Dot gave birth to her and Stan's third child, their first and only boy. For almost 20 years, the coach had served as something of a surrogate father to numerous high school football players. Now he had a son of his own. He and Dot wasted no time in naming the boy David, in memory of David Coughlin.

When the preseason rolled around, the *Item's* Red Hoffman provided brief assessments of local teams. He wrote that, with some good veterans and promising rookies, the Big Blue's fortunes depended on how well the players jelled. Hoffman's guarded comment was understandable. While the 1961 team had lost only once, it had played a shortened seven-game schedule and stumbled badly in the finale against the Headers. And in the most recent season, the Blue had barely managed a winning record, finishing 5–4 while again losing to Marblehead. None of Bondy's prior SHS teams had lost more than three games. It seemed unlikely that another championship was on the horizon.

Yet there were a number of talented veterans on the roster, particularly at the skill positions. Returning regulars included Peter Cohen at quarterback, Barry Gallup at end, Walter Costello, Billy Conigliaro and Bill Herlihy in the backfield, and linemen Steve Buswell and Paul Legere.

Less experienced players like juniors Paige Cullen, Phil Gapinski, and Norman Jacobs and seniors Marty McKenney and Norm DeRobertis had to fill the vacancies in the line. Cullen and Gapinski soon became fixtures at center and left tackle, while Jacobs and DeRobertis were each seeing regular playing time at left guard. All four had decent size, although none weighed more than 200 pounds. McKenney, at about 180, moved into the end position that had been so ably filled by Hinch. Versatile junior Mike Maselbas joined Costello and Conigliaro in the defensive backfield. Maselbas, a talented 3-sport athlete, also assumed the punting duties.

It was Bondy's eleventh season in Swampscott and he and Dick Lynch decided to add a new wrinkle to the offensive scheme. Since his arrival, Stan's offense had operated out of the wing-T. During that period high school teams, whether using a T, single-wing, or wing-T formation, generally stuck with tight alignments, bunching all 11 offensive players closely together. Open or spread formations, utilizing ends or backs split out toward the sideline, were rarely seen, other than at the professional level where they were featured by passing teams like the San Diego Chargers.

However, in 1963 the coaches decided to open up the offense to take advantage of a talented passer in Peter Cohen and outstanding receivers like Costello and Gallup. They frequently positioned halfback Costello well beyond the offensive end toward the sideline, transforming the wing-T into something more akin to a pro-T. Costello was well-suited to play the role of flanker/wide-receiver. He was fast and athletic, with the ability to make quick moves to get open. And he had good hands, evidenced by his numerous interceptions during the prior season.

After the team played well in scrimmages against Malden Catholic and Waltham, and in the Jamboree against Lynn English, the *Item* sounded a more positive note, reporting that Swampscott was "highly regarded as the dark-horse to win the Northeastern Conference title."

The first game at Andover had originally been scheduled for Saturday, September 28, which was the Jewish high holy day of Yom Kippur. Peter Cohen, Norman Jacobs, and others had missed games played on Jewish holidays in prior seasons and Bondy wanted to assure that it did not happen again. He was successful in rescheduling the game to Friday afternoon.

The team traveled to Andover and won, 38–22. It was an impressive start for the offense. Billy Conigliaro rushed for 107, including two touchdowns and a conversion. He also returned a punt 53 yards. Herlihy scored twice and ran for a total of 128 yards. Gallup ended the day with seven receptions, good for 80 yards, a touchdown, and a conversion, and Costello hauled in two more Cohen PAT passes.

The well-balanced attack and explosion of points was a welcome sign after the prior year's offensive struggles. But while the offense scored more points in its opener than it had in any game during the prior season, the defense gave up more than it had in any 1962 contest. And Bondy expressed concern about the strength of the conference. "I saw Newburyport beat Woburn 16–6 and both teams along with Danvers and Amesbury looked terrific," he said. "The Northeastern Conference is loaded this year with powerful teams." He could have included Marblehead and Winthrop, both talented squads.

The Blue next hosted Woburn and won decisively, 28–12. Cohen connected with Gallup for 138 yards and two touchdowns. Costello caught a pass for another score and Herlihy ran one in. While the visitors rushed for 184 yards, Swampscott's defense turned in a "bend but don't break" performance, generally keeping the opponent from the end zone. The team was aided in that effort by Paul Legere's two fumble recoveries.

A veteran Danvers club visited Blocksidge Field for the next game. Having defeated the Big Blue in 1962, the Oniontowners were 2–0 in the current season, with wins over Gloucester and Andover. The game was billed as a battle between Swampscott's prolific offense and Danvers' stout defense. Although the *Item* rated it a toss-up, Swampscott won 26–6.

Danvers moved the ball, amassing 286 yards rushing, but was undone by an incredible eight fumbles and a touchdown nullified by an infraction. There were five instances when the visitors drove inside the 10-yard line but failed to score, including once due to a Gallup interception. Meanwhile, the offense produced again. Conigliaro raced 64 yards for the game's first touchdown. McKenney caught Cohen's pass for the two-point conversion. Thereafter, Cohen connected on long passes for touchdowns with both Gallup and Costello. The fourth score came off a Danvers fumble, recovered in the end zone by tackle Phil Gapinski.

With victories over Woburn and Danvers, 3–0 Swampscott was now the conference frontrunner. But Winthrop loomed. The Vikings were 2–0–1, having beaten Amesbury and Saugus and battled Newburyport to a tie. The Winthrop players always seemed to get up for Swampscott and now there was the added incentive of ending the Big Blue's unbeaten season while extending their own.

Bondy and his staff prepared the squad for the usual hard-hitting game with Winthrop. Providing added incentive and continuing his emphasis on family and community involvement, he announced that Saturday would be "Parents Day." A section of Blocksidge Field stands was reserved for players' parents, and all of the boys involved in the high school program, including JVs, suited up for the varsity contest. The band, drill team, and cheerleaders planned a special half-time program in honor of the parents.

The Vikings almost spoiled the day for the Swampscott parents, but the Blue claimed a tight 8–6 victory. It was a low-scoring yet exciting game. The visitors scored first, but the conversion kick failed. Swampscott responded with a 70-yard, Cohen-engineered drive, with completions to Conigliaro, Gallup, Gapinski (as an eligible tackle), and finally Costello for the touchdown. Peter again connected with Costello for the two-point conversion, giving the home team an 8–6 halftime lead. Thereafter Winthrop threatened for a good part of the second half and ultimately finished with more yardage than the Big Blue.

The frustrated Vikings lost possession five times on four fumbles and an interception. As in past games, Swampscott's defense surrendered yardage but generated multiple turnovers and yielded few points. However, while the opportunistic defensive performance was no longer surprising, the struggles on the other side of the line were. What had been a productive, high-scoring offense sputtered as the team managed just a single touchdown.

Swampscott was 4–0 and preparing for an away game against Amesbury. Beginning with the upset victory in 1953, Bondy's teams had dominated the series, winning 10 times, including the last seven, while losing just once. The undefeated 1963 squad was heavily favored over the winless Carriagemakers.

The game, however, was hardly a blow-out. The once-prolific offense was missing again. The teams seemed headed to a scoreless first half until Barry Gallup intercepted a deflected pass and raced 74 yards for a touchdown. Peter Cohen teamed with McKenney for the two-point conversion and SHS took an 8–0 lead into the locker room.

In the second half, the Carriagemakers picked off a Cohen pass for a touchdown and evened the score with a successful conversion. Late in the third quarter, Gallup turned in his second spectacular play of the afternoon, blocking a punt at the Amesbury 39-yard line. He had been blocking punts since his first varsity game as a sophomore. Gallup's play led to a Herlihy score and conversion and the defense held the home team in check for a hard-fought 16–8 victory.

Swampscott was assured a winning season. It had not always been pretty. When the defense was porous, the offense was prolific; when the offense struggled, the defense was stout. As a result, SHS, along with rival Marblehead, stood atop the conference. The question was whether the boys could keep finding ways to win. Recognizing the important role that turnovers played in the team's success, Bondy rewarded players with blue star helmet stickers for causing or recovering fumbles, making interceptions and blocking kicks. Not surprisingly, after the first five games, Gallup had the most stickers—11.

Saugus was the first of two Class A teams on the schedule. Swampscott's record against the Sachems had changed dramatically since Bondy's arrival. Saugus had been dropped in 1952 after the then-Sculpins had fallen seven consecutive times. But Bondy's teams had lost only once to Saugus since the series had resumed in 1957. Another win was probable, with Swampscott undefeated and the Sachems winless. Bondy, of course, issued dire warnings, contending that Saugus was the most dangerous type of team, with nothing to lose and everything to gain. However, he acknowledged that, despite the Blue's recent struggles to generate points, his team had a balanced offense capable of scoring on the ground via Herlihy and Conigliaro or through the air with Cohen, Gallup, Costello, and McKenney.

The Big Blue beat Saugus 24–6, with the defense again playing a key role. The first score came on a Conigliaro 47-yard interception return. Herlihy then blocked a punt giving the offense possession on the Sachems' 39-yard line and setting up his own touchdown run. Later Cohen connected on scoring passes to Costello and McKenney.

Swampscott, now atop the Class B rankings, prepared to visit Manning Bowl to take on 1–4–1 Classical. When the teams had met a year earlier SHS had upended the undefeated Rams 8–6. Classical now had a chance to return the favor and would be sky high for the rematch. If the Big Blue players needed more motivation to match the Rams' intensity, they found it when they arrived at Blocksidge on the day before the game.

Stan Bondelevitch was particularly protective of Swampscott's game field. It was maintained in pristine condition by the town's public works department and no activities were allowed there during the fall except for games played by Big Blue football teams. There was one exception. Practice on the day before a varsity game was typically held on the Blocksidge playing surface rather than the practice field. These brief, non-contact sessions, sometimes referred to as "walk-throughs," were performed in game uniforms without pads. The squad typically ran through its plays, schemes, and formations and was then sent home.

When the boys arrived at Blocksidge Field on Friday afternoon for their walk-through they discovered a large letter *C* burned into the game field near the end zone closest to the Fieldhouse. For them, it was an ugly scar on hallowed ground. Before sending the team to the locker room after the walk-through Bondy pointed to the *C* and offered some choice words about vandalism and disrespect. The perpetrators of the burned *C* were never identified. But the Big Blue players had added incentive for their game against the Rams, which proved unnecessary when miserably wet weather on Saturday morning caused it to be canceled.

While Swampscott remained undefeated and continued atop the Class B rankings, the team was tied for the conference lead with Marblehead. If the boys could prevail at home over Newburyport and Marblehead could do the same at Woburn, they would battle on Thanksgiving for the championship. Newburyport had won only once in the conference and most recently had fallen to the Headers, 37–20. Bondy, of course, warned that the Marblehead loss gave the Clippers even more incentive to beat his squad. As he put it, "Newburyport, after that trouncing by Marblehead on Monday, is going to be honed razor sharp for us...."

Despite or because of Bondy's expressed concerns, his boys did fine against Newburyport, winning 26–12. Walter Costello had a big day, catching a couple of touchdown passes and another for a two-point conversion. He also intercepted a pass which helped set up a touchdown drive. Barry Gallup made a diving catch for another score shortly after he returned a Newburyport kickoff to the Clippers' 30-yard line. The other six points were tallied by Conigliaro on an 18-yard run. Cohen played well, passing for three touchdowns and a two-point conversion. Meanwhile, Marblehead drubbed Woburn 34–6, setting the stage for the hoped-for championship game between the 7–1 Headers and the 7–0 Big Blue.

The passing offense again seemed to be running on all cylinders, challenging opposing defenses with Cohen's willingness to spread the ball around to his talented group of receivers. Gallup and Costello, in particular, were not shy in urging Cohen to throw the ball in their direction, always assuring the quarterback that they could get open. Believing that Peter had a tendency to pass to the player who most recently pled his case, each tried to get in the last word prior to breaking the huddle. Swampscott's aerial attack was giving opponents fits.

The *Item* wasted no time in billing the Thanksgiving tilt in Marblehead as the "Game of the Year." It certainly was the biggest game of the season on the North Shore. If Marblehead could beat Swampscott, the Headers could finish unbeaten in the conference, take the title, and retain an outside chance for the Class B crown. The Big Blue had even more at stake because a win would secure an unbeaten, untied record, and both the conference and Class B titles. The icing on the cake for either squad would be a win over the traditional rival in the final game of the season. For

Bondy, a victory would also end a frustrating streak of three consecutive Thanksgiving Day losses to Noel Reebenacker and the Headers. Under Stan Bondelevitch, SHS owned a winning record over every conference team except Marblehead, against whom the Blue was 5–5.

Swampscott received plenty of media attention in the period leading up to Thanksgiving. On Sunday, November 17, the band, accompanied by the 16-member drill team, performed for 20 minutes at halftime of the nationally televised game at Fenway Park between the Boston Patriots and the Kansas City Chiefs. *Item* Sports Editor Ed Cahill lavished praise on the kids, writing it was "as polished a performance as these tired old eyes have ever seen presented by a high school unit, winning a thunderous roar of appreciation from the usually sophisticated pro football fans." He noted that the drill team was particularly impressive when the girls performed a number of intricate steps. Directed by Mrs. Flora McLearn, who coached the highly successful field hockey and basketball teams, they always delivered exceptional performances.

On November 20, Swampscott got more publicity on the weekly television show *Date-Line Boston*, which featured Bondy in a 25-minute segment that included assistant coaches Lynch and Marden and a number of players. The boys executed some plays while Bondy explained the team's game-preparation routine. All of the positive media exposure furthered the sense of pride and accomplishment at the high school and within the community.

With another local "game of the year" scheduled for Thanksgiving, Red Hoffman started beating the drum for a change to a larger venue. Since Manning Bowl would not be available due to the annual Classical v. English tilt, Hoffman suggested that the game be moved to Salem's Bertram Field. It could accommodate more than twice the number of fans who could squeeze into the Marblehead stands. Noting that there was great interest in the game throughout the North Shore, Hoffman argued that Bertram Field would be packed and that thousands of fans would be prevented from attending if it remained in Marblehead. As an alternative, he suggested that the Thursday morning match be postponed to Saturday when it could be played at Manning Bowl. For many in both communities, the Thanksgiving game was an essential part of their holiday tradition. Postponing would not be a popular option.

Hoffman took an informal poll and learned that the Marblehead school committee was not receptive. However, before throwing in the towel he took one more stab, enlisting an obvious ally. Bondy, having laughed off any thought that the 1962 Classical game might be moved away from little Blocksidge Field to accommodate the fans, now declared that transferring this game from host Marblehead to a larger stadium was a great idea. He must have had trouble keeping a straight face as he told Hoffman, "The more people see this game, the better it is...."

Stories and related excitement about the upcoming game would have continued throughout the weekend, but the assassination of President Kennedy on Friday, November 22, 1963, changed everything. By the end of that day, Swampscott v. Marblehead was likely the last thing on anyone's mind. Interest in high school football had been replaced by shock and grief following the events in Dallas, Texas.

The President's assassination was, like the bombing of Pearl Harbor 22 years earlier and the 9/11 terrorist attacks almost 38 years later, the kind of shocking event that permanently imprints itself on the American psyche. As was the case with Pearl Harbor and 9/11, most people who lived through those days could always recall exactly where they were and what they were doing when they heard the news.

The shooting occurred at 1:30 p.m. (EST), and President Kennedy was pronounced dead half an hour later. Big Blue football players were still in classrooms or just leaving the high school when they heard the news. Afternoon practice was canceled. Many players, like millions of other Americans everywhere, spent the remainder of the day glued to television sets, watching and listening as the surreal story unfolded. The President's body was flown back to the D.C. area on Air Force One. Vice President Lyndon Johnson was sworn in as President before the plane took off. Meanwhile, reports were coming in that a suspect named Lee Harvey Oswald had been apprehended.

On Sunday, millions were stunned anew when they witnessed perhaps the first murder ever shown on live television. As the suspected assassin was being led through a corridor in the basement of the Dallas Police Station, a man named Jack Ruby stepped into his path and shot him with a pistol at point blank range. Oswald died shortly thereafter.

On that same day, Kennedy's flag-draped casket was carried on a horse-drawn caisson to the Capitol building and placed in the Rotunda where it lay in state for a number of hours as thousands of mourners shuffled past. On the following day, a state funeral was held. After a requiem mass in Saint Matthews Cathedral, the slain president was buried at Arlington National Cemetery. It was all televised. A great many Americans, young and old, suffered through four days that felt like an endless nightmare.

No football games were played on the North Shore on Saturday, November 23, but few, if any, were scheduled. The larger question was what to do about the traditional Thanksgiving Day matches. Most schools decided to play those games, no doubt in the hope of restoring some sense of normalcy in the area's communities. Thus, as of Tuesday, many high school football teams and their fans tried to re-focus on the upcoming traditional contests. None generated more interest and excitement locally than the Big Blue's date with the Headers.

The teams were seemingly well-matched. The Headers' only loss had come at the hands of powerful 7-1 Salem, a club that the Big Blue had not faced. Like SHS, the Magicians frequently attacked through the air. Marblehead's senior quarterback Daynor Prince was, like Peter Cohen, a highly capable passer and field general. Both teams had outstanding receivers. Prince had thrown 13 touchdown passes while Cohen had connected for 12.

Marblehead averaged fewer points per game than Swampscott and had surrendered slightly more. However, those statistics were skewed by its 27–0 loss to Salem. Disregarding that result, and considering their conference games against common opponents, the rivals were statistically almost dead even. Both offenses could put points on the board, while both defenses had a tendency to give up yardage.

Two years earlier, the Headers had hosted Swampscott on Thanksgiving and ruined the Big Blue's perfect season. Would they do it again? In fact, while everything seemed to point to a nail-biter, the anticipated close contest never materialized. Swampscott soundly defeated Marblehead, 34–14. The defensive players followed a familiar script, yielding yardage but generally doing what was necessary to keep the Headers from scoring. They pressured Prince and recovered four of eight fumbles, with each recovery leading to points for the visitors.

An opportunistic defense combined with a productive offense to produce the team's strongest game. Conigliaro, Herlihy, Costello, and Cohen all participated in the scoring. According to the Big Blue coach, "It was a great team effort. They made mistakes and we didn't." During the post-game locker room celebration, the ecstatic players seized Bondy, Lynch, and Marden and dragged them into the showers.

Swampscott won both the Northeastern Conference and Class B championships. While the boys did not dominate every opponent, they always made the plays that brought home victories. They became the third Bondelevitch-coached SHS squad to post a perfect record—unbeaten and untied. The seniors, who had seen the Headers prevail in each of the prior three years, concluded their careers with a highly satisfying win over their rivals.

Bill Herlihy, Walter Costello, and Barry Gallup were three major con-tributors to the championship season. Co-captain Herlihy was a quiet leader. The hard-charging fullback/linebacker had typically delivered when called upon. He went on to play football at Holy Cross. As for Costello, for two seasons he had excelled as a ball hawking safety and in 1963 had also been a highly productive, play-making receiver, consistently breaking open to haul in Cohen passes for first downs, touchdowns, and conversions. And Walter Costello was a physical player who did not hesi-tate to block and tackle. Bondy said that, pound for pound, he may have been his toughest player. Coach Lynch still raves about Costello's hit on the much bigger Bobby Nash during the 1962 Classical game.

Barry Gallup's three-year performance was remarkable. In addition to many receptions and touchdowns, Barry blocked eight punts, recovered 14 fumbles, and intercepted passes, including one that he returned for a touchdown. Among other postseason honors, he was named a *Boston Globe* and *Boston Herald* All-Scholastic and a *Parade Magazine* and *Scho-lastic Coach Magazine* High School All-American. And while he may not have been football captain, the three-sport star captained both the Big Blue basketball and baseball teams. He was one of the best athletes and leaders in SHS history.

Shortly after the season ended, Bondy called Costello and Gallup into his office to suggest that both would benefit from a year of prep school. He added that Connecticut's prestigious Taft School would be the perfect place for Costello. For Gallup, it was Deerfield Academy in Western Massachusetts. Costello loved Taft, finding himself challenged both athletically and academically. Gallup was equally enamored of Deer-field. Walter went on to attend Boston University and Boston College Law School. Today he is one of the most recognized and successful trial lawyers on the North Shore. He and his wife have lived in Swampscott for many years. Like so many from the Bondelevitch era, Costello spends a good deal of time watching his grandchildren play sports.

Barry Gallup set receiving records at Boston College, where he also played on the basketball team coached by Dick Lynch's old rival, Bob Cousy. Thereafter, with the exception of a stint as head football coach and athletic director at Northeastern University, Barry's professional life has been closely associated with BC, where he now serves as Senior Associate Athletic Director, Football and Alumni Relations. There are few, if any, who have given so much of themselves to the college. Barry has also always worn his love for Swampscott on his sleeve. In 1994, he followed his father Earl into the SHS Hall of Fame. Bondy's Big Blue football program never produced a more exemplary representative than Barry Gallup. During and after his playing career, he served as a role model for, and generously mentored, many young athletes.

With his 1963 Thanksgiving Day victory, Bondy had improved to six wins versus five losses against Marblehead, and he could now boast of a winning record against every conference opponent. Many years later, as he reminisced about his various championships, Stan would say that he had been most surprised by his undefeated 1963 team. More than any-thing else, he felt that those boys had done it on guts and determination. Overall, they were not the most explosive or talented of Bondy's unbeaten teams, but they had almost certainly shown the most grit.

Following the win over Marblehead, Bondy publicly praised Doc Marden for his handling of the defensive line and Dick Lynch for his work on the team's pass defense, asserting that the two were the equal of any coaching staff in Eastern Massachusetts and deserved a major share of the credit for the team's success.

While Marden took a relatively low-key approach to coaching, there was nothing low-key about Lynch. Bondy was not the only strong per-sonality involved with Swampscott sports. His backfield coach matched him in energy, passion, and persistence, as did Flora McLearn, the girls' longtime gym teacher, and sports coach. Dick and Flora were about to butt heads as coaches of the boys' and girls' basketball teams. Athletic Director Bondelevitch was caught in the middle.

In 1963 Lynch, who had coached basketball at Saint John's Prep since 1956, took over SHS's team after Harold Martin stepped down. He soon encountered opposition much tougher than any his team would be facing. Her name was Flora McLearn and she oversaw SHS girls' athletics. She was a tough, no-nonsense taskmaster. And she was super competitive. As one of her former captains put it, "*Lose* was not in her vocabulary!"

To her credit, Mrs. McLearn strongly resisted anything that she felt put the girls' sports teams at a disadvantage. This brought her into conflict with new varsity coach Lynch. He could not believe that during prime practice time in the late afternoon he was restricted to using just one half of the high school's small gym because Mrs. McLearn had reserved the other half, separated by a sliding wall, for her girls.

Lynch favored aggressive man-to-man defenses with frequent full-court presses. He also emphasized a fast-breaking offense. He required well-conditioned players who knew how to apply pressure and move quickly up and down the full court. In his view, it was ridiculous to expect him to effectively coach the team if he was limited to having the boys practice in just half a gym.

He complained to Bondy, who knew how tough McLearn could be and did not want to tangle with her, particularly on a matter involving basketball, which was never one of his priorities. "Why don't you try to work something out with Flora?" he suggested. Lynch tried but got nowhere. He convinced Stan to schedule a meeting to inform Flora that changes in the practice schedules needed to be made to allow the boys' basketball team full use of the gym. When the message was delivered Flora said nothing, but her eyes filled with tears. Bondy backed off, announcing that there would be no changes until he gave the matter further consideration.

If Stan thought Lynch would drop the issue he was wrong. Dick soon informed his boss that if he could not have use of the full gym he would quit. He'd forced Bondy's hand. They worked out a schedule that they felt would be fair for Flora while allowing Lynch the entire gym for his practices. At their next meeting, Stan announced that his decision was final. Flora did not shed any more tears. She turned to face Dick Lynch and hissed, "You dirty bastard!" and then stormed out of the office.

While Mrs. McLearn lost that battle, she always fought fiercely for her girls' programs. It was sometimes not easy but Lynch, McLearn, and their mutual boss usually found ways to resolve differences. Yet there could be no doubt that, with Stan Bondelevitch as the town's athletic director, a certain boys' fall sport would always receive special attention. ☐

Harvard and Yale can move over—this is THE GAME!

In 1953 Bondy had greeted 38 football candidates. Fieldhouse manager Vinny Easterbrooks now distributed equipment to well over 100. Sustaining those numbers required more than convincing kids to initially sign up. The coaches had to continually find ways to keep the reserve players involved and energized. Otherwise, many would not remain with the team.

Regular recognition and encouragement, such as Stan had given to reserve players like Arthur Palleschi in 1958–59, certainly helped. Assuring that reserves saw action in games whenever possible also returned major dividends. Rather than running up the score, Stan preferred to give his reserves a chance to play. In addition to replacing starters once a contest was in hand, Bondy liked to use younger reserves on the kickoff squad. It made good sense for many reasons, including resting regulars, keeping more players actively involved, and filling the kickoff unit with boys who were highly motivated to prove themselves by rushing downfield and making big plays. Bondy also performed regular ceremonies where he recognized some sophomore JVs by handing them varsity jerseys while announcing that they had earned the right to dress for Saturday's game.

Looking at the large number of players reporting in 1964, the coach decided to do even more to try to sustain participation. "We must keep every boy who wants to play football active," he said. To further accomplish that goal, he announced that the Big Blue would field a junior varsity "B team" comprised of underclassmen who were not seeing regular action with the JVs. The plan was to have the B team play a separate six-game schedule.

Yet while plenty of players reported for preseason practice in 1964, there were not too many starters back from the championship squad. Still, according to the *Item*, the all-senior backfield was "blessed with size, great speed, and versatility." Peter Cohen, the 5-foot, 9-inch, 190-pound senior, may have been the premier passing quarterback on the North Shore. For the third consecutive year, halfback Billy Conigliaro was starting both ways. He was clearly one of the area's stellar athletes. With Costello gone, 170-pound defensive veteran Mike Maselbas took over at right halfback. Mike was another great athlete, excelling in hockey and baseball as well as football, where he performed as a runner, receiver, punter, and defensive back. Rugged fullback Bob Frizzell, yet another former Big Blue waterboy, completed the backfield.

Paige Cullen and Phil Gapinski were the only returning linemen who had been regular starters. In hope of providing Cohen with a new, reliable receiver, the coaches moved Gapinski, who was big, strong, and a good athlete, from tackle to end. A quick, tough 165-pound sophomore named Tony Blood performed well enough in preseason to claim the other starting end position as well as a spot in the defensive backfield.

Senior linemen Mickey DePaolo and Larry Mangini, who had played during the latter half of the 1963 season, were counted on to solidify the forward wall. Their classmates Dean Andersen, Norman Jacobs, and Dennis DiPietro, and juniors Mike Collins, Gary Earle, Ricky Jacobs, and Arthur Clippinger were among those who would also be seeing some action up front.

In the annual Jamboree Swampscott made a good showing against a strong Beverly squad, prevailing 8–6. The Class A Panthers went on to finish the regular season with a perfect record. As had been the case since 1958, the Blue opened with Andover. It was the final meeting between the schools, as Andover was leaving the conference at year's end. The Big Blue had never lost to this opponent and made it six in a row, winning 12–7. Cohen connected on a pass to Frizzell for one touchdown and scored the second on a quarterback sneak. Interceptions by Conigliaro and Blood helped.

SHS next took its nine-game winning streak to Woburn, where it played the inaugural game on the Tanners' new field. The streak ended with an 8–8 tie. It could have been worse had the defense not made four stops of Woburn drives inside Swampscott's 25-yard line.

Mike Maselbas was unavailable against Danvers due to injury and Tony Blood, already an accomplished player, filled Mike's spot in the backfield, while 150-pound junior receiver Tommy Boyce took over at end. The coaches frequently positioned Boyce as a wide receiver where, like predecessor Costello, he would have more room to maneuver and make better use of his speed and pass-catching ability. The offense came to life as SHS easily took down the Oniontowners, 28–6. Cohen threw two touchdown passes to Boyce, and one to both Gapinski and Blood.

On the following Saturday, the team traveled to Miller Field to face the 3–0 Vikings, a very strong team with a number of veterans, including powerful running back Steve "Tank" Adamson. Tank had scored seven touchdowns against Swampscott's Baby Blue while a freshman. The hefty Vikings line included twin tackles Bill and Ron Olsson, tipping in at 220 and 230 pounds respectively, and 215-pound end John Miles. Bondy said, "If we're going to lose this season, Winthrop is the team that could beat us."

Winthrop did beat them, 14–0, handing the Blue its first loss in 12 games. As in 1962, this contest was played on a muddy field in driving rain. The Vikings relied on their size advantage, rushing for 228 yards compared to 41 for Swampscott. Unable to sustain anything on the ground, SHS turned to the air but Cohen struggled with the wet ball, completing only four of 11 passes while throwing two interceptions. While the weather favored the Vikings, they were also the better team, ultimately winning the conference title.

With the Blue having now lost one game and tied another, Swampscott's fans could put aside dreams of back-to-back championships reminiscent of 1957–58. And it seemed the boys faced another stiff challenge against 2–2 Amesbury. The Carriagemakers had beaten Marblehead 26–14 and Newton South 12–8. Their two losses had come against undefeated Winthrop, and what the *Item* described as "a great Classical team." Yet this was Amesbury, a school that had lost eight straight to Swampscott.

Bondy tended to be conservative and resisted change when his teams were experiencing success, but he seldom stood pat after they struggled and lost. In something resembling a game of musical chairs, several players were moved to new positions. While Maselbas had recovered from his injury, he did not return to right halfback. Tony Blood, who was performing well, remained in the backfield, while Mike was inserted at right end, enabling the coaches to move Gapinski to the tackle position he had held as a junior. With Gapinski available for the interior line, Mickey DePaolo was transferred from tackle to fullback, sharing the position with Frizzell. The 200-pound DePaolo may have enjoyed contact too much, causing Coach Lynch to suggest that he consider running around, rather than into, tacklers.

Bondy mentioned that junior Ken Kinsey might see action at quarterback, while asserting, "We're going to throw and keep throwing." However, Cohen missed on all seven of his attempts against Amesbury and Kinsey, playing in the fourth quarter, connected on just two of six for 35 yards. Despite the absence of an aerial attack, the team scored 26 points while surrendering just six. Billy Conigliaro rushed for two touchdowns and a two-point conversion, the highlight being his 82-yard sprint to pay dirt in the second period. Maselbas and DePaolo also each scored.

It seemed that the line-up shuffling had paid off. It also seemed that Bondy's confident pregame assertions about the Swampscott passing attack may have been a ruse designed to mislead the Carriagemakers. During the week following the game, he revealed that Cohen had injured his arm late in the Danvers contest, which may have explained his recent passing struggles.

The Blue took its 3–1–1 record to Saugus. New coach Walter Sheridan had been hired away from Salem in the spring of 1964 after his 8–1 Witches claimed the Class A championship. Prior to Sheridan's arrival, Saugus had won just one game in three seasons, and the Sachems continued to lose in their first three games under the new coach. But they finally won in their fourth outing, thereby ending a 20-game losing streak. They then won again, raising their record to 2–3.

Coach Sheridan operated under his normal cloak of secrecy. Third parties, including reporters, were barred from Saugus practice sessions. Although young and inexperienced, the Sachems were improving. Games between Saugus and Swampscott always seemed to generate considerable interest, and a standing-room-only crowd of 7,500 was expected at Stackpole Field. Bondy predicted, "They'll be sky high for us."

If the Sachems were "sky high," the Blue, riding the healthy arm of Peter Cohen, quickly brought them plummeting down. Cohen fired touchdown passes to Blood and Maselbas and ran 12 yards for a third, as SHS again took the measure of the Sachems, this time by a score of 18–0. Conigliaro, while not scoring, enjoyed a productive afternoon, running and receiving for a combined 122 yards.

Swampscott's next opponent was visiting Lynn Classical. My dad had lost the Classical coaching job and his position as a history teacher in late spring of 1964. How had a former Little All-American Coach of the Year reached a point where he was unable to hold a high school teaching/coaching position? For years he had been sabotaging his career with alcohol. He had developed a serious drinking problem that had worsened to a point that it controlled his life. In May of 1964, an alcohol-fueled altercation with the Classical principal resulted in loss of his positions at the school. The ugly episode was reported in a front-page story in the *Item*. Not only had he lost his job, he was close to losing his family and perhaps his life. He was near rock bottom.

It was a difficult period for our family, particularly for our mother who was trying to hold down a full-time clerical job in Lynn, care for her children's needs, and figure out how to deal with the crisis. I had just graduated from junior high school and had been planning to meet some friends at a dance in Lynn on the evening following my dad's run-in with the principal. When I saw the headlines and story in the newspaper, I felt embarrassed and dreaded having to face others who were aware of what had happened.

Our older brother Wayne had just returned home after finishing his freshman year at Princeton. After I told him how I felt, he insisted that I attend the dance and drove me there. In the car, he told me to keep my head up. Then, as I was exiting, he grabbed my arm and said, "Don't take any crap from anybody!" While my younger brothers and I would all grow to be much taller than Wayne, we never stopped looking up to him. He became a highly capable corporate attorney but tragically suffered sudden fatal heart failure in 1989, leaving behind his wife and two young daughters.

It may have been a week or so after that dance in late spring of 1964 when I returned home one evening and encountered my father sitting in the kitchen. There were several empty liquor bottles on the table in front of him. He had been absent for several days, was unshaven, and looked like hell. I wanted to walk back out the door, but he asked me to sit down, saying that there was something he needed to tell me. "Robert," he said, "I dumped all the booze down the drain. I'm finished with drinking. I'm an alcoholic and I've joined AA. I am sorry for what I've put you all through." I had never before heard him talk like that. Shocked and relieved, I could think of nothing to say in response, other than "OK," as I retreated upstairs to bed. What neither he nor I envisioned that night was that his joining AA would take him down a path that would soon land our family in Swampscott.

George Moriarty, having returned in 1964 to assume the Classical coaching job, brought his 4-1 team to Blocksidge to face the Big Blue. The Rams were led by his son, Richie. The senior quarterback was an outstanding two-way player. In addition to Moriarty, the Rams had some other dangerous weapons, including running backs Walter Abernathy and Billy Mahoney. The *Item* rated the contest a "tossup", predicting a thrilling game. A large crowd was anticipated, particularly because it was Swampscott's Homecoming.

After the teams traded interceptions, Classical, relying heavily on the run game, reached the end zone but failed on the conversion attempt. Swampscott quickly responded, with Cohen completing passes to Maselbas, Blood, and then Boyce for the touchdown. He connected again with Maselbas for the conversion, and SHS took an 8–6 halftime lead into the locker room.

Early in the second half, Classical evened the score after forcing the home team to attempt a punt from its end zone. Trying to field a high snap, Swampscott's punter leaped and caught the ball but landed out of bounds, giving Classical a safety which knotted the score at 8–8. The next points came when the Rams' outstanding junior linebacker, Nick Ciarlante, picked off a Cohen pass and returned it 38 yards for a touchdown. Moriarty connected with Abernathy for the conversion and the visitors led, 16–8.

After Classical's Dick Knight registered his second interception, the Rams drove for another touchdown. The conversion failed. Classical led 22–8. Cohen then quickly moved SHS downfield, firing passes to Maselbas and Boyce before finding Blood in the end zone. After he connected with Boyce for the conversion Swampscott trailed 22–16.

The defense held and forced a punt. The Blue took over on its own 30 with only about 90 seconds remaining. Needing a big play, the offense tried what is known as a "hook and lateral." Cohen connected on a pass over the middle to Maselbas who then pitched the ball back to Conigliaro as he cut behind the play. Billy raced down the sideline some 69 yards before being caught by Moriarty just short of the goal line. Swampscott had a first down on the 1-foot-line with just over a minute remaining.

A touchdown would tie the game and Swampscott could then take the lead with a successful conversion. But as Cohen tried to push into the end zone on a quarterback sneak, the ball came loose and was recovered by the Rams who hung on for a 22–16 victory.

Classical won while only attempting three passes, two of which were picked off by Conigliaro deep in Swampscott territory. In contrast, SHS threw 25 passes. The offense could do nothing on the ground. Swampscott's 23 rushing attempts yielded a paltry 20 yards. Peter Cohen passed for an impressive 250 yards and all of his team's points, but also turned the ball over four times with the interceptions and lost fumble.

It was a big victory for the Rams and some revenge for the 1962 heartbreaker that had robbed them of an undefeated season. For Swampscott, it was a painful, unexpected loss. Big Blue fans were accustomed to Bondy's teams winning such close, hard-fought battles. But for the spectators on both sides, it was one of the most exciting games they would ever witness.

In addition to losing the game, the Blue lost three of its top playmakers to injuries. Maselbas was out again and was joined on the disabled list by Blood and Conigliaro, hobbling on crutches. None were available for the Newburyport game and all were questionable for the finale against Marblehead.

Because of the injuries, Bondy made further line-up changes. Among the new starters were junior David Corcoran and sophomores Tommy Murray and Brian Bates, filling in for Blood, Conigliaro, and Maselbas respectively. While Cohen was still slated as starting quarterback, Bondy planned to give Kinsey more playing time.

Despite the Classical loss and the injuries, SHS was favored over a Newburyport squad that had been blown away by Marblehead in its last game, 32–0. Yet the Clippers surprisingly battled Swampscott to an 8–8 tie. Bob Frizzell scored Swampscott's only touchdown on a 70-yard punt return. The team struggled without the three injured playmakers.

It was late November and again time to end the season by playing the boys from Marblehead. For the first time in five years, no titles or perfect records were at stake. It was just the 4–2–2 Big Blue against the 4–4 Headers. Yet, as Red Hoffman observed in his pregame article, as far as Swampscott and Marblehead fans were concerned, "Harvard and Yale can move over—this is THE Game." As always when the opponent was Marblehead, Big Blue spirit was at fever pitch. "Whip the Whips" chants echoed at the pep rally and the student body sprang for a full-page ad in the *Item* that read:

GO BIG BLUE. BEAT MARBLEHEAD. GOOD LUCK, BOYS!

The *Item* rated the Headers a slight favorite despite their 4–4 record because they had looked better in recent games, winning three of their last four. The newspaper predicted a passing duel between Cohen and Marblehead's sophomore quarterback Peter Brown. Noel Reebenacker was the only conference coach with a winning record against Bondy, but an SHS victory would even things between them. The big question for Swampscott was whether the three injured stars would be in the line-up. When they were absent against Newburyport, the offense had failed to score a single touchdown.

The football gods then smiled on Swampscott, as heavy Thanksgiving rains forced a postponement to Saturday, which allowed the boys another two days to heal. By game time, all three were able to play. Conigliaro and Blood each scored twice and Conigliaro intercepted a pass. As in 1963, the anticipated tight game never materialized, with SHS crushing the Headers, 30–6.

The team finished with a somewhat disappointing 5–2–2 record. The most frustrating loss had been the thriller against Classical. However, the season ended with a solid drubbing of Marblehead, something that the seniors could take away and recall happily in future years.

Peter Cohen, Billy Conigliaro, and Mike Maselbas had played their final game for Swampscott. As a sophomore, Cohen had led the team to victory over undefeated Lynn Classical, and as a junior had quarterbacked the Blue to a perfect record and conference and Class B titles. While his senior season had not always gone smoothly, he finished his high school career as one of Swampscott's most prolific passing quarterbacks. He went on to star in the position at Tufts University.

Versatile Mike Maselbas excelled in three sports, making major contributions to the football, hockey, and baseball teams. Performing as running back, end, defensive back, and punter, Mike was one of those athletes who could do everything well. After starring as a pitcher at American International College, he became a 1968 first round draft pick of the Saint Louis Cardinals. Mike spent three years pitching in the minor leagues before an arm injury ended his career.

Billy Conigliaro had started both ways since his sophomore season. While he may have been even more gifted as a baseball player, Billy's contributions to the football team were extraordinary. Among other things, he had sparkled on kick returns, runs from the backfield, pass receptions, and interception returns. Like his older brother, Billy pursued a baseball career. He was a 1965 first round draft pick of the Boston Red Sox. And, like Tony, he played in the outfield for The Olde Towne Team. But looking back on his athletic career, Billy said that the biggest sports thrill he ever had was not in the major leagues, but on Saturdays playing for the Big Blue.

Cohen, Conigliaro, and Maselbas were all destined for the SHS Hall of Fame.

The Aberrant Season

Bondy began his thirteenth year at the SHS helm. None of his past 12 teams had suffered a losing season. Some believe that "13" is an unlucky number. By the time the 1965 football season ended, Bondy likely shared that superstition.

I experienced the season firsthand, as our family had just moved into town from Lynn. When our dad had reached a low point in the spring of 1964, several acquaintances offered help. Two of them hailed from Swampscott and had some other things in common. Both were World War II combat marine veterans, having fought in the South Pacific. Both were successful in their careers, with one a well-established, politically active attorney and the other a prominent businessman and community leader. Both were enthusiastic followers of high school football. And both were members of Alcoholics Anonymous. They told our dad their stories and urged him to give AA a try. By doing so those men and several others helped him save and rebuild his life.

Following the loss of his teaching/coaching position at Classical, he embarked upon a new career in sporting goods, initially working for several companies before establishing his own business and opening a store. He supplemented his income by scouting games for other coaches who recognized and welcomed his exceptional football knowledge and unique analytical talent. Eventually, he also served in various coaching positions at the high school, college, and semi-professional level.

Our parents decided that it would be better if we did not attend public high school in Lynn. Therefore, when September rolled around in 1964, I entered Saint Mary's as a sophomore. But my dad's Swampscott friends were encouraging him to consider their town for a possible new home. He, of course, knew something about Bondy and SHS sports, while our mother was attracted to the small seaside community with its quality schools. A search was undertaken for suitable, affordable housing in Swampscott.

In the summer of 1965, the perfect place was found. We moved into a large rental property in a duplex owned by a local couple named Roz and Myron Stone. Roz was a teacher at the Machon School. Myron, a lifelong Swampscott resident, and World War II U.S. Marine veteran, worked in the shoe industry. He was also one of the most active and loyal members of the Big Blue Boosters. The house was in an ideal location, situated on a hill above Humphrey Street, overlooking the Surf Theatre and Fish House. It was just a short walk from our place down to Phillips Park and an even shorter one up the hill to the high school. The view across Swampscott Harbor to Nahant and the Boston Skyline was spectacular.

Regardless of the advantages of our new home, my brother Dick and I were initially unhappy with the idea of joining Big Blue sports. I was entering my junior year in high school, and Dick enrolled in Alice Shaw as a ninth grader. The quality educational system and other town attributes meant little to us compared to Swampscott's having ruined our dad's and older brother Wayne's perfect season with Classical in 1962. As a result, we disliked everything having to do with Big Blue sports, even though we did not know the coaches or any of the players.

Our feelings soon changed. Not long after we arrived, Bondy stopped by to welcome us and leave a book of Grantland Rice sports stories and a typewriter. Those gifts revealed something about Stan Bondelevitch. We were not aware that his parents were illiterate, but by gifting a book and typewriter the coach was telegraphing his feelings about the importance of literacy and education.

Barry Gallup, about to begin his freshman season at Boston College, also paid a visit. Barry, probably at the behest of Stan, introduced himself and offered to give us a tour of the town in his yellow jeep. We quickly became acquainted with some of the other Swampscott athletes and realized that they were kids much like our former teammates in Lynn. When football practices started, we liked the coaches, men like Brock Maher and Dick Connors, who were coaching the freshmen, and Stan Bondelevitch and Dick Lynch at the varsity level.

Bondy liked to talk about "the Big Blue family," and there was a definite community and family feeling to SHS football. There were typically quite a few players with brothers or cousins also participating in the program at the same time. Three sets of twins were playing at SHS in 1965. But the family connection went well beyond players. A great many parents, other students, and townspeople were involved in supportive activities. Our family became a typical example. My brother Dick was on the ninth-grade squad and would be joining me on the varsity the following year, while youngest brother Michael served as a waterboy. Susan, our only sister, became a Big Blue cheerleader after she arrived at SHS in 1967.

In 1965 the coaches had to contend with the departures of talents like Cohen, Conigliaro, and Maselbas. The only returning backfield starter was junior right halfback Tony Blood. Senior Steve DiPietro took over on the left side. Nicknamed "Link" (shorthand for "the missing link"), Steve had good size, speed, and power. Mark Stevenson was the new starting fullback. Mark, who also started as a linebacker, was Dick Stevenson's son. The six-foot, 180-pound junior was a good all-around athlete and perhaps the hardest-working and most coachable kid on the team. He had mastered fundamentals of blocking and tackling and was on his way to becoming an outstanding player.

Tall, wiry senior Ken Kinsey, who would go on to excel as a record-setting passer at Nebraska's Hiram Scott College, battled junior Bobby Hopkins for the starting quarterback job. Both had good arms and would be seeing plenty of action. Other backs in the mix included seniors Tony Benevento, Charlie Rizzo, and Dave Corcoran (no relation to 1961 star Ronny), and juniors Gary Savatsky and the Serino twins, Al and Vinny.

Up front, seven players who had started or seen regular action is 1964 had graduated. The most experienced returning linemen were seniors Gary Earle, Mike Collins, and Rick Jacobs. They, together with center Arthur Clippinger and junior guard Steve Sheperd, formed the new interior offensive line. Other seniors who would be working as varsity linemen, ends or linebackers, either on offense, defense, or both, included Tim Greeley, Billy Porter, Donny Petersen, Barry Ryan, Steve "Silky" Shapiro, Bob Smith, Mark Hatch, and Mike and Steve Farrer. They were joined by juniors Philip "Bimbo" Berkeley and Alan "Rugs" Gardner. Split end Tommy Boyce led the receiving corps. Brian Bates was the starting tight end. Earle and Boyce were co-captains.

At the outset of the season, I was competing for a spot at running back but would be starting (as a linebacker) on a defensive unit that included a number of other juniors, including Blood, Stevenson, Savatsky, Berkeley, Sheperd, and Vin and/or Al Serino.

Dick Baldacci, a stocky, colorful guy who had played his college football as a very good lineman at Brandeis, arrived at SHS to oversee the Art Department. He also joined Bondy's staff where he worked with the varsity linemen and the JVs. Unfortunately; he almost immediately antagonized his new boss when he exited the Fieldhouse for the start of preseason drills armed with a clipboard and papers. No one had thought to warn him about Bondy's absolute ban on written materials at practice. When Stan noticed the papers he heatedly ordered Baldacci to get rid of them, even suggesting that they might best be shoved into a certain body orifice.

Coach Baldacci was hardly the only assistant to suffer a Bondy tongue-lashing after engaging in well-intentioned, innocuous action. While Stan usually managed to control his temper, there were memorable exceptions when he erupted. Dick Lynch was not averse to using unsuspecting young assistants as dupes in order to bring about such meltdowns, which he found enormously entertaining.

An opportunity had presented itself during a recent season prior to the start of a game in Winthrop. Typically, Bondy put on his "game face" early, projecting an image of someone entirely focused on the upcoming battle. Any assistant who distracted the boss ran the risk of having his head bitten off. On such occasions, Bondy seemed so emotionally charged that Lynch and others questioned how much of it was genuine and how much was for show. Stan was, after all, part showman.

As the team was warming up at Miller Field, affable young assistant Billy Gillis had ambled over to Coach Lynch. Mentioning that he was hungry and pointing to a refreshment stand located a short distance from the field, he informed Lynch that he was going to walk over and buy a hot dog. He asked whether Dick would also like one. Rather than counseling Billy against his ill-conceived plan, Lynch said that while he was not hungry, Bondy might be. Gillis walked over to the head coach and offered to get him a pregame frankfurter.

Bondy's ensuing wild explosion was even worse than Lynch had expected. In fact, Stan lit into Gillis to the point that Dick Lynch almost felt guilty about his role in the episode. Billy survived the chewing-out but presumably went hungry that afternoon.

Yet, while Bondy could be harshly critical, he more often used humor to defuse tension and lighten the mood. As an example, early in the 1965 season, we hosted Central High School of Manchester, New Hampshire, in a scrimmage. Central coach Billy Hall's team was one year away from an undefeated season and state championship. But even in 1965, many of the Central Little Green players were hardly "little." They were big and tough. Their short, volatile coach was all about physicality, seemingly as intent on beating-up, as beating, the opposition.

When the scrimmage commenced, one of Central's linebackers positioned himself directly across from our top wide receiver, Tommy Boyce. The player probably outweighed Boyce by 40 pounds. As soon as the ball was snapped he charged across the line and belted Tommy. This happened several more times before Boyce lost his temper and went after the Central player. Bondy immediately ran onto the field, dramatically shouting, "Boyce, get away from that kid. He'll kill you!" He pulled our talented co-captain away from the big linebacker and escorted him to the sideline, out of harm's way.

Then there was a practice when nothing seemed to be going right. The mood of the team, like the sky, was growing darker by the moment. While our coach was generally positive and upbeat, on that afternoon he had been loudly voicing his frustrations for some time. Late into an intrasquad scrimmage, Bondy really exploded after one of the backs failed to perform an end run to his satisfaction. He inserted a new running back, but the result was no better. At that point, he somehow must have sensed that his continued expressed anger was not achieving positive results.

He thereupon switched to the melodramatic. He threw a mock temper tantrum, dropping to his knees and wailing while pounding his fists on the ground. This was one of a number of the coach's sight gags, occasionally performed to entertain the troops. In addition to lightening the mood, such antics were a means of feeding his penchant for theatrics. The performance elicited hoots and guffaws from players and assorted adults watching from the sidelines.

"Please," he begged, "run this play the way that it is designed—you guys are killing me!" After yet a third unsuccessful attempt Bondy cried,

"Oh, my god, I'm going to be sick! Somebody bring me a bucket. I'm going to puke in Technicolor! My grandmother could do better than you guys." The coach liked to point out a player's shortcomings by comparing the kid's athletic skills to those of his grandmother. She must have been quite an athlete since, according to him, she could run faster than a number of his starters, even while carrying a piano on her back. He ranted on, exclaiming that any other player on the team could do a better job.

He paused for a moment, surveying the field. Suddenly he yelled, "Carl Reardon, get in there at halfback and run that sweep!" Carl was a near-sighted, overweight, reserve senior lineman. He was not a great player. But Carl was at the top of his class when it came to school spirit. He rabidly supported everything related to SHS, both as a student and later as a custodian at the school, a position that he held until shortly before his death in 2008.

Carl was almost certainly the slowest kid on the team. Yet, in response to Bondy's command, he stepped into the backfield and crouched in a stance next to the fullback. Knowing that Bondy wasn't serious about a promotion, Carl was willing to play his role. When the football was pitched to him he managed to catch it.

The whole scene unfolded in slow motion. Cradling the ball as if it were an infant, big Carl staggered slowly toward the sideline. He could neither evade nor run over tacklers. As the first defender hit him, Carl emitted a roar and continued to stumble slightly forward. A second defender made contact, but Carl just roared louder. Several others piled on as he shook his head and slowly moved his feet, with little, if any, forward progress. Yet, despite the multiple hits and clinging tacklers, raging Reardon refused to go down.

Eventually, it seemed that Carl was supporting the weight of most of the defensive team. After what seemed an eternity a coach blew a whistle and the whole mass of humanity collapsed in one giant heap. Reardon had managed to only traverse a short distance, almost all of it laterally. The pile of players lay well behind the line of scrimmage. By the time the ridiculous spectacle had ended players, coaches and other onlookers were practically doubled over in fits of laughter. Bringing the practice to a conclusion, Bondy hollered, "Great job, Carl Reardon! I think we've found a new halfback. Okay, boys, head on in." Practice was over.

Despite Stan's efforts to inject humor, there was cause for concern as we were not performing too well in scrimmages. Then things got worse when Dick Lynch, who had been struggling with stomach pains since the start of preseason, was rushed to the hospital where he underwent emergency surgery for ulcerative colitis. Coach Lynch barely survived and was lost for the season. Not only would he miss football, he would be unable to return to work for the entire year.

Since the absence was unexpected, there was no one available to take over. Walter Costello, only two years out of high school and attending Boston University, tried to help by working with the running backs. Yet there was no way that Bondy, Walter, and the rest of the staff could completely fill the void from the loss of our savvy backfield coach.

We faced a tough opponent in our first game. Bondy noted that the Revere High School Patriots fielded a big, veteran line and some promising newcomers. In describing our squad, he said, "There will be a lot of new faces, but we'll win some games."

On Saturday, September 25, 1965, Swampscott entertained Revere at Blocksidge Field. Revere was no doubt "entertained." Swampscott was not. We were crushed, losing 40–18. It was an uncharacteristic and humiliating loss. The Patriots jumped to an early 20–0 lead and never looked back. While Revere started a couple of its scoring drives after Swampscott turnovers, our defense was unable to contend with the visitors' passing attack, while our offense struggled to put together sustained drives. The game was never close.

Following the loss, Bondy refrained from criticism, marveling at Revere's speed and size:

> We knew we had our hands full, but we didn't realize Revere was so fast.… You can beat a big team or you can beat a fast team, but it's hard as the dickens to beat a big, fast team.

Was the Revere loss a harbinger of things to come? The answer was both yes and no. While our team would never again lose a game by more than 14 points, we would continue to lose games—a lot of them.

The most bizarre of those losses occurred the following weekend when we hosted Woburn. We led by a score of 26–14 late in the fourth quarter.

Link DiPietro played exceptionally well, running for three touchdowns. Hopkins connected with Boyce on a 44-yard touchdown pass and on a two-point conversion to Tony Blood. It seemed we were on our way to victory in our conference opener. None of us envisioned the pathetic comedy of errors that was about to unfold.

With only a couple of minutes remaining we had possession near the 50-yard line and were preparing to punt. As Greg Murray, our punter, started to kick, one of our blockers, positioned several yards in front, and to the left, of Murray moved laterally, directly into the path of the football. It hit him squarely in the rear end, ricocheting backward toward our end zone. The Tanners recovered on our 11 and then quickly scored. While the PAT attempt failed, our lead was down to 26–20.

Following the kickoff, our offense didn't pick up a first down. But with less than a minute remaining, a decent punt would likely have sealed our victory. This time an errant long snap sailed over our punter's head. He retrieved the ball but was immediately brought down on our 33.

After an incompletion, Woburn tried a desperation pass to a receiver who was surrounded by several of our guys near the goal line. They all went for the ball and it was deflected into the end zone where it fell into the arms of another Woburn player. Their quarterback then ran for the decisive two-point conversion.

The joyous visitors departed with a miraculous 28–26 victory. We were stunned. It was hard to believe that we had blown the game. Nothing had gone right during the final minutes. We'd fallen woefully short in all phases. Our team never really recovered from that debacle. We had truly snatched defeat from the jaws of victory.

While Bondy had not been critical after the Revere rout, this time we came in for well-deserved blame. Among other things, he told the *Item*, "Our entire defense fell apart in the final period, allowing Woburn to score two touchdowns in the final two minutes plus the go-ahead conversion." But even in the wake of our disintegration, he pointed to some positives, including the overall play of DiPietro and Hopkins. He also singled out Mark Stevenson as the team's best defensive player.

We were 0–2, but many expected we'd right the ship against Danvers. The Oniontowners were in the midst of a 12-game losing streak. Even Bondy sounded optimistic, noting that Danvers was "no Revere", nor was it as good as the Woburn team that only managed to win as a result of our late-game bumbling.

But Danvers was good enough to beat us, 14–6. This time our loss was no fluke, as they amassed 243 yards of offense while we managed a modest 148. Most of those gains came on long passes from Hopkins to Boyce. We could not mount any real running attack as our backs gained just 27 yards. The *Item* observed, "You could cut the gloom with a knife in the Swampscott dressing room after the Danvers game Saturday…."

Our coach publicly charged that his defensive players were "too nice," uncharacteristically adding that "nice guys seldom win." He then recognized big senior defensive tackle Barry Ryan as a "rock 'em and knock 'em player", suggesting that others try to emulate him. It seemed a contradiction because Barry was one of the nicest guys on the team. He was a popular, good-natured kid with a ready smile. Moreover, Barry had been a frequent target of the coach's sarcasm during preseason practices. Some of Bondy's critiques had referenced a popular movie starring Frank Sinatra titled *Von Ryan's Express*. During a few scrimmages, Bondy had repeatedly shouted out messages like, "Go ahead boys—just keep running the ball down Von Ryan's Express—he's not even going to collect a toll—you're free to go!"

Presumably, Bondy's comments had their intended effect, and Barry became one of the few defensive players to impress the coach in early conference games. There were certainly plenty of "nice guys" over the years who were very tough football players. Bruce Jordan, co-captain of the 1959 squad, was a prime example.

Our struggling club next fell to the visiting Winthrop Vikings, defending conference champions. But the game was at least closer than the 20–8 score suggested. Our defense surrendered some long drives but also made several big plays. And our offense moved the ball well but twice turned it over deep in Winthrop territory. As Bondy put it, "A couple of bad breaks hurt us. If we had been able to score when we were on their two instead of fumbling, the entire game might have been different."

Interestingly, the abnormal losing streak did little to dampen school spirit. If anything, it seemed that SHS students cheered louder. As usual, Stan heaped praise on the cheerleaders, drill team, band, and entire student body. Some of these kids continued to appear outside players' homes on Friday evenings to distribute supportive signs and conduct impromptu rallies. Our games continued to be well-attended, as were the weekly Boosters Club dances at the high school or Ionic Social Club.

While disappointed in our performance, we still felt special to be part of the Big Blue program thanks to the efforts of the community, including coaches, parents, students, and Boosters. As noted in the *Item*:

> Swampscott may be in the throes of a losing grid season for the first time in more than a dozen years, but enthusiasm is still rampant among the players and students alike, as evidenced by the fact that a squad of 75 players report daily.

While the varsity was losing, the freshman squad was winning. On October 14, the unbeaten Baby Blues destroyed Danvers by a score of 30–6. The *Item* reported that "Dickie Jauron was all over the field and had a hand in all of the scoring…." Help was on the way, but it would not be arriving until 1966. In the meantime, we needed to win a game.

Bondy juggled the line-up, hoping to find a winning formula. But, to his credit, he continued to play many seniors. In the face of a poor season, he was not going to switch to younger kids simply to give them experience and build for next year. All things being close to equal, the seniors had paid their dues and deserved an opportunity to play.

Fortunately, it was time to meet the 0–3–1 Amesbury Indians. Ironically, the high school that had once dominated the pre-Bondelevitch Sculpins had become something of a guaranteed win for Bondy's teams. Playing in our first road game, we notched our first victory, beating the Carriagemakers, 22–0. Ken Kinsey passed for a touchdown. Steve DiPietro scored twice, once on a 55-yard run. And our defense held the opposition scoreless.

Next, we hosted Saugus. Bondy was 2–0 against the highly regarded Walter Sheridan, having bested him when he coached an opposing All-Star squad in 1959, and again when Swampscott beat Saugus in 1964. The 1965 Sachems, like Swampscott, had won only once. But they had also tied Beverly and Woburn. Several days before the game, Bondy announced that Tommy Boyce was probably lost for the remainder of the year due to an ankle injury. But Boyce healed quickly. Playing on Saturday, he caught four touchdown passes, all thrown by Kinsey. He pulled in the last with seconds remaining, sealing our exciting 42–37 come-from-behind victory. Unfortunately, it was our last.

We lost the following week by two points (14–12) in Manning Bowl to a strong Classical team, and Bondy did some further roster-shuffling. I was one of the beneficiaries, becoming a two-way starter when I was permanently switched from the backfield to tight end on offense.

On the Tuesday following the Classical game, as we showered after practice, all of the lights suddenly went out. We were left to dress in the dark. We assumed that the problem was something like a blown fuse, but when we stepped outside no lights were visible anywhere. A massive power failure, originating in a Canadian plant, impacted some 80,000 square miles and left approximately 30 million people in the dark, including folks throughout New England and in New York City. It became known as the Blackout of 1965.

Power was restored in Swampscott later that evening, but it was in short supply for our football team on Saturday as we lost again; falling to eventual conference champion, Newburyport, and its standout junior quarterback, Larry Russell. The southpaw ran for one touchdown and passed for another while leading his team to an 18–6 win. The Clippers finished the season with a perfect 7–0 conference record.

As Thanksgiving approached, Bondy was assured of his first losing season in Swampscott. The 5–2–1 Headers were good. The game was played at Marblehead High School on what may have been the worst playing surface in the conference. When we arrived, the field, more dirt than grass, was frozen hard. By mid-morning it started to thaw. Shortly after the opening kickoff, we were playing in what seemed a large mud hole. The Headers did a good job pressuring our quarterbacks and shutting down our passing attack. On offense, they ran the ball effectively. Talented sophomore back Bobby Blood was outstanding, gaining 146 yards on only eight carries. We lost 16–2.

Our final record was 2–7, making 1965 the worst season since the pre-Bondy days of the early 1950s. The reasons for the poor record remained something of a mystery. Most of the boys had played in Bondy's system for years. The seniors had been associated with undefeated JV and varsity squads. And we had some strong performers at skill positions.

Furthermore, the 1965 club did not lack size. In fact, we may have had more players in the 200-pound range than any of Stan's previous teams.

Yet, a number of bigger players had been beaten out for starting jobs by smaller boys. This caused Bondy to once quip that he was going to dig a ditch in front of our bench and force the heavyweight reserves to stand in it so that the fans would not notice their sizes and wonder what was wrong with the coach. We also did not have great overall team speed. And Bondy had certainly missed Dick Lynch.

It was disappointing for the seniors to conclude their high school careers with a losing record. Nonetheless, they had played football for Stan Bondelevitch and Swampscott High School. For most, if not all, it had still been a special, positive experience. But we juniors were hoping for much better results when we would be returning in 1966.

One of the players we expected would help was a sophomore lineman named Billy Adams. He had been promoted from the JVs early in the 1965 season, and I had played a role in that promotion. For most of us who competed in sports, there came a time when we realized that there were limits on how far we could go—that there were others who played the game at a level beyond what we could reach. In football, that moment arrived for me on the practice field at Phillips Park one day in 1965 when I made the acquaintance of William Adams.

It was a humiliating and, therefore, unforgettable experience. Our varsity defense was scrimmaging against the JVs and I was on the field as a linebacker. The JVs ran a play, and as I moved into what seemed a hole in the line and prepared to make a tackle I was obliterated. I had not seen the block coming and had never before been hit that hard on a football field. I looked up from the ground in time to see the running back scampering toward the goal line and a large kid in a red jersey stepping over me to return to the JV huddle.

I next heard Bondy's loud melodramatic lament. "Oh, somebody give me a bucket, I'm going to be sick … P-U-K-E … Pathetic! Robert Jauron, how did you let a little sophomore knock you on your butt?" I wondered whether Bondy had actually seen the player who had knocked me down because there seemed nothing about him that could be described as *little*.

"Run the play again," Bondy ordered. I had a chance for redemption. When the ball was snapped I charged forward, turned and braced to fight through the block and make the tackle. The big kid ran me over again. Bondy shouted to one of his assistants, "Get Jauron out of there and put somebody in who wants to play."

My backup ran in as I made the walk of shame to the sideline. He fared no better against the *little* sophomore and was helped off the field with an injury. Bondy had seen enough. "Stop everything!" he barked as he made his way over to the big JV player. "You're Billy Adams, right?" The kid acknowledged the fact, whereupon Bondy placed an affectionate arm on Adams' shoulder. "Take off that red jersey, son. You're on the varsity now. Someone find us a blue jersey for Billy." That was the first "battlefield promotion" that I witnessed in Swampscott. Others would follow, always involving the ceremony wherein the honored player's red JV shirt was removed and replaced with a varsity blue practice jersey.

As a young boy, Billy lived with his family in a three-decker in the McDonough Square area of West Lynn. The Santangelos, his maternal grandparents, were Italian-speaking immigrants who resided in the same building. Billy's mother and her parents and siblings were a typically close-knit Italian-American family.

An uncle named Fred Santangelo captained the 1949 Classical football team and had played with the Golden Greek, Harry Agganis. One of Billy's early childhood memories was accompanying his mother Lola to the Agganis wake at the Greek Orthodox Church. The line of mourners ran out the door and down the street for as far as the eye could see.

Although he was a big youngster, Billy was quiet and shy. He wore glasses and felt socially awkward. Regardless of his size, a shy, quiet, spectacled kid living in West Lynn's McDonough Square was bound to encounter more than his share of teasing and physical challenges. But it is not likely that any bully challenged Adams more than once. When provoked, he was fully capable of responding in decisive fashion.

During the December school holiday when he was a sixth grader, Billy's family moved into Swampscott. By that point, he was a veteran of many schoolyard and neighborhood brawls, virtually all of which he had won. The Adams family settled into their new home on King Street, just a stone's throw from SHS. After the holiday break, Billy reported to nearby Hadley School but was informed that due to overcrowding he would have to attend Stanley instead. The shy sixth grader was placed in a car and driven across town to his new school.

Billy's path home from Stanley led past Shaw Junior High School, where older kids yelled at him, teasing from a distance. He kept his head down and avoided eye contact. In some ways, he took after his father, a quiet, hard-working man, forced to quit school and go to work to help support his family during the Depression. To say that the senior Adams was a man of few words was an understatement. If asked a direct question requiring a response, Mr. Adams might, after considerable delay, respond with a simple yes or no.

Billy, though not as reticent as his dad, was hardly outgoing. However, he eventually became better acquainted with a few classmates. One of the favorite discussion topics was "tough kids." There seemed to be a consensus that a certain Hadley School boy was "the toughest sixth grader in town." Yet, as some of Billy's new friends took further notice of his size and athleticism they questioned whether he just might be tougher.

When the fall of 1962 arrived, Billy reported to Blocksidge Field for the first day of seventh-grade practice. One of his classmates approached and asked for protection from a bully. Adams told the bully to leave the kid alone. The bully wanted no part of Adams and instead asked a friend to intercede. That friend was the former Hadley boy, now "the toughest seventh grader in town." He issued a challenge. The fight ended quickly. When it was over, Billy Adams was the new "toughest seventh grader in town." While he continued to be quiet, shy, and a bit socially awkward, Billy Adams was never again teased or challenged by any kid in Swampscott.

Adams played halfback and safety on the seventh-grade team. As an eighth grader, he was a fullback and linebacker. As a ninth grader, he was a two-way end. As Billy continued to grow, the coaches continued to reposition him closer to the interior line. His future was foretold. While he had the speed and athleticism to play as a back or end, he was simply too big and strong to avoid the interior line. By the time sophomore tackle Billy Adams knocked me on my butt, he was near 6-foot, 3-inches and weighed in the vicinity of 210 pounds. He was destined to become a legendary SHS player and personality, considered by many the most dominating of all Big Blue linemen.

The Bandito Resurgence

When we arrived at Phillips Park to start the 1966 season, we found something resembling an oversized lifeguard chair planted near the sideline of our practice field. Bondy had reportedly been inspired by a photograph of Alabama coach Bear Bryant on an observation tower. But Stan's elevated chair was soon rendered useless when some mischievous vandals sawed off its legs.

Not to be deterred, he replaced it with an elevated, wooden platform. The thing may have been 15 feet high, supported by four sturdy beams. Bondy used a ladder to access his tower. The coach spent portions of each practice perched atop the structure where he used a megaphone to shout various commands, compliments, jokes, taunts, and exhortations.

Stan obviously enjoyed his new tower. Visitors sometimes joined him there, and he occasionally rewarded a player by letting him rest beneath the platform, shielded from the sun. When not atop his lookout, he often stood near the sidelines, chatting with reporters or other visitors. But while his assistants performed much of the "hands-on" coaching at practice, Bondy's frequently shouted comments reminded us that he kept at least one eye on the field.

Despite our rough 1965 campaign, we were generally optimistic, with varsity veterans returning at a number of positions, including quarterback, fullback, guard, tackle, middle guard, linebacker, and end. Unfortunately, our most experienced senior could not take the field with us. Co-captain Tony Blood, who missed the latter part of the prior season with a torn cartilage, had not recovered sufficiently to play as a senior. While surely disappointed, Tony pitched in and helped the JV coaches develop younger players. He remained a quietly supportive sideline presence on game days, but we missed his skill and leadership on the field.

There were, however, some notable positive additions. The first was Coach Lynch; back in his familiar position as Stan's key assistant. It was not coincidental that the Big Blue had suffered its worst season when he had been absent. While Coach Lynch may have been physically smaller than most of the players, it never seemed that way to us. When he spoke we listened, and then did our best to follow his instructions. Nobody wanted to disappoint our tough, highly respected backfield coach.

Then there was Frank DeFelice, a new assistant who would be working with the linemen. He was the same fellow whose fumble recovery for Winthrop had helped send SHS to its first defeat of the 1956 season. Frank's father had introduced him and younger brother Bobby to baseball at a young age and both boys eventually became high school football and baseball stars. After a postgraduate year at Worcester Academy, Frank, a 210-pound lineman, received a football scholarship to Boston College.

He was the first in his family to attend college but flunked out as a freshman. He was embarrassed and his parents were devastated. It was the only time that Frank had ever seen his dad cry. He enlisted in the army but promised his father that he would return to college.

After two years in the service, Frank re-enrolled at Boston College and his football scholarship was restored. He played three seasons as a varsity lineman. Frank wanted to continue playing after graduation and found an opportunity in 1965 with the Boston Steamrollers. This was the same team that Bondy had played for in the 1940s, then known as the Providence Steamrollers. Another coincidence was that one of Frank's Steamroller teammates was Jimmy Lyons, who had starred for the 1959 Big Blue.

However, when Frank returned to Winthrop to live with his parents, his mother fretted that her college-educated son should be doing more than playing semi-professional football for the princely sum of $100 per game. Not knowing where to turn, Frank decided to re-join the military, this time the marines. But on the evening prior to enlistment, his mother told him that he needed to call Stan Bondelevitch.

With Dick Lynch hospitalized, Bondy was looking for someone to fill in as a temporary gym teacher. He had offered the job to Lyons who begged off but suggested that teammate DeFelice might be interested. Bondy asked Mrs. DeFelice to have her son contact him. But, like many in Winthrop, DeFelice did not have warm feelings for Swampscott or Bondelevitch. He wanted nothing to do with the Big Blue.

However, Mrs. DeFelice pleaded with her son: "Please just do this for me." The reluctant caller heard Stan explain the situation and ask if he might fill in for a few days.

On a Thursday morning in early November of 1965, Frank drove north to the small school on the hill. When he met Bondy he exclaimed, "Hey Coach, having a losing season … tough year, huh?" DeFelice was not interested in tact or diplomacy. He was not planning to spend much time in Swampscott and was enjoying his chance to needle the Big Blue coach.

However, he discovered that he enjoyed teaching gym, which included plenty of interaction with high school athletes. That evening, he told his brother Bobby that things had gone fairly well, but that some kids had been inattentive and hard to control. The brothers discussed how he might go about instilling more order and discipline. Frank mentioned that in boot camp the technique used by drill instructors had been to immediately call out and physically intimidate the biggest, toughest guys in the unit. "That should work," Bobby replied.

Frank was intent on establishing his authority. With no training as a teacher or understanding of the disciplinary measures that were or were not appropriate, he planned to employ the drill instructor intimidation strategy as soon as possible.

A boy in Frank's senior gym class was generally acknowledged as the toughest kid at SHS. He was big, muscular, and reportedly held a black belt in karate. Frank had observed the kid's size and confident swagger. At the start of class Frank grabbed him and issued a challenge, "I'm not going to have any problems with you, am I?"

DeFelice was in his mid-twenties, weighed over 200 pounds, and was in great shape. He was also a teacher. Not surprisingly, the senior assured Frank that there would be no problems. He received a similar response from the tough-looking 200-pounder he selected for his Junior Class demonstration.

Frank chose Billy Adams as his sophomore target. Adams was clearly the largest, strongest boy in the gym. Frank held the mistaken belief that Adams was a bit of a troublemaker. Billy was nothing of the kind. He was generally soft-spoken and mild-mannered. However, while never disrespectful, he could sometimes appear inattentive and seem to lollygag as he made his way around the school.

Billy was nonchalantly shooting baskets when Frank barked the command for the class to line up. Adams did not immediately respond, instead firing another shot at the hoop. DeFelice, who was looking for a chance to go after the big sophomore, slammed Billy in the upper torso with a forearm. Adams did not even flinch. He simply looked bewildered. "What did you do that for?" he asked. "I didn't do anything." Adams was confused but hardly intimidated. Frank DeFelice was impressed.

As Frank had hoped, word quickly spread about the tough new guy running the gym classes. The message was clear, "Don't mess with him or piss him off." By Friday afternoon, the only sound in the gym was the authoritative voice of Frank DeFelice. Stan took notice. When it became clear that Dick Lynch would not be returning that year, Bondy offered Frank the job. DeFelice forgot about the marines and embarked on a new career.

With Lynch unavailable, JV basketball coach Brad Sheridan stepped into the varsity position. Bondy suggested that DeFelice take over the JVs but wanted Lynch's approval. Sheridan and DeFelice visited Lynch, still confined to bed in his Swampscott home, to discuss the coaching change. While Lynch correctly surmised that basketball was not Frank's forte, he recognized that DeFelice would assure that the kids were tough and played hard. He gave his blessing.

DeFelice was not one for the finer points of roundball. One of his favorite drills was to roll the ball into a circle of players; the boy who emerged with it would be rewarded with a starting assignment. After Lynch returned the following year and Sheridan departed for a head coaching opportunity, DeFelice became Lynch's assistant. Coach Lynch asked him to do two things. First, make sure the boys were aggressive rebounders. Second, assure that every player always hustled. Frank had no problem handling those assignments.

In February of 1966, Bondy returned from a coaching conference and told DeFelice about his plan to install a new 4–3 defense. When Frank told him that the scheme would not work, Stan heatedly berated his new gym teacher as a clueless, smartass, Winthrop know-it-all. DeFelice held his ground and urged Bondy to calm down and listen. After Frank finished his explanation Stan remained silent, seemingly mulling things over. Finally, he said, "Okay, I get your point." Two days later Bondy asked Frank DeFelice to join his coaching staff.

A third major addition to the 1966 football squad was a 170-pound, 6-foot sophomore who happened to be my younger brother. Dick Jauron was one of a few players during Bondy's reign that never spent a moment on the JV squad. Bondy felt certain, even before laying eyes on him, that Dick would be a special player.

When we moved into town, our dad told Bondy that he had three sons who would be playing football and that his boy Richard was "a good player." Bondy knew that our dad had been one of the best athletes to come out of Nashua, New Hampshire and that he was an outstanding coach. He also knew that Coach Jauron was hardly one to overstate the abilities of high school players. If he was prepared to describe his own 14-year-old son as a "good player," Bondelevitch expected that the kid would be exceptional.

Dick was exceptional. Given a ball, bat, glove, racket, golf club, or any other sports object and a brief explanation of the rules, he could master the game and excel in little time. Yet from the day that he was born in Peoria, Illinois, he had a special connection to football. On that day, our dad was coaching the football team at Peoria Manual Training High School and the boys were involved in a tight battle. In an effort to motivate his players, Coach Jauron told them that if they won he would name his new son after the team.

The boys won and our dad made the trip to the hospital and sheepishly informed our mother of his pledge. Kay Jauron was not pleased with the news, and insisted that her son would be named Richard, not "Peoria." Ultimately, they reached a compromise. The birth certificate confirmed that the name of Bob and Kay's newborn son was Richard Manual Jauron. Years later, our mother said that she was only happy her husband had not been coaching Marblehead at the time.

As youngsters in Rensselaer, Indiana, Dick and I passed and kicked footballs at Saint Joseph's College near the field where the Chicago Bears were holding their preseason workouts. When their practice sessions ended, we were allowed into the locker room where we sought autographs from coaches and players. Ironically, Dick would one day become the Bears' head coach.

We spent many hours in sandlot games played in the neighborhoods near our successive homes in Indiana, Ontario, and finally, New Hampshire. It seemed that, regardless of where, or with whom, we played, my skinny younger brother always excelled. He was talented and also quietly, but fiercely, competitive. He approached all contests with a focused determination to win and almost always did.

From early childhood, it was obvious that of Coach Jauron's five children, Dick had the most athletic ability. He also inherited our dad's love for sports and his instinctive grasp of the nuances of the games, particularly football. Yet, in other ways, the two were quite different.

Our dad was something of an immoderate man, often ruled by emotion. He was bright and could be witty and amusing, but also outspoken and short-tempered. He held strong opinions about many people, which he did not always hide. He sometimes did not seem to realize or care how his comments might be received. As a result, while he had many close, loyal friends and admiring former players, there were at least a few whose feelings about him were less positive.

Dick was more like our mother in manner and outlook. Early in life, he started to practice disciplined living habits. He maintained a quiet, attentive, and supportive demeanor. To the extent that he may have harbored negative opinions about people; he generally kept them to himself. He directed his focus outward, taking a genuine interest in others. He did not complain and always sought to deflect attention and praise. Popular and respected, he was a quiet leader.

Bondy's assumptions about Dick's abilities were confirmed when he watched my brother quarterback the ninth-grade team. Then, in a preseason article concerning our 1966 squad, the *Item* reported that the sophomore had made his presence felt among the quarterbacks. Bondy, noting that Dick had no varsity experience, told the paper's Bill Beaton, "We'll be hearing quite a bit from this boy before the season's over."

The starting quarterback was senior Bobby Hopkins. Bobby had been determined to play football for the Big Blue since Thanksgiving of 1957. On that day, nine-year-old Hopkins, accompanied by his brother and cousin, walked from Swampscott to Spanish War Veterans Memorial Field in Marblehead to watch star fullback Billy Carlyn and his mates complete their undefeated, state championship season.

His father, a dentist, died when Bobby was only a year old, and the boy and his three siblings were raised by their mother in a house bordering Phillips Beach. Hopkins loved sports, playing basketball in the winter, baseball in the spring and summer, and, of course, football in the fall.

While, as a sophomore, he led the JVs to a successful season, his fondest memory from that year was the varsity's one-sided victory over Marblehead on Thanksgiving. During the fourth quarter, Bondy sent him into the contest to play quarterback, telling him to throw a touchdown pass. Bobby connected with the receiver but it did not result in a score. Later Bondy sent him back into the game, again confidently telling him to throw for a touchdown. Bobby did just that, connecting with Tony Blood for the final points in the 35–7 rout.

The experience did wonders for the boy's confidence, as he recognized that the coach firmly believed in his ability to get the job done. As a junior, he started a number of games. Now in his senior season, he was the leader of the offense. Hopkins was a pinpoint passer and steady field general; typically cool in the heat of battle. It made no sense to even consider moving him out of the quarterback position. But it also made no sense to keep sophomore Dick Jauron off the playing field.

So the coaches had Dick run a few plays from the halfback position. When he took the hand-off and burst into the defensive backfield, Coach Lynch turned to Stan in wonderment with a look that asked: "Do you realize what we have here?" Bondy nodded his head, while quickly pushing his palms downward in a "cool it" motion, signaling that he understood and nothing need be said. Dick's quarterbacking days were over.

However, the coaches did not immediately insert my brother into the starting backfield. They went with four seniors: Hopkins at quarterback, Gary Savatsky at fullback, Tom Murray and Brian Bates as halfbacks.

Hard-running, 195-pound fullback Gary Savatsky was a muscular, bright, and personable kid. After moving into town from Great Neck, New York in 1965, he quickly became an active, popular member of the Junior Class. Like most of the 1966 offensive starters, he played both ways, also serving as our defensive middle guard. Recognizing Gary's contributions to the team, Bondy installed a special, new formation he dubbed "the Great Neck Spread." While Gary presumably appreciated the recognition, I'm not sure we ever actually used the formation in a game.

Tommy "Rabbit" Murray, our right halfback, was a track team sprinter and good all-around back, with breakaway speed and the ability to release out of the backfield and catch the football. His father, Richard, had been co-captain of Harold Martin's 1943 championship Sculpins. Tommy had other talents. Like his older brother Greg, he was a musician, playing guitar in a popular local rock band. And he was an outstanding student—ranking near the top of the senior class.

Unlike Murray, big Brian Bates, the 200-pound left halfback, was not particularly interested in school work, nor was he a musician. He was, however, a well-built, reasonably fast kid, who had past experience playing as an end. Brian relished his new role as a running back, perhaps because his idol was Green Bay Packers fullback Jimmy Taylor. A poster of Taylor adorned the wall of his room at home, and he asked for, and was assigned, game jersey number "31"—Taylor's number.

Many SHS players were saddled with nicknames, and we had our share on the 1966 squad, most of them Bondy creations. For example, there was "Bimbo" Berkeley, "Stumpy" Cordette, "Rugs" Gardner, and "Rabbit" Murray. But Bondy seemed to have the most fun inventing names for Brian Bates. While Brian's pals, of course, joked that he should change his first name to "Master," two of Bondy's favorites were "the Big Stud" and "the Golden Palomino." Depending on Brian's performance, our coach's tone could make those terms of either praise or derision.

While co-captain Mark Stevenson had played regularly as a fullback in 1965, he transferred to the offensive line where he took over as our center. It was a good move for Stevenson and the team. Mark was an exceptional blocker and a bright kid, able to easily read and respond to defensive alignments at the line of scrimmage. He quickly adapted and did a fine job anchoring the offensive line. At the same time, he continued to lead the defense as our middle linebacker.

Stevenson epitomized the kind of kid that Bondy liked to boast about. He was not only a hard-working, dedicated player, but an honor student who did not drink, smoke, or swear. He listened to his parents, coaches, and teachers and tried his best to do what was asked of him. Stan was well aware of those qualities. This became apparent one day when an irate teacher barged into his office while he was meeting with Frank DeFelice. She informed Bondy that all of his football players had been drunk at the Boosters Club dance on the preceding Saturday night. "All of them?" asked Stan. She repeated her accusation.

At that point Bondy, while continuing to eyeball the teacher, picked up the phone and called John Ingalls, a school committee member. The coach felt certain that at least most of his players, including Mark Stevenson, my brother and I, would not have been drunk at the Boosters Club dance. Knowing that Ingalls shared that certainty, he announced that he'd just been given disturbing news and that someone would need to call Mrs. Stevenson and Mrs. Jauron and inform them that their boys had been drunk on Saturday night and were in big trouble. After a moment's silence, the teacher shook her head, and in a resigned tone muttered, "Oh, just forget about it," as she retreated out of Stan's office.

Other than Bill Adams, seniors held every starting line position. Joining Stevenson, Adams, and the other tackle—6-foot, 3-inch, 240-pound Phil "Bimbo" Berkeley—were guards Steve Sheperd and Steve Mosho. Sheperd, at about 5-foot, 10-inches, and 180 pounds, also started as a cornerback or outside linebacker.

We continued to operate the modified wing-T and 6-foot, 2-inch Jeff Rossman became our new split end. Jeff's older brother Neil had played on the 1963 championship team. I would be playing as a two-way end in 1966, returning to my tight end spot, while switching from linebacker to end on defense. Mike Shumrak, a quiet 6-foot, 2-inch, 200-pound senior, was the other defensive end and also filled in at times in the offensive line. Other seniors seeing regular action on the defensive side included hefty, good-natured, interior lineman Rugs Gardner, twin utility backs/linebackers Al and Vinny Serino, and reliable cornerback Jeff Collier, the SHS baseball captain.

Jeff had been prohibited from playing high school football prior to his senior year due to a chronic back condition. He managed to finally secure the medical release and quickly earned a spot as one of our starting cornerbacks. At about 150 pounds, he was a solid tackler and heady player.

While we opened the season with an all-senior offensive backfield, the coaches also intended to regularly insert their new sophomore. In addition to running back, my brother was used as a safety, kick and punt returner, and placekicker. In the 1950s and 1960s, reliable high school placekickers were scarce. Dick, like virtually all schoolboys, kicked the ball in the straight-forward manner of Cleveland Browns tackle Lou "The Toe" Groza. Kicking, even at the professional level, was handled by guys like Groza who regularly played other positions. That started to change when the Hungarian-born Gogolak brothers, Pete and Charlie, popularized soccer-style placekicking. But few high school players were skilled in that method in the 1960s, perhaps due in part to the fact that many public high schools, including Swampscott, did not field soccer teams.

We did fairly well in preseason scrimmages against solid teams like Revere and Melrose, but Bondy did not want us to forget our 1965 struggles. At one point, after seeing me on the ground during a scrimmage, he exclaimed, "Are you going to lie around and let them run over you again this year?" While I felt embarrassed and resentful, his comment motivated me to lift my performance, which was exactly what he intended.

In typical fashion, Bondy balanced such criticism with positive reinforcement. After I did something right, he rushed over, slapped me on the back, and shouted, "That's the way to play that position!" He then added, "I remember another defensive end who made many plays like that." Bondy paused before whispering, "He played at Saint Anselm and his name was Stanley." He winked and ambled away.

Nothing in Frank DeFelice's background prepared him for some of the things he encountered at our practices. No doubt influenced by the Coughlin tragedy, Bondy was focused on hydration. He dispensed with the unsanitary water buckets that were common sights at high school games in the sixties. Instead, our student manager wheeled out a state-of-the-art, cylindrical, water-dispensing machine, containing a multi-gallon, insulated tank connected to two fountains and a spray hose. Players could lean down, press a button and take a long drink of water, and thereafter cool off by spraying themselves with the hose.

During one particularly hot, dusty preseason practice Frank spotted a lineman attempting to take a drink. "Get away from there," he growled, "I'll tell you when you can drink!" The next sound came from the big man with the megaphone. "Frank, can I see you over here, now?"

DeFelice crossed the field and looked up at the boss standing atop his tower. Bondy dispensed with the megaphone but everyone on the field could hear him yell, "Don't you *ever* tell a kid he can't take a drink while he is out here!" Before resuming the drills, the chastised new assistant reluctantly told us that if we wanted to take a drink we could do so. His words said one thing. His tone said another. No one dared approach the machine until an official water break was declared.

Frank was even more astonished on the first day of practice when the team manager drove Bondy's station wagon onto the field and Stan yelled that it was time to take a break. He beckoned us to the open tailgate where the manager dispensed popsicles. We took off our helmets, knelt on the grass, and enjoyed popsicles while Bondy regaled us with jokes and wisecracks. Occasionally he'd become more serious and discuss what was expected of us as SHS players, emphasizing our responsibilities to family, school, and community. Frank learned that such refreshment breaks, with popsicles, ice cream and/or cans of soda were common during preseason practices.

Frank was also surprised that Bondy didn't regularly conclude practices with wind sprints and never used them to the point where players were totally exhausted. There was something to be said for such "gassers" as conditioning tools and a means to measure quickness, speed, and endurance. However, used to excess, as they were in some programs, they became tortuous. Bondy was not a proponent of drawn-out, punishing gassers. When sprints were employed, he often turned them into contests, offering small prizes or adding some other gimmick to trigger more interest and excitement. Not wanting to "stunt the enthusiasm," he preferred that players build stamina while focusing on something other than simply sprinting as fast as they could up and down a field to the point of exhaustion.

Despite limited sprints there was plenty of running. It seemed we spent much of each practice session running from one point to another. For example, several offensive units successively executed plays at full speed while reserves held blocking pads. Each player completed his assignment; which might include handing off or passing, throwing, catching, ball-handling, or blocking, and then sprinted downfield, usually some 10 or 20 yards. "Run it out" may have been the phrase most often shouted by coaches. Having run out the play, the unit would turn back, jog along the sideline and reform a huddle while the second team executed the same play. The defense and special teams engaged in similar fast-paced drills.

These more closely replicated the combined physical and mental exertion required during a football game.

One exercise that Bondy dearly loved and regularly employed, sometimes to the point of exhaustion, was the "grass drill." We ran in place until a whistle blew at which point we threw ourselves to the ground and then quickly jumped up and resumed running in place until again hitting the ground on the next whistle. The whistles and resulting quick visits to the ground could continue for what seemed an eternity, but the hated drill not only improved physical condition, it emphasized something critically important to football success—the need to immediately bounce back after hits.

Coach DeFelice soon began to see the logic in Bondy's approach and recognized that the team was well-conditioned and morale was high. Frank also knew we had some extraordinary players such as junior Billy Adams and sophomore Dick Jauron, even telling his brother that they had the ability to someday play professional football. Bobby was profanely dismissive. He reminded Frank that as a novice with little coaching experience he was hardly qualified to recognize potential professional talent. But Frank persisted. In another six or seven years, he could have said to Bobby, "I told you so."

As preseason practices continued, Frank became even more impressed with Adams' abilities and potential. Then, in one of the coaches' meetings, Bondy threw out a question, asking his assistants whether Adams or another of the team's starters was the better lineman. One of the assistants suggested that the other kid might be the better player.

DeFelice was shocked. "You've got to be kidding!" he shouted. "That kid is okay but Adams is unbelievable. They aren't in the same league!" Frank continued his rant until the head coach brought the discussion to a close. Shortly thereafter Bondy informed his staff that DeFelice was in charge of offensive and defensive line drills and techniques. It was an unspoken but clearly understood promotion. In a short time, Frank DeFelice had become Swampscott's primary line coach.

DeFelice had some things in common with predecessor Dick "Chipmunk" Stevenson. Both were Winthrop natives. Both played college football. Both excelled at drilling fundamentals of line play. But there were also differences. By the 1960s Stevenson was a middle-aged married man with three children. The relatively low-key school administrator was respectful in his treatment of players. Most people would have described him as a gentleman. By contrast, Frank was not much older than some of the boys on the team. He was living a young bachelor's life, staying out late and playing as hard as he worked. His coaching style was pretty much "in your face." It was not unheard of for Frank to get down in a stance and do battle with some of the stronger linemen. And it is questionable whether anyone would have described the brash, young coach as "a gentleman".

After beating Wakefield in the Jamboree with a 6–0 win, we seemed ready to open the season. According to an *Item* poll of local coaches, one of the squads expected to be among the North Shore's strongest was "surprisingly Swampscott." But most of the accolades went to Saugus, a team with eight offensive starters returning, including its entire backfield. Marblehead was another seasoned club with a number of skilled players. Yet while the *Item* was writing about Saugus, Marblehead, and Swampscott, a team in Newburyport was preparing for what it hoped would be a historic run.

In our opener at Blocksidge, we faced an opponent that Swampscott had last played in 1954. Back then, the Class B Gloucester Fishermen had easily romped over Bondy's smaller Class C team. It had been the Fishermen's eighteenth consecutive triumph over SHS. Gloucester was now back on our schedule, having just joined the Northeastern Conference, filling the vacancy resulting from Andover's withdrawal.

Bondy scheduled the game for a Friday afternoon, recognizing that the Jewish holiday of Yom Kippur would otherwise prevent some players from participating and many students and fans from attending. We passed our first test with flying colors, soundly defeating the Fishermen, 35–0. The highlight may have been my brother's 74-yard punt return for a touchdown. In his first varsity game, he also kicked three conversions, while logging considerable minutes in the offensive and defensive backfields. Not only did we win convincingly, we finished before sundown. The Jewish players immediately raced home without showering or removing the tape from their ankles.

Woburn was next. There was no repeat of the 1965 debacle as we trounced the Tanners, 38–0. We next traveled to Danvers and posted our third consecutive shutout, 35–0. Over our first three games, we outscored our opponents, 108–0. Bobby Hopkins played brilliantly, connecting on eight touchdown passes, including three each to Rossman and to me. The running game with Savatsky, Murray, Bates, and my brother was also very productive.

Most impressive, however, was the exceptional play of the defense. In three consecutive shutouts, the team forced numerous turnovers. Because of all the takeaways, someone dubbed our defensive unit the "Banditos." Throughout the rest of the season, the spirit squad prepared posters and signs depicting banditos, the newspapers printed cartoons, and some of our supporters arrived at the games in ponchos and sombreros.

The string of shutouts ended at Winthrop. Swampscott-Winthrop games were often close, hard-fought contests played in bad weather. On a raw, overcast, rainy day we managed to beat the Vikings, 20–12.

While our fifth game was at home against Amesbury, it seemed that we were concentrating on preparing for the following week when we would be facing Saugus. In one of the private coaches' meetings, Frank DeFelice voiced concern that we could be making a mistake by failing to focus more attention on our next opponent. Bondy just rolled his eyes and, glancing toward Coach Lynch, said, "Tell him, Dick."

Lynch informed Frank that we would have no trouble beating Ames-bury and that the big challenge was Saugus on the following Saturday. While true, Bondy and Lynch would never have said this publicly or to us players. We romped over the Carriagemakers, beating them 31–0.

There was always keen interest when Saugus and Swampscott met, probably in part because the towns are almost neighbors. Only Lynn separates the two communities. The 1966 Sachems were undefeated and stood atop Class A. To remain there, they needed to beat us, which most observers predicted they would do. Coach Sheridan had been building the squad since his arrival in 1964. Every offensive starter was a senior, and many were starting for their third consecutive year.

Their anchor up front was rugged John Dancewicz, an outstanding tackle and linebacker. Saugus pounded opponents with a fearsome run-ning attack, featuring powerful star fullback Ed Maguire, complemented by talented halfbacks Jim Paolini and Mike Kimball. But Saugus was not one-dimensional. Chris Serino, a three-year starter at quarterback, was a skilled passer, able to pick apart defenses. The Sachems were averaging 34.4 points while surrendering just 6.6. In their two most recent games they outscored opponents 69–0, including bludgeoning a good, veteran Marblehead squad, 29–0.

Our match-up was billed in the local media as the game of the year. The *Item's* Red Hoffman predicted that the host Sachems would win, 20–12. The weather was perfect on game day as an estimated 11,000 fans jammed every inch of Stackpole Field, filling the stands, crowding the sidelines, and perching on walls and whatever other structures might offer a view.

After warming up, we retreated through the throngs of excited spectators to the small building behind the field that housed the visitors' meeting room. Anything that our coaches tried to say was drowned out by the earsplitting noise from outside. A group of kids climbed on to the roof above us and banged away with feet, hands, and whatever else was available. There was also the blaring music of the nearby competing school bands. But by that point, nothing really needed to be said. Adrenalin was soaring and we were ready to go.

Following the opening kickoff, we took advantage of a Saugus fumble and ran the ball successfully in a drive that ended when my brother crossed the goal line. By this point, he had taken over at left halfback and would start in that position for the rest of his high school career. For the first time all season, the Sachems trailed an opponent. But they quickly engineered their own scoring drive. Their conversion attempt failed, leaving the teams knotted at 6–6 when the first quarter ended.

Later in the second quarter the most memorable play of the game, if not the season, occurred when Saugus punted. Dick received it on his own 34-yard line, but quickly reversed field and retreated to the 18, thereby evading a Saugus player who arrived almost simultaneously with the ball. Then, as a number of other Sachems closed in, he cut sharply and accelerated, outracing them down the sideline. He avoided a final tackler by cutting back across the field and then sprinted to the end zone. The electrifying return put us back in the lead. Dick's PAT kick was good. Saugus trailed 13–6.

With less than a minute remaining in the half, a punt return gave the Sachems good field position at our 36. On the next play, they scored on a pass and then went for the two-point conversion and the lead when Serino threw to Paolini in the right flat. Our cornerback Jeff Collier managed to bring him down just short of the goal line, allowing us to hold on to our 13–12 lead as the first half ended.

The second half was all about defense. Two of the most prolific offenses in Eastern Massachusetts struggled to generate scoring opportunities. However, late in the fourth quarter the Sachems took possession on their 18 and marched downfield in eight plays where they had a first down on our 14. Serino tried to pass but was sacked. On second down Paolini ran to the 10, but a third down pass fell incomplete. With the clock winding down, Saugus faced a fourth down, needing six yards for a first down and 10 for a touchdown.

Our coaches had prepared us for a play favored by Coach Sheridan in which Chris Serino rolled to his right, while Maguire and several linemen brush-blocked and then drifted into the left flat to set up a screen pass. Serino would stop, turn, and throw back across the field to Maguire. This was the play they attempted, but we were ready. As reported in the *Item*:

> When his pass crossed the field, there were as many defenders awaiting it as there were Sachems, and when it was batted down the ball game was to all intents and purposes, over.

Taking over on downs, we ran out the clock and made our way to the bus, squeezing through a mob of despondent Sachems fans and our own jubilant supporters. Red Hoffman, ducking his head in to congratulate us, was greeted by a chorus of loud, good-natured jeers and boos, a reminder that he had wrongly predicted that Saugus would win. He departed with a wave and a smile. In 1967, he moved his family from Lynn to Swampscott and his sons joined Bondy's football program.

It was one wild, rowdy bus ride back to Swampscott.

One of the nice postgame stories involved a nine-year-old Saugus boy named Kevin Cronin, who caught the football that Dick kicked for the decisive point. He traveled with his parents from Saugus to our Swampscott home to give that ball to my brother and ask for his autograph. Although embarrassed, Dick obliged with an autograph but told the boy that he could keep the football. However, Kevin and his family ultimately insisted that Dick take the football and our mother found a prominent spot for it on a trophy shelf in our house.

Playing at home, we rolled over winless Classical, 40–6, and then prepared for a trip up Route 95 to Newburyport. While we were routing Classical, the Clippers were crushing Marblehead, 53–28. They shared the conference lead with us and were also unbeaten. Clipper senior Larry Russell may have been the best quarterback in the state. Following high school, he starred at Wake Forest, leading the Demon Deacons to an ACC championship. The left-hander did everything well. And the Clippers had a number of other weapons, including quick, strong running backs in Bill Cashman, Dan Sullivan, and Ed O'Bara and a couple of superior, pass-catching ends in tall Kevin Lucy and speedy George Chaisson.

Newburyport's dismantling of talented Marblehead had been particularly impressive. Following the game, Headers coach Noel Reebenacker described Newburyport as the best high school machine he had ever seen. Clippers coach Jim Stehlin had arrived in 1964 and very quickly put in place an outstanding program, generating much support, excitement, and pride in the town. The 1965 squad had claimed the conference title while finishing 8–1. Folks in the Port City were looking forward to winning it again.

Football fever was burning in both communities, and this was our latest "biggest game of the year." While the weather for our pivotal conference tilt was wet and raw, it did not prevent another sell-out crowd, even in Newburyport's larger World War Memorial Stadium. The winner needed only to prevail on Thanksgiving to secure a perfect, championship season.

We believed that we were ready for Stehlin's team. We were wrong. Our magical ride ended on that damp, dismal day. The offense struggled. The defense struggled. Nothing seemed to work. The Banditos surrendered more points than we had given up in the first seven games combined.

Russell was a dazzling ball handler. He was so adept at faking handoffs and hiding the football that we often had trouble identifying the ball carrier. Late in the first quarter, they notched their first touchdown, covering 79 yards in just three running plays. In the second quarter, they did it again, going 60 yards in six plays. With Russell's conversion kicks, the home team held a 14–0 halftime lead.

We entered our locker room, stunned and disheartened. Two weeks earlier we had beaten the team that many considered unbeatable. Now our defense seemed helpless against the relentless, lightning-quick Newburyport attack. Meanwhile, our offense had managed 18 yards during the entire first half. Frustration got the better of Billy Adams as he erupted in an emotional outburst, attacking all inanimate objects within reach. The coaches huddled and then did their best to rally the troops.

We returned to the field determined to give it everything we had, but our confidence was shaken. Then, on their first possession of the third quarter, our opponents needed only three plays to rush 48 yards to our end zone. Russell again kicked the extra point and we trailed 21–0. Finally, we responded, with Hopkins completing four passes, the last to Rossman for the touchdown. We faked the conversion kick and passed for an additional two points, making it a 21–8 game and offering a glimmer of hope.

That glimmer was quickly extinguished when the Clippers launched another drive. We halted their advance near our 20, but Russell kicked a 36-yard field goal. Trailing 24–8, we tried to rally through the air, but Hopkins was pursued and harassed relentlessly. Ultimately, he was sacked six times for a total of 82 yards and was forced to throw the ball away on several other occasions. At one point, we needed something like 43 yards for a first down.

The Clippers did not let up and crossed our goal line again in the fourth quarter, this time on a Russell pass. The score rose to 31–8. As the clock ran down we managed to drive the length of the field and score as time expired.

Bondy later said that it had been the first time in his career that he and his assistants could not spot an exploitable weakness in an opponent. "We just couldn't come up with anything," he confessed. We rode back to Swampscott in cheerless silence, our dreams of an undefeated season and conference and state championships shattered. But we could eventually take some solace in realizing that we had been beaten by one of the best high school football teams ever produced in Eastern Massachusetts.

We needed to regroup for Marblehead. Because it was the Headers, there was plenty of motivation. Yet it is hard to overstate the impact of the beating we suffered in Newburyport. We not only lost that game but some of the swagger and sense of invulnerability that had grown over the remarkable season. We also incurred injuries to key players, including Jeff Collier and Mark Stevenson, both hobbling with lower leg damage. Perhaps most alarming was a knee injury suffered by Bill Adams, who was doubtful for Thanksgiving.

We faced a gifted, experienced opponent. Senior quarterback Don "Toot" Cahoon and junior running back Bobby Blood were two of the North Shore's most versatile, exciting players. Other veteran Marblehead playmakers included halfback John Ormiston and former quarterback Peter Brown, now an end. However, like us, the Headers were at less than full strength, having lost their captain, strong senior fullback Tom Livingston, to a serious head injury.

Don Cahoon's older brother Frank had been a standout 190-pound fullback/linebacker on the Big Blue championship teams of the fifties. Don was "little brother" in size as well as age. Even as a high school senior he was only about 5-foot, 7-inches and weighed in the neighborhood of 150 pounds. Frank was "Truck," while Don was "Toot." But what he lacked in size he made up for with athleticism and heart. He excelled in all youth sports but was a truly outstanding hockey player. According to legend, some dismissive comments by Bondy about that sport had caused Mr. Cahoon to relocate his family to Marblehead. Whatever the cause, the move proved a blessing for Swampscott's rival.

The 5–3 Magicians had lost only one conference game—to Newburyport. They had beaten all of the same conference teams that we had beaten and, like us, had a theoretical chance of tying for the title if they could win on Thanksgiving and Amesbury could somehow find a way to take down the Clippers. Of course, there was no way that Newburyport would lose to Amesbury—they concluded their perfect season by hammering the Indians, 49–0.

Stan Bondelevitch was not a "one size fits all" coach. He used the psychological approach with each boy that he believed would be most effective, regularly riding some while never saying a critical word to others. In general, he knew which buttons to push on which kid to generate maximum performance.

During my two seasons on the team, Bondy treated me like he treated many SHS players; with good-natured ribbing and encouragement. He liked to joke about my ankles, which I had sprained several times. As I'd jog out to practice, he might announce something like, "Oh no, it's Glass Ankles Jauron. I hope you triple-taped those things." He also liked to needle me about my girlfriend. But he rarely yelled at, or criticized me. Perhaps as a result, when he did, those verbal barbs really stung.

Our final practice was the brief walk-through in game uniforms on the afternoon before Thanksgiving. For some foolish reason, I was tardy. I'd missed warm-ups, but the team had not yet begun the walk-through. As I approached the field, Bondy approached me. He was not smiling. He was livid. "Where the hell have you been?" I tried to offer some weak excuse, but he cut me off. "You missed the team picture. You are not in it! I hope you are proud of yourself. What is the matter with you?"

I'm not sure that I had ever seen the coach more upset. I know that I'd never seen him more upset with me. And, ever clueless, I could not understand. Why was he fuming over my having missed a photo shoot? He was acting like I'd burned down the high school. As he stormed off, shaking his head, I was asking myself, "What is his problem?" It was only years later that it dawned on me. Perhaps he had been so disturbed because he sensed how much I would eventually regret being absent from our team picture.

SHS students worked all week to boost school spirit and inspire the players. A lively pep rally was held in the decorated gym. The theme, as always, was "Whip the Whips." Then, on the evening before the game, supporters marched around town to homes of various players where they performed cheers and posted personal signs.

Thanksgiving morning dawned crisp and cool, a perfect day for football. We had already played before sold-out, standing-room-only crowds at Saugus and Newburyport and now would do so again, this time at home before what was reportedly the largest crowd ever at Blocksidge Field. Mark Stevenson and Jeff Collier would be playing, although neither was close to 100 percent. Bill Adams' limited mobility kept him out of the offensive line. Tony Blood, while still unable to play, dressed for the game and joined Mark Stevenson to lead us out of the Fieldhouse and through the large "Big Blue hoop" held by the cheerleaders.

The Headers scored first, capping an impressive 82-yard drive. After exchanging punts, we mounted our own touchdown drive, with my brother scoring and kicking the extra point, giving us a 7–6 lead. One play after the ensuing kickoff, Dick intercepted a Cahoon pass at our 30. After two Hopkins passes, we were in the end zone again, with the big play being a completion to Tommy Murray who caught the ball at midfield and sprinted down the sideline for the score. The PAT kick was good and the half ended with us ahead, 14–6.

We held the lead but had further injury problems. Gary Savatsky was hurt and lost for the remainder of the contest. While Billy Adams had been able to play as our right defensive tackle, by halftime his knee had swollen badly and he was sidelined. Thus, we were missing our starting fullback/middle guard and our best two-way lineman for the entire second half.

On our first possession of the third quarter, Dick sprang through the line behind solid blocks, cut to his right and turned on the jets, racing 60 yards to the end zone. His conversion kick was good and we led 21–6. But after the teams exchanged punts, the Headers narrowed the gap, with Bobby Blood finishing off the drive with a 13-yard touchdown run. Marblehead went to Blood again for the two-point conversion. Our rivals were now frequently attacking our weakened defensive line by running behind their left guard and tackle.

We thought that we had expanded our lead when Rabbit Murray broke through on the 22-trap and bolted 65 yards to pay dirt. However, we were flagged for backfield-in-motion and the touchdown was negated. This penalty was later bitterly recalled in some Swampscott circles as a "phantom motion call" because the coaches had difficulty spotting the infraction when they reviewed the game films.

Later in the fourth quarter, after we were forced to punt, the Headers put together the key drive of the game, with almost all of it accomplished on the ground. Cahoon converted on several third down scrambles and Bobby Blood ultimately ran it in from the 2-yard line for his third touchdown. They then wisely ran John Ormiston behind their left tackle for the critical two-point conversion. The Headers had overcome a 15-point second-half deficit and now held a one-point lead, 22–21.

However, there was still time on the clock. After our offenses traded possessions, we took over on our own 15 and quickly moved to midfield. We were running out of time and needed to advance to at least field goal range. Several passes fell incomplete and we faced fourth down.

The play sent in from the sidelines was the "Happy Jack Pass." This was a hook and lateral like the one that had almost secured a last-second victory over Classical in 1964. As designed for our offense, Hopkins was to throw to me and I would then toss the ball back to Dick as he trailed the play and cut behind me. I caught the pass and as I was being hit from behind spotted Dick cutting across the field and underhanded the ball toward him. But the play did not work. Perhaps our timing was off and/or the Headers did a nice job defending it. Whatever the reason, we were finished.

Our locker room was like a tomb, muted and mournful. While Newburyport had ruined our dreams of finishing unbeaten, this loss, in which we had surrendered a 15-point lead in the second half and fallen by the slimmest margin, was the most painful. Many of us, players and coaches alike, were despondent. Frank DeFelice always looked forward to his family's Thanksgiving feast but could not eat a bite. We all hurt on that holiday.

Of course, our rivals were experiencing very different feelings. Rallying in the second half to beat Swampscott on Thanksgiving had been exhilarating. After high school, Don Cahoon continued his athletic career at Boston University, where he starred on two national championship hockey teams. Thereafter he coached collegiate hockey for almost 40 years, including an early stint as an assistant to Jack Parker at BU. At one point, Cahoon and Parker were about to send the BU team onto the ice to play in another NCAA championship game. As part of his motivational strategy, Parker said, "Coach Cahoon tell these players about the most exciting experience you ever had as an athlete."

Jack Parker felt certain that his assistant would rave about the thrill of having won national championships. But Cahoon, concerned that the players were already overstressed, told them that nothing in his sports experience could compare with having led Marblehead to victory over Swampscott on Thanksgiving morning.

His surprise declaration had the intended effect on Parker and others, who burst out laughing. But if beating us may not have been as thrilling as winning a national championship in college, it certainly remains one of Don's most treasured sports memories. And with the benefit of the passing years, even those of us who came away on the losing end realize how special it was to have played for Swampscott in that season-ending game against Marblehead.

Years later Bondy had this to say about the traditional Thanksgiving contest between the rivals:

The thing about the game is that nothing in a boy's sports life can take the place of the Thanksgiving Day game. Whether he goes on to play in college, nothing is like it.

Postseason honors were bestowed on a number of SHS players, including Mark Stevenson, who was named to several All-State squads and was honored as a high school All-American by Scholastic Coaches Magazine. He went on to become a two-year starting center and All-Ivy selection at Dartmouth College. After graduating, Mark worked in the sporting goods field before ultimately establishing his own marketing company. His Swampscott and Dartmouth classmate Gary Savatsky became an orthopedic surgeon, while Tom "Rabbit" Murray attended Harvard before finding success with a career in international finance, retiring in his mid-forties.

Jeff Collier credits his high school baseball coach Frank DeFelice for helping him secure a scholarship to Florida's Rollins College. Frank had originally pressed Collier to seek a Boston College football scholarship, promising that he would help him win the award. Jeff tried to explain that he was too small, but Frank persisted. Finally, Jeff confessed that he had no intention of trying to play college football at BC or anyplace else. He'd been banged up enough in his only season playing the high school game. Jeff's sport was baseball. DeFelice refocused and sang Collier's praises to the baseball coach at Rollins. After playing ball throughout his undergraduate years at Rollins and remaining for an MBA, Jeff embarked on a highly productive business career.

Bob Hopkins set an SHS record by completing 15 touchdown passes in his final season and then starred as an All-Conference and All-New England quarterback for the University of New Hampshire. Following college, he decided on an acting career and left for California. After studying with legendary acting coach Lee Strasberg, he built an acting and filmmaking career as Bobb Hopkins, much of it related to American hobo culture. His fascination with that wandering lifestyle led him to ride the rails recreationally and become the founding director of the National

Hobo Association. He credits his Swampscott sports experience for the self-assurance that helped him beat the odds in the competitive acting and filmmaking world, and also embrace an unusual and perilous past-time—riding freight cars for fun and adventure.

A number of us played for Bondy a final time in August of 1967 as members of the North Shore team in the Agganis All-Star Game. The best thing about that experience was being able to meet and play with some of our former opponents from places like Saugus, Newburyport, and Marblehead.

Despite our disappointing finish, 1966 was clearly a resurgent season for Big Blue football. But that period remains my favorite for another reason. It was my only chance to play on football and basketball squads with my younger brother. He was the best teammate that I ever had.

Dickie, Speed, and
the Harpooned Whale

While it was not unusual for groups of players to meet at Phillips Park on summer evenings to work out in preparation for the upcoming season, something more organized and effective occurred during the summer of 1967. Bondy arranged with Barry Gallup to oversee a strength and conditioning program. Barry, who would return to BC in the fall where he was a starting end for the Eagles, was the perfect choice. He ran a structured, formalized program featuring weight training and agility drills that greatly benefited the players.

Bondy also added a new assistant. Former star Ronny Corcoran, who had assisted part-time as a student-coach in 1966 while finishing an education degree at Salem State College, was hired to coach the JVs with Dick Baldacci and also help with the varsity. Corcoran intended to make a career of coaching and could not envision a better start than with Swampscott.

When preseason practice commenced in August, it was time for another Bondy innovation. Rather than attend double sessions at Phillips Park as in past years, the varsity players packed their bags, climbed aboard a bus, and traveled to New Hampshire for a training camp at Saint Anselm College. The "Count" had returned to his alma mater.

According to the *Item*, from the moment the team arrived, it was all "football, food and fun." Yet there were at least a couple of tense moments. Not surprisingly, they involved the team's captain, Bill Adams. The soft-spoken lineman was highly respected. He was also feared. His teammates were not fooled by his normally relaxed, quiet demeanor. They had witnessed, or at least heard of, some of his monumental meltdowns.

One such control malfunction occurred after the first half in New-buryport when he exploded in the locker room. There was also a track meet when Billy was trailing in the shot put competition. On his final attempt, he heaved the shot past his opponent's mark and it seemed that he had clinched first place. However, as cheers arose from teammates and supporters, he struggled unsuccessfully to regain his balance before finally falling across the foul line. As the Swampscott cheers turned to groans, Billy's own tearful disappointment turned to rage when some kids from the other school started laughing. Picking up another of the large metal balls and spinning toward his tormentors, he screamed something to the effect that they would not be laughing for long.

Swampscott's Hall-of-Fame track coach Charley Kimball, who never needed a bullhorn to be heard in crowds, saw the potential donnybrook unfolding from a distance and instantly barked, "BILLY, TAKE A LAP!" Kimball may have been the only person who could have protected the foolish kids from the enraged Adams. Nobody disobeyed Charley Kimball. Weeping and infuriated, and still toting the shot, Billy sprinted around the field. By the time he returned to the site of the altercation, the hecklers had come to their senses and departed.

As the 1967 team dressed for its first practice at Saint Anselm, Adams shouted, "Who has my cleats?" No one responded. He repeated the question several times but nobody answered. Finally, one of the smaller reserve players sheepishly delivered the cleats and scurried away. Billy, terribly frustrated, was the last person to reach the field, a fact that did not escape Bondy's notice.

After practice, the head coach spoke harshly to Adams, telling him that his tardy arrival was unacceptable. Explaining that the team required a captain who set a good example, Bondy stripped him of his captaincy. While Billy was soon restored to the leadership position, the experience left him in a foul mood.

That mood darkened considerably several days later when he made a disturbing discovery while dressing after practice. This time it was money, rather than cleats, that had disappeared. He walked to the locker room door, turned, and faced his teammates. Announcing that five dollars were missing from his wallet, he said that no one could exit the room until the thief confessed and returned the stolen loot.

Had the ultimatum been issued by anyone else some of the players may have ignored it and continued out the door. But it had come from Adams, and no one made the slightest attempt to leave. The clock ticked while the players, showered, dressed and growing hungry, waited silently. Finally, one of Billy's most respected teammates spoke up; trying to reason with the captain that if anyone had taken the money that kid was not going to admit it in front of the entire squad, especially Adams. But he refused to acknowledge the futility of his continued imprisonment of the team.

The stalemate continued until a concerned coach discovered and freed the hostages. If one of the players had taken Billy's cash, the thief never owned up to the crime, no doubt fearing that cruel and unusual punishment would have been administered by the captain.

Billy was never reluctant to address a perceived injustice. As an example, during the preceding track season, he was walking to the team bus when he noticed sophomore Lloyd Benson struggling to lug a bag loaded with shots and other weighty materials. When questioned by Adams, Benson explained that he had been told by two seniors that, as a lowly sophomore, he had to collect, bag, and carry the stuff to and from the locker room and bus. The seniors were both over six feet in height and likely weighed a combined 440 pounds.

Adams was not amused. Telling Benson to drop the bag, he walked to the bus. Billy announced that neither Benson nor anyone else was obligated to carry equipment for other members of the team. Eyeballing the two seniors, he asked whether anyone had a problem with his message. Neither was reckless enough to say a word. There would be no hazing on Billy's watch.

Despite Billy's early frustrations, the Saint Anselm camp proved a smashing success, with Bondy proclaiming it the best thing he had ever done to prepare a team for the upcoming season. He stated that the squad's best assets would be "speed and Dickie Jauron." He could have mentioned a third asset in the formidable Adams. Yet while the team had the two proven standouts, it lacked experience and depth.

The only other players who had logged significant varsity playing time—Dick Polisson, Mark Bogardus, and Ricky Anderson—had done so on defense. The three now vied for positions in the starting backfield. However, Polisson and Anderson would, at times, be moved to other positions.

In the team's first scrimmage against Manchester's Bishop Bradley High School, my brother ran 70 yards for a touchdown, caught a 45-yard pass from quarterback Dan Videtta for a second score, and kicked a 40-yard field goal. He had added some weight and strength during the off-season through participation in Barry Gallup's program, augmented by his personal workout regimen.

The Blue would scrimmage other teams in 1967 and 1968, but with the exception of appearances in the Jamboree, Dick was never allowed to participate. Coach Lynch argued with Bondy, maintaining that Dick needed to experience more contact prior to the regular season. Lynch also knew that Dick wanted to be on the field playing with his teammates. But Bondy was adamant. As he eventually explained to the newspaper, "When you have a valuable commodity like Jauron you just can't gamble with him…. You use him sparingly to protect him from overeager defensive linemen." His response to Coach Lynch was more succinct, "We are not going to lose Saturday's game on a Tuesday."

Coming out of the Saint Anselm camp, there were plenty of new players. Although the boys had little varsity experience, many had played regularly as JVs. Among them were seniors Ed Clippinger, Mike Hoffman, Fran Mayo, Gerry McGettrick, Ben Williams, John Carden, and Bobby Rebholz and juniors Carl Kester, Phil Abram, Andy Rose, Bob Brand, Ray MacCallum, Lloyd Benson, Brian Moore, John Squires, Ralph Floria, and Paul Hayes.

There was also a fast, lean, rugged 185-pound newcomer named Tommy Toner. The football-playing Toner family had just moved in from Lynn. Tom's oldest brother, Ed, had been a standout in high school and college and played for the Boston Patriots. Two other brothers, Paul and Mark, were members of the University of Massachusetts football squad. And Tommy's younger brothers Billy and John would be contributing to future Big Blue teams.

Tommy reported to Coach Lynch with the hope of playing quarterback. He may have had the strongest throwing arm on the team, but Lynch was satisfied with Danny Videtta. After Toner almost knocked out a couple of other backs during tackling drills, Lynch shouted to his counterpart DeFelice, "Frank, I'm sending over another lineman for you." Tommy was not happy, complaining that he had dreamed of being a quarterback. "If I keep you here," said Lynch, "I won't have any healthy backs left by the time the season starts." DeFelice worked the promising junior at both tackle and end. Instead of starring as a quarterback, Toner would become one of the best two-way line players in Big Blue history.

One other boy who was pushing for a starting nod was Alexander "Sandy" Tennant, the only sophomore invited to Saint Anselm. Tennant was a special player. He was one of those kids who seemed born to play the game. When he was very young, Sandy and his sister had moved with their parents from Swampscott to Australia. Several years later his parents divorced and his mother returned with her children and soon remarried.

Sandy was naturally athletic and physically aggressive. As a result of the disruptions related to his time in Australia, and the differences in school systems, he repeated the fourth grade and was older and stronger than most of the other kids in his class. As soon as he was eligible, he joined the Pop Warner team and played well in his first season. He returned the following year and was an intimidating fullback and linebacker. Mike DiPrisco, who eventually became a strong two-year starting Big Blue lineman, recalled that his own Pop Warner career lasted a single day because of Sandy. DiPrisco reported for try-outs and encountered Tennant in a blocking drill. Sandy hit him so hard that Mike wasn't sure his head remained attached to his body. He went home and never returned.

Sandy had the potential to become an outstanding high school player. However, he'd gotten into a number of elementary school scraps and difficulties. He had not worried about such matters until the day that Bondy heard of another incident and sternly warned the youngster that unless his conduct improved he would never play football for SHS. Sandy could not have imagined anything much worse.

Like so many Swampscott kids, Tennant dreamed of the day when he might be able to play for the high school team. He loved everything about Big Blue football. As a seventh grader, he rode his bike to the Burrill Street firehouse on Sunday nights where he sat in the back row of the upstairs meeting room, watching the film of the team's most recent game narrated by Coach Bondelevitch for the Boosters Club. And in 1966, ninth grader Sandy had biked all the way to Winthrop in the rain to watch the Big Blue play.

While Sandy could be a bit mischievous, he focused on controlling himself sufficiently to satisfy Coach Bondelevitch. By the time he showed up as a sophomore at Saint Anselm, he was already an exceptionally aggressive, competitive, and tough player. He thrived on the physical nature of the game, relishing contact.

Coaches and commentators will sometimes refer to players who have a mean streak. Sandy was such a player. There were times when it seemed he was intent on more than just blocking or tackling. He wanted to destroy. At about 5-foot, 10-inches, and 175 pounds, the sophomore was not the biggest kid on the field. Yet, with all his other attributes; he was capable of dominating many older, larger opponents. The coaches recognized that he could immediately help the varsity.

Despite Adams and Jauron and promising newcomers like Toner and Tennant, the lack of varsity experience at most positions led some to believe the squad would struggle to match the 7–2 record of the 1966 squad. When Bondy and Marblehead's Reebenacker were asked by the *Item* for their assessments, they predicted that the conference's best teams would be Danvers, Winthrop, and Newburyport.

Jim Stehlin had been building his program in Newburyport and establishing a pipeline of trained, talented players. The Clippers varsity was riding a 14-game winning streak. Some observers thought that the 1967 squad, fueled by a new crop of players who had been undefeated as JVs, could be almost as good as the prior season's championship team. However, pundits should not have been quick to rule out Swampscott, with a program that had produced three undefeated teams while suffering just one losing season since Bondy's arrival.

After returning from Saint Anselm, the Big Blue struggled in a scrimmage against the Salem Witches. When the team again faced the Witches in the Jamboree, Dick was allowed to play and Swampscott prevailed, with the winning score set up by his 44-yard gallop.

SHS opened against a Gloucester squad that was stronger than the one that had been shut out a year earlier. But the Fishermen still came out on the short end, 25–16. Swampscott's seniors led the way, with Bogardus running for one touchdown and returning an interception for a second. Another key play occurred with 20 seconds left in the half when Videtta connected with Ricky Anderson near midfield and he went the distance.

Junior Andy Rose was credited with a strong defensive game. Andy had hit some rough bumps on his way to becoming a starter. Growing up just a stone's throw from Stanley School, he had followed the SHS teams, typically walking to the games at Blocksidge Field and thereafter joining his friends for touch football. Like so many Swampscott youngsters, young Andy had dreamed of becoming an elite Big Blue player, making miraculous catches and racing past defenders to score game-winning touchdowns.

But kids in the less affluent areas of town were not impressed by Rose and his classmates. The boys at Hadley and Machon viewed their counterparts from the east side as privileged, soft, and spoiled. This opinion was reinforced after Andy and his buddies met some Hadley-schoolers in a tackle football game. The Stanley kids arrived with helmets, pads, and matching jerseys, accompanied by supporting cheerleaders. By contrast, the ragtag Hadley boys wore old jeans, T-shirts, or whatever other clothing they managed to locate that day. Yet once the game started the Stanley girls had nothing to cheer about because the Hadley kids beat up on Andy and his friends, most of whom played like it was touch football.

As a JV sophomore receiver, Andy enjoyed some success as the favorite target of quarterback Fran Sheehan. Fran, a slightly built, long-haired kid, had been told by Coach Lynch that he would never amount to anything unless he cut his hair and cleaned up his appearance. While he did not go on to quarterback the varsity, he did amount to something as the original bass player for *Boston*, one of the era's most spectacular rock bands. Today Sheehan laughs about the coach's faulty prediction, while Lynch is thankful that he was not a guidance counselor.

Andy played well enough on the JVs that he was told he would dress with the varsity for the big Newburyport game. Unfortunately, prior to that game, he sustained a brutal injury when his ankle and nose were both broken during a JV contest. There would be no more football for Rose in 1966.

During the following summer, Andy participated in Gallup's program and then reported to the Saint Anselm camp. After several days of practice, he was moved from end to center. He was not happy. Centers did not catch passes and score touchdowns. Centers were stuck in the middle of the line and had to block opponents—usually large opponents—on virtually every play.

Andy did not want to block opposing players; he wanted to run past them and make highlight film catches. Instead, he was laboring with the other linemen under the less-than-gentle ministrations of Coach DeFelice. He struggled at center, playing with the second or third teams. His varsity career was not following the script that he had written in his mind. Then, a few days after the team returned to Swampscott things got worse.

Every player except Andy was using the tan, generic rubber mouth guards that were distributed when the boys reported to camp. But Andy had arrived with a black, custom-designed, form-fitted mouthpiece. When Bondy first noticed, he made a disapproving comment but otherwise left the matter alone. Insisting that he would not tolerate prima donnas, Bondy occasionally decided that a boy needed to be taken down a few pegs. It seems likely that Andy unknowingly did something to antagonize the coach beyond wearing the customized mouth guard. Perhaps Stan believed that Andy was pouting or resentful about having been moved to the offensive line.

In any case, several days after the return from Saint Anselm, Bondy brought practice to a sudden halt. Calling out Rose, he blasted the kid for thinking himself too special. "Who the hell do you think you are?" he barked. "Get off this field and don't come back." His teammates stood, silently watching, as Andy walked past them, off the field, down the track, and into the Fieldhouse. He changed quickly, left the locker room, and trudged homeward in a kind of stupor. He could not believe that his football career was over almost before it had started.

As he shuffled along a blue station wagon pulled up. "Get in," growled Bondy. Andy cannot recall what the Big Blue boss said as he drove the crestfallen junior home. Chances are the comments revolved around things like vanity, team, and commitment. But by the time Andy exited the car he knew that he had another chance.

On the following day when he reported to practice, Andy was moved to offensive tackle and defensive end. He finally understood that if he was going to live his dream of playing for the Big Blue, he would have to do so by blocking and tackling rather than catching passes and scoring touchdowns. Accepting this reality, he focused on becoming the best lineman that he could be. He was surprised to discover that he enjoyed the physical nature of line play. Naturally athletic, he was particularly quick off the mark.

By opening day, Rose had secured starting positions as an offensive tackle and defensive end. One of the things that impressed Coach DeFelice was Andy's performance in drills against Billy Adams. Frank was hard on all of the linemen, but particularly tough on Adams, recognizing that he had almost unlimited potential. Frank knew how to push all the buttons to drive the big senior to maximum effort. One of those buttons was Andy Rose.

For example, the line coach would have Rose and Adams team up to drive the blocking sled. He would then frequently yell at Adams, "Rose is turning you!" The coach's message, whether true or not, was that Andy was driving harder than was Adams. This typically motivated Adams to maximize his effort which in turn made things even tougher for Rose.

Then there were the one-on-one blocking drills in what the players called "the pit." This was probably Frank's favorite part of practice. He would call out two players while the other linemen looked on. The boys took opposing stances, with DeFelice typically crouching nearby. On Frank's signal, they would drive into one another and try to win the line-of-scrimmage battle, with the coach typically shouting exhortations. While Adams was unquestionably the best lineman on the squad, Andy managed to get the better of him several times in the pit one day. DeFelice went berserk, screaming at Adams that he was losing to the smaller junior. Frank continued to relentlessly berate Billy before having the two square off one last time. An enraged Adams exploded on poor Rose, driving him out of the circle and across the field, and dumping him into the bushes. That was the thanks Andy received for his strong performance. Yet the junior was on his way to becoming an outstanding high school player.

In its second game of the season, the Blue hosted Woburn. Ricky Anderson was moved to end and his place in the backfield was taken by 170-pound junior Phil Abram, a fine athlete who had been the lead halfback on the ninth-grade team quarterbacked by my brother. Now he joined Dick in the starting varsity backfield. Bondy also announced the promotion of two JVs. End/linebacker David Caras and back Richie Conigliaro, Billy's younger brother, joined fellow sophomore Tennant on the varsity.

The *Item's* report on the Woburn contest began:

Swampscott's star halfback, Dick Jauron, completely demoralized Woburn Saturday in leading the Big Blue to a 40–24 victory over the Tanners at Blocksidge Field in Swampscott. The 6–1, 182-pound junior scored four touchdowns and kicked four extra points while amassing a total offense of 256 yards. Jauron struck twice in each half as he averaged 16 yards every time he got his hands on the ball.

Phil Abram was solid in his first offensive start, carrying five times for 53 yards. He also picked off a Woburn pass. Caras joined Tennant at linebacker on defense and both sophomores played well, as did linemen Adams and Rose.

In the third game, Swampscott faced Danvers, a team that Bondy and Reebenacker had expected to contend for the conference title. The Blue dominated, winning 28–0 while rolling up 380 total yards of offense. Celebrating his seventeenth birthday, Dick scored 16 points, which included two touchdowns and four placements. Bogardus also scored twice, while he, Tennant, and Caras were major factors in derailing the Danvers running game. Videtta, Abram, Anderson, and John Squires contributed with big plays.

Having soundly defeated each of its first three conference opponents, the Blue prepared to host 2–1 Winthrop. The Vikings had beaten Amesbury and Danvers before falling to Newburyport, winners of 16 straight. They had held the Clippers scoreless for three quarters before giving up two touchdowns in the fourth. Concern about the Winthrop game and the season skyrocketed early in the week when Billy Adams went down hard in practice and rolled in agony while clutching his leg. It seemed that the captain had sustained a serious injury. The field fell silent and the mood turned somber. Coaches and players alike recognized that a healthy Adams was essential to their continued success.

Suddenly the silence was broken by a loud, melodramatic bellow from the big man atop the tower. There was only one person who thought that it was a good moment for some levity. "Oh no, our great white whale has been harpooned!" moaned Bondy. "Well, help him off the field and let's get back to work." The head coach's seemingly insensitive, but amusing, histrionics broke the spell. With the mood lightened, the players resumed practice. Bondy continued with a few extra "harpooned whale" metaphors during the remainder of the session. The implied message was clear. Billy Adams was their leader and best lineman, but if he was hurt the boys needed to regroup and work harder to find a way to win. Yet Bondy's efforts could not completely erase a plain truth. Winning a championship without Adams would be almost impossible.

Billy's injury was diagnosed as a severe ankle sprain. While the Winthrop game was scheduled for Sunday, which allowed for an extra day of healing, it seemed unlikely that he would be able to play. He did not set foot on the practice field again that week and was still limping on game day. He was allowed to suit up, but as he was putting on his equipment Bondy quietly informed him that he would not be seeing any action. Billy felt crushed that he could not lead the team in a crucial game.

After inspiring the boys with typical pregame exhortations, Bondy suddenly shouted, "Billy Adams, what do you want to tell the team?" The coach was expecting his captain to deliver a fiery, confident message. There was an air of tense anticipation as the big tackle, who was sitting in a far corner of the room, slowly rose to his feet. For a moment Billy said nothing. He then lowered his head, started to sob, and muttered, "Gee, I hope we can win." While great coaches know how to deliver inspirational messages, great players, especially adolescents, often do not. Stan had to spend some additional time regenerating confidence and excitement before sending the boys onto the field.

The team managed a touchdown in the early minutes on a long Videtta to Jauron pass play. Winthrop responded with a touchdown drive of its own. The Vikings' two-point conversion attempt failed, and the Blue clung to a 7–6 lead. However, the defensive line continued to yield yardage to Winthrop's ground attack, and it seemed inevitable that the visitors would score again before the half ended. In an attempt to bolster the defense, Bondy changed his mind and inserted Adams with a couple of minutes remaining in the half. Although hampered by lack of mobility, Billy made some plays. The teams left the field with Swampscott still ahead.

When the second half commenced, Captain Adams was back on the field. Though slowed by the damaged ankle, he helped disrupt Winthrop's run game. On a play when he was unable to break loose from a double team, he reached with one arm and managed to drag down the ball carrier. The defense stiffened, seemingly galvanized by Billy's presence. Winthrop had rushed for almost 100 yards during the first half. But with Billy, the "harpooned whale," back in the defensive line for the entire second half the visitors managed only 34.

With its ground game stymied, Winthrop took to the air and paid a price as both Jauron and Abram intercepted. While Winthrop's tough defense was also making things difficult for Swampscott, the Blue finally put together a scoring drive after recovering a fumble at the Vikings 42. The player making the recovery was Adams, the team's hobbled leader. Dick ultimately ran the ball in from the six. Winthrop tried to strike back through the air and Abram picked off his second pass. He followed that play with a beautiful 41-yard touchdown run. SHS had its fourth consecutive win, 20–6.

As midseason approached, the Big Blue remained unbeaten at 4–0 and had taken down two of the three teams that Bondy and Reebenacker had expected would be top conference contenders. The third squad, Newburyport, would be visiting later in November. The Port City team continued to roll during its first four games of 1967, unbeaten, untied, and un-scored upon.

Bondy teased Adams mercilessly after the Winthrop game; pointing out that his weeping expression of *hope* had not exactly energized the team. It seemed unlikely that the coach would risk asking his captain to deliver another pregame "pep talk." But there was no need for a pep talk from Bondy, Billy, or anyone else prior to the next game at winless Amesbury. The Blue clobbered the Carriagemakers, 47–7. The defense held the Indians to a total of 9 yards rushing. Amesbury, the team that had amassed 31 straight wins before Bondy's 1953 club ended the streak, had now suffered its twenty-second consecutive loss.

Despite the one-sided win, John "Squirrel" Squires paid the price for a couple of mistakes. John was a reasonably tall, fairly thin kid who had been one of five sophomores to dress with the varsity in 1966. Now a junior, he had nailed down starting spots at end and cornerback. However, during the Amesbury game, he was beaten badly twice by an Indians receiver. While neither play resulted in a completion, let alone a touchdown, Squires found himself benched, replaced by the sophomore Caras.

John Squires had long dreamed of playing for the Big Blue. His father Jack, a former athlete who spent considerable time refereeing sports as an adult, had moved his family into town from Revere in 1953. One of the factors that Jack Squires considered in choosing Swampscott was the winning reputation of the town's new athletic director/coach, Stan Bondelevitch.

Jack took his son to the 1958 Thanksgiving game at Blocksidge Field, and they watched George Blais and company roll over the Magicians. After the game, John told his dad that when he got older he wanted to play football for the Big Blue. Jack Squires could not have been happier. Soon thereafter, when young John was a third grader at Saint John's, Bondy sought him out and gave him a football, predicting that he would someday be one of the Big Blue's great quarterbacks. He also told him that he could serve as a waterboy during the following season.

John was a waterboy during the Barry Gallup era and loved it. A good athlete, he played youth football, basketball, and baseball. Now, in 1967, he was on his way to being a Big Blue starter in all three sports (he had started for the baseball team as a sophomore). Knowing that Squires would struggle with the news that he was being replaced by Caras, Bondy told him that his leadership was needed on special teams and that Squirrel would be serving as the captain of those units. That helped. During the rest of the season, John stood out on special teams, particularly as an aggressive downfield tackler on the kickoff squad. One year later he would be playing linebacker for the 1968 squad.

Winless Saugus was the next opponent for the 1967 Big Blue. With practically all of his 1966 starters gone, Walter Sheridan had thought it a good time to retire, leaving new coach Paul Maguire with mostly young, untested boys who were struggling to play well. While Bondy was predictably cautious, preaching against overconfidence, the Blue easily prevailed 28–0.

Saugus had not presented a real threat, but the next opponent did. The Classical Rams had made it no secret that, other than Thanksgiving foe Lynn English, SHS was their biggest rival. With the exception of the 1966 game in which Swampscott had trounced Classical, every contest between the teams since Bondy's arrival had been close. The Blue had lost as many as it had won, with an overall series record of 3–3. Described by Bondy as a fine football team, the 1967 Rams had won four straight before falling in successive weeks to Newburyport and Melrose, both undefeated.

The Rams' strength was up-front, where they were bigger and more experienced than Swampscott, a fact acknowledged by Coach Moriarty. However, he qualified his statement, mentioning that aside from Adams his line should have the advantage. But Classical had more than just a strong front line. Junior Peter Mazareas had already picked off five passes from his middle linebacker position. Quick, with good reflexes and decent size, Mazareas excelled in basketball as well as football. His classmate, quarterback/safety Jimmy Silvonic, Joe's younger brother, was speedy and an outstanding all-around player. In short, Classical matched up well against the Blue.

Of course, Swampscott had a few strong players of its own. In his November 1, 1967, column, Red Hoffman wrote:

> When you think of post-World War II great ones, the mind skips from Harry Agganis to Tippy Johnson to Pete Pedro to Dick Jauron. That's how good this lad is.

In Lynn, the late Harry Agganis, "the Golden Greek," was idolized as something close to a sports god. Some must have considered it almost sacrilegious to suggest that another local high school player, let alone a junior from little Swampscott, could come close to Agganis in talent or performance. But while praising my brother, Hoffman made clear that the game would see a clash of two very talented squads.

The Rams were motivated. Swampscott had spoiled Classical's undefeated season in 1962 and now the Rams could return the favor. Moreover, there was the matter of trying to avenge the 1966 humiliation. Moriarty told the *Item:*

> Six of the boys in our starting lineup Saturday were starters in last year's loss to Swampscott and they haven't forgotten the score. Actually, with Swampscott being so close to Lynn it makes a natural rivalry and their being undefeated adds a bit more incentive to the game.

Bondy always found opportunities for hyperbole in upcoming battles with schools from the neighboring city. He loved to moan about his little boys having to face the massive urban brutes and enjoyed coming up with new ways to describe Lynn's players and fans. Always somewhat tongue-in-cheek; he'd lay it on thick with embellished descriptions of those "tough thugs" from the hard-scrabble city, offering warnings like the following:

> Those Classical players have been shaving for years, and they not only drive to the games, they bring their wives and children with them! When you run through that tunnel at Manning Bowl make sure you have your helmets on because they'll be throwing rocks and spitting on you! They'll treat it like a street fight but we need to focus on playing good football. They'll be yelling that the baby blues are soft, little Jews!

Stan maintained a strong relationship with leaders of Swampscott's Jewish community, likely triggered by both an interest in building support for his program and a genuine respect and affinity for the Jewish people. While Stan was officially Catholic, he suspected that he may have been part Jewish, recalling that his parents had understood and spoken some Yiddish. He was capable of using stereotypes but applied them to his players in a positive and/or humorous way. There were a number of Jewish kids on every roster who contributed to the Big Blue's football success. Bondy liked to boast about all of his "smart Jewish players".

Stan's overblown blusterings about the terrors that waited in Lynn were designed to both motivate and amuse. But many of his top players, including Bill Adams, Dick Jauron, Tom Toner, and Carl Kester, had moved into Swampscott from Lynn. They knew that although Lynn kids were tough, they and their fans were typically no more nasty or bigoted than players and fans in other towns. Big Blue players rarely, if ever, heard anti-Semitic comments from opponents or opposing fans.

The Rams were sky-high when the teams met at Manning Bowl and gave SHS all that it could handle in a hard-fought battle. As advertised, their linemen were big and good. According to Bondy, they controlled the game. But Swampscott managed a score early in the second quarter, with the big play a Videtta to Abram pass covering 41 yards. Dick's PAT kick made it 7–0. Both teams threatened several other times, but there was no more scoring until seven and a half minutes remained in the contest when the Rams crossed the Swampscott goal line. After the touchdown, Coach Moriarty spoke with Jim Silvonic on the sideline. The Rams did not have a reliable kicker and were considering the play that would give them the best chance for a two-point conversion and the lead.

As their offensive players then broke the huddle and approached the line of scrimmage one of them looked up and sarcastically shouted "Baby Blues!" Billy Adams somehow found the taunt extremely inflammatory and reacted with a violent outburst. Gesticulating wildly, he screamed at his teammates, "Did you hear that? Are we going to take that? Did you hear what he said?" Adams seemed on the verge of single-handedly attacking and destroying the offending Rams player before the ball was snapped.

Participants on both sides were not sure what to do. The other SHS players were shocked by their captain's volcanic reaction to what seemed a rather mild insult. On the other side, things came to a halt. The Rams stared at the large, seemingly maniacal Swampscott tackle and then turned toward each other, uncertain how to proceed. Finally, one of them signaled for time-out and they retreated to a huddle.

When Adams cooled down, the Rams again broke their huddle and ran their play. Silvonic dropped back to pass, but a strong rush led by defensive end Gerry McGettrick forced him to release the ball quickly and it sailed out of the end zone. They were not able to challenge again and the game ended with the undefeated visitors in possession of the ball on Classical's 17-yard line.

Dick finished the day with just one point, but it was the point that proved the difference. Coach Moriarty, explaining the decision to try for a two-point conversion, said: "We didn't have any Dick Jauron to kick it for us...." While it had been the only time all season that Dick failed to score a touchdown, Bondy singled him out, saying, "People sometimes overlook the fact that this boy plays both ways and that he does a tremendous job both offensively and defensively.... We never would have won it without Jauron."

Another player that they needed for the victory was Adams. The coaches had played a guessing game on defense, strategically positioning him where he could have the most impact. He might line up at tackle on one down, linebacker on the next, and then move to end or middle guard. His shifting defensive presence had been a key factor in Swampscott's ability to slow the Classical attack.

No one recalled any further taunts or comments following Billy's outburst. That is just as well. The offending Rams player was center Dave Dempsey. His sister eventually became Mrs. William Adams. It's a safe bet that the term "baby blues" is not heard when Bill and his brother-in-law get together at family gatherings.

Following the game, a brief story about my brother appeared in the *Item*. For some reason, Dick was delayed leaving the Fieldhouse after the team returned from Lynn, and only he and building manager Vinny Easterbrooks remained. Apparently, Vinny had to run an errand and asked Dick to lock the outside door when he eventually also exited the building. When Vinny returned sometime later he discovered that all of the towels had been picked up and the floor swept.

Bondy could not resist telling the story to the *Item's* Ed Cahill who, of course, printed it. Titling the piece, "Big Blue Football Star Real All-Around Boy," he led with the line, "Everybody has heard about the football star who could do everything but clean out the locker room. Swampscott High has come up with one who can do even that." Dick was a bit embarrassed by the whole thing. Vinny Easterbrooks was a great guy, well-liked by all of the players. In Dick's view, helping Vinny by cleaning up after yourself and your teammates was hardly newsworthy. It was common courtesy and any number of players would have done the same. Nonetheless, the story had "legs" and became part of Big Blue lore.

On November 7, 1967, the *Item* wrote about the upcoming battle between the Big Blue and Clippers football teams. Both were unbeaten, although the Clippers had just been tied by Marblehead. Newburyport was 6–0–1 and riding a 20-game unbeaten streak, the longest in the state. Meanwhile, Swampscott owned a perfect 7–0 record and needed to beat the Clippers if it was going to reach its goal of an undefeated, championship season.

The newspaper also published another article about Swampscott athletics on that date. It focused on Mrs. Flora McLearn, who had made winning a tradition for Swampscott girls well before Bondy's arrival. After 46 years she was retiring. As the school's longtime girls' gym teacher, field hockey coach, basketball coach, softball coach, and cheerleading and drill team director, she had taught and coached hundreds of girls and then had taught and coached hundreds of their daughters. And they had shared a common experience, winning all, or almost all, of their games.

The Floradora Girls, as they were known, consistently performed at an extremely high level. They had no choice. She yelled at her field hockey players to "Play It!" until the ball either rolled well out of bounds or into the net. She drilled and pushed the girls relentlessly, shouting, "Run until your lungs hurt!" The girls were so well coached and skilled that they typically routed all local teams.

Flora searched far and wide for more competitive opponents. At times, they traveled hours by bus to distant locations in search of stronger teams that might present more of a challenge. Occasionally, they defeated college squads. As of her announced retirement, Flora's basketball teams had lost only once in 11 years. Her field hockey team had recently suffered its first loss in several years, which ended the state's longest winning streak. Mrs. McLearn and her husband retired to Florida, where she planned to play golf every day. □

The Newburyport tilt was the latest "biggest game ever" for Swampscott. Prior to the Clippers' game against Marblehead, Noel Reebenacker proclaimed them "the best schoolboy football team in the state." Up to that point, Newburyport had easily cut through all opposition and seemed on course to duplicate the remarkable achievements of the 1966 champions. Marblehead, however, battled the Port City team to a draw that may have revealed more about the Headers' strength than Newburyport's weakness. The Clippers still held the state's longest unbeaten streak.

My brother and his classmates had lost one game as freshmen—to Newburyport. Then, when he was the only sophomore starter on our 7–0 senior-laden squad, the Clippers had easily beaten us. Dick hated losing those games but recognized that Newburyport had been the better team. In his view, if SHS wanted to experience a different result in 1967, the returning players needed to improve. He and most of his teammates dedicated themselves to doing just that, particularly during the summer strength and conditioning program and at the Saint Anselm camp. Some augmented those efforts with individual workouts. As a result, they had grown bigger and stronger and increased their speed and agility. The game would test those sacrifices.

Newburyport's big gun was senior Eddie O'Bara. "Ed is the finest running back I've had the privilege of coaching," said Coach Stehlin. O'Bara could burn opponents by running, receiving, passing, kicking, and great defensive play. And the Clippers had other backfield weapons. The other halfback, Pat Ladd, was a strong runner and great complement to O'Bara. While not Larry Russell, quarterback Mike Sullivan was a highly capable field general and could hurt defenses with his arm and his legs. Newburyport's linemen were solid and, on average, about 10 pounds heavier than Swampscott's.

Although the Big Blue remained unbeaten, after further review of the low-scoring, razor-thin win over Classical, Bondy and his staff decided to make some line-up adjustments. The changes included switching Polisson to end and middle guard, with Tennant taking his place at fullback, inserting John Carden at left end, and moving Ray MacCallum from middle guard to tackle.

The excitement for the upcoming game reached a fever-pitch. At SHS, instead of saying "hi," students greeted one another with "Beat Newburyport!" Some 25 buses would be transporting Clippers fans to Blocksidge Field. On game day, the size of the crowd exceeded expectations. The ticket booth closed one hour before kickoff. Large numbers of disappointed fans were turned away. There was simply no more room for sitting or standing. The refreshment stand sold out its supply of hot dogs well before the game started. Of the many overflow, energized crowds that filled Blocksidge Field during the Bondelevitch era, this may have been the largest.

The visitors were the first to threaten, advancing to the Blue 17 in the opening quarter before being stopped. Shortly thereafter, Swampscott struck when Videtta connected with Polisson at the visitors' 35 and, with the help of a great block by Abram, the senior took it all the way. The conversion kick gave SHS a 7–0 lead. The Clippers responded with a long drive capped by O'Bara, who then ran for the two-point conversion and an 8–7 lead. The Blue quickly took it back. On the offense's second play following the kickoff, Phil Abram galloped 57 yards to the Clippers' 1-yard line. Videtta snuck it in for the score, but Dick's conversion attempt was wide right.

After forcing the Clippers to punt, the Blue took over on the 20 and moved methodically for its third touchdown, covering 80 yards in eight plays. After the conversion kick, the score was Big Blue 20, Clippers 8. Newburyport again responded, this time going 57 yards, with Ladd scoring from two yards out and O'Bara kicking the extra point. Later, after Tommy Toner recovered a Clipper fumble on the SHS 41-yard line with just seconds remaining on the clock, it seemed that the teams would be heading to their locker rooms with Swampscott ahead, 20–15.

The next play remains etched in the minds of many who witnessed it. Videtta dropped back and threw a long, high pass down the middle of the field to Jauron, who had to leap up and try to make the catch near the 1-yard line. As described by the *Item*, "Dick stole it from the grasp of three Newburyport defenders. Before he hit the turf he was signaling for a timeout and the clock stopped with four seconds left." On the next play, Dick ran it in for the touchdown as time expired. Videtta connected with Polisson for the two-point conversion and the team left the field with more breathing room, leading 28–15.

The boys had a couple of third quarter opportunities to widen that lead. At one point, they advanced to the Clippers 19 but were stopped there, and Dick's field goal attempt deflected off the crossbar. They had another chance when Ray MacCallum recovered a fumble on the Clippers' 28 and the offense marched to the 13 before turning it over on downs.

Would those failures to score eventually haunt the Big Blue? It seemed possible after a good Clippers punt return set up O'Bara's 19-yard touchdown jaunt. But Tommy Toner broke through to block O'Bara's extra-point kick. Swampscott led, 28–21, with less than six minutes remaining.

The Clippers got the ball back with four minutes left and launched another impressive touchdown drive, covering 65 yards in 11 plays. They trailed by just one point, 28–27. With little time left it was unlikely that they would have another chance to score. No doubt expecting that SHS would be keying on O'Bara, they turned instead to Ladd for the crucial two-point conversion try, running him wide on a quick pitch. Ladd barely escaped Toner and Tennant who both broke into the backfield. But he was then brought down by linebacker Fran Mayo and cornerback John Carden just short of the goal line.

However, the game was not over. The Clippers recovered an onside kick near midfield and had one final chance. That evaporated when David Caras intercepted a pass and the Big Blue ran out the clock. It had been one more memorable game at Blocksidge Field.

Coach Stehlin was philosophical and gracious, telling the press:

I've always figured that if we lost I'd like it to be to a team with class.… Swampscott is a fine team and deserved to win today … we're not going to cry at all.… Jauron's catch was the key play.…

Stehlin visited the SHS locker room to congratulate the players, a classy move that showed his respect for Bondy and his team.

The Blue offense finished with 321 total yards, compared to 245 for the Clippers. O'Bara scored 15 of his team's 27 points, while Jauron scored 14 of his team's 28. While Stehlin cited Dick's acrobatic catch as the back-breaker, the game was full of key plays. The touchdown in the last seconds of the first half could not have happened if the defense, led by Toner, had not come up with the fumble recovery, and it may not have mattered if Videtta and Polisson had not connected for the PATs, or Toner had not blocked O'Bara's extra-point kick, or Mayo and Carden had not been able to stop Ladd's late-game conversion attempt. It had been a total team effort.

In retrospect, the line-up changes looked brilliant. As an end, Polisson teamed with Videtta for a touchdown and conversion. MacCallum was in on a number of key stops and recovered a Clippers fumble. Carden contributed to the all-important defensive stop at the goal line. The Clippers gave up more points to Swampscott than they had given up in the previous seven games combined. Ironically, in the 1966 contest, we had given up more points to the Clippers than we had in our previous seven games combined.

For the fifth time, Stan Bondelevitch took an undefeated team into the Thanksgiving Day contest with Marblehead. On all but one of the past occasions his team won. Winning this time would not be easy. The Headers, like the Big Blue, were unbeaten in the conference. Their only loss had been to Class A Salem. At the beginning of the season, Bondy and Reebenacker had predicted that Danvers, Winthrop, and Newburyport would be the conference's best teams. Now the two coaches were a combined 5–0–1 against those three opponents.

Tootie Cahoon was gone but Bobby Blood remained. He had starred in the Magician's victories over Swampscott in 1965 and 1966, and the Headers were hoping that he would lead them to a third consecutive Thanksgiving Day win in his final high school game. In an attempt to take full advantage of Blood's overall athleticism, his coach had been playing him, at least part of the time, at quarterback. Swampscott went into the game with one roster change. Bobby Rebholz, a hard-working senior back, made his first offensive start.

As in 1966, the Headers scored first, this time off Blood's 50-yard run. The two-point conversion attempt failed. They narrowly missed increasing that lead after driving to the 1-yard line before fumbling. Tom Toner, who was making a habit of such plays, recovered near the goal line and the offense then moved the ball out of the danger zone.

As in 1966 Swampscott next put up 21 unanswered points. The first score came on Dick's 29-yard touchdown run. His conversion kick was true and SHS led 7–6. Then, as it had against Newburyport, the Blue grabbed another touchdown just before the end of the half. This time the score was set up by Dick's 63-yard sprint to the Headers three. On the next play, he ran to the 1, and then, with only 13 seconds left, carried in for the score. Videtta threw to Abram for the two-point conversion and the Big Blue took a 15–6 lead into the locker room, which mirrored the halftime score of the 1966 Thanksgiving game.

At the beginning of the second half, Swampscott quickly scored its third touchdown with Rebholz running it in. The conversion attempt failed and the Blue led 21–6, as it had in the third quarter of the 1966 game. At this point, there was an eerie sense of déjà vu. According to the 1966 script, Marblehead would next cut the lead to 21–14. But Swampscott re-wrote the script, marching 80 yards to the Headers' 10-yard line, where Dick kicked a 27-yard field goal, boosting the lead to 24–6, which was the final score.

Bobby Blood, one of Marblehead's all-time greats, played a tremendous final game for the Magicians, but the better team won. The Blue offense rushed for 295 yards, while the Headers managed 167. Bobby Rebholz played well, rushing for 75 yards and a touchdown. Dick accounted for 172 of Swampscott's rushing yards, while scoring two touchdowns, and kicking a point-after and field goal.

The 1967 team exceeded expectations. While Adams and Jauron were great players, they had been the only returning starters. There were many reasons for the team's success. Danny Videtta was an effective field general and reliable protector of the football. Over the course of nine games, he did not throw an interception until the third quarter of the season's finale.

Boys with no varsity experience, like Carl Kester, Andy Rose, and Phil Abram, capably filled voids left by the departed seniors. Tommy Toner, the new kid from Lynn, became a disruptive defensive force, and sophomores Tennant and Caras made major contributions to the team's success. Collectively, these players and a number of others combined with the handful of seasoned veterans to lead SHS to another championship. The team's success was a testament to the boys themselves and to a program that prepared them to play well at the varsity level.

This was Bondy's fourth Swampscott team to finish undefeated and untied. Three of the boys on the 1967 squad, Adams, Jauron, and Toner, would eventually become professionals, each playing for a number of seasons in the NFL. Few, if any, other small public high schools could ever boast of such a phenomenon.

Bill Adams and Dick Jauron were named to various All-Star teams, and Dick was also named a first team high school All-American. Yale-bound Richard Polisson became the fifth of Bondy's players to win the coveted Thom McAn Shoe Award. Adams deservedly finished his high school football career by leading his team to a championship. He was not simply a great player; he was a fine leader and teammate.

Billy's high school football days had ended, but the basketball season loomed. As a center, he was a strong defensive player and rebounder. He also continued to experience the occasional control malfunction. During one game, some students from the competing school were heckling the

Big Blue players. Finally, Billy bolted into the stands with the intention of silencing the group. Coach Lynch quickly followed, ordering Adams back to the bench. But the coach then shouted a warning that if the taunting continued he would give Adams the green light. It stopped.

The most widely repeated of all Adams stories involved his exit from Swampscott's biggest basketball game, not only of the season but of its entire history. The team was competing for the Eastern Massachusetts Class B championship in the old Boston Garden, home of the Celtics. Billy, who had played a strong game, collected his fifth foul and was forced to take a seat on the bench. He was inconsolable, believing that he had let down his teammates at a crucial time, costing them the state title. As he left the court in despair he ripped off his eyeglasses and fired them high into the upper balcony of the ancient arena.

He sat on the bench in tears, head in hands, as the game wound down to its dramatic conclusion. But Adams had not cost his team the championship; he had played an essential role in helping to achieve it. While Dick Jauron sank the winning basket in overtime, Coach Lynch named Adams the team's MVP, saying that without Billy's' tenacious defense and rebounding the boys would not have reached, let alone won, the final game.

After starring as a lineman for Holy Cross, where he also served as team captain, Bill Adams played a number of years with the Buffalo Bills. Following his NFL retirement, he returned to the North Shore and, after working briefly as an assistant for Stan Bondelevitch, served for a long time as the highly respected and successful head football and basketball coach and athletic director at Lynnfield High School. Away from the playing field, he remains the same soft-spoken, shy fellow that he was as an SHS student. While Bill Adams was a somewhat socially awkward teenager, prone to occasional emotional meltdowns, he is most fondly remembered in Swampscott as the fierce competitor who helped lead the Big Blue to football and basketball championships.

Juggernaut

S wampscott put together back-to-back undefeated seasons in 1957 and 1958. Could it happen again a decade later? While the incomparable Adams was gone, along with Thom McAn Shoe winner Polisson, quarterback Videtta, and some other capable players, the 1968 team was loaded. As reported by the *Item*, the Big Blue had "experience, depth and speed."

Phil Abram, a superior athlete, returned to the offensive and defensive backfields. Tom Toner, Andy Rose, and Carl Kester, seasoned starters, remained front-line stalwarts. Linebacker/end Bobby Brand, linebacker/receiver John Squires and linemen Lloyd Benson, Ray MacCallum and Ralph Floria were five more experienced seniors. Juniors Sandy Tennant and David Caras returned in prominent defensive roles and both would be seeing plenty of action on offense.

A sturdy 200-pound sophomore named Jim Carone impressed the coaches, nailing down the starting fullback slot. Peter Beatrice, having performed well as the 1967 JV quarterback, became the varsity signal caller. At 6-foot, 1-inch, and 190 pounds, the junior had size, a strong arm and a good head on his shoulders. He could also run when necessary. Lastly, the Big Blue had a special star in its captain, Dick Jauron.

This talented, veteran-heavy club benefited from another off-season of structured strength and conditioning work-outs with Barry Gallup. The players who reported for preseason camp at Saint Anselm in 1968 were a confident bunch. In addition to their perfect 1967 football campaign, a number of them, including Jauron, Abram, Tennant, Caras, Brand, Squires, and MacCallum, had played on the state championship basketball team.

One addition was made to the coaching staff. William Parsons, an SHS biology teacher with considerable coaching experience, signed on with the football program where he spent most of his time working with the JVs. Sadly, Mr. Parsons only coached with the Big Blue for two years before passing away from illness following the 1969 season.

Bondy generated an early season sports page headline by announcing that the players, not the coaches, would select the starting line-up for the Jamboree. He said that he disagreed with those who feared the election would be a popularity contest. In reality, Bondy risked little in allowing the players to elect the starters. He could reasonably assume that they would choose either the boy currently holding the position or a strong challenger. In any case, regardless of the election results, he and his assistants would determine the starters for the first official game.

The election was a clever way of involving the players while gaining favorable publicity. His decision may have been influenced in part by recognition that, with the extreme unpopularity of the Vietnam War and on-going cultural changes, there was a growing anti-establishment, anti-authority sentiment among many young people. Stan could be seen as a coach willing to surrender some of that authority, trusting that the boys were mature enough to handle the responsibility.

The team performed well in several preseason scrimmages against strong opponents, even with Dick not participating. But there was growing interest in knowing whether he would play against Lynn English in the Jamboree, something he wanted to do. Despite Bondy's reservations, the coach announced that Dick would play, which came as good news not only for fans and media representatives but also for the Jamboree's organizer, Bondy's friend Elmo Benedetto.

Dick scored all the points in a 14–0 win, running 13 and 18 yards for touchdowns and kicking the PAT's. Red Hoffman's column on the Jamboree opened with, "Dick Jauron is terrific", and thereafter repeated the statement several times. He also returned to the Agganis comparison, asserting, "Jauron is the nearest thing to Harry since Harry" while raving about Dick's blocking, kicking, and defense.

What caused such effusive praise? Although he broke through many tackles, at six feet and about 180 solid pounds, Dick had decent, but not extraordinary, size and power. He was, however, an outstanding all-around athlete and competitor with great balance and reflexes. He was also as fast as, or faster than, virtually any other player on the field. And he had excellent football skills, including the ability to block, tackle, catch, and kick accurately. All of that surely mattered, but what truly stood out, putting him into the elite, rarely seen category, was an uncanny ability to see and avoid tacklers and break into the open. He made opponents miss. He did it instinctively, using sudden, lightning-quick, perfectly timed changes in speed and direction, and explosive acceleration.

However, the team's Jamboree performance confirmed that it had much more than its star halfback. English, a highly rated team going into the event, was held to a total of just 19 yards rushing. Strong, experienced defensive players like Rose, Abram, Toner, Kester, Tennant, Caras, Squires, and Bobby Brand frustrated the Bulldogs.

The first regular season game against a much-improved Gloucester club resulted in an easy win, 34–12. Dick scored 16 points and Frank DeFelice praised the defensive work of Rose, Tennant, and Kester. As an example of the growing regional interest in the Big Blue, the *Item* reported that films of the Gloucester game would be shown on a Boston television station with Bondy narrating.

The second game was at Woburn, "a good club", according to Stan. But the Tanners were not good enough to avoid a 40–20 pasting, administered despite multiple Swampscott miscues, including a blocked punt, 80 yards in penalties, and a staggering six lost fumbles. The team still rushed for 282 yards, while holding the Tanners to a mere 36. Dick covered 163 yards in 13 carries and scored twice. John Squires had a strong game, with two sensational catches and an interception.

Tom Toner was by now a major defensive force. He'd grown bigger and stronger since his junior year. He used his strength, quickness, and football instincts to fight through blocks, penetrate backfields, and run down ball carriers, frequently stripping them of the football and recovering it. He seemed particularly adept at doing so near either goal line.

Toner's ability to dominate opposing linemen reminded some of Billy Adams. But the two were radically different in personality and temperament. Tommy was not shy. He was supremely confident in almost any social setting. An irrepressible prankster, he was uninhibited and fun-loving. In some ways, he resembled 1957 star, Billy Carlyn. Both were good-looking, good-natured, popular kids with ready smiles. When they walked into a room, others gravitated to them.

Randy Werner was one of four sophomores (other than starter Jim Carone) who had the chance to dress for the Woburn game. He was surprised by the atmosphere on the bus ride home. Instead of celebrating, the veteran players seemed upset. They knew that blocked punts, multiple penalties, and fumbles were not acceptable, regardless of the outcome. They did not need to hear it from the coaches. Werner realized that these guys held themselves to very high standards.

Despite its sloppy Woburn performance, the team was attracting national attention. The *Item* reported that *Scholastic Roto Magazine*, a national publication based in New York, named SHS the fifth best high school football team in America. No other New England school was included on its list of the top 20.

Bondy loved to boast about his players' academic, as well as athletic, performances, and he had much to talk about when it came to the 1968 squad. Senior starters Rose, Benson, Abram, Jauron, and Kester were all top students. The coach sometimes asked such players to speak at certain functions. While being interviewed on a radio program earlier in the year, Carl Kester had commented: "Football in Swampscott is not just a game, it is a way of life." Bondy heard and loved it. From that point, the coach had used Carl as something of a poster boy for Big Blue football.

According to the *Item*, Kester, who was also class president, had recently attended a Gridiron Girls meeting and spoken about time management for the student-athlete. The Gridiron Girls were comprised of players' mothers and other women interested in SHS football. Bondy helped to organize the group and championed their activities, which included weekly evening meetings during the season at which coaches and/or players spoke.

Kester reportedly made quite an impression, appearing before the group dressed more like a Wall Street executive than a high school teenager. He hardly looked as polished on the football field. During the first game of his junior year, he suffered a broken nose while making a tackle. His appearance was captured on camera after he reached the sideline and removed his helmet. He was smeared with blood and grime, his hair was matted down with sweat, and he had a particularly ferocious, snarling look on his face.

During the following week, teammates were passing around the photograph and Gerry McGettrick exclaimed, "Kester, you mad dog!" From that point forward, to players and coaches alike, Carl was "Mad Dog Kester." It seemed to fit him perfectly—not because of his appearance but his style of play. He made up for lack of size with fierce tenacity. He played with a wild abandon, taking pride in his ability to hit as hard as anyone on the field.

Carl Kester had wanted to play football for as long as he could remember. His father was a Swampscott native who had played for Harold Martin. On a freezing cold Thanksgiving morning when Carl was about five years old, his dad took him from their home in Lynn to the game at Blocksidge Field. Not arriving in time to find seats, they were forced to stand with a mob of other onlookers on the track behind one of the end zones.

Young Kester was enthralled by the crush of fans and smell of cigar smoke in the cold, crisp air. He relished the sights and sounds of the band, drill team, and cheerleaders. Above all, he was fascinated by the action on the field. To the small boy, the players in their helmets and pads looked like giant warriors as they crashed into one another. At one point, a pack of them tumbled toward the back of the end zone near the spot where he and his dad stood. It was the most exciting thing that he could imagine, and he dreamed of one day being able to play the game.

A few years later, Carl's family moved to Swampscott where he enrolled at the Clarke School. For some weeks, the shy newcomer walked back to Lynn's Kiley playground each day after school to play with old friends. But eventually, he drifted to Abbott Park and joined in the informal tackle football games. As the unimposing new kid, he was the last selected when choosing up sides. The other boys generally ignored him until a moment when the biggest player was returning a kick. Carl raced ahead of his teammates and launched himself at the big kid, knocking him to the ground where he lay moaning. The boys looked at Carl differently after that play. When he showed up on the following afternoon, he was the first player chosen.

What Carl most enjoyed about the game was the contact. He thought that it was wonderful to be able to knock kids down and not get into trouble. Kester had other talents, including being a promising clarinet player in the school music program. When he reached the eighth grade, he made the decision to forego band in favor of football, disappointing his mother and high school band director Donald Hammond. However, his football season ended quickly when he suffered a ruptured appendix.

Carl returned a year later and, though slightly built, played guard and linebacker on the ninth-grade team. That is when Bondy seemed to take notice. During one game, Carl made a block near a spot where Coach Bondelevitch stood watching and he heard the big man exclaim, "Who made that block? Who is that kid?" When he got up he took his time returning to the huddle, hoping that Stan would get a good look at him. Then, in 1966 he was playing as a JV linebacker in a scrimmage against the varsity when he brought down a running back with a hard hit. An excited Bondy shouted from his tower, "Was that Kester making the tackle?" Those brief moments of recognition made him feel terrific.

As a junior, Carl reported to the Saint Anselm camp where he had a chance to compete for a starting position. Line coach DeFelice initially seemed unsure about him. As a somewhat thin, quiet kid, Carl did not fit Frank's profile of an ideal high school lineman. Moreover, he was an honor student. That may have impressed Bondy but, if anything, it made Frank more skeptical. The line coach sometimes sarcastically addressed Carl as Einstein and groused, "Never trust a *Phi Beta Kappa!*"

Nevertheless, DeFelice loved that Kester hit hard and was physically tough, showing no concern for his own safety. Carl became a two-way starter. At one point during a preseason scrimmage, Carl overheard Bondy talking about him to an onlooker, saying enthusiastically, "That kid loves to hit!" Kester was thrilled. He certainly voiced no objections when teammates and coaches called him "Mad Dog."

After starting the first two games of his junior season, Carl suffered a hamstring strain that prevented him from going full speed. Thinking it his obligation, he informed the coaches. They sidelined him for the next game and continued to hold him out after he felt fully recovered. Frustration set in as it seemed reporting the injury had cost him his starting job. Finally, he was inserted as the right guard at the start of the third quarter of the critical seventh game of the season at Lynn Classical and played the entire second half in that one-point victory.

After the team returned to the Fieldhouse, Carl was called upstairs and found Coaches Lynch, DeFelice, and Bondelevitch waiting. As the assistants looked on, Bondy said, "You had a very good game. That's what we want from you. Keep it up and glad to have you back."

Several days later he suffered a painful injury when another player's helmet came down hard on his hand during practice. Determined to remain in the starting line-up, Carl did not mention it to his coaches. Instead, he iced the hand and played with the pain for the final two games of his junior year. Now he was a senior. While the hand continued to bother him, Mad Dog kept that to himself. There was no way that he was going to miss out on playing guard and defensive end in his final season.

Carl and his 1968 teammates kept rolling, playing a more error-free game while dismantling Danvers, 41–20. Dick scored 21 points and the offense put up 473 yards. Further national media attention came Swampscott's way as Dick was named *Sport Magazine's* "Teenage Athlete of the Month." Bondy said, "In my 24 years of coaching I've never seen anything like him."

In Swampscott, my brother had become the subject of much adulation. He maintained a quiet, understated demeanor and an obvious concern for those around him. Dick recognized that his accomplishments with the Big Blue were the result of not only his talent, hard work, and determination, but a tremendous amount of help and support from coaches, teammates, and the entire community. He did not like to talk about himself, preferring to single out others for credit. There was nothing contrived or insincere about it, which was one of the things that made him a great teammate.

Meanwhile, despite the team's continuing success, senior guard Lloyd Benson was in jeopardy of losing his starting job. It struck him as highly unfair. As a young boy, Lloyd's sports heroes had not played for the Patriots, Red Sox, or Celtics. They had played for Swampscott High School. In 1961, he watched the undefeated Big Blue lose at Marblehead and cried in the car ride home. He cheered for and idolized Barry Gallup, Walter Costello, and the rest of the 1963 championship team.

Lloyd dreamed of becoming a Big Blue player since the time that Bondy mesmerized his Pop Warner team. It was something he would never forget. One afternoon as practice was concluding, the coaches informed the youngsters that the next day would be special. Mr. Bondelevitch would be coming to speak to them. Lloyd and his teammates could hardly wait.

On the following day, they all listened reverently as Coach Bond-elevitch delivered "the speech." It was the same talk that hundreds of Swampscott grammar school kids had heard or would hear over the years. But on that day, Lloyd felt that Coach Bondelevitch was speaking just to him. Bondy promised that if Lloyd diligently applied himself, got good grades, listened to his parents, behaved properly, and otherwise acted as a model young citizen, he would someday be able to run on to Blocksidge Field as a member of the Big Blue. From that time forward Lloyd Benson wanted nothing more than to play varsity football for SHS.

As a sophomore, Lloyd managed to play on the JVs but saw no action with the senior-laden varsity. After that season ended, he received a message to report to Mr. Bondelevitch. With considerable trepidation, he walked down the hall to the athletic director's office, located across from the gym entrance. He knocked on the closed door and heard a booming, almost jovial, voice bid him enter.

The coach sat behind his desk, wearing his trademark broad smile. Several seniors from the prior year's team were seated across from him, including All-American Mark Stevenson. Bondy looked up at Lloyd. The smile disappeared and his face took on a contemplative expression. While continuing to stare at Benson he asked, "So what do you think Stevenson, can Lloyd Benson play in the big arena? Will he be able to cut the mustard?"

Bondy liked to talk about players who could "cut the mustard" and perform in "the big arena." Stevenson, correctly surmising that the question was rhetorical, said nothing.

Bondy continued: "Lloyd Benson, we think that you have a chance to help us next year, but it is going to take a lot of hard work and dedication. Are you ready to commit and do what is necessary to play for the Big Blue?"

Benson was ecstatic, "Yes sir!"

The smile returned to Bondy's face. "Good. Now we are going to need you stronger and faster, so you'll be training with the track team this spring, okay?"

So, in the spring of 1967, Lloyd reported for track where he first encountered Coach DeFelice. He could vividly recall that day in the southwest corner of Blocksidge Field, struggling against a biting wind while trying to toss a heavy metal sphere known as the "shot." A steady drizzle added to his discomfort. It was one cold, wet March afternoon.

Bundled in a hooded sweat suit worn over a double layer of tee-shirts, he was still feeling the chill. He braced against the elements and tried to focus on proper technique. Track was hardly his sport of choice. But while Lloyd never dreamed of becoming a shot-putter, he did dream of becoming a starter on the Big Blue varsity football team. Bondy told him what he needed to do if he wanted to play and Benson was determined to do it.

Gazing up he saw a solitary figure exit the Fieldhouse and step on to the dirt track. Benson could not identify the man, but he looked to be at least 200 pounds and in good shape. Incredibly, the guy wore only a pair of sneakers, a tee-shirt, and gym shorts. He paused for a moment and then seemed to focus on Lloyd and started walking toward him. As he came closer Lloyd realized that it was Frank DeFelice, the varsity line coach. As a JV, he had never dealt directly with DeFelice, but he had heard a lot about him—most of it troubling. Frank was reportedly a demanding hard-ass.

DeFelice continued over the length of the field directly toward Benson's corner. While ostensibly concentrating on the shot put, Lloyd wondered whether the line coach wanted to speak with him. Lloyd was feeling pretty good about the rugged image he projected—out there on a raw, wet, miserable day, training so as to better contribute to next year's team.

DeFelice arrived and observed Lloyd for a moment before asking in a gruff voice, "You Benson?" Lloyd quickly confirmed the fact. Frank stared for another moment. Then, shaking his head with a look of utter disgust, he growled, "Well, you are about as coordinated as an African Pissant!" With that, the coach turned and made his way back to the Fieldhouse.

Frank DeFelice had been less than impressed with Lloyd's potential as a varsity lineman. The former Boston College player had a picture in his mind of the kind of hard-nosed, athletic kid he wanted to coach. The spectacled, awkward-appearing boy he had been watching struggle with the shot did not fit that image.

However, as the 1967 football season approached, DeFelice had to contend with the exodus of almost all the experienced varsity linemen. Benson was one of a handful of former JVs who competed for starting jobs. Ultimately, Lloyd became the backup to senior Mike Hoffman and junior Carl Kester but logged considerable playing time as a result of injuries. When the 1968 season commenced, Lloyd took over at left guard. But he was hardly a DeFelice favorite.

As Frank considered the 1968 roster, he believed there were others who could better handle the position. He was also determined to hold Bondy to a promise. During the prior season, Frank grew dissatisfied with one of the starting linemen and told Bondy that he was going to bench the kid. The head coach refused to allow it. The two engaged in quite a dustup over the matter. Finally, Bondy told his line coach that if he would stop pressing the issue and forget about benching the player in question, Frank would have the final say on starting linemen in the future.

Now Frank saw Benson as his test case, viewing him as one of Bondy's pets. When Frank criticized Lloyd's play, Stan generally came to the kid's defense. But Frank started to push Bondy to have Lloyd replaced. During their discussions, Bondy mentioned that he believed Lloyd was one of Dick Jauron's best friends. That struck Frank as irrelevant to the question of who should start at left guard.

Frank was still a young coach and would ultimately realize that Bondy may have been making a valid point with his "best friends" comment. Teams reached their full potential only when the players cared about each other. Knowing that he would be blocking for a boy that he liked and admired would help drive Benson to do his best. Running behind a line comprised of players who were his friends might similarly further motivate Jauron. Relationships mattered in team sports.

But there was clearly more to Bondy's support for Benson than the kid's relationship with the team's star. He had observed Lloyd for a number of years and had seen that he desperately wanted to play football for the Big Blue. "Want to" was highly valued by the head coach. And there was something else that Stan liked. Benson was smart.

Frank remained determined to make the change and looked for his opportunity. It was no secret that the line coach was monitoring Lloyd's every move. Before the Danvers game, he stopped Andy Rose and snarled, "Tell your friend Benson that if he screws up today he'll never play again." Rose relayed that message, which of course made Lloyd even more anxious.

After Frank reviewed the Danvers game film, he was convinced that Benson had screwed up, costing the team a touchdown. The offense had driven to the 2-yard line whereupon Dick ran the ball on a simple dive play (the "33") behind left guard and tackle. Watching the film, Frank saw that Lloyd was slow off the mark and a Danvers lineman penetrated into the backfield, bottling up the play, and preventing Dick from reaching the end zone. It made no difference to DeFelice that the Blue had easily won the game or that the film appeared to show Dick slipping as he left his stance. Not scoring on that play from the 2-yard line was unacceptable. In Frank's view, only one player was to blame—Benson.

Frank had his evidence and ran the film of that play repeatedly for Bondy. The head coach relented, saying that if one of the reserves clearly beat out Benson at practice he could be replaced. Bondy made certain that Lloyd was aware of his precarious hold on the job, as the *Item* reported that the coaches were considering making a change at left guard. Thus, Lloyd would have to battle to try to keep his starting job—one that he had coveted and worked so hard to earn. He knew that Coach DeFelice wanted him benched and felt that only Bondy believed in him.

Greg Brand was the top contender. Greg was the younger brother of senior defensive standout Bobby Brand. He was taller and more athletic than Benson, and at least as heavy. He played regularly on defense and was the number one reserve on the offensive line. As a senior, Greg would become an outstanding two-way lineman for the Big Blue and then go on to play as a starting guard at BC before spending some time with a few professional teams. Frank planned to have Benson and Brand battle on the practice field, certain that Greg would prevail and he'd have his new left guard.

On Tuesday, Frank informed the linemen that there would be a competition in the pit. He called Benson and Brand forward and explained that they would be going full contact. The boys squared off, each in a three-point stance. Frank hollered "Go" and was amazed at what happened.

Benson exploded out of his stance and drove hard into Brand's midsection, knocking him backward and well off the line. DeFelice was dumbfounded. He could only assume that Greg must not have been ready. "Let's go again," Frank yelled. Once again Benson powered forward and won the contest. Coach DeFelice had the two players collide several more times with similar results. "We'll do it again tomorrow," Frank growled.

The outcome was no different on Wednesday. Frank remained unconvinced. "Be ready tomorrow, Benson," he warned. For the third consecutive day Benson fought off Brand. As the players returned to the locker room after Thursday's practice, some of Lloyd's friends congratulated him on having weathered the storm.

On the following afternoon, the players were preparing to take the field in their game uniforms without pads. It would be the Friday walkthrough, a brief, non-contact session. DeFelice entered the locker room. "Benson and Brand," he hollered, "Full gear. Let's do it one more time." He then walked over to Benson and warned that if he let up just once he would be spending the rest of the season on the bench.

While the rest of the team waltzed through the walk-through, the two guards battled for the fourth consecutive day. Lloyd Benson, "about as coordinated as an African Pissant," never faltered. Not only did Lloyd keep his starting position but, according to the line coach himself, he thereafter performed as well or better than any other Big Blue lineman. The irony was that the player whom DeFelice was so intent on replacing had used everything he had learned from Frank to meet the challenge. The coach had taught Lloyd Benson a great deal about offensive line play but Benson also taught DeFelice something. Frank learned an important lesson about the power of "want to."

Having breezed through their first three opponents, the boys prepared to visit Miller Field to take on Winthrop, a team that would surely love to end Swampscott's winning streak. On the morning of the game, recently married Frank DeFelice told his wife Susan that he felt bad for her younger brother, Robert "Shorty" Mahegan because he was not going to have a good day. Shorty was a rugged starting tackle for the Vikings. When Susan asked Frank to explain, he said that Shorty would be across the line from Tom Toner. Susan replied that Shorty could take care of himself. "Normally yes," said Frank, "but not today."

Winthrop usually gave Swampscott a battle, and Bondy had predicted that his team would be "in for some trouble." But the Vikings could not create much trouble this time, surrendering 320 yards on the ground while losing 35–8. The game ball was awarded to Frank DeFelice. The Winthrop native had been instrumental in derailing an undefeated Swampscott team in 1956 but now had helped to coach the Big Blue to an impressive win over his alma mater. Brother-in-law Shorty was a good player but could not have enjoyed his outing against Toner. At least he could feel grateful that the worst was over. He would not be facing anyone else like the Swampscott lineman.

The team kept winning. Dick scored three touchdowns in a 33–6 victory over Amesbury. The Blue crushed Saugus, 56–32. In that game, Swampscott had 33 first downs, 404 yards rushing, and 8 touchdowns. The boys managed 390 yards of offense in the first half alone. Saugus scored most of its points later against the reserves. In truth, opponents like Amesbury and Saugus had fallen on hard times and were not what they had once been. But Swampscott would now be facing the two biggest obstacles to reaching its goal of a second perfect season—Classical and Newburyport.

The 1967 team had managed to get past each of those rivals by the slimmest of margins. They were both strong again, perhaps even stronger than their predecessors. The visiting Rams welcomed a second chance to bring down their unbeaten neighbors. Classical (5–1) was led by senior quarterback Jimmy Silvonic, one of the North Shore's most talented and exciting players. He and his teammates turned in a gutsy performance, especially in the first half when they kept the Blue off the scoreboard. But the home team's offense broke through after intermission, posting 21 points, all scored by Jauron. Meanwhile, the Swampscott defense shut out the Rams as the boys recorded their seventh win.

At one point during the game, Dick was on his knees after the whistle had blown the play dead when a Classical defender hit him with a vicious shot that could have caused serious injury. In the ensuing huddle, Peter Beatrice's attempt to call the play was drowned out by center Sandy Tennant's furious command that everyone nail the offending Rams player. When the ball was next snapped the entire offensive line, led by the enraged Tennant, battered the Classical kid. Swampscott ultimately rushed for 248 yards while Classical was held to 89. Silvonic played a sterling game, especially on defense where he was credited with 18 tackles and assisting on a number of others. But Swampscott was the superior team.

The team was sailing along smoothly, but the seas had grown rough for Frank DeFelice. Stan could be tough on assistants and Frank felt that Bondy had too often criticized and belittled him while ignoring his contributions. On the Monday morning following the Classical game, Stan told Frank that he wanted him to speak to the Gridiron Girls at their evening meeting that week. Frank, already feeling abused, resented being volunteered by Bondy and replied that he had other plans. Bondy stormed away in a huff. Frank expected repercussions.

On the following day, he was about to teach a gym class at Shaw when custodian/athletic manager Frank Coletti approached and announced that Bondy wanted to see him right away at the high school. Still upset, DeFelice said that he wasn't going. "What," asked Coletti, "should I tell Mr. Bondelevitch?" DeFelice heatedly suggested that Coletti tell Bondy to perform an impossible, unilateral sexual act. Coletti was aghast. "I can't tell him that!" He begged the upset line coach to go and talk to Stan.

Frank DeFelice finally agreed to visit Bondy while the custodian filled in as gym teacher. It was time to clear the air. When he arrived at Stan's office, he bitterly recited a litany of Bondy's slights and insults. When the boss suggested that his assistant was being disrespectful, Frank barked back, "Respect is a two-way street!" Bondy, seemingly shocked by DeFelice's anger, suggested they put off further discussion until they both calmed down.

Later that day during the regular coaching staff meeting upstairs at the Fieldhouse, Bondy spent much of the session praising DeFelice. He raved about how lucky they were to have Frank, gushing that he was the best line coach on the North Shore. When he concluded and the other assistants were departing, Stan asked Frank to remain. Once they were alone, he respectfully asked if it might be possible for Frank to help out by speaking at the Gridiron Girls meeting that week. "No problem," replied the smiling line coach. While Stan regularly used flattery to motivate some players, he was not averse to doing the same to smooth his assistant's ruffled feathers.

With the air cleared, the coaches worked to prepare the team for Newburyport. For the third consecutive year, Swampscott v. Newburyport was the biggest conference game of the season and would be played before a standing-room-only crowd. The Clippers won handily in 1966, while the Blue prevailed by a razor-thin margin in 1967 to end Newburyport's 20-game unbeaten streak in one of the most unforgettable victories ever forged at Blocksidge Field. Now Swampscott was the visiting team.

While Eddie O'Bara had graduated, the 1968 Clippers were loaded with veteran players. They shared the conference lead with the Big Blue but were not undefeated, having lost to non-conference Stoneham. They had a chance to do to Swampscott what Swampscott did to them in 1967—end an opponent's long undefeated streak while becoming the front-runner for the conference crown.

For away games, SHS players put on their jerseys, pants, and cleats at Blocksidge Field, but carried their shoulder pads and helmets with them on the bus ride. When the bus arrived at Newburyport's World War Memorial Stadium, it parked at the end farthest from the visitors' locker room. The boys, carrying their helmets and pads, had to walk the length of the field in front of the packed visitors' stands. As they entered the stadium, Swampscott supporters rose from their seats. Before long the boys were receiving an extended standing ovation.

After they warmed up and returned to the locker room for final preparations, Bondy stood to address the team. The players expected to hear the usual emotional appeal, but their coach remained silent. The 1968 team did not lack for confidence and had every reason for optimism. Perhaps nothing needed to be said.

Just as it seemed they would take the field without any message from the coach Bondy broke the silence, telling them, "The following players will be starting on offense today … for the *Best High School Football Team in America!*" He then mentioned each starting player and the boys roared out of the locker room. While objective observers might consider Bondy's description of his team hyperbole, it had the intended emotional impact. The Big Blue dominated and returned home with an 8–0 record after claiming a 24–6 victory.

On November 24, 1968, Lynn Sunday Post reporter Matt Rillovick commemorated Bondy's recent 100th win as SHS coach with a lengthy article, accompanied by drawings, photographs, and congratulatory messages from dozens of area businesses and organizations, writing,

This is a form of "reverse PR," as it were, for Bondelevitch is recognized among the sporting gentry locally as one of the leading tacticians of promotion and public relations for the good of his teams and players.…

The article noted that Bondy's plan of organization, education, and implementation had been realized through "untold hours of loves' labor, both physical and administrative." He praised Swampscott as "a town second to none, as evidenced by the spirit of people like Henry and Paul Gibbs, Ed Shub, Brad Moore, Tony Pierre, and Tom Collins." Those men, together with others like Rollie Booma, Marty Goldman, and Myron Stone, were, at different times, actively involved in the support of Big Blue football through the strong Boosters organization.

Commenting on Stan's "truly amazing coaching record," and also noting that the coach was "directly instrumental in sending off more than 300 boys to college with athletic assistance," Rillovick asked, "Is this any way to run high school football?" Answering his own question, he wrote, "You better believe it is!"

Meanwhile, the "tactician of promotion and public relations" was busy generating more media attention for his program. Swampscott authorities decided to put together an exhibit at town hall commemorating "S.H.S. Teams of Yesterday." A large glass display case held banners, photos, clippings, and other memorabilia of past high school teams dating back to the early twentieth century. Seeing a photo opportunity, Bondy enlisted his favorite poster boy, Carl "Mad Dog" Kester, as well as Carl's dad Waldemar who had played for the 1938–40 SHS teams when he was known as "Cowboy." Painted footballs recognizing the undefeated 1957, 1958, 1963, and 1967 teams were included in the exhibit, and the *Item* published a photograph of Carl, standing in front of the display case with his dad and former 1928–29 Sculpin player Mike "Skip" Pagnotti. In the photo, all three looked down at a ball held by Carl marked for the undefeated 1967 championship team, likely hoping that they would soon be adding another for the 1968 squad.

Only Marblehead remained. Time-worn clichés were bandied about. There was talk about "throwing away the record books" and that "anything could happen" when the two rivals collided on Thanksgiving. But a victory by the 3–5 Headers over this 8–0 juggernaut might qualify as the most shocking miracle in conference history.

On Thanksgiving morning, as Lloyd Benson donned his Big Blue uniform for the last time, a nearby familiar voice expressed the hope that Lloyd knew how fortunate he was to be able to play against Marblehead. Coach DeFelice continued for a couple of minutes, exclaiming on the thrill of playing in the traditional season-ending game. "I hope you know how lucky you are," DeFelice told him as he walked away. "Yes," Lloyd thought, "I know exactly how lucky I am." On that Thanksgiving, Benson was most grateful that he would never again have to contend with the demands of the hard-driving line coach.

To their credit, the out-gunned Magicians managed to keep the game close in the first half and went to the locker room trailing only 8–0. But they had staved off the inevitable. The dam broke after the second half started. Leading 33–0 in the fourth quarter, the Blue drove to a spot a few yards from the Headers' end zone. Dick's teammates, particularly Benson and Rose, knew that with one more touchdown their friend would break the all-time Massachusetts career scoring record.

Beatrice called Dick's number, a 33-dive. This was a play that Bondy dubbed "the Kosher dive," since it was run between Benson and Rose, the two Jewish kids in the line. Lloyd and Andy were never more motivated to block for their friend. They wiped out the defensive linemen and Richard Jauron waltzed into the end zone for the final, record-breaking touchdown of his high school career. Following the kickoff, Dick joined the defense on the field. After Marblehead's first play, Coach Lynch's son, sophomore Mike Lynch, was sent into the game to replace my brother at safety. Dick left to a standing ovation from the packed home stands and embraces from coaches and teammates.

Young Michael Lynch was caught up in the moment. He watched, misty-eyed from the field as the sideline celebration continued. Meanwhile, the Headers snapped the ball and one of their receivers streaked past the oblivious Lynch. By the time Mike came to his senses the receiver was a good 20 yards downfield. Luckily the Header quarterback did not throw the ball, thereby saving Lynch from certain ridicule when the coaches and players later watched the game film. Time on the scoreboard clock ran out, and the 1968 team ended its perfect season by posting its largest margin of victory and shutting out the rival Headers, 40–0.

In the Fieldhouse, as Andy Rose started to remove his jersey for the last time, Coach DeFelice walked over, grabbed it and said, "Let me help you with that." Andy was shocked. The gesture and comment were so out of character. Then DeFelice smiled broadly, adding, "It's the least that I can do after all of the shit I've given you over the past two years." For Andy, it was a revelation that Coach DeFelice was not some sadist who enjoyed making their lives miserable. Instead, he was a man who had done his best, in the best way that he knew how to do it, to help Andy and his teammates reach their full potential.

Postseason honors poured in. The boys were again conference champions. They were also Class B champions. Dick was again an All-American. He finished the season as the highest point-scorer in the state and his total career points of 360 broke the Massachusetts schoolboy career scoring record. Locally, he became the second consecutive Swampscott player to win the Thom McAn Shoe Award. Andy Rose and Bobby Brand joined him on the first team of the *Item's* North Shore All-Stars. Phil Abram was named to the second team. Tom Toner was somehow left off both squads, a glaring oversight. Stan Bondelevitch was named Massachusetts Coach of the Year. The 1968 team scored 324 points, which was, as of that time, the most ever scored by a Swampscott team in a season.

The media, having pretty much run out of superlatives for my brother, turned again to the ultimate gold standard of North Shore athletic performance, the late, great Harry Agganis. In his column summing up Dick's career, the *Item's* J. F. Williams, noting that the time period when Harry had thrilled North Shore fans had become commonly known as "the Agganis era," predicted that the more recent years when the Swampscott player graced local playing fields might likewise ultimately be remembered as the "the Jauron era." Dick cared little about that. His college coach, Carmen Cozza, in speaking about him a few years later, summed it up nicely when he said, "Compliments don't go to his head. They go to his heart." What Dick most valued about football in Swampscott was being able to play a game that he loved with friends like Rose, Benson, Kester, Toner, and Tennant.

My brother went to Yale, where he became an All-American running back and was drafted by the Detroit Lions. After playing a number of years in the NFL as a defensive back and kick returner, he enjoyed a long coaching career, including serving as the head coach of the Chicago Bears and the Buffalo Bills.

Dick's Swampscott teammate Tommy Toner never realized his boyhood dream of becoming a star quarterback. But as a football player, he just kept getting bigger, stronger, and better. After playing for the Big Blue, he became a defensive star for Idaho State. Thereafter he was drafted by the Green Bay Packers and played a number of years as a 240-pound linebacker.

Carl "Mad Dog" Kester attended Amherst College, playing football until knee damage made it impossible to continue. He also learned, as a result of an x-ray at Amherst, that the hand injury he had sustained and kept quiet about during his junior year at SHS had been a fracture. Following college, he attended the London School of Economics before returning to Cambridge, where he obtained both MBA and doctorate degrees from Harvard. Carl became a professor, and ultimately a dean, of the Harvard Business School.

Andy Rose attended Harvard and played freshman football. His playing days ended when he suffered a serious hand injury. Following graduation, Andy earned an MBA from Boston College. He has resided in Swampscott for the past 30 years while enjoying success operating his own real estate investment and development business.

After a year at prep school, John Squires attended the University of Maine, where he had a strong career as a receiver on the Black Bears football squad. Thereafter, he returned to the North Shore, where he spent a number of years as a teacher and administrator and also worked a couple of seasons as an assistant coach with Bondy.

After graduating from Colby College, Lloyd Benson also returned to the North Shore and built a career in marketing. His feelings about his high school line coach changed over time as he and Frank became close friends. They meet most Saturday mornings at Dunkin Donuts in Swampscott, where they discuss and debate almost anything. Talk can become especially heated when it turns to the glory days of Big Blue football.

Exactly 10 years after the Big Blue completed consecutive undefeated seasons, it did so again. As in 1958, Bondy's success led to speculation about his departure to the college level, in particular, Holy Cross College. Ed Cahill devoted an entire column to the possibility, suggesting that Swampscott's Jim Hughes, a Holy Cross alumnus, may have been courting the Big Blue mentor. Cahill observed that, should Bondy take over there, he would be reunited with former captain Bill Adams, who had just completed his freshman football season at the school. The speculation increased after Bondy was the featured speaker at the O'Melia Award Banquet, an annual event honoring the most valuable player in the

Holy Cross-Boston College game. He turned his speech into something of a rousing pep talk for the assembled Crusader faithful and concluded to a standing ovation. Despite rumors and speculation, Bondy remained in Swampscott.

Sixteen football seasons had passed since his arrival, and the townspeople decided to honor their high school coach with a testimonial dinner. Perhaps it was seen as a way of not only thanking him for what he had accomplished but for his decision to remain. Approximately 50 individuals worked on one or more of seven planning committees. John P. Ingalls Jr., a direct descendant of Swampscott's earliest resident, served as general chairman and toastmaster.

The testimonial was held at the Harvard Club in Boston on March 8, 1969. A 28-page commemorative program was produced. Speakers included Dick Lynch and former players Winslow Shaw, Bob Carlin, Barry Gallup, Dick Jauron, and Al Viola. Viola had been the captain and MVP of one of Bondy's Maynard High School teams. After serving as a marine in the Korean War, he attended Northwestern University where he captained the football team and became the school's first Academic All-American. The rugged lineman once made an NCAA record-setting five fumble recoveries in a single game. Perhaps the most memorable line of the evening came during Viola's speech. Having flown in from Chicago, Viola looked at his former mentor and said, "Coach, I did not travel all this distance for the chicken dinner. I did it to tell you that I love you."

Determined to Do Well

O
n May 8, 1969, a fire started in the lobby of the vacant New Ocean House. It quickly spread through the sprawling complex and could not be extinguished. Over the years the hotel had played host to many of the country's most famous citizens. Lucille Ball, Calvin Coolidge, Herbert Hoover, Helen Keller, John F. Kennedy, Sinclair Lewis, Harpo Marx, and Babe Ruth were among those who visited. Many Swampscotters fondly remembered the place as the glamorous site of their high school proms. Reconstruction was out of the question. The era when wealthy vacationers made the New Ocean House their summer home had passed. Nonetheless, it was a sudden, poignant, and sad ending to a once elegant Grand Lady.

Big Blue football players would never again be able to look up from their practice field and see the flag waving atop the roof of what had been one of New England's most renowned seaside resorts. However, they could continue to look up and see Stan Bondelevitch atop his tower. While the gala testimonial dinner in March had seemed like a send-off at the conclusion of a remarkable high school coaching career, Bondy remained. He was not finished with his work in Swampscott.

Only four offensive regulars returned. Dick Jauron and Phil Abram were gone from the backfield. Other than center Sandy Tennant, the entire starting offensive line had departed. The defense was similarly decimated, as most of the seniors who started on offense played both ways. Defensive specialist and *Item* All-Star Bobby Brand had also graduated, as had middle guard/punter Ralph Floria. And there was the need to find the players who could assume the kicking and kick-returning duties that Dick had handled. Not surprisingly, an article in the *Item* titled, "Big Blue's 18-Game Streak In Danger This Fall," implied that Swampscott's reign would soon end.

However, the returning veterans were impact players. As a sophomore, 200-pound Jimmy Carone had been a steady presence at fullback, blocking well and running hard when given the opportunity. Quarterback Peter Beatrice had played well as a junior and would again direct the offense. Captain Sandy Tennant and classmate David Caras were exceptionally versatile two-way performers who had helped the Big Blue secure championships in 1967 and 1968. The six-foot, 180-pound Caras started the 1969 season as an offensive end, while handling the punting duties and continuing to perform as a cornerback or linebacker. As for Tennant, Bondy told the *Item's* Bill Beaton:

> Tennant is the finest linebacker in the state and you won't find many better than him as an offensive center either. He loves to hit, has good size, and is a fine team leader.

Seniors Richie Conigliaro and Steven Dushan were the leading halfback candidates. Having suffered a badly broken leg as a freshman, Richie had struggled over the past two years to fully return from that trauma. He had the size, speed, and athleticism to make major contributions on both sides of the line of scrimmage. Undersized Dushan had seen some varsity action in 1968 and, when given the chance, had been solid. Lou DeFelice (no relation to Frank) was another capable, hard-nosed back who was anxious to step up and play regularly.

The seniors would be pressed by some talented younger kids who had been undefeated as freshmen. In 1967, despite the fact that almost the entire starting team from the prior season had graduated, only one sophomore (Tennant) was invited to the Saint Anselm camp. The story was different in 1969. "We're going to lean on our sophomores as much as possible," Bondy said. Underclassmen Danny Losano, Billy Leone, and Charlie Cardillo were all backfield candidates. Losano had broken the state Pop Warner scoring record and had been the leading scorer on the ninth-grade team.

While Tennant was the only lineman who had started on offense in 1968, his classmate Greg Brand possessed the size and skill to excel as a two-way tackle. Greg had gotten bigger and stronger in the off-season. He stood 6-foot, 3-inches and weighed about 210 pounds. Others vying for positions up-front included ends Jerry Mangini, Billy Goade, Randy

Gibbs, and Billy Toner; tackles Stu Greeley, Ron Tamborini, and Ben Mosho and guards Mark Adelson, Randy Werner, and Mike DiPrisco.

Most of the players had participated in the summer strength and conditioning program. For seniors like Tennant and Caras, it was their third consecutive summer of such training. While Bondy expressed concern that the team could struggle early as the younger players gained experience, he wasn't about to concede the crown, asserting, "Swampscott is still the Class B champion until someone takes the title away from us."

The boys did little in the Jamboree to lessen Bondy's worries about early season struggles, losing to Revere in the abbreviated game. But the bigger concern was the loss of fullback/linebacker Carone who suffered a broken ankle. Much had been expected of Jimmy, who had been the only sophomore starter on the 1968 championship team. Now he was gone.

Carone's injury left a big hole in the backfield. The coaches turned to their leader and best football player. Sandy Tennant shifted from center to fullback. Tennant was a hard runner and, more importantly, a ferocious blocker. But with Carone gone from a roster already short on experienced varsity players, there was concern about the Blue's ability to continue the winning streak by beating Gloucester in the opener. That concern vanished when SHS blasted the Fishermen 42–8.

This Big Blue team was blessed with a number of very good football players, some of whom had been flying under the radar. Bondy was pleasantly surprised by several things, including the fine performances of both offensive and defensive lines, several of the running backs, the kicking game, and a couple of sophomore cornerbacks.

Quite a few playmakers emerged. Tennant, in addition to his blocking and tackling, scored twice, blocked a punt, and ran for 55 yards on 13 carries. Richie Conigliaro, looking like older brother Billy, scored a touchdown, ran and caught for a combined 88 yards, and intercepted a pass, returning it 27 yards to the 1-yard line. Dave Caras, who saw limited action due to illness, caught a touchdown pass and pulled in an interception. Senior backs Dushan and DeFelice both scored, with DeFelice's touchdown coming off an interception which he returned 45 yards. And the Big Blue again unveiled a reliable kicking game. Junior Mike Lynch converted all six of his PAT attempts. With the victory over the Fishermen, Swampscott matched its 19-game winning streak from 1957–59.

SHS had not played its next opponent, the Lynn English Bulldogs, since 1927. While English had fallen to Salem in its opener, 38–12, Bulldogs coach Charlie Ruddock sounded optimistic, telling the *Item* that, according to his reports, Salem was better than Swampscott. One thing his reports apparently did not tell Ruddock was how to beat Swampscott, as the Big Blue easily defeated English, 26–6.

The score may have been even more one-sided had Swampscott not fumbled five times. The Blue was so dominant it never punted. Tennant, Caras, Dushan, and Cardillo all scored, and Lynch stretched his consecutive PATs to eight. The Bulldogs notched their only touchdown late in the fourth quarter when the SHS regulars were on the bench. After the game, Bondy commented, "I must say these kids have surprised me. They're the hardest working bunch I've ever had. They're determined to do well, and they will." They were also now part of the longest winning streak in SHS history.

Swampscott, riding its 20-game streak, now faced undefeated Danvers, a team that had not lost since its last meeting with the Big Blue. The Falcons, as they were now known, were very good. After winning a close game in the opener, they easily beat both Winthrop and Saint John's Prep by a combined 77–6. They had plenty of offensive weapons, including fullback Ken St. Pierre ("Mr. Inside"), halfback Chuck Flint ("Mr. Outside"), and gifted quarterback Bruce Madden. In their last game, St. Pierre had scored three touchdowns.

This was one more in the growing number of "huge games" during the Bondy era. Fans were advised to arrive at Blocksidge Field early if they wanted to get in. While Bondy never needed help motivating his players, he got some. Despite the Big Blue's 20 consecutive victories, the *Item* declared Danvers the favorite. Next, anti-Big Blue graffiti appeared on the walls of the Fieldhouse on the morning of the game. One message included the words, "Tennant Dies!" Danvers coach Russ Fravel could not have been happy with those developments. Bondy knew how to use such things for maximum motivational impact. In fact, some cynical observers speculated that the Swampscott coach was responsible for the graffiti as well as the large *C* that had been burned into the Blocksidge grass prior to the 1963 Classical game.

In any case, if the underdog designation and anti-Tennant graffiti were not enough to inspire the Big Blue captain, a pregame comment by

Coach DeFelice certainly was. Frank told Sandy that while many folks were saying St. Pierre was the best football player on the North Shore, a few thought that Tennant might be better. He mused, "Well, I guess we'll find out today." Sandy's assignment—stop St. Pierre.

When the dust settled at Blocksidge Field several hours later, there could be no doubt that Swampscott was still king of the hill. The boys outplayed Danvers, beating the Falcons 31–22. Bondy explained that the coaching staff had pulled the 38 Hurricane out of mothballs. This was the unbalanced line/end sweep that had been so effective in the huge upset win over Amesbury in 1953. Although Bondy implied that Danvers may have been surprised by the play, Coach Fravel's explanation was simpler. "We have no excuses. They just out-hit us and they were the better team today. That's all there is to it," he said.

According to the *Item*, there were plenty of stand-out performers for Swampscott, including Caras, Conigliaro, Dushan, Beatrice, DeFelice, Brand, and Tennant. Caras alternated between fullback, halfback, and end on offense and cornerback and linebacker on defense. He performed well as a ball carrier, receiver, kick-returner, and punter, and scored a touchdown and two-point conversion. Conigliaro ran for 84 yards and caught a 53-yard touchdown pass, while also intercepting two passes. Beatrice completed six of seven passes for 143 yards, two touchdowns, and two conversions. Dushan ran for almost 100 yards and scored a touchdown and a two-point conversion. Lou DeFelice was another Swampscott ball hawk, picking off two passes. He also made a great defensive play to break up what appeared to be a likely Danvers TD pass, while pulling in a reception for a conversion. The team rolled up 422 yards in total offense.

Led by their ferocious, fired–up captain, Swampscott's defensive players shut down the Falcons' running game. On his first carry, St. Pierre was met head-on by Tennant in a staggering collision at the line of scrimmage. It was a harbinger of things to come. The Danvers star, having averaged over 100 yards per game, was held to a mere four yards on seven carries. The entire Danvers offense registered just two yards rushing in the first half and 19 for the entire game.

The solid win over highly touted Danvers was impressive, but there was no time to relax. The Vikings were coming. Winthrop, troublesome for SHS even in down years, had just beaten Newburyport, 22–0. Now the Vikings invaded Blocksidge Field intent on battling the Blue tooth and nail. They did just that. Whether due to exhaustion from its Danvers performance, the strong play of the Winthrop defense, or both, the SHS offense was far less productive than in any of its first three games.

The team had been averaging 33 points per game but could only muster 14 against the Vikings. Fortunately, the defense excelled, holding Winthrop to a single score and the boys prevailed, 14–6. Conigliaro and DeFelice scored the touchdowns, and Mike Lynch nailed the points after. Kicking and defense were keys to the win. Dave Caras punted the Blue out of trouble multiple times, with several kicks traveling more than 50 yards. Tennant and DeFelice were two-way standouts.

Swampscott would be facing further challenges down the road. According to Marblehead coach Reebenacker, whose team had just lost to unbeaten Saugus, the Sachems were a strong club, as was the Blue's next opponent, Amesbury. While the Indians were a mediocre 1–2–1, Reebenacker rated them highly, noting that they were well-organized and effectively executed their plays. They also had a special incentive because Swampscott had ended their historic 31-game unbeaten streak in 1953. Now the Carriagemakers had the chance to return the favor and end the Blue's 22-game run. According to their coach Doug Wood, in the week leading up to the contest his players were thinking about that 1953 game, having heard about it from nearly every fan in town. As described by the *Item*,

> Amesbury was a town with a dream when Swampscott came to town on Saturday.... The dream was weaved around a memory, the recollection of an 18–14 Swampscott win over the Indians back in 1953, first year at the helm for Stan Bondelevitch.

The dream was that the two teams would reverse roles and the Indians would pull off a similar historic upset.

It looked like that might happen after Swampscott fumbled on the game's first play, and Amesbury drove to the end zone and followed with a two-point conversion to take an 8–0 lead. While the Blue managed a score at the end of the first quarter, the conversion attempt failed, and Amesbury held an 8–6 lead when the first half ended. Unfortunately for the Indians, there was another half to play.

As Coach Wood described it,

We were in man-to-man in our pass defense, and it worked for a
while. Then Stan figured out what we were doing and it was all
over. I'm just thankful it took him as long as it did.

Actually, it's more likely that Dick Lynch figured out what Amesbury was
doing with its pass defense and dictated the effective counter-measures.
He excelled at recognizing opponents' strategies and prescribing necessary
adjustments.

Swampscott completed a 93-yard scoring drive toward the end of the
third quarter, and then extended its lead to 15–8 on Mike Lynch's 26-yard
field goal. The visitors scored again when Cardillo returned an interception 37 yards, but the touchdown was nullified by a clipping penalty. On
the next play, Beatrice ran for a score, but that too was called back on a
motion penalty. Shortly thereafter Caras ran 34 yards for a touchdown
that was not called back. The handwriting was on the wall. The home
squad could not stand up to the relentless attack. There would be no
celebration and return to glory for the Indians and their fans, as the Big
Blue left town with a 36–8 victory, its fourteenth consecutive triumph
over the Carriagemakers.

Often when sports teams dominate for a lengthy period, whether on
the professional, college, or high school level, many who are not part of
the successful organization and its fan base become increasingly resentful
of the attention given the winning program. Such was the case for the Big
Blue. The constant media coverage riled fans from opposing schools. An
example can be seen below in an excerpt from a letter signed by 37 female
Saugus supporters and reprinted by Ed Cahill in his *Item* column shortly
before the 1969 game between Swampscott and undefeated Saugus.

TO WHOM IT MAY CONCERN: I am writing this letter to
you not just for myself, but for many people from Saugus. In your
sports pages, all attention is focused on Swampscott. It did this, or
it did that. Swampscott is not the only football team around here.
Saugus and other towns have teams who have won all their games
so far, also. Why should Swampscott be highly referred to in this

section of the newspaper?… Every day you look at the newspaper and all you see is SWAMPSCOTT! Why don't you have more about other towns? We're playing football games too. I realize that Swampscott has a good team, but isn't the *Item* Sports overdoing it?

Cahill's rebuttal, after detailing the extensive *Item* coverage of the Sachems, noted that Swampscott, undefeated over the past three seasons, merited its share of attention.

However, the Big Blue's football success only partly explained the media coverage. Stan Bondelevitch was the program's unofficial press agent. He was in regular contact with sports writers and media personnel. He socialized with them and provided information, ideas, and stories. If several days passed without seeing anything positive in the newspapers, he was not averse to picking up the phone and demanding explanations from sports editors. He got results because he made their jobs easier, being so accessible, quotable, and ready with material that they could use to fill their columns and meet deadlines.

It took a unique person like Bondy to accomplish dual tasks of running a successful program and promoting it to the public. He had built a sustainable, winning football program, characterized by superb organization, effective cultivation, excellent coaching, and enthusiastic community support. He may have been fortunate at times in having some truly outstanding athletes on his teams, but he and his assistants knew how to properly handle and use such players and to motivate, develop, and train the less-talented.

With regard to promotion, many coaches were either unable or unwilling to hype their teams to the media. Some lacked the necessary outgoing personality, while others no doubt considered it unseemly. Not Bondy. He was masterful in generating favorable publicity.

One step the 1969 Sachems could have taken to assure more positive coverage was beating Swampscott in what looked to be the biggest game of the season for both clubs. Each team was undefeated. The 5–0 Sachems were riding an eight-game winning streak, with their last loss having come at the hands of the Big Blue, 56–32.

The *Item* had favored Danvers over Swampscott, but the Blue had won convincingly. Now, facing unbeaten Saugus, Swampscott was in the midst of a 23-game winning streak, had easily beaten the Sachems in 1968, and was winning its games by an average of almost 20 points. Saugus, having faced comparable opponents, was winning by an average of just over eight points. Yet, according to the *Item*, North Shore football experts were rating the game a "toss-up."

Bondy, of course, would have preferred that his squad be the perceived underdog, as unreasonable as that would seem. In pregame interviews, both coaches were asked which team should be favored and by how much. Saugus coach Maguire offered no opinion. Bondy proclaimed that Saugus should be favored by one point, adding, "And I mean just that." It is hard to believe that he could have made the statement with a straight face.

Red Hoffman further fueled the build-up with a brief story that one of the coaches, unidentified, had received a note that read, "Coach, if you lose this game, there's a train leaving Saturday night at 9 o'clock … be under it." It seemed unlikely that such a message could have been directed to the well-established and remarkably successful Swampscott coach. On the other hand, it was just the kind of short, amusing story that Bondy would have enjoyed feeding to the *Item*.

Swampscott's battle with Saugus became the new "biggest game of the year." Bob Osgood, their standout quarterback, was the key man for the Sachems. According to Bondy, Osgood was capable of throwing very well, both short and long, but was perhaps most dangerous when unable to find a receiver. He was a strong runner who could beat you with his feet.

Swampscott drew first blood, driving 43 yards for a touchdown. The offense increased the lead to 13–0 after an 80-yard touchdown drive. The Sachems then cut the Blue's lead to 13–6 when they scored after recovering a Swampscott fumble. They never scored again. Swampscott dominated, particularly in the second half, and beat the previously unbeaten Sachems, 27–6. David Caras scored twice while Richie Conigliaro and sophomore Danny Losano each tallied once. Lynch added three conversion kicks.

Conigliaro's touchdown came off a fake field goal. According to Coach Maguire, the Sachems expected it but still could not stop it because of perfect execution. The Swampscott defensive line, including Jerry Mangini, Greg Brand, Marty Orloff, Mike DiPrisco, and Jay Coughlin (younger brother of David), recorded four quarterback sacks in the second half. This would be the only blemish for the Sachems in 1969. They were very good, but Swampscott was much better. Coach Maguire sounded like Danvers coach Fravel, conceding, "I must say we were simply out-played by a better team today."

With undefeated Swampscott riding a 24-game winning streak, the *Item* decided that it was time for another article about the secret of the Big Blue's success. Bondy typically credited parents and players:

> The most important thing about any football program is you can't win unless you play your best players. Thanks to the Big Blue football parents our boys have great character. Coaches here don't build character; they leave that to the parents and spend more time coaching football.

In all probability players in places like Lynn, Marblehead, Danvers, and Newburyport had no less character than Swampscott boys. That didn't matter to Bondy since the folks that he was intent on reaching were his players' parents. They undoubtedly appreciated his comments. Stan's frequent words of praise for parents likely reflected both his genuine gratitude for their contributions and his strategy for assuring continued widespread support for his program.

Respect for parents was a favorite Bondy theme. Among his many talks on the subject was his *white socks* speech. Bondy told the players that they should never feel embarrassed by the way their parents dressed, using as an example a father who showed up at a somewhat formal function wearing black shoes and white socks. He stressed that it did not matter how their parents dressed or spoke. What mattered were the sacrifices that they made to provide their children with food, shelter, and guidance. On occasion, he let slip that he had once, years ago, been embarrassed that his parents were immigrants who could not speak or write English and that it was wrong for him to have ever felt that way. It was something he deeply regretted.

Swampscott great Bill Adams never forgot the white socks talks. It seemed the head coach was speaking directly to him. His father, who had been forced to quit school and go to work during the Depression, was a "white socks with black shoes" guy. Bill had felt somewhat embarrassed about that until he listened to Bondy. The coach helped him appreciate that the color of his dad's socks meant nothing compared to his gifts of love and support.

After rolling over Saugus, the still-unbeaten team prepared to travel to Lynn to play Classical. The Rams had won only once and had lost most of their games by large margins. While most Swampscott v. Classical games were close battles, particularly when played at Manning Bowl, this one was not. It was no contest as the Blue won 55–14. The offensive starters left the field in the second quarter after bursting to a 21–0 lead. Swampscott held Classical to minus 12 yards rushing. Eight Big Blue players scored.

The 4–3 Newburyport Clippers could no longer roll over strong opponents and they could not contend with this Swampscott team. Bondy's club increased its record to 8–0, beating the Clippers, 34–22. The game was never close, with the boys riding second-half leads of 27–6 and 34–14, and holding the ball on the Newburyport 17-yard line when the final whistle blew.

While a number of players scored and played well on defense, the most credit went to lineman Greg Brand, adding to his reputation as one of the area's best players. The consensus from the coaching staff was that SHS had won by running behind Brand. As reported by the *Item*:

> The 200-pound senior tackle had demolished one side of the Newburyport line in an outstanding two-way effort, blocking for ball carriers and, alternately, dumping others.

In commenting on Swampscott's victory, Coach Stehlin stated, "The line did it … they get off the mark quickly." He also noted that the Swampscott players made no mistakes and read well on defense. Coaching obviously played a role in such performance, and key assistants Lynch and DeFelice deserved much of the credit.

Thanksgiving and Marblehead loomed. This would be the seventh time that a Bondelevitch-coached team sought to complete an undefeated season by beating the Headers. It had failed in that mission only once—in 1961 at Marblehead. Now, traveling again to Memorial Stadium, the Big Blue had even more at stake. In addition to securing another conference and state title, the state's longest high school winning streak was on the line.

It had been a disappointing season for Headers fans and Coach Ree-benacker, who had felt he had "quite a team" and whose quarterback Frankie Legro had been described by Saugus coach Maguire as "one of the finest backs I've ever seen." Yet the Headers were going to finish with a losing record, having registered only three wins in their first eight games. Seeking improvement, the coach had made a number of changes, including moving Legro from quarterback to halfback where, according to Reebenacker, his performance had been "absolutely fantastic." The coach also lauded his defensive linemen, noting that they had played well and were improving all the time. "They can do the job," he had promised.

The losing record may have led to Reebenacker's announcement that he would step down at season's end. During his decade at the helm, he had coached the Headers to two championships. While he had not enjoyed Bondy's level of success, the two men were even in their match-ups, at five wins apiece. If the Magicians could find a way to win on Thanksgiving, it would not only spoil Swampscott's unbeaten season, end the state's longest winning streak, and be the biggest upset of the year on the North Shore, but also enable Reebenacker to retire with a winning 6–5 career record over Bondy.

As Thanksgiving morning dawned, there was tremendous incentive for both longtime rivals to play their best game. But the Big Blue was heavily favored. According to the *Item,* the Headers were 26-point under-dogs. As it turned out, the game was not a rout, it was a stunner. In reporting on the outcome, Red Hoffman wrote, "It is doubtful whether any winning or losing team in the series has ever played better football than the rivals played yesterday."

Shockingly, the Headers dominated in the early going. They took the opening kickoff and put together a long scoring drive, with sophomore quarterback Randy Rundle completing a short pass for the touchdown. Legro, running an option, threw to Paul Zagaeski for the two-point con-version. Marblehead led 8–0. The teams then kept trading possessions, including an exchange of interceptions, first by Swampscott's Caras, then by Legro. Near the end of the first half, the Headers mounted another drive that included a 44-yard gain on a pass from Rundle to Zagaeski. Legro finished it off from eight yards out after catching a pass over the middle. But the conversion attempt failed. When the half ended, the Big

Blue, having been favored by 26 points, retreated to the locker room on the short end of a 14–0 score.

The offense had struggled to get anything going. In addition to the tenacious Header defense, Swampscott was hampered by the loss of its two top scorers. Richie Conigliaro sprained his back in a freak accident during warm-ups and missed the final game of his senior year. Leading scorer Caras aggravated an injury suffered against Newburyport while intercepting Rundle's pass in the first quarter. He limped off the field, never to return. Not only were the two athletes the team's leading scorers and Beatrice's favorite targets, they were critically important to the defense. Now Swampscott had to find a way to win without them. The coaches opted to run directly at the defense at the start of the second half, hoping that the strategy would ultimately open up some better passing opportunities.

Swampscott began to dig itself out of the hole in the third quarter. The team established good field position when Mike Lynch, filling in for the injured Caras, punted 46 yards to the Headers' 6. Several plays later, Marblehead punted and Lou DeFelice returned the ball to the Magicians' 32. After runs by Dushan and DeFelice, Beatrice connected with end Jerry Mangini for the touchdown. The conversion pass fell incomplete. The Header lead was down to 14–6.

Then, after Marblehead took possession, Lou DeFelice did what he had been doing consistently all season. He intercepted—this one at his own 35. From there, Swampscott put together another scoring drive, with huge plays by DeFelice, who made a diving catch at the Header 23, and Beatrice, who first ran to the one and then snuck in for the score to bring the Blue within two points. But the conversion pass attempt again fell incomplete.

The Headers still held the lead and appeared on their way to expanding it after the ensuing kickoff as they drove to the Swampscott 24 before Mangini's tackle of Legro for a 7-yard loss and a holding penalty allowed the Blue to regain possession. But unable to move the ball, the boys punted back to Marblehead and SHS fans grew anxious as the game clock continued to wind down.

With slightly more than two minutes remaining, Marblehead was forced to punt. Lou DeFelice had been making plays all over the field. Now he snatched the punt in heavy traffic near midfield and, breaking a number of tackles, raced all the way to the Marblehead 22. From there the offense advanced the ball methodically against the stubborn Headers front wall. Swampscott reached the 3-yard line but faced a fourth down with 1:02 remaining, needing two yards for a first down and three for the touchdown.

After a time-out and sideline discussion, Bondy sent Mike Lynch in to attempt a field goal that would give the Blue a 15–14 lead. Peter Beatrice did a tremendous job fielding a high snap and placing it so Lynch could make the kick. Mike coolly booted it through the uprights and the Big Blue achieved its dramatic, comeback victory.

The Headers, playing exceptionally well, almost pulled off a historic upset. Frankie Legro lived up to his billing, carrying 21 times for 130 yards, catching a touchdown pass, throwing for a two-point conversion, intercepting a pass, returning kicks, including one for 44 yards, and turning in a strong performance as his team's punter. But the Swampscott players refused to lose.

However, Sandy Tennant's postgame celebration was cut short. As fans and players surged over the field, Jerry Mangini's dad toppled to the ground, felled by a heart attack. Sandy was one of the players closest to him. No one was able to locate Jerry in the ensuing chaos as an ambulance was quickly summoned. Tennant, still in his game uniform, climbed into the ambulance and tried to comfort his teammate's father as they rushed to the hospital. Thankfully, Mr. Mangini survived.

The 1969 Big Blue football team far exceeded expectations. SHS again claimed the Class B title. For the third consecutive year, Swampscott won on Thanksgiving, took home the conference championship, and finished the season unbeaten and untied. The state's longest winning streak now stretched to 27 games. Stan Bondelevitch was again Coach of the Year.

The depth of backfield talent was critical to the Blue's success, with Conigliaro, Caras, Tennant, Dushan, DeFelice, Losano, Cardillo, Leone, Beatrice, and Lynch all contributing. Peter Beatrice finished his two-year stint as varsity signal caller with 25 touchdown passes. He never lost a game and went go on to a highly productive college career as a quarterback at Brown University. Junior Mike Lynch successfully booted 28 extra points and two field goals, including the crucial game-winner in Marblehead.

Shortly before the Marblehead game, Bondy said that his team's defensive backfield was the best in Big Blue history; high praise indeed considering some of the stellar units of the past. Lou DeFelice finished the season with six interceptions, while Richie Conigliaro ended with five. Caras, Tennant, and Lynch each had two. Swampscott's line, one of the most inexperienced in Big Blue history, performed extremely well. Greg Brand was a dominant force, while two-way end Jerry Mangini made a number of big plays. Mike DiPrisco was solid all year at offensive guard and defensive end.

Seniors David Caras and Sandy Tennant were remarkably versatile players. In addition to serving as the team's punter, Caras played end, fullback, halfback, linebacker and defensive back. After a year of prep school, he went on to star at Bowdoin. Sandy, at different times, filled no less than eight separate positions. During his three years with the varsity, he started all 27 varsity games and never lost. Sandy was named to numerous All-Star squads and became the third consecutive Swampscott senior to win the coveted Thom McAn Shoe Award. He was a great high school football player.

Sandy planned to attend Boston College on a football scholarship but was encouraged by his high school guidance counselor to apply to Harvard. She assured him that if he put in the effort he would do fine. He put in the effort and did fine, earning separate Harvard bachelor's, master's, and doctoral degrees, the last in Educational Planning, Social Policy and Administration. He also played football for the Crimson and was named an All-New England linebacker. He returned to Swampscott, entered politics, and served on the school committee. He also became active as a consultant and lobbyist while he and his wife raised five children. Today he operates his own consulting business and is involved with organizations addressing the issue of concussions in sports. One lesson that Sandy is certain he learned through his Swampscott football experience was to never give up.

While Bondy had expressed some concerns at the outset of the 1969 season, he also noted that Swampscott was still the Class B Champion until someone took the title away. No one took it away. After the second game of the season, he also said that the boys were determined to do well. They did.

1961 tri-captains Dana Coughlin (8), Ronny Corcoran (9), and Richie Fuller (64) with Coach Bondelevitch. 1962 *Seagull*

David Coughlin. 1962 *Seagull*

Walter Costello is escorted from the field by two Denver Broncos linemen. Courtesy *Daily Item*

1963—Seniors Paul Legere (75), Walter Costello (22), and Barry Gallup (82). Paul J. Maguire photo. Courtesy *Boston Globe*

Costello catches pass against Marblehead as Gallup (82) turns upfield. 1964 *Seagull*

1963 cheerleaders, pregame with Big Blue hoop. 1964 *Seagull*

Flora McLearn, Stan Bondelevitch, and Dick Lynch. 1964 *Seagull*

1964 Coaches Gillis, Lynch, Bondelevitch, and Marden. 1965 *Seagull*

1966 co-captains Tony Blood (l) and Mark Stevenson (r) with Bondy. Edison Farrand photo, courtesy *Boston Globe*

Our mother took this photo of my brother Dick (5) and me following 1966 Danvers game.

1966—Big Blue Banditos cartoon by Hank Collins, courtesy *Daily Item*

Typical gathering in Bondy's office. Standing behind Bondy (l-r): Vin Serino, Alan "Rugs" Gardner, Bobby Hopkins, Coach Bill Gillis, Steve Sheperd, and Dick Jauron. 1967 *Seagull*

1967—kneeling (l-r) Ben Williams, Bill Adams, Carl Kester, Ed Clippinger, Mike Hoffman, Andy Rose, John Carden; standing (l-r) Dick Polisson, Phil Abram, Gerry McGettrick, Dan Videtta, Dick Jauron, Tom Toner, Ray MacCallum. Adams, Jauron, and Toner went on to eventually play multiple seasons in the NFL.

1968 coaches: (l-r) Stan Bondelevitch, Frank DeFelice, Dick Lynch, Ron Corcoran.

November 1968—Carl "Mad Dog" Kester (r) poses with his dad Waldemar "Cowboy" Kester (m) and Mike "Skip" Pagnotti (l), both former Sculpin players, in front of a town hall exhibit commemorating prior SHS teams. Courtesy *Daily Item*

1969—"Stan the Man"

The '70s

Bondy standing on his tower, above 1972 senior linemen; front row (l-r), John Hoffman, Greg Beatrice, Roy Ostrovitz; second row (l-r), Wayne Smith, Steve Zuchero, John Toner; top, Richard Dedrick. Smith photo, courtesy *Daily Item*

Homegrown Heartbreaker

S HS had not lost in three years, but it *had* lost 18 seniors to graduation. Only two offensive starters remained—both interior linemen. Yet once again, there were very good players to fill vacated skill positions. As sophomores, backs Danny Losano and Charlie Cardillo played regularly on defense. Now they would be starting both ways. Captain Jimmy Carone, having missed his junior season, was ready to return at fullback. Rugged junior Billy Leone, who had established himself as a hard-hitting sophomore linebacker in 1969, was also fully capable of filling in at fullback. Six-foot junior receiver/defensive back Larry Moran, who weighed close to 200 pounds, was a gifted athlete, with the hands, speed, strength, and reflexes to excel on the football field.

With Peter Beatrice gone, Mike Lynch stepped in as the starting quarterback. If anyone could be described as having been raised in the Big Blue culture it was Lynch. As the oldest son of the team's longtime backfield coach, he could not recall a time when Swampscott sports had not played an integral role in his life. In 1961, Mike and several friends had served as waterboys. The buckets had felt so heavy that it took two of the youngsters to lug them to the huddles during time-outs. He had been in awe of varsity players like Ronny Corcoran and Richie Fuller.

Prior to playing organized football, Mike spent countless hours in sandlot contests, including many in the neighboring Faulkners' yard, where Mr. Faulkner had erected a goalpost. From an early age, Mike focused on learning to pass, punt, and placekick. He and younger brother Terry had both won local punting and passing championships and advanced to statewide competitions. By the time he reached the eighth grade, it seemed clear that Mike was destined to play quarterback. While he was not especially fast, nor a ferocious hitter like Sandy Tennant, Mike was athletic and intelligent, playing basketball and baseball as well as football. Yet he and his classmates struggled as members of the ninth-grade squad. They did not win many games and were not even competitive against the Danvers freshmen.

When they reported for preseason in 1968, Lynch and the other sophomores were issued red JV jerseys. However, Jimmy Carone soon disappeared from the JVs, becoming the starting varsity fullback. Then, on the Thursday before the season's opener, Coach Bondelevitch conducted a little ceremony during which he awarded varsity jerseys to four more sophomores, including Mike Lynch.

What most impressed Mike and his friends about dressing for games as sophomores was their treatment by the squad's senior leaders. In all respects, they were welcomed and accepted as full team members, including being invited to social events like the Sunday night player-only gatherings where they watched game films while enjoying pizza and other treats. They were not subjected to hazing or disrespectful treatment by the older, more experienced boys. They concluded that this was the way leaders and champions behaved.

As a junior in 1969, Lynch backed up quarterback Peter Beatrice, while further contributing to the team's success in other ways, including kicking the all-important winning field goal at Marblehead. As soon as that season ended, Bondy handed him a football and told him to throw 50 passes each day, predicting that if he worked hard he could become one of the top quarterbacks in Big Blue history. Following the coach's instruction, he focused on improving his passing and kicking skills during the off-season.

Veteran guards Randy Werner and Mike DiPrisco returned to the front line. However, much to DiPrisco's dismay, the coaches decided to move him to offensive end. He loved playing guard and was so upset with the change that he begged Coach DeFelice to return him to his former position. When Frank said that it was out of his control, DiPrisco actually started to cry.

Stu Greeley, who had played linebacker in 1969, became the starting varsity center. Bobby Murray (no relation to Greg and Tom) and Kevin Riley, two good-sized juniors, were named starting tackles, while Steve Kruger would be used as an offensive end. Murray and senior Randy Kline joined Billy Leone as linebackers. Larry Moran was versatile enough to play different skill positions.

Bondy continued to invent nicknames, not just for individual players, but for various units. Like many of his generation, he had no concern for what now would be termed "political correctness." Realizing that there were a number of Jewish kids playing on the defensive side, he announced to the *Item* that he would be relying on a "Kosher Defense." Aware that many of his leading backs (Carone, Losano, Cardillo, and Leone) were Italian-Americans, Stan lauded his "pizza backfield". His players didn't seem to mind the ethnic references, as the coach's tone was light-hearted and complimentary. Most, if not all, enjoyed the humor and recognition.

One of the newcomers who performed well during preseason was Peter Beatrice's younger brother, Greg. Although he was only 14 years old, the 6-foot, 3-inch sophomore was the biggest player on the team. While his reported weight was 235, some teammates believed that it was under-stated. Yet Greg was more than just a big kid. He was athletic enough to have played quarterback as a freshman and in his sophomore year would be working as an offensive end and defensive tackle.

In 1969, Jim Carone had suffered a season-ending injury during the Joyce Jamboree. Despite the loss of a key player in what might seem a meaningless exhibition game, Bondy had been quick to praise the event. "I think the Jamboree is the greatest thing that's ever happened to local schoolboy football, and I hope nothing ever happens to it," he had said. Unfortunately, despite Bondy's hopes, in 1970 the event lost much of its luster and appeal after organizers made the decision to move it to a Saturday afternoon. Many complained and some teams held out their starters, playing only reserves. While the Big Blue participated and managed to take down Class A Peabody, 7–6, Stan publicly expressed his unhappiness, telling the *Item*:

When we go into the Jamboree, we go in with class. I don't want any part of the Jamboree again if it's going to be run like it was this year. Why should I risk getting my starters hurt when other coaches use their second and third stringers? If the Jamboree is held again next year, I'd have to give it a great deal of consideration before agreeing to play in it.

It was the beginning of the end for the once-popular Friday night extravaganza.

On September 24, 1970, the *Item's* Cahill devoted his entire column to Stan Bondelevitch and the Big Blue. He wrote that, according to Bondy, Swampscott football players were "taught to respect their parents, do their school work conscientiously, and give the coaches their undivided dedication from 3 to 5 every afternoon during football season."

In discussing game preparation, Stan explained that on Friday afternoons before Saturday games the team engaged in a light workout and the captains then conducted a private, players-only meeting. Later in the evening, Stan met with the team's defensive signal caller and then with the quarterback. Describing his remaining activities, Bondy said he usually stared blankly at the television for an hour or two and then retired to bed and read until falling to sleep. Noting that he liked to read historical biographies, Bondy told Cahill that he was in the process of reading *The Life of Bismarck,* joking that it might be dull enough to put him to sleep quickly.

Bondy spent some time discussing the pressure of the long winning streak, telling Cahill:

Sometimes I think some people, very good people, like parents, may expect too much of the boys. They are teenagers, not professionals, and they're only human.

He mentioned that the Blue's schedule was its toughest ever. "Every team on it will be sky high against us, hoping to end our streak," he said. He described opening opponent Gloucester as improved and well coached, adding with a smile, "There are a lot of football players in Gloucester this very moment who can't wait to get at us."

On September 26, 1970, Swampscott hosted the big Fishermen, three of whose linemen weighed over 210 pounds. They also had a couple of fast, explosive backs in Wayne Saunders and Ambrose Orlando. SHS did not impress in the early going. Saunders returned the opening kickoff 81 yards to the 4-yard line. He subsequently ran it in for the score. After Swampscott responded with a Lynch to Losano TD pass to take a 7–6 lead, Orlando ran back the ensuing kick 85 yards into the end zone. When

Gloucester, continuing to play well, surged to a 28–13 second-half lead it seemed that the streak had run its course.

However, the Blue stormed back as Carone and Losano each ran for two touchdowns. Lynch's conversion kick following the second Losano score gave the home team a 39–28 lead with only a couple of minutes left. While Gloucester closed the gap following another long kick return, Swampscott hung on to win, 39–36. It was the eighth time during the streak that the boys had come from behind to win.

Swampscott posted some massive numbers against the Fishermen, including 20 first downs and over 500 yards of total offense. The Achilles heel was poor kick coverage; Gloucester amassed a jaw-dropping 268 yards in returns. Yet the boys were resilient and displayed considerable firepower and an ability to score quickly on big plays as well as through long, sustained drives.

By 1970, Bondy had grown so comfortable with the smooth operations of his program that he no longer paid much attention to what was happening daily at JV and freshman practices. However, he tried to attend the games. A new man was working as the freshman coach. Opting to de-emphasize the Big Blue's standard wing-T, the fellow drilled the ninth graders in an offensive scheme that employed quarterback options run out of a wishbone formation. He did not mention the changes to Stan before the first freshman game, played at Blocksidge Field with Bondy watching from the stands.

When the players broke from the huddle to run their first play and set up in a wishbone formation, a shocked Bondelevitch bellowed, "STOP! STOP EVERYTHING!" And everything did stop, as coaches, players, and officials looked up and saw the irate Big Blue boss barreling down from the bleachers. Bondy demanded to know just what the hell was going on. In a brief and heated exchange with the new coach, Stan explained that the ninth-grade squad should be operating in the same fashion as every other Swampscott football team. The players returned to the wing-T, running the offense that served as almost a trademark of Big Blue football.

The varsity's second game was against Saugus. Bondy tried to downplay talk of the 28-game winning streak, telling the *Item* that most of the current players had played little if any role in past unbeaten seasons. "It's not fair," he said, "to burden them with thoughts of defending an undefeated streak such as we have now. It just puts added pressure on them every game." Fair or not, the players could not escape the pressure of the streak.

The coaches made some changes for the game. Reluctant offensive end Mike DiPrisco had fumbled after catching a pass against Gloucester and was now happily back in his treasured left guard position. Tall, athletic junior Richard Fromer replaced him at end while Randy Kline moved from guard to tackle. The team made a strong statement at Saugus, clobbering the Sachems, 42–14. Carone rushed for 123 yards and two touchdowns, and Losano ran for over 100 yards and scored. Lynch passed for two touchdowns and also scored on a sneak. The defense did what Swampscott defenses so often did—create turnovers. In addition to recovering a fumble, the boys intercepted five passes.

The team now faced one of those big games that seemed to come along once or twice every season. As in 1969, the opponent was Danvers, a school that had struggled in the past against most of Bondy's teams but had ended the Big Blue's 19-win run in 1959. Now the Falcons had a chance to ruin an even longer streak.

Their only loss in the last 17 outings had been to the Big Blue when the Tennant-led defense shut down Danvers and its great fullback Ken St. Pierre. Since that defeat, they had won nine straight.

The pressure was squarely on the Big Blue as it traveled to Danvers. The game was a sell out with the largest crowd in Danvers football history on hand to watch the unbeaten squads battle. While Bondelevitch-coached teams seldom lacked confidence, Stan apparently felt that this club needed a boost, perhaps recalling that three years earlier Mike Lynch and his teammates had been humiliated by the Danvers freshmen. Bondy told the *Item* that his players were a dedicated bunch and believed that they would win. On game day, the *Item* carried a surprising headline on its sports page, "'We Think We'll Win': Bondelevitch."

Swampscott did win, 35–22, rolling up an incredible 556 yards in total offense, including 352 yards rushing. Red Hoffman suggested that the "awesome offense" might be the best in Swampscott's history. Danny Losano alone accounted for 230 yards, while Charlie Cardillo rushed for 147 and Mike Lynch threw for 100 yards and two touchdowns.

While not quite as stingy as the 1969 defense, the boys on the first unit again slammed the door, limiting the Falcons to just 84 yards rushing, while the Blue built a 35–8 cushion. Danvers did most of its damage against reserves late in the second half. According to Stan, the "Kosher Defense" was now the "Kool Kat Defense." He told Hoffman, "We try to keep our kids cool because they're young and can't afford to become emotional." It was a different strategy from that used to inspire Tennant and company, but Bondy did not hesitate to vary his motivational approach to better match a particular team's personality.

The first third of the season exceeded expectations, particularly the domination over previously unbeaten Danvers. Swampscott, having won 30 consecutive games, practiced at Phillips Park in preparation for its trip to Winthrop. As he had been doing since his playing days at Saint Anselm, Bondy decided that it was time to inject some humor to lighten the mood. When a plane approaching Boston's Logan Airport flew over the practice field at a low altitude, the coach, with perfect timing, dropped to the ground, yelling, "Hit the deck! It's a Winthrop spy plane." He continued with the comic relief, ordering the offense to run some fake plays to confuse the spies in the aircraft.

The Vikings, now coached by Frank DeFelice's brother Bob, were no match for the Blue, falling 35–6. Speedy Charlie Cardillo, whose father Joseph "Jo-Jo" Cardillo had captained the 1940 Sculpins, had a banner day, rushing for 148 yards, including touchdown scampers of 75 and 50 yards, while scoring a third on a 26-yard interception return. In addition to the Cardillo pick, the defense recovered four Winthrop fumbles.

It seemed that in every season some SHS player managed to find unique ways to antagonize Coach DeFelice. In 1970, that unlucky fellow was 185-pound guard Randy Werner. Randy was a fourth grader when his family moved into town. He soon learned about Big Blue football. He lived near Phillips Park and often watched the team practice. On one occasion, Coach Bondelevitch heartily assured the youngster that one day he too would be playing for the Big Blue. Randy yearned to do just that.

Although he lived in a large house in an affluent neighborhood, Randy could never think of it as *home*. Randy's father was killed in an accident when he was three years old. His mother remarried and moved to Swampscott. The boy felt that the adults who were supposed to act as supportive, affectionate parents did the opposite. He sensed that, for reasons he could not fathom, they despised him. Randy found his family circumstances so abhorrent that, to this day, he has difficulty referring to the woman who gave birth to him as his mother. Rather, he talks about "the people that I lived with." He spent as much time as possible staying with friends like Mike DiPrisco or Mike Lynch, or with his grandparents in Revere. Not surprisingly, he struggled in school, finding it hard to complete homework assignments. He sometimes also acted out and got into minor difficulties of one sort or another.

He turned to sports in search of acceptance and a sense of belonging. He joined in games of tackle-fumble football with kids at Stanley School and, although he was not a natural athlete, loved the rough-and-tumble game. When he grew older, he played Babe Ruth baseball. His team was coached by former Big Blue football co-captains Bobby Carlin and Billy Nelson. Randy had wavy, blond hair and after he arrived at a game wearing sunglasses and sweat bands, the coaches remarked that he looked like the right fielder for the Boston Red Sox, Ken (Hawk) Harrelson. Thereafter, Randy would forever be known to many in Swampscott as simply, "Hawk."

Hawk started playing organized football in the eighth grade. He was the kind of kid that Bondy loved to talk about, making up for limited ability with desire, spirit, and a positive outlook. When he reached high school, Randy played as a guard on the JVs but his biggest thrill was dressing for varsity games. He had a chance to hear Bondy's pregame speech when the coach recited the name and position of each starting player. Hawk looked forward to the day when his name would be one of those mentioned.

Because the 1968 team was so strong, there was usually a time in the second half when Bondy cleared his bench. Late in those one-sided affairs, Hawk stood close to Stan, knowing that the coach had a habit of grabbing a nearby reserve and pushing him onto the field while shouting something like, "Get in there at defensive end and sack the quarterback!" When the team returned from away games and the players exited the bus amidst a crowd of cheerleaders, spirit squad members, and other supporters, Hawk always tarried outside, hoping that onlookers, particularly girls, might recognize him in his varsity uniform.

But it was not always fun. Coaches Lynch and DeFelice sometimes made Hawk feel that, like Rodney Dangerfield, he got no respect. But at least they paid attention to him. He was a high-spirited kid and sometimes found himself in trouble at school. Coach Lynch was aware of Hawk's family circumstances and tried to extend him some "tough love." At one point, having heard of another Werner incident, he called Hawk into his gym office. Coach DeFelice was also present. Lynch promised that if Randy stepped out of line once more, he and DeFelice were going use him as the ball in a game of ping pong. DeFelice added, "And I ping a little harder than he pongs!"

Hawk experienced some DeFelice "ping" when he joined the JV basketball squad as a sophomore. Aggressive football players had a good chance of making Frank's JVs regardless of their roundball skills. It took no basketball ability to battle other kids in a scrum on the gym floor and come away with the ball, but it seemed to impress DeFelice, as did fighting through Frank's no-holds-barred rebound drill, or standing perfectly still and being run over when Frank had the boys practice "taking a charge." Randy was willing to absorb some blows in such drills as he saw it as a chance to showcase for football.

During the following summer, Hawk worked various jobs and regularly attended Barry Gallup's strength and conditioning workouts, staying away from home as much as possible. However, despite his scrappy performance in the JV basketball scrums and loyal participation in the summer workouts, when football practice started in 1969, he struggled, toiling in obscurity on the third team. Then he caught a weird break.

He and other reserves were standing on the sideline during a scrimmage and someone mentioned history teacher Waldemar Kester. Hawk commented that he loved Mr. Kester. Coach DeFelice, who also thought highly of Carl's father, was standing nearby and heard the comment. He turned and asked, "Who said that about Mr. Kester?" Randy identified himself. Frank had a second question. "Do you know your plays at right guard?" When Hawk said yes, he was promptly sent into the scrimmage. He must have done the job because he was thereafter named the starting right guard. While Hawk was not the kind of player who could beat up and dominate opposing linemen, he was determined to get the job done and usually found a way to accomplish the task.

After the 1969 football season ended, Hawk failed to make the varsity basketball squad. But Coach DeFelice not only gave the junior a spot on the JVs, he named Randy captain. However, there was at least one occasion when Hawk failed to act like the captain. During a practice, Coach DeFelice, dissatisfied with Werner's soft in-bounding pass, grabbed a ball with both hands and fired it at him, shouting, "This is how you pass the ball!" Hawk did not react in time and the ball bounced off his face. In thoughtless anger, he quickly picked the ball up and rifled it toward a nearby small teammate. The ball flew through the boy's hands and smashed into his face, shattering the poor kid's glasses and leaving him with a bruised and bloody nose.

Before Hawk could apologize, he was confronted by DeFelice, who was furious. Meanwhile, the varsity players were ascending the stairs from the locker room to the gym. Suddenly the Hawk came hurtling down upon them. The mechanism of his launch through the gym door remains a matter of some dispute. His friend Mike DiPrisco broke his fall, but Randy landed in a heap at the base of the staircase. There was much commotion and Coach Lynch was in the midst of asking what the problem was when he came upon the boy sprawled on the floor in front of him. "Oh," he said dismissively, as he stepped over the dazed kid and continued up to the gym, "it's only Werner." For Hawk, it was another Dangerfield moment.

When the fall of 1970 rolled around, senior Randy Werner was the starting right guard. But life at home was worse than ever. It seemed that there were constant confrontations. One night, the police were called to the residence after a major blow-up. When Randy had left the Fieldhouse earlier that evening following practice, he found his younger sister waiting outside. She was disheveled and in tears following some kind of argument with her mother and stepfather. It was getting colder and darker as Randy returned with her to the house. But the adults refused to let them in. Finally, after repeated futile requests that they be allowed inside, Randy forced his way in and a brawl ensued.

Bondy and Dick Lynch knew many, if not all, of the men on the Swampscott police force. If the police came upon an issue involving a Swampscott athlete, the coaches were usually quickly notified. Soon after the police arrived at Werner's house, so did Coach Lynch and Marty Goldman, a local attorney and special friend of Big Blue sports. Ultimately, Hawk was transported to the home of a local family more than willing to welcome him.

At practice on the following day, a distracted Hawk made repeated mistakes. Finally, Coach DeFelice intervened and walked with the boy a few yards away from the other players. If onlookers expected that the coach was going to express compassion or cut Randy some slack, they were mistaken. Instead, Frank promised that if Hawk continued to screw up, he would find himself on the bench. While confirming that he knew about Randy's difficult family situation, Frank emphasized that when any player stepped onto the field, he had to be ready to perform. Hawk desperately wanted to continue to start for the Big Blue. He refocused and held on to his starting job. In so doing, he took his mind off his other troubles, at least temporarily.

Although Hawk avoided further major performance issues on the football field, the same could not be said of his off-field activities. Soon after that day, as he entered the Fieldhouse for practice he heard a sharp command, "Werner, come over here!" Randy was always apprehensive when Coach DeFelice demanded his presence. His anxiety only increased as he listened to the line coach. "I'm planning to steal Coach Bondelevitch's car," DeFelice whispered. "I need you to serve as my lookout. Can I rely on you?" Randy was bewildered. He stammered that he did not understand.

Frank raised his voice: "You heard me. I need your help. You stay here and let me know if you see Coach Bondelevitch coming because I'm going to steal his car and I don't want to get caught. Got it?"

Hawk had no idea what to say or do. He was struggling to come up with some kind of response when DeFelice hissed, "What is wrong with you? My defensive end is in detention! How stupid can you be?" Suddenly Hawk understood the message.

At school that day, a problem kid who played defensive end had told him that he was going to enter Mr. Kester's classroom, rifle through the teacher's briefcase, and find and remove the history exam. He wanted Hawk to wait at the top of the stairs, and shout a warning if he saw the teacher approaching. Rather than trying to talk the kid out of such a harebrained scheme or at least refuse to participate himself, Hawk foolishly agreed to act as sentry.

He was daydreaming at his post when a whistling Mr. Kester suddenly ambled around the corner and up the stairs. "Hey, Randy Werner, how ya doing?" he called out merrily, as he continued quickly toward his classroom. Hawk, having no time to sound the alarm, bolted away. At the same time, Mr. Kester's tone changed when he entered the classroom. Hearing the teacher's shocked, angry voice yelling the culprit's name, Hawk continued to scamper from the scene of the crime.

The hapless teenager had forgotten about his latest screw-up until he was rudely reminded by his fuming line coach. Hawk was not sure whether Frank was more troubled by his involvement in the wacky misconduct or his failure to properly carry out his agreed assignment. But Werner was beginning to examine some of his past actions, realizing that there were perhaps good reasons for the Dangerfield treatment.

Yet, while Randy could sometimes get under Frank's skin, he just seemed to amuse Bondy. The head coach, aware of Randy's rough family situation, liked the boy and treated him well. Hawk may not have felt welcome at his family's home, but he always felt welcome at Stan's. And he spent a good deal of time there, listening to Bondy talk about various subjects, helping with work in the garden and other chores, and laughing at the big man's jokes.

At practices, Stan also directed some good-natured kidding at Randy. One of his favorite routines, when the boy faltered or seemed to be wearing down, was to pretend to wind him up by turning an imaginary screw in the middle of Hawk's back while chanting something like, "Oh, it's time to rewind our robot, Randy Werner.... Okay, now you are good to go for another 10 hours." Actually, Hawk was good to go for as long as necessary to remain part of the Big Blue family.

In its fourth consecutive road game, Swampscott traveled to Manning Bowl and defeated Lynn English, 33–20. The score was misleading since the Blue led 33–0 when Bondy pulled his starters. Mike Lynch threw three touchdown passes and the team produced over 500 yards.

At 5–0, the Big Blue was more than halfway home to a fourth consecutive undefeated season. But a unique challenge lay ahead. For the first time, a Bondelevitch team would play the Eagles of Saint John's Preparatory School. The Prep, as it is commonly known, had a distinct advantage. As a private school, it accepted students from all over the North Shore and beyond. With such a wide pool of potential talent, the Prep typically produced strong teams. The 1967 squad had claimed the Class B championship based on its having faced more Class A schools than had the Big Blue.

But the 2–3 Eagles did not seem much of a threat in 1970. They had suffered a 29–6 thrashing by Danvers, a squad that the Blue had easily beaten. And they were coming off a 26–0 pounding by Peabody, a team that SHS had handled in the Jamboree. Moreover, after four road games, the Big Blue was finally returning to Blocksidge Field. Yet, the Prep always had a number of good athletes, and this squad held a substantial weight advantage over Swampscott. Like every opponent, they had extra incentive—an opportunity to end the state's longest winning streak, now numbering 32 consecutive victories.

The well coached Eagles arrived at Blocksidge Field and, playing before another full house, surprisingly put the clamps on an offense that had been averaging over 39 points per game. At halftime, Swampscott held a slim 7–0 lead. Receiving the kickoff to start the third quarter, the Prep put together a scoring drive that included a successful fake punt on fourth down. The conversion attempt failed, so the Blue clung to a one-point lead. That disappeared when the Prep scored again with eight minutes remaining in the contest.

Trailing 12–7, the home team fought back and reclaimed the lead when Larry Moran caught Lynch's pass in the corner of the end zone. Leading 13–12 the boys were only a couple of minutes away from extending the streak. But after first returning the ensuing kickoff to its 41-yard line, the Prep shocked the Big Blue faithful when quarterback Dave Handy fired a 40-yard pass down the middle of the field, hitting halfback Dana Hughes in stride. Hughes sprinted all the way to the end zone. The PAT-kick was good and Swampscott trailed again, 19–13.

Bondy's squad had just over a minute to avert its first loss in more than three-and-a-half seasons. Billy Leone ran back the kick to the Blue 33. On first down Lynch connected with Moran who took it all the way to the Prep 27. After an incompletion, Losano carried to the 17 and Lynch then completed a pass to Fromer. Swampscott called a final time-out. It was first and goal with the ball resting on the 9-yard line and 26 seconds remaining.

With no timeouts available, the offense could not risk a running play. Three consecutive passes toward well-covered receivers proved unsuccessful. The team had one final chance. Mike Lynch called a play designed to free up a receiver in the corner of the end zone. But there was some confusion and it was not run as designed. As a result, no Blue player made it into the corner and Lynch was left looking for another option as the pass rush bore down on him. Finally, he released the ball to avoid being sacked, but it fell incomplete.

The streak was now history. Speaking shortly after the final whistle, Stan lauded the Prep. "They beat us right up front where it counts," he told the *Item*. "We can point to no mistakes, no bad calls, no excuses. They just beat us in every department." Bondy had taught many kids how to win. Now he was showing the boys how to be gracious in defeat. The players had no reason for head-hanging. They had fought valiantly down the stretch, first responding late in the fourth quarter to reclaim the lead and then driving almost the length of the field in a last-ditch effort to seize victory.

Statistically, the game was almost dead even. Ultimately, the difference was the dramatic 59-yard touchdown by Hughes. Red Hoffman expressed great respect for Swampscott's fans, who, he reported, stood and applauded for a full five minutes after the game, recognizing both teams, but especially their own for its record-breaking run.

Ironically, a team traditionally known for excellent pass defense saw its historic string of victories broken by a long touchdown pass. It was even more ironic that Prep hero Dana Hughes could have easily walked home after the game. He was a homegrown Swampscott boy who lived just a stone's throw from Blocksidge Field. Dana grew up playing sandlot football with Mike Lynch, Mike DiPrisco, and many of the other SHS players. As a youngster, he served as a Big Blue waterboy. But his parents enrolled him in the private secondary school in Danvers. He had returned to help end the long winning streak, breaking the hearts of the Big Blue faithful.

That night some of the boys gathered in the large parking lot in front of Friendly's Restaurant in Swampscott's Vinnin Square and sadly rehashed the game, voicing regrets about miscues that led to the loss. They were in the midst of various self-recriminations when a honking car pulled into the lot and Dana Hughes, still in his Prep game jersey, stepped out. He was carrying the game ball which had been awarded him during his team's postgame celebration. Several teammates were with him.

The crestfallen Swampscott players were in no mood to socialize with guys who were responsible for ending their winning streak and ruining their undefeated season. But several SHS cheerleaders felt no such constraints. They chatted amiably with Dana and his pals before climbing into the vehicle and riding away with them, adding insult to injury.

The boys were still in the doldrums when they arrived at school on Monday and an announcement was made that all students were to report to the gym for a special assembly. When the players arrived, they discovered that the purpose of the assembly was to recognize and honor the Big Blue football team. The spirit squad and cheerleaders led the rest of the students in the celebration. Bondy and others congratulated the boys on everything that they had accomplished. Principal Bertrand Roger, after thanking the team and coaches for "an absolutely incredible win streak", proclaimed that it was "Big Blue Week". It was the best thing that could have been done to raise the spirits of the players and help them cope with the staggering loss to the Prep.

The streak was over, but the team could still win a championship. The 5–1 Blue was unbeaten in the Northeastern Conference. There were three games remaining. Could the boys regroup and return to their winning ways after the disappointing loss?

As a result of injuries suffered against English and the Prep, the team faced Classical without defensive tackles Kevin Riley and Greg Beatrice, flanker/safety Larry Moran, center Stu Greeley, and fullback Jimmy Carone. Fortunately, there was good depth in players like junior Billy Leone and sophomores Jeff Hegan, Ray DiPietro, and Roy Ostrovitz, all of whom stepped up and contributed, as Swampscott beat the Rams at Blocksidge, 35–14. For the fourth time, the team amassed over 500 yards of total offense.

On the following Saturday at Newburyport, Swampscott won again, 28–18. The team was still missing a number of its regulars, but outstanding junior halfback Dan Losano had a monster game, carrying 21 times for 231 yards and a touchdown. Lynch also had a strong outing, passing for two touchdowns and kicking four extra points.

The 7–1 varsity only needed a Thanksgiving win over Marblehead to claim the conference crown. The 4-4 Headers, now coached by Alex Kulevich, had a good quarterback in Randy Rundle who had played well as a sophomore in the 1969 near-upset. The 1970 game at Blocksidge Field was initially a tight contest. Only Mike Lynch's 37-yard field goal with five seconds left in the first half enabled the Blue to enter the locker room with a 9–7 lead. But Swampscott was ultimately too strong for Rundle and his mates. The team exploded in the third quarter, first scoring off a blazing 75-yard Losano dash and then on a 4-yard ramble by Jimmy Carone.

The senior fullback had to deal with more than his share of frustrations during his three varsity seasons. While he was a member of consecutive undefeated teams, he did not play a single down as a junior due to the season-ending injury sustained in the Jamboree. He continued to struggle with injuries as team captain in 1970, missing several more games. But he recovered in time to return to the line-up on Thanksgiving and cap his SHS career by leading his team to a third consecutive conference title, bashing the Headers, 35–6.

The *Boston Globe* named Michael Lynch its Class B All-Scholastic quarterback. As a junior, he helped SHS preserve an undefeated season and secure a twenty-seventh straight victory by kicking the critical game-winning field goal against Marblehead. As a senior, he led the team to a conference championship, and his 15 touchdown passes tied the SHS single-season record set by Bobby Hopkins. In his two seasons as the Blue's placekicker, Mike also made 60 PAT kicks and three field goals. Following a year at Exeter, Lynch attended Harvard, played football, and ultimately became an award-winning sports anchor for a major Boston television network.

Randy Werner's Swampscott family situation never improved, but he received support from many, including SHS guidance counselor Jack Curry, who helped him gain admission to Northeastern University. Curry would ultimately become president of that institution. When Frank DeFelice became head football coach at Xaverian Brothers High School in 1971, Hawk worked part-time as one of Frank's assistants. They became good friends.

Randy eventually transferred to Western Michigan University to be closer to his fiancée, ironically named Randi. Following graduation, he worked as an innovative elementary school teacher before meeting a salesman from the Shakespeare Fishing Company. Hawk was so impressed by the man, that he decided to join Shakespeare and applied for a sales job. Despite countless rejections, Hawk persisted. Finally, he flew to South Carolina and convinced Shakespeare's president to hire him. He became a highly productive salesman and eventually established his own successful business.

In 2002, Werner, who had struggled academically at SHS, was inducted into the Alumni Honor Academy of Western Michigan University's Department of Health, Physical Education and Recreation. Randy and Randi have been happily married for many years and have two grown children, one of whom recently made them grandparents. Hawk is certain that his Swampscott sports experience taught him how to overcome obstacles and fulfill his ambitions.

The 1970 Big Blue players had come within a hair of completing the school's fourth consecutive undefeated season, falling just short due to the last-minute exploits of one of their Swampscott neighbors. Despite that heart-breaking loss, they were still champions. For the fourth consecutive year, SHS won the conference title. And the good news was that many veterans, including three pizza backfield regulars, would be returning in 1971.

I Wonder Who Will Beat This Team

Most of the staff remained in 1971. Coach Lynch, tough, capable, and highly respected, embarked on his eighteenth season in Swampscott. Ronny Corcoran continued as JV coach, while also helping with the varsity. Corcoran manned the headsets on the sidelines during varsity games, staying in touch with Lynch, who watched and strategized from the press box. Ronny was somewhat low-key, popular with the boys, and destined to become legendary as a Hall of Fame coach at Triton Regional High School.

One major change was the departure of Frank DeFelice, who left to become the head football coach at Xaverian Brothers High School in Westwood, Massachusetts. During his five years as a Swampscott assistant, the Blue had posted 40 wins and three losses. That incredible record could not have been achieved without the strong performances of Frank's offensive and defensive lines. Mark Stevenson and Bill Adams have credited DeFelice's coaching as essential to their becoming outstanding high school and college players. Adams, who also played professionally, asserts that he never had a better line coach at any level. But Frank DeFelice also learned and matured as a member of Bondy's staff. While he had sometimes bristled at the head coach's rebukes and criticisms, he came to realize that he received a remarkable coaching education working with Stan Bondelevitch and Dick Lynch.

Former Big Blue player George Pleau, who had been working with the JVs, became the new line coach. Pleau's coaching style was different from Frank's. Compared to DeFelice, he was almost passive. He rarely yelled or got in players' faces. Like Frank, he knew and could teach line play, but used different communication skills. He was well-liked and respected by the players.

Fran York, a Lynn Classical grad, joined the staff and worked primarily with the JVs. Bondy, reminded of professional baseball's Rudy York, immediately dubbed the new man "Rudy" and eventually had difficulty recalling York's actual first name. On one occasion, Fran's wife interrupted a coaches meeting, telephoning due to an emergency at home. When she told Bondy that she needed to speak with Fran, he informed her that she had the wrong number and hung up. She called again, with the same result. Phyllis York dialed a third time. As soon as Bondy answered she explained that her husband, Fran York, was one of his assistants and that she urgently needed to speak with him. "Oh, you want Rudy!" replied Stan as he handed the phone to York.

As the new assistant at the bottom of the totem pole, "Rudy" was assigned "get back" responsibility during varsity games. He, therefore, spent his time constantly shouting at the players to get back as they continually surged forward, crowding the sideline to watch the action on the field. York's duties increased considerably over time, as did his understanding of many ingredients in Bondy's winning formula, which he, like Corcoran, eventually utilized in building his own Hall of Fame career as a football coach of championship teams in Manchester, Massachusetts.

Swampscott's fans were excited about the upcoming season. The team featured a run-dominated offense fueled by a number of strong performers. The starting backfield showcased four gifted seniors: Charlie Cardillo, Billy Leone, Danny Losano, and Larry Moran. Fast and slippery Cardillo played right halfback. Hardnosed fullback Leone, an exceptional hitter, had super football instincts. Explosive left halfback Losano was a shining talent; a real star. Six-foot, 1-inch, 205-pound starting quarterback Moran was a three-sport standout who had seen regular action in 1970 on defense and at receiver.

Two other superior athletes, juniors Jeff Hegan and Ray DiPietro, pressed for minutes in the backfield. Jeff, nephew of professional baseball's Jim Hegan, was big, fast, and athletic, with all the tools to excel at both fullback and linebacker/defensive end. Ray, a cousin of 1965's Steve "Link" DiPietro, was a fast, shifty halfback. He helped lead the 1970 JVs to an undefeated season, including a 40–14 mauling of Newburyport in what had been billed as a title contest between two 6–0 teams. Ray ran wild in that game, delivering a first-quarter performance that may never be duplicated at any level of North Shore football. He scored on each of the offense's first three plays, with consecutive end runs of 55, 45, and 64 yards. Then, on Swampscott's fifth play of the game Ray-Ray, as he was known, sprinted 22 yards on another sweep to notch his fourth touchdown.

The roster held sufficient depth to enable the coaches to start many different players on defense, including a number of juniors from the prior season's undefeated JVs. Donnie Page was a track star slotted as a safety, alongside another junior, hard-hitting, 6-foot, 3-inch Richard Dedrick. Seniors Losano and Rick Young and junior DiPietro were among those playing the cornerback positions. Senior linebacker Leone and juniors Hegan and John Toner, younger brother of Tom and Billy, were all able to consistently fight through blockers and demolish ball carriers. Peter Cassidy, also a junior and the son of the quarterback of Bondy's 1953 team, was another good-sized kid who would be seeing time as a linebacker. While Mike Lynch's dependable kicking skills were hard to replace, both Leone and Cassidy could kick extra points and field goals.

Most of the starting linemen on the 1970 team had been seniors but the new squad still had up-front depth, with a number of returning veterans joined by an unusually strong group of new arrivals from the prior year's outstanding JVs. Among the key linemen were seniors Bruce Savatsky, Ken Carpenzano, Kevin Riley, Jim Morash, and Bob Moses, and juniors Roy Ostrovitz, John Hoffman, Gary Orloff, Steve Zuchero, Greg Beatrice, Fred Keach, Wayne Smith, and Bill Wharff. Most of them weighed around 200 pounds, but Ostrovitz tipped in at around 230 and Beatrice was bigger. The offensive ends were led by seniors Steve Kruger and Richard Fromer and junior John Toner.

Bondy remained oblivious to political correctness. With quite a few Jewish players manning the line and a number of Italian-Americans running with the ball, he now bragged about having both a "wailing wall" and "spaghetti backfield".

There was much to like about the 1971 roster, but the coaches were missing one player whom they had been counting on to anchor the offensive line and lead the defense. Captain Bobby Murray had been a solid linebacker and tackle in 1970 but suffered a broken jaw during the summer while playing American Legion baseball. Bondy feared that Murray was lost for most, if not all, of the season.

Despite Murray's absence, Bondy acknowledged that this might be one of his best teams. In a scrimmage on the final day of Saint Anselm camp, Swampscott played very well against a Manchester Memorial team that would go on to win the New Hampshire championship. The *Item* predicted that Swampscott and Bob DeFelice's Winthrop squad would be the top teams in the conference. According to the newspaper, the Big Blue was "an experienced team with good size, plenty of speed, and most important of all, depth."

The team traveled to Gloucester for the opener and shut out the Fishermen, 29–0. The statistics were typical of the dominance displayed by SHS in recent years, with the Blue holding huge advantages in first downs (18–7), rushing (194–61), and total yards (411–179). The game's most exciting play occurred in the first quarter, with Swampscott leading 7–0. Instead of letting Gloucester's punt carry into the end zone, Cardillo picked it up on the 9-yard line and, aided by good blocking, streaked down the left sideline 91 yards for the touchdown. Losano, Moran, and end Richard Fromer also scored and Cassidy successfully kicked four extra points. Larry Moran threw for 120 yards and a touchdown.

Prior to the next game against visiting Saugus, the team received surprisingly good news. Bobby Murray, who had been feared lost for the season, was cleared to play. Given the performance and depth of the offensive line and the challenges Murray faced to regain weight and strength, the coaches decided to use him only as a linebacker.

Saugus had started its season with a victory over Newburyport, winning the game despite seven fumbles. The *Item* expected Saugus v. Swampscott to be "a real battle." The game, though initially close, did not turn out to be much of a battle, as the home squad overpowered the Sachems, 38–14. The ground attack fired on all cylinders as the Blue rolled up 338 yards.

The next opponent, Danvers, had been generally frustrated in its games against the Big Blue. Undefeated Danvers teams were dispatched by Swampscott in both 1969 and 1970. Unlike the past two seasons, the Falcons were not unbeaten entering the 1971 game, having lost twice. However, they may have been inspired by their victory over the Prep on the preceding weekend. They came into Swampscott intent on pulling off an even bigger upset and trailed by only seven points at the end of the first half.

It was not a good day for the Big Blue passing attack as it yielded four interceptions. Partially as a result, the boys generated less than 200 total yards. Despite a weak offensive performance, Swampscott did enough to win. With a 7–0 lead in the third quarter, DiPietro grabbed a Danvers punt and returned it 66 yards to the end zone. Leone's second successful conversion kick made it 14–0. A Losano TD then made it 20–0. Danvers managed to avoid a shutout with a late touchdown, but the Blue won 20–6. SHS remained unbeaten and turned its focus to the upcoming Winthrop game.

Swampscott and Winthrop owned identical 3–0 records as they prepared to meet at Blocksidge Field. Both offenses featured strong ground games. The Vikings attacked with a number of weapons, including quarterback Pat DiGregorio, speedy junior halfbacks Mike DeMarco and Mark DiGregorio, and fullback Jim Davie. Winthrop was a ball-control team, as evidenced by a win over Classical when the Vikings ran 60 plays compared to the Rams' 23. This was another contest between conference-leaders played in Swampscott before a standing-room-only crowd. It ended in another Big Blue victory.

Swampscott scored first on a Cardillo run that completed a 51-yard drive. Losano got the second score when he broke through the right side behind a great John Hoffman block, cut left and sprinted 36 yards to the end zone. Leone's kick was good and the Blue led 13–0. But the Vikings bounced back and scored on a wild 71-yard play that involved a scramble and ensuing fumble by Pat DiGregorio that was then picked up and run into the end zone by his cousin, Mark. The Vikings almost scored again before the half ended when Pat DiGregorio raced down the sideline but was caught by Losano and pushed out of bounds on the 1-yard line as time expired.

As happened so often in Swampscott games, the Big Blue took control in the third quarter, scoring on its first two possessions. First, Larry Moran orchestrated a 10-play, 69-yard drive, finishing it with his own touchdown scramble. Next, after Losano and Don Page teamed in a fumble recovery, the Blue marched 67 yards in seven plays. Moran connected with Fromer for a 17-yard touchdown to complete the drive. Leone and Page thereafter helped seal the 26–12 victory with interceptions. After its anemic Danvers performance, the offense seemed fully recovered, amassing 373 yards, with 268 gained on the ground.

Winthrop coach Bob DeFelice was gracious in defeat, stating, "Swampscott always rises to the occasion. You have to give that team credit. They win the big ones. Stan Bondelevitch is a super coach." He also lauded Swampscott's linebacking corps of Murray, Leone, and Toner.

Next came visiting 3–1 Lynn English. Described by the *Item* as "rejuvenated" and "powerful," the Class A Bulldogs were mentored by Billy Hall, the same coaching terror who had brought his Manchester Central team from New Hampshire to scrimmage the 1965 Swampscott squad. Hall was in his second year at English and, according to the *Item's* J. F. Williams, had "put it all together into a winning combination capable of challenging every opponent on the schedule."

English had been particularly impressive in its most recent game, destroying a previously unbeaten Peabody team, 35–0. The Tanners were perennial Class A powers and had beaten Lowell, Lawrence, and Beverly on successive weekends before being chewed up by the Bulldogs. Bondy viewed the upcoming opponent as the "fastest, biggest and best" English team he had seen. Many rated the game a toss-up, considering the squads to be evenly matched based upon the Bulldogs' dismantling of Peabody and the fact that each team had scored 17 touchdowns over their first four games. Another overflow crowd was expected at Blocksidge.

As it turned out, the teams were not evenly matched. Swampscott routed the Bulldogs, 41–14. The home team took control early. English fumbled the opening kickoff and Fromer recovered on the Bulldogs' 21. Five plays later Losano ran for the touchdown. After Swampscott got the ball back on a Steve Kruger interception the offense embarked on a 66-yard march that ended when Jeff Hegan scored from the one. Then, after DiPietro returned an English punt to the 50, Swampscott scored again, this time in only two plays. First Losano blasted over right guard and ran 31 yards. On the next play Moran found Fromer who made a great catch in the end zone, giving Swampscott a 19–0 lead.

Hegan and Fromer each scored again, and defensive end Billy Wharff finished off the barrage when he caught a ball deflected by teammate

Kevin Riley and returned it all the way to the end zone. The Blue rushed for 322 yards, compared to 162 for English. Prior to the game, Coach Hall said that Swampscott was the type of team that would quickly capitalize on opponents' errors. That was what happened. But there was more to it than that. According to Hall, "They out-hit us from the beginning."

When it was over Billy Hall mused, "I wonder who will beat this team." Four opponents remained and the first was Saint John's Prep, the only school that had been able to beat Swampscott in four years. The boys were not going to let it happen again. The Prep scored first, but those points were all that the Eagles could muster. The Big Blue scored five consecutive touchdowns in the one-sided affair, winning 35–6.

SHS next traveled to Manning Bowl to meet Lynn Classical. The star of the 4–2 Rams was a 5-foot, 8-inch, 155-pound halfback named Mike Murphy. He had been making plays on both sides of the line of scrimmage all season. The Rams turned the ball over early deep in their own territory when a fourth down snap from center sailed over the punter's head. Soon thereafter Swampscott scored on a Moran to Fromer pass, and Leone kicked the extra point. The teams slugged it out without points on either side for the remainder of the first half.

But in the third quarter, Losano broke away on a 33-yard scoring jaunt. Leone's kick made it 14–0. Losano also tallied the final touchdown in the fourth quarter, running in from the 11-yard line to make it 20–0. Thanks in large part to solid blocking by the line, including Savatsky, Morash, Hoffman, and Smith, the team rushed for 241 yards. Meanwhile, the boys did a masterful job shutting out the Rams. Defensive stalwarts Hegan, Leone, Murray, and Toner helped to limit Classical star Murphy to only 28 yards on 10 carries.

Just two games lay ahead for 7–0 Swampscott, as it prepared to host the Newburyport Clippers. The Port City team had fallen on hard times, with a record of seven losses and no victories. The Clippers had little chance of beating the Big Blue, but hung tough and trailed at the end of the first half by only a touchdown and conversion kick. In the second half, first Hegan and then Losano ran for touchdowns and both PAT kicks were good, raising the score to 21–0. Finally, with less than a minute to play, ball hawking junior defensive back Richard Dedrick grabbed his second interception of the day and returned it 38 yards for the Blue's fourth score.

Cassidy's kick was good to complete the 28–0 shutout. The win was aided by multiple turnovers. In addition to Dedrick's two interceptions, Hegan, Losano, Ostrovitz, Smith, and Wharff recovered fumbles.

With a record of five victories against three losses, the Marblehead Magicians were assured a winning season. They could finish in glorious fashion by taking down their unbeaten rivals in Marblehead. Veteran quarterback Randy Rundle was again at the controls. With the Blue heavily favored, local sports writers harkened back to Thanksgiving of 1961 when another unbeaten visiting Swampscott team was ambushed by the Whips, losing 35–14. Bondy brushed aside suggestions of another upset, stating, "We're determined that nothing like that will happen this year."

The last two Swampscott teams that played in Marblehead on Thanksgiving (1969 and 1967) had beaten the Headers to cap undefeated seasons and win conference crowns. The 1971 team hoped to do the same but would have to wait until Saturday as the game was postponed from Thanksgiving due to bad weather. While Bondy voiced concern that his players might be emotionally drained, he suggested that simply playing Marblehead would be enough to get them up for the game. Apparently, it wasn't.

The offense was stuck in neutral for the first half and the rivals returned to the locker rooms knotted at 0–0. Shockingly, the Blue managed a mere 31 yards rushing and just eight passing. The only big offensive play was a 60-yard Losano touchdown that was nullified by a penalty. Marblehead's defense was outstanding. But so was Swampscott's. Through the first half the Magicians were held to just four yards.

With the start of the third quarter, the Big Blue got untracked. On the second play from scrimmage, DiPietro tore off a long run to the Marblehead 37. Several plays later, with the ball on the 28, Losano broke loose and sprinted to the end zone for the game's first points. The conversion kick was blocked, but on Marblehead's next series Bobby Murray picked off a Rundle pass and returned it 30 yards to the Whips' seven, setting up Moran's eventual touchdown sneak. Larry added a bootleg for the two-point conversion, as the lead increased to 14–0. After another penalty call again wiped out a Losano touchdown, Swampscott regained possession on a Hegan interception. The Blue notched its final points when Cardillo raced across the goal line to cap a 10-play drive. The final score was 20–0.

The story of the game, according to Bondy, was the second-half performance of the offensive line and the play of the linebackers. The defense sacked Rundle six times, picked off two of his passes, and held the Headers to minus seven yards rushing and only 22 yards of total offense. It was the team's third consecutive shutout.

After Swampscott destroyed English, Bill Hall had wondered who would beat the Big Blue. No one did. The 1971 undefeated team brought home a fifth consecutive Northeastern Conference title and a Class B championship.

A number of players were recognized in the postseason. Guard Bruce Savatsky, younger brother of former fullback Gary, was named a *Boston Globe* All-Scholastic. Bruce was a major cog in the Blue rushing machine, consistently helping to create openings for the running backs.

Danny Losano was a tremendous two-way player, registering 29 touchdowns in his varsity career. During a single game against Danvers, he intercepted three passes. He was named to the *Boston Globe* and *Boston Herald* All-Scholastic teams and became the eighth of Bondy's players to win the Thom McAn Shoe Award. Danny went on to a highly productive football career at the University of New Hampshire where, among other things, he set records as a punt returner.

The hardest-hitting, toughest, player on the 1971 team may have been fullback/linebacker Billy Leone. Major college football programs took notice. He ultimately accepted a scholarship offer to play at the University of Pittsburg.

Marvin Cohen was another member of the team who earned a scholarship. But Marvin was not a player; he was the student manager and one more kid who saw Bondy as a mentor. He recalls how Bondy would write a single word on the blackboard and use it as the theme for an instructive, inspirational talk. An example was "Execution!" Stan told the boys that, regardless of their sizes, if they carried out their assignments, making the correct blocks and runs at the right times, the team would succeed. At times, he asked Marv to come up with the "word of the day" for the blackboard, emphasizing to the team that the manager was just as important as the starting 11.

The coach commended Cohen for being meticulous about player uniforms and equipment and assuring that things such as tackling dummies were properly placed on the field before practice started. Marvin was also charged with keeping players hydrated, and Bondy always made certain that the manager had what he needed to accomplish that task. Because of such support, Marvin never doubted that his contributions were import-ant and appreciated.

Bondy's letter of recommendation helped win Cohen a partial scholar-ship to Northeastern University, where he served as the team's equipment manager, becoming, he says, "the first, last, and only" student to receive such a scholarship. Marvin's recollections of Stan include the following:

> I remember that his office was always open to anyone who needed a place to talk about anything in life. The team was not just about the current roster, it was always about them, the cheerleaders, the junior varsity and freshman squads/coaches and the community. He stressed that without them we were not a complete team.

The theme of team extending beyond the starting 11 and varsity roster to encompass a larger community was central to the long-term success of Bondy's program. In typical fashion, he spent time throughout the 1971 season publicly praising the contributions of various starters, reserves, JVs, and supportive non-players. He understood that teens and adults alike appreciated words of recognition and he spread them around liberally. One of his vehicles for doing so was his unsigned column in the game programs, titled *Big Blue Notes*.

According to the 1971 *Big Blue Notes*: linebacker Bill Leone was "considered by experts as the best in a long list at Swampscott"; Bobby Murray was "an excellent pass defender"; Billy Wharff and Richard Ded-rick "make things happen"; Steve Kruger "goes about his business of being a top player in the Northeast Conference without noise or fanfare"; Bruce Savatsky "a top student, is rated as the best guard on the North Shore."

He added that defensive ends Wayne Smith and Jeff Hegan "remind people of Rose and Kester on the great 1968 team"; and that center Roy Ostrovitz was "being compared to Mark Stevenson—captain of the 1966 team—That in itself tells the story." By comparing some of his 1971 players to outstanding boys on past Big Blue teams, Bondy effectively furthered a sense of community and family—that Swampscott players were linked to one another over the years.

But the recognition in *Big Blue Notes* never ended with the stars and front-liners. Bondy made sure to credit many others, as in the following:

> Our boys that don't play as much deserve a great deal of credit. It takes quite a lad to be at practice every day.

> Our Jayvees are playing great football.

> Our squad and coaches have great confidence in Dr. Bessom, our team doctor. We are proud to have such a qualified man with us over the years.

> It's always nice to see Dr. Patrinos, Superintendent of Schools and Mr. Bertrand Roger, our high school principal, at all games, home and away. All students involved appreciate this backing.

After praising all seven starting offensive linemen individually, Bondy added the following, applicable to all of Swampscott's offensive linemen who often toiled in obscurity:

> To play in the offensive line at Swampscott the most important requirements are speed and intelligence. You must get there to block, you must change your assignment at the last moment for a change in defense. Our offensive line has been a prime factor in the long winning streak. Playing in the offensive line is a great honor for a Swampscott boy.

Bondy also used *Big Blue Notes* to assure readers, especially parents, that Swampscott football instilled strong values. For example, *Big Blue Notes* in the Program for the 1971 Danvers game contained the following:

> Violence means "to abuse" according to Webster—Swampscott football does not require violence. We have respect for rules. With four officials, coaches and spectators by the thousands observing

the boy he has no time to be "violent." His assignment is to block or tackle. To carry out his assignment he must be intelligent, quick and well-conditioned. Breaking a law is not playing good football. A good football player has to have pride, dignity and strong human feelings.

Another example can be seen in these comments from the Program for the 1969 Saugus game where he stressed the importance of character, family, and performance:

When all else is gone character should remain. This is a lesson our youth is learning everyday as part of the athletic program at Swampscott High School. To have a good team we must have not only good boys, but also good parents. In Swampscott, this appears to be the case…. Religion, race or color makes no difference in a first string player, but performance, dependability and conduct do.

Big Blue Notes was just one of the myriad ways in which Bondy built support for his program, crediting many contributors and explaining that players learned valuable lessons through football. Of course, the incredible record of success also surely helped. Since 1967, the team had completed four undefeated seasons, won five consecutive conference titles, and posted a cumulative record of 44–1. A large sign, complete with a smiley face, adorned the Fieldhouse roof and smaller copies were also spread around town by the spirit squad, reminding Swampscotters to appreciate and enjoy their high school team. The message was, "Smile, you're in Big Blue Country."

Super Champs

In June of 1972, Eastern Massachusetts high schools were re-classified into four athletic divisions. All Northeastern Conference teams were classified Division II. Under the new system, the two top-rated Division II teams would be meeting in a postseason championship game, as would those in Division I. These quickly became known as the high school Super Bowls.

The returning SHS seniors may have comprised the largest (in physical size and numbers) group of experienced players from a single class in Big Blue history. They included backs Ray DiPietro, Donnie Page, Al Barbanel, Jeff Hegan, and Peter Cassidy; ends Richard Dedrick, John Toner, and Billy Wharff; and interior linemen Greg Beatrice, John Hoffman, Gary Orloff, Steve Zuchero, Roy Ostrovitz, Wayne Smith, and Fred Keach. Almost all had been playing together for years; many formed the nucleus of the undefeated 1970 JVs and contributed to the success of the undefeated 1971 varsity.

Ray DiPietro and Donnie Page, each weighing about 175 pounds, would be starting in the offensive and defensive backfields. Firmly in place at fullback was the team's captain, 220-pound Jeff Hegan. A bruising runner and blocker with good speed, Jeff also excelled at defensive end. Six-foot, 200-pound starting linebacker Peter Cassidy served as the reserve fullback. Two other seniors, Terry Fitzgerald and Al Barbanel, would be seeing considerable action on defense and special teams. Richard Dedrick, a play-making defensive back throughout the 1971 season, was slated as a two-way starter. He was a tough, sure tackler, also capable of catching any pass thrown in his direction.

Up front, the two biggest linemen traded places. Roy Ostrovitz, the 240-pound former center, switched to tackle, while Greg Beatrice, who had been a two-way tackle, replaced him at center. According to some reports, Greg weighed more than his listed 265 pounds. John ("Hoffa") Hoffman, a rugged 210-pounder, was firmly in place at right offensive guard. The other veteran senior linemen generally weighed in the neighborhood of 200 pounds.

Wayne Smith started as an offensive tackle and defensive end, while Toner switched from offensive end to linebacker when the defense took the field. While the other veteran linemen were also capable of playing both ways, there was so much depth and experience that the coaches elected to platoon in many spots. For example, they regularly used Beatrice, Hoffman, and Zuchero on offense, while plugging Keach, Wharff, and Orloff into the defensive line. Orloff manned the middle guard spot throughout the season despite playing with a shoulder that frequently popped out of joint and needed to be pushed back into place.

Acknowledging that he had a big squad, Bondy told the *Item*, "But you don't win football games with size ... no matter what the fan may think. You win with quickness." This team, however, was plenty quick, with speedsters DiPietro and Page in the backfield, and a number of agile big guys up front who could really move.

It was perhaps the most senior-dominated line-up during Bondy's tenure. There was only one spot where varsity experience was lacking—quarterback. Larry Moran was no longer behind center. His backup had been Rusty Walker; a 170-pound southpaw who had capably quarterbacked the unbeaten 1970 JVs. Rusty competed for the starting job with Michael Jauron, my youngest brother.

Mike had been a Big Blue waterboy in 1966 when, among other things, he kept track of Dick's kicking shoe. Since then he had grown into a 200-pound, 6-foot, 2-inch high school junior. A strong athlete, he had been the starting signal caller on the prior year's JV squad. He was an accomplished ball handler and classic drop-back passer, with good arm strength and accuracy. In short, he had the skill set possessed by most of the highly successful Big Blue quarterbacks of the past. Ultimately, Bondy named him the starting quarterback and the team's placekicker.

The boys faced a big test in their opener. For the first time, the Big Blue would be playing the high school team from Swampscott's much larger neighbor, Salem. The match against the big, veteran Class A Witches generated great interest on the North Shore. Playing at Salem's Bertram Field, Swampscott passed the test, winning 19–7.

The game was not as close as the score suggested, as Swampscott dominated on both sides of the line, rushing for 326 yards while holding the Witches to only 98 in total offense. Jeff Hegan ran for 122 yards on 18 carries, intercepted a pass, and helped lead the defense. Donnie Page carried only seven times but accumulated 126 yards and scored a touchdown. He also intercepted a pass, as did Billy Wharff. Salem coach Jackie Farland commented after the game that he was certain his team would not be meeting a better opponent. The margin of victory could have been greater if the offense had not frequently shot itself in the foot with miscues that prevented touchdowns.

On the following Saturday, the team delivered a cleaner performance, pasting Gloucester, 42–0. Several days later, Bondy praised two of his seniors, recognizing tackle Wayne Smith as a great blocker, critical to the success of the Blue's trap plays, and Billy Wharff as one of the best defensive linemen he had ever coached. Over the preceding 11 games, Wharff had recovered six fumbles, intercepted three passes, returning one for a touchdown, and blocked two punts.

On the following Saturday, Smith, Wharff, and company took care of business at Stackpole Field, easily besting Saugus, 33–6. The Big Blue rolled up 444 total yards compared to 191 for Saugus. The current streak stood at 15, and the Blue had won 47 of its last 48 games.

The halfback tandem of DiPietro and Page was proving every bit as lethal as the 1971 Losano-Cardillo duo. Both were explosive ball carriers, capable of breaking away for long gains and touchdowns. Moreover, Don Page, according to Dick Lynch, was one of the best defensive safeties he'd ever coached, and Bondy recognized Ray DiPietro as one of the top three blocking backs during his tenure in Swampscott.

Playing their next game against Danvers on a rare Sunday, the Blue fell behind for the first time all season when their opponent capitalized on an early turnover to seize a 6–0 lead. But John Toner, looking like his brother Tom, blocked the attempted placement and Swampscott thereafter literally ran away with the game, churning out 347 rushing yards. DiPietro ran for 222 yards on 19 carries and scored a touchdown. Page intercepted three passes and scored three touchdowns. Michael Jauron completed three of his four attempted passes, including one for six points, and made all five of his PAT kicks. Swampscott generated over 600 yards while rolling over the Falcons, 35–6. Danvers coach Fravel described the Blue's running attack as "definitely awesome."

It was obvious that SHS was again a powerhouse, featuring a big, veteran line; talented, explosive running backs; and a passing and kicking game that could produce when called upon. In only four games, the Big Blue rolled up 1,282 yards rushing, while surrendering just 323. Defensively, the squad attacked with a strong front five, agile, punishing linebackers, and quick, ball hawking backs who had intercepted nine passes in the first four games. According to the *Item*, the current squad was "described by opposing coaches as certainly better than 1971 and possibly the best Big Blue team ever." The same question that Bill Hall had asked in 1971 could be asked again. Who was going to beat this team? The two clubs with the best chance were Hall's own English Bulldogs and Swampscott's next opponent, the unbeaten Winthrop Vikings.

Going into the Winthrop tilt, the Blue had won 38 consecutive conference games, dating back to 1967. From that time, it seemed that in every season there was at least one opponent riding its own unbeaten streak. In the past, there had been Newburyport, Danvers, and Saugus. Now it was Winthrop. The 3–0 Vikings had been unbeaten in 1971, prior to losing to SHS, and then went on to win out, finishing 8–1. Now they were again undefeated as they faced the Big Blue. Would they be able to get past Swampscott this time?

Winthrop was a big, veteran club, relying primarily on seasoned halfbacks Mike DeMarco and Mark DiGregorio in a highly productive running attack. Swampscott, however, dominated both sides of the line at Miller Field. Ahead 7–0 after the first half, the visitors blew it open in the third quarter, scoring on their first three possessions to take a 27–0 lead. Winthrop's only points came with just 33 seconds remaining. The Vikings were held to 89 yards rushing, while Ray DiPietro alone ran for 113 and two touchdowns. Hegan added another 85 and two more scores. Defensively, John Toner made nine unassisted tackles, and Wharff, Keach, Cassidy, Orloff, Hegan, and Page were among those also contributing with key plays.

In 1971, English and Swampscott had been unbeaten when they met at Blocksidge Field in what many expected would be a tight game.

But the hosts, on their way to a perfect season, hammered the Bulldogs, 41–14. This time English would be hosting Swampscott on a Friday night at Manning Bowl. The Bulldogs were strong again, having lost only once in five outings. Red Hoffman's pregame write-up emphasized Swampscott's potent running game and English's lethal passing attack, led by senior quarterback Clark Crowley. In a closing note, Hoffman mentioned that Michael Jauron kicked "with enough authority to be a definite three-point threat."

Our family was well acquainted with English coach Billy Hall. Prior to 1960, Manchester, New Hampshire, had maintained two high schools, Central and West. When a third school was opened—Manchester Memorial—the school board drew new lines resulting in a number of former Central players transferring to Memorial. In 1960, our dad was hired to teach history and serve as the football and basketball coach at the new high school. The team's first game was against Central, coached by Billy Hall. Many former teammates faced each other. Our dad's Memorial Crusaders beat Hall's Central Little Green, 8–6. While it was the only time that Hall and Jauron would coach against one another, it was just the beginning of their friendship.

Hall was now in his third year as coach at Lynn English. During the summer of 1972, he sometimes ventured to Phillips Park in the evening and stood at the end of the practice field watching the Swampscott players, including my brother Michael, engage in their off-season work-outs. He also stopped by my parents' home in Swampscott to visit our dad. Occasionally, he talked football with Michael, giving him tips on passing and kicking. But in Lynn's Manning Bowl on Friday night, October 21, 1972, Hall was not giving any tips to the Swampscott quarterback. He was doing his best to coach his team to a victory over Michael and his Big Blue teammates. With seconds remaining in the contest, Swampscott held the ball on the English 13-yard line with the score tied, 12–12.

It had been quite a game. Swampscott scored twice in the first half on two short touchdown plunges by Hegan. After the first score, the team tried unsuccessfully to run for the conversion after an English penalty put the ball on the 1½-yard line. After the second touchdown, the Blue faked the extra-point kick and holder Rusty Walker connected with Hegan on a screen pass. But a procedure penalty nullified the score and pushed Swampscott back.

Intent on going for two, the boys again faked the kick but failed to convert. SHS took a 12–0 lead into the locker room at halftime.

While Swampscott teams frequently blew close games open in the third quarter, it did not happen against the energized Bulldogs. The home team's first scoring drive came after Swampscott ran on fourth down from its own 40, making it past the first-down marker but fumbling in the process. English took over and reached the end zone after a series of runs. A bad snap from center foiled the conversion attempt. After the Bulldogs scored a second time, again doing it all on the ground, Smith and Cassidy blocked the PAT kick.

Late in the fourth quarter, Swampscott took possession on its own 27 after English failed on a fourth-and-one attempt. The offense drove all the way to the English seven; with the big gainer—a 42-yard DiPietro breakaway. The team seemed poised to win by either pushing in for the touchdown or kicking a field goal.

However, the offense went into reverse. A penalty pushed the boys back to the 12, and then Hegan was caught for a 2-yard loss. With the ball on the 14, the team tried to run again, but DiPietro only gained a yard. Swampscott called its final timeout. It was fourth and goal with the ball resting on the 13 and only seconds remaining. The team had one last chance. The options were to try some kind of a running or pass play for a touchdown or to attempt a field goal.

As he typically did, Dick Lynch observed from the press box. With only a few seconds left and the score tied, he knew that it boiled down to Michael Jauron kicking a 30-yard field goal which was within the junior's range. But now he watched, dumbfounded, as Peter Cassidy entered the huddle while Michael remained on the sideline.

Cassidy, a starting linebacker and backup fullback to Hegan, was a big, strong player who had shared kicking duties with Leone in 1971. But my brother was now the Blue's regular placekicker. The coaches had carefully tracked and charted distance and accuracy of both Michael and Peter throughout the season, most recently at practice on the preceding day. There was no question in Lynch's mind that Mike was the kicker for this crucial situation. There was no time to question or debate. It came down to this moment. Make the kick or say goodbye to the winning streak and chance to play for a Division II title in the State's first high school Super Bowl.

Coach Lynch hurried from the press box and down the Manning Bowl steps. Spotting Michael standing on the sideline, Lynch grabbed and pushed him onto the field, yelling, "Get in there and kick it!" He ran out to the huddle, replacing Peter. The team lined up. Greg Beatrice's snap and Rusty Walker's hold were perfect, as was Michael's kick, which was high and through the uprights. The kid whom the *Item* had said could be a "definite three-point threat" won the game with a 30-yard field goal, preserving Swampscott's winning streak and championship hopes.

It was a dramatic end to a remarkable game. Hall's tactic of overloading his defensive line to hinder Swampscott's running game was not a surprise, but his offensive approach was. The Bulldogs abandoned the passing attack, thought to be their strong suit. Hall knew that SHS would prepare all week to defend the pass. The Blue's pressure pass defense typically garnered multiple sacks and interceptions. The English coach deprived the visitors of that opportunity, turning almost exclusively to a ground game that ate up time, giving Swampscott's offense fewer chances to take the field.

Hall's strategy proved very effective. The Bulldogs committed no turnovers and ran for 134 yards and two touchdowns. But Swampscott's ground game was just good enough to put the team in position to win. The offense rushed for 140 yards in the second half and finished the game with a total of 247.

After the game, Michael Jauron walked over to Coach Hall, shook his hand and thanked him for all of his help and advice. Hall congratulated my brother but then asked whether Mike was trying to get him killed with that kind of talk. He suggested that they curtail further pleasantries and go their separate ways. Later that evening, Hall barged into our parents' Swampscott home and entertained us with a mock, melodramatic accusation; shouting that our dad had ruined his coaching career by allowing Mike to play for the Big Blue. The two friends then spent some time discussing the game.

Dick Lynch never asked Bondy or any of the other coaches why Michael had been left standing on the sideline when the team was about to attempt the crucial field goal, nor did Bondy ever say a word to him about the matter. Lynch had acted instinctively, never giving a second thought to the possible ramifications.

The team survived its biggest scare, barely getting past English. Next, it faced another Lynn school when Classical visited Blocksidge Field. The closest that the 0–6 Rams had come to victory was a 21–12 loss to Gloucester. It was unlikely that they would mount much of a challenge, and they did not. Don Page scored a 61-yard touchdown on Swampscott's first play and later raced 87 yards for a second TD. Hegan added two more as the Blue romped 27–0, amassing 15 first downs compared to two for the Rams, and running for 336 yards while holding Classical to minus 29.

As the boys prepared to play 4–3 Newburyport, Swampscott fans worried that they might miss out on the Super Bowl. Changes had been made in the ranking formula to factor in the records of a team's opponents. Because some Swampscott opponents were having poor seasons, the Blue trailed five other teams in the Division II rankings, with only two games remaining. It seemed unthinkable that if Swampscott finished undefeated and untied, thereby extending its winning streak to 21 straight and 53 of its last 54, it might still be deprived of a chance to play in the Super Bowl. While agreeing that such a result would be "ridiculous," Bondy emphasized that the team had to beat both Newburyport and Marblehead before any possibility of a postseason, championship game.

The contest at Newburyport was the last in the series between the teams because the Clippers were exiting the conference at season's end to join the Cape Ann League where they would enjoy great success. There had been some truly memorable games between the schools, especially during 1966-68 when they had dueled three consecutive times in pivotal contests before standing-room-only crowds. But it was now history, a fact recognized by the high school band as it played "Auld Lang Syne" at World War Memorial Stadium.

The 1972 Big Blue squad was simply too strong for the Clippers and romped, 35–7. It was business as usual; SHS churned out 359 yards. All three starting running backs found the end zone, with Page and Hegan each scoring twice. One of Page's touchdowns came on a pass from Jauron, the only one attempted all day. Ray DiPietro was immense, finishing with 172 yards on 16 carries. John Toner also had a big day, particularly on defense where he intercepted a pass, sacked the quarterback, and made a couple of big tackles to kill Clipper drives. Defensive back Marc Weiss picked off a pass, Hegan and junior Billy Dedrick recovered fumbles, and Wayne Smith had three quarterback sacks. Other defensive linemen combined on several more takedowns.

Traditional Thanksgiving rival Marblehead was in the midst of a good season, having won five of its first eight games. But the Big Blue was not about to falter with so much at stake. Swampscott completed its perfect regular season at Blocksidge Field on Thanksgiving morning, shutting out Marblehead, 29–0. The defense was outstanding. DiPietro intercepted two passes and sophomore Tom Kelliher picked off a third. Wharff and Orloff recovered fumbles. Toner downed a Swampscott punt on the visitors' 1-yard line and then broke through on the next play to tackle the ball carrier in the end zone for a safety. Wayne Smith had a monster day, with five sacks. All totaled, Blue defenders brought down the quarterback almost a dozen times. The decimated Magicians finished the day with minus 48 yards rushing and a mere 15 in total offense.

Both head coaches lauded Swampscott. Marblehead's Kulevich, noting that his plan had been to combine outside running with passing, lamented that his offense could do neither, describing SHS as one of the most balanced teams he had ever seen in high school football. In the home team's locker room, Bondy simply called his squad "the best I've ever had." While "best" and "ever" were words that the coach used frequently throughout his career to describe numerous teams, groups of boys, and individual players, he would repeat this comment about his 1972 team many times in future years.

With its Thanksgiving victory, the Big Blue secured a sixth consecutive conference championship and extended its latest winning streak to 21 games. By beating the Clippers and Headers, the team also secured the top spot in the Division II rankings. The boys had, therefore, earned a chance to play on Saturday morning, December 2, 1972, at Boston University's Nickerson Field in the first-ever Eastern Massachusetts Super Bowl game.

Swampscott would be facing the undefeated Knights of Catholic Memorial High School. Like the Prep, Catholic Memorial was a private school with the advantage of being able to draw its athletes from a large talent pool. Located in Boston's West Roxbury neighborhood, the school, frequently simply called "Memorial" or "CM," attracted players from throughout the heavily populated Greater Boston metropolis.

The Knights won the Catholic League championship, demolishing all opponents. The closest game was a 21–2 victory over Saint Peter's of Worcester. Other established, respected teams crushed by CM included Archbishop Williams, Lawrence Central Catholic, Malden Catholic, Boston College High School, and Frank DeFelice's Xaverian squad. Over the course of the season, the Knights had scored more points than Swampscott and allowed fewer.

CM attacked with a punishing, explosive ground game. Operating out of a Wishbone-T, the team featured 195-pound workhorse fullback Paul Ragucci, described by his coach as "the finest two-way player in the state." Ragucci ran for 720 yards on the season, averaged 6.4 yards per carry, and scored 108 points. He also led the defense from his linebacking spot, making tackles all over the field as he aggressively ran down ball carriers from sideline to sideline. Fleet-footed halfback Dave Singleton scored 70 points, having rushed for 916 yards while averaging six yards per carry.

Memorial quarterback Joey O'Brien, the *Boston Globe* high school player of the year, was fully capable of beating opponents by either running or passing. Described by his coach as "accurate both long and short," O'Brien threw 11 touchdown passes during the regular season despite his team's emphasis on a ground attack. The Knights had good size, with an offensive line averaging over 200 pounds. Freshmen were eligible to play varsity football in the Catholic League, and they had a good one in placekicker Ron Perry, who made 36 of 42 PATs during the season.

Catholic Memorial was undoubtedly a great high school team, but so was Swampscott. Ray DiPietro had run for over 1,000 yards and Donnie Page for more than 900. Fullback Jeff Hegan led the team in scoring with 16 touchdowns. Overall, SHS was bigger than CM, with players like Beatrice, Ostrovitz, Hoffman, Smith, and Wharff up front. Like Memorial, the Big Blue also had a reliable kicker. Michael Jauron was 26 for 29 in extra points and had kicked the 30-yard field goal.

Yet Bondy was worried. He and his assistants were having trouble finding weaknesses in the Knights. He described them as probably better than any team Swampscott had faced during the preceding six seasons. The Memorial offense seemed practically unstoppable, and no opponent had been able to move the ball effectively against their tough defense, which had posted four shutouts and given up only five TDs all season, with the starters having surrendered just one on the ground.

Swampscott relied heavily on its run game and fullback Hegan. He had scored close to half of the Blue's touchdowns and was either the lead blocker or decoy on many others. Now Bondy was concerned that Hegan, who was also a mainstay on the defensive side, might not play due to a pinched nerve suffered in the Marblehead game. Without the captain, it was difficult to envision a win.

Stan and his assistants met with Frank DeFelice and my dad to review the game film of Xaverian's loss to Memorial. Initially, it was a discouraging session because CM looked as strong as advertised. The Knights were big, fast, and athletic. Perhaps most impressive was their defensive pursuit. They reacted and moved to the football better than any team Swampscott had faced since at least 1966.

But as the coaches further analyzed the film they saw opportunity. The Big Blue had been effective in running its power sweeps throughout the season. A strong fullback and some large, agile linemen had cleared the way and provided running room for the explosive, fleet-footed halfbacks. The question was whether they could do it against CM's vaunted defense. Hegan's lead blocking had been a major factor in assuring the effectiveness of the sweeps. Now Bondy disclosed that the team might be going into the biggest game in school history without its outstanding fullback. Who, asked DeFelice, is the backup? "Peter Cassidy," said Bondy. "Wow," said Frank, "That's some backup!"

Even with Hegan unavailable, the coaches concluded that they could have some success with the power sweeps, run behind the big line, with Cassidy as lead blocker and a player like end John Toner clearing the way at the point of attack. While not as big as older brothers Ed and Tom, John was an outstanding two-way player, able to handle and often dominate much larger opponents.

Knowing that Memorial's coaches would surely plan to try to defend against the power sweeps, the Big Blue staff added some wrinkles designed to surprise the Knights. In 1953, Swampscott had upset unbeaten Amesbury and ended its 31-game winning streak by attacking with an unbalanced line and some quick-hitting sweeps, which Bondy referred to as the hurricane series. The Big Blue had also sprung the hurricane on Danvers in a huge game between undefeated North Shore powers in 1969. The coaches decided that it was hurricane season again.

The offensive strategy, with or without Hegan, was to set up in an unbalanced formation and run the fleet halfbacks wide on quick counts. If the Big Blue could sting Memorial early with such plays, Ragucci, and his teammates would likely focus even more on lateral movement in an attempt to stop the sweeps. Swampscott might then be able to take advantage with its patented counter plays, like the 22-trap, run back against the flow of the defensive pursuit.

As the game approached, there remained some concern that the team from the little town of Swampscott might be in over its head against the Catholic League power. Over the preceding 16 years, the SHS football program had achieved remarkable success, including numerous conference and Class B titles, and three lengthy winning streaks. But now the Big Blue would be traveling away from the North Shore and trying, for the first time, to beat a favored undefeated champion from a larger conference.

The news on the day before the game must have shaken even the most optimistic Big Blue fan. Bondy announced that captain, leading scorer, and outstanding defensive end, Jeff Hegan, would not play in the biggest game in SHS history. While CM coach Jim O'Connor believed that his fullback Ragucci was the finest two-way player in the state, there were others who argued that Hegan was as good or even better. When Hegan's pinched cervical nerve had not healed despite nine days of rest, the team's doctor ruled him out. It was a major blow, but there was great depth on the roster. Peter Cassidy would be Swampscott's fullback in the Super Bowl. Another talented player, junior Bill Dedrick, younger brother of Richard, was inserted at Hegan's defensive end position.

The team needed to make another adjustment. For the first time, Swampscott would be playing on an artificial surface. The grass at Nickerson Field had been replaced by a synthetic covering known as AstroTurf. Catholic Memorial had played on AstroTurf as recently as Thanksgiving Day and had spent the entire week before Thanksgiving practicing on it. But Bondy had no complaints, commending BU for allowing his team access to the facility in preparation for the game and for providing an ample supply of special cleats for use by his players.

The boys practiced on the turf on Thursday and, according to the coach, handled it well. He expected the artificial surface would help his team's kicking game and that his speedy halfbacks would be even faster. "It certainly was one of the best practices we've ever had," he said. "The boys are sky high and looking forward to the game."

Despite the fact that the Big Blue had won 21 straight games, four more than CM, the *Item* described the upcoming contest as David (Swampscott) against Goliath (Memorial). Bondy's team had not been an underdog all season, and he undoubtedly relished the role. It was time for the two teams to meet and for one of the streaks to end.

On Saturday morning, December 2, 1972, Frank DeFelice was standing near the Nickerson Field entrance when the Swampscott team walked past him. Frank looked at Bondy, who did not make eye contact. Yet, watching his former boss, DeFelice suddenly felt confident that the team would win. There was something about the hard, determined look of the man that seemed to say, "We're ready for everything you've got—let's do it!"

After kicking off to open the game, Swampscott forced a Memorial punt. The Big Blue offense took over, running consecutive, quick-hitting hurricane sweeps from unbalanced formations, both for considerable yardage. Then on its third play from scrimmage, the Blue sprang Donnie Page on an inside trap and he sprinted 41 yards to the end zone. It had taken Swampscott only three running plays to score on CM's acclaimed defense. With Michael's conversion kick the Blue took a 7–0 lead. But the Knights struck back on their next possession, driving 76 yards, with Ragucci doing most of the damage until Singleton reached the end zone on a 13-yard run. The point after kick was wide right.

Both teams' offenses continued to move the ball. First, Swampscott put together a drive highlighted by a 29-yard pass from Jauron to Toner but then bogged down. When Memorial got possession Ragucci broke loose on a 52-yard ramble. Ultimately, the Knights drove to Swampscott's 9-yard line before Cassidy put a jarring hit on Ragucci who fumbled. Terry Fitzgerald recovered. However, Swampscott turned it back over, fumbling on its 23 and this time the Knights found the end zone as O'Brien connected with Singleton. O'Brien then made it 14–7 by running up the middle for the conversion.

Swampscott immediately responded with an impressive 80-yard drive. The big plays were a 23-yard pass from Jauron to Page and a Page burst through the right side of the line and cut-back for a 43-yard touchdown. Michael's kick made it 14–14, and the score remained unchanged for the rest of the first half.

The offensive strategy was working well, but, as the half ended, Coach Lynch was worried about the opponent's rushing attack. Memorial had been finding big holes through the middle of the defense. Lynch was convinced that the defensive tackles needed to pinch down closer toward the center during the second half in order to plug those holes. But as he was speaking to Michael Jauron in the locker room, he glanced over the quarterback's shoulder and was shocked by what he saw.

Another assistant was diagramming a defensive change on the blackboard that had both tackles slanting out, away from the center. Lynch felt certain that would spell disaster. There was no time for debate. He walked over to Bondy. Pointing to the diagram, he forcefully told him, "If we do that we will lose!" When the head man asked for clarification, Lynch simply said, "We need to have the tackles pinch in, not slant out." Coach Lynch was clearly the most experienced assistant on the staff. Stan was convinced that he knew what he was talking about. Bondy asked no more questions, telling him to take the chalk and make the change. Lynch erased the diagram and replaced it with another, emphasizing to the defensive tackles that they needed to pinch in rather than slant out.

With those adjustments, CM found it tougher to pick up good yardage running up the middle. After the teams exchanged punts in the third quarter, Swampscott pieced together another touchdown drive, covering 88 yards in nine plays. This time, it was flashy Ray DiPietro with the big gainer, a 51-yard run, during which he broke through the right side, cut to the middle, evaded one defender, but then slipped and went down on the Memorial 29. From there Peter Cassidy carried to the 15 and then ultimately scored on a 2-yard plunge. SHS had now scored three rushing touchdowns on a defense that had previously only given up one over the entire season. Michael again split the uprights and Swampscott led, 21–14.

Memorial fumbled on its next possession and DiPietro recovered on Swampscott's 38. Runs by Page, DiPietro, and Cassidy and a pass from Jauron to Toner moved the ball to Memorial's 34. SHS again took to the air. End Scottie MacCallum, a six-foot, 190-pound junior, had become an offensive starter earlier in the season after two-way stalwart Richard Dedrick first struggled with a concussion and then was lost with a ruptured spleen. It was a testament to the depth of Swampscott's roster that the offense was able to absorb the loss of Dedrick with another strong player like MacCallum.

Scott ran a short down-and-out toward the right sideline, while Don Page streaked deeper down the same side of the field. Mike threw long and both Page and CM's Singleton went up for the ball near the 15. Meanwhile, MacCallum, having seen that Jauron was passing downfield, broke off his pattern and raced along the sideline in the direction of Page, hoping to assist with a block if the pass was completed. Page and Singleton, battling for possession, deflected the ball back toward the sideline and into the hands of the sprinting MacCallum who continued unmolested into the Memorial end zone.

Mike Jauron and Scottie MacCallum were childhood friends when their families lived in Lynn. They were practically next-door neighbors and played many sandlot games together. When both families moved to Swampscott Mike and Scottie reconnected. Now their connection at Nickerson Field gave the Blue a two-touchdown lead. With Michael's fourth conversion kick, Swampscott led 28–14 with about one minute gone in the fourth quarter.

Memorial attempted its comeback through an aerial attack but was stymied by Swampscott's pass defense, with Page playing a key role, ultimately breaking up a number of O'Brien's passes. The Big Blue threatened to increase its lead when Page broke away on a 45-yard run to Memorial's 24. But Michael missed his 28-yard field goal attempt. The Knights then took over and drove 80 yards in eight plays, with O'Brien running the final six for the score. The kick was good and CM trailed by seven points with just over four minutes remaining.

After a good kick return by DiPietro, Memorial's defense forced a Swampscott punt that it partially blocked. But after Roy Ostrovitz threw O'Brien for a 10-yard loss, Al Barbanel recovered a Knights fumble on the next play at the Memorial 27. The Big Blue ultimately set up for another field goal attempt but faked the kick with holder Rusty Walker scrambling for what seemed a first down. That might have allowed the Blue to run out the clock, but the play was nullified by a penalty.

When Swampscott then failed to convert on fourth down the CM offense returned to the field with a final opportunity. O'Brien took the snap, rolled out, stopped, and threw long toward Singleton, who seemed open as he streaked down the right sideline. But Don Page, sprinting from his safety position, leaped at the last second and deflected the ball before it could reach its target. O'Brien attempted another long pass and this time it was picked off by Page on the Swampscott 32 and returned to Memorial's 25. Seconds later it was over.

The Big Blue had won the first Eastern Massachusetts High School Super Bowl Game, securing a Division II championship. Going into the contest, Don Page may have been the least heralded of Swampscott's starting running backs. Unlike Hegan and DiPietro, he had not seen much varsity action on offense until his senior year, having previously operated as a specialist in the defensive backfield. During the 1972 regular season, DiPietro led the team in rushing, while Hegan led in scoring. Prior to the start of the CM game, Page had been fighting a virus and suffering from swollen glands in his throat. He had also sustained bruised ribs on Thanksgiving and was worried that they might hamper his running.

Yet in the biggest game in Swampscott football history, Donald Page delivered one of the greatest individual performances in Swampscott history. He rushed for 251 yards on 31 carries, scored twice on runs of 41 and 43 yards, caught a pass for 23 yards, and returned a kick 24 yards. From his safety position, Page knocked away four passes in the fourth quarter alone, including a critical deflection that likely prevented a late touchdown reception by Singleton. Finally, Page intercepted and ran back O'Brien's last pass to seal the victory.

While Donnie Page was justifiably recognized as the game's most valuable player, he had plenty of help. The coaches game-planned perfectly and made important adjustments as the contest wore on. Ray DiPietro carried 22 times for 97 yards. He also returned kicks for another 49 and recovered a fumble. Interior offensive linemen Smith, Hoffman, Beatrice, Zuchero, and Ostrovitz did a fine job opening holes in the line for the running backs and pass blocking. John Toner was immense, making key blocks on the edge that enabled the backs to turn the corner and run to daylight. He also hauled in several passes and turned in his typical solid defensive performance. Fitzgerald, Barbanel, Orloff,

Keach, and Billy Dedrick all contributed to the Blue's strong defensive performance. Then there was Scottie MacCallum's heads-up reception, grabbing the deflected ball along the sideline and running it in for what proved the decisive points. According to the *Item's* Red Hoffman, Michael Jauron's team direction was flawless, and he was perfect on PAT kicks, nailing all four.

Countless boys made big plays throughout the contest. Peter Cassidy was certainly one of them. He had been ready to take over at fullback, blocking and running well, and scoring the third touchdown. And he played his usual strong defensive game, which included forcing a turnover with his hit on Ragucci at the 9-yard line. Cassidy's father had quarter-backed Bondy's first Swampscott team in 1953. Now the senior Cassidy watched his son help SHS win the Super Bowl game. He and his old coach had come full circle. The victory seemed the fitting culmination of the football program that Stan Bondelevitch had been building over the preceding 20 years.

Donnie Page went on to the University of Pennsylvania where he played for the Quakers. A number of the other seniors, including Ray DiPietro, Jeff Hegan, Wayne Smith, and Billy Wharff, joined Danny Losano and Jim Morash at UNH where they had an opportunity to play against the University of Massachusetts, eventually captained by their high school teammate, John Toner.

Three days after Swampscott won the Super Bowl, the *Item* reported on scuttlebutt that both Bondy and Lynch would not be returning in 1973. Red Hoffman hoped that the rumors were false, noting, "The two coaches, in tandem harness, have led the Big Blue to some of the greatest feats ever accomplished in schoolboy ranks." As in past years, the reports about Bondy's imminent departure proved false. However, those about Coach Lynch were only too true.

Soon after the story appeared, Dick Lynch confirmed that he would be leaving his positions in Swampscott to become the Danvers athletic director. It was hard to imagine SHS sports without Coach Lynch. In his short, three-year stint as Swampscott's baseball coach, his teams won two conference titles and were twice finalists in the state tournament. He coached Big Blue basketball for eight years, and in that period his teams consistently posted winning records, claimed multiple conference titles, including finishing 14–0 in league play in 1967 and won the Eastern Massachusetts Class B championship in 1968. And he was, of course, Bondy's longtime assistant football coach. His essential role in helping to shape the Big Blue football dynasty was undeniable. In 1972 alone, he had not only coached one of the strongest, most productive backfields (on both sides of the line) in Swampscott history, but had been there to shove Mike Jauron from the sidelines to kick the winning field goal against English and had insisted on the critical defensive adjustments at halftime of the Super Bowl game.

Most importantly, however, in his role as gym teacher and coach, Richard Lynch had helped hundreds of teenage boys grow into young men, pushing them to become the best that they could be.

End of the Reign

After hinting that he might not be returning, Bondy announced in February that he planned to coach for at least two more years. However, he suggested that it was becoming tougher to coach in Swampscott, predicting that people in the town, spoiled by football success, would not appreciate winning again until the Blue first experienced a period of failure. He added:

> I really don't know who'd apply for a head coach's position in a town where so many championship teams are produced. A new man coming to Swampscott would be placing himself in a very tortuous position.

Bondy also had to try to keep winning without Dick Lynch by his side. Fortunately, he could turn to another member of the Big Blue family as his new backfield coach. Ronny Corcoran was well prepared, having served what he described as an "apprenticeship in Coaching 101" by observing and assisting Lynch for the past seven years.

Young Bill Bush, who had played at the University of Massachusetts and whose father Lou had led the country in scoring at the school in 1931, joined the staff. Bush helped Fran York with the JVs and assumed York's old job as the "get back" assistant on the sidelines at varsity games. When Bondy looked at his new assistant, he thought of Bill's famous dad. As a result, in Stan's mind, the JVs were now coached by "Rudy" York and "Lou" Bush.

Swampscott was the defending Division II champion and had won 22 straight games and six consecutive conference titles. But some observers saw another championship in 1973 as a pipe dream. The *Item's* Bill Beaton observed, "The size, the depth, the experience is no longer there." Unlike the prior year, the list of returning players was shockingly short. All of the starting running backs and interior linemen from the Super Bowl champs had graduated. Only quarterback Mike Jauron and end Scott MacCallum had been starters. Moreover, Peter Cassidy's brother Reid, a tall senior who could have supplied some added size and skill to the 1973 squad, accepted a scholarship offer from a prestigious prep school and left SHS.

However, those who predicted that Swampscott could no longer contend may have overlooked an important factor. New assistant Bill Bush was awed by the well-organized, deeply layered football program in the small town. It seemed that everywhere he looked he saw youngsters being schooled in Big Blue football. In addition to the blue-shirted varsity and red-shirted JVs, there were separate teams of ninth, eighth, and seventh graders, and below them, large numbers of Pop Warner players. This was all part of a well-coordinated system that had been functioning for years with coaches like Doc Marden, Brock Maher, Dick Connors, Fran Chiary and Bob Andersen helping to prepare boys at the junior high school level so that they were ready to perform when they reached SHS.

In explaining how little Swampscott, like Green Bay, Wisconsin, became the unlikely site of a football dynasty, the *Boston Herald's* Kevin Mannix wrote that it was "Just a matter of organization, dedication, cooperation and pride," for which he credited Stan Bondelevitch. There was, at least, one other key factor. It was also a matter of inspiration. Bondy was the master motivator, and his efforts with most players started well before they reached high school. He regularly spoke to elementary school classes, kids in the summer parks program, Pop Warner teams, and numerous boys individually.

One of many examples involved a boy who loved playing Pop Warner football but was doing poorly in school and did not seem to care about learning. His mother involved counselors without much change. She initially scoffed at her brother's suggestion that she talk with Stan Bondelevitch about the problem, dismissing him as "just a football coach." But, reminded that the boy's one passion seemed to be football, she finally contacted Stan and asked if he would help.

Stan sought out her son and complimented him on his fine Pop Warner performance, predicting that he would be a great high school player for the Big Blue. Then, as almost an afterthought, Bondy asked how he was doing in school. When the boy confessed that he was not doing well at all, the coach expressed great disappointment, delivering a clear message that unless that situation changed the kid would never be able to play football for SHS. By the time the boy reached high school a few years later, his academic performance had markedly improved, and he played as a two-year starter on championship Big Blue teams. Like most SHS players, he then went on to college.

Stan worked to motivate not only his players but the cheerleaders, spirit squad, drill team, band, and entire student body. In fact, on at least one occasion, Bondy even motivated the school's acclaimed math team. In the early 1970s, the high school math team was continuing a tradition of excellence, undefeated in its various matches. Bondy, aware that the "mathletes" were facing another school in a match that would determine the league championship, called custodian Louis Gallo into his office and asked that he prepare signs of support and affix them to the cafeteria walls. Gallo, assisted by custodian and former player Carl Reardon, prepared several signs, such as one with the message "÷ and Conquer!" After reviewing and approving the signs, Bondy addressed the bright students on the math team.

He congratulated them, emphasizing that the entire school was proud of their performance. He then delivered one of his classic pep talks, raising his voice and increasing his tempo as he urged them to finish the mission by winning the final match and expressed his confidence that they would get the job done. Carl Reardon remarked to Gallo that it was the same kind of talk he and his teammates had heard many times in the Fieldhouse back in the 1960s. Bondy told the math team that he would be waiting in his office to hear the good news of victory. When the match ended some of the young wizards hurried to his office to report that they had won.

Naturally, Bondy's primary motivational efforts were directed to the boys on his teams. The 1973 players could not match their predecessors in size or experience, but they remained confident. Most had spent years playing in the Swampscott program. They were well-drilled in Big Blue football and accustomed to winning. There were some quick, capable linemen and fast, athletic backs. A number of upperclassmen, including Captain David Faulkner, Bobby Lippa, John McKenney, Kevin Donelan,

Bill Palleschi, Mike Tumulty, Mark O'Brien, and George DePaolo were available to step up and fill vacancies in the interior lines and at linebacker. The end positions seemed in good hands, with veteran seniors Scott Mac-Callum and Bill Dedrick returning.

The primary backs included seniors Ken Bane, Don DiLisio, and Ralph Boyce, junior Ricky Bessom, and sophomores Tommy Beatrice, Mike Snyder, and Jimmy Harris. At 175 pounds, DiLisio, a hard-running fullback with good speed, may have been the largest of the bunch. Bessom, the son of the team's longtime doctor, was likely the smallest but was quick and shifty. Bane and Boyce were speedsters. Tommy Beatrice, the younger brother of Peter and Greg, was a former Pop Warner star. He was talented and athletic, as were fellow sophomores Snyder and Harris. The three would be seeing action on defense and special teams and Beatrice would also soon find a spot in the offensive backfield. Senior quarterback Mike Jauron would again be directing the offense. He was the only player on the 1973 roster who had started every game for the undefeated Super Bowl champs.

The team's first game was at Blocksidge Field against Salem. The Witches, one year away from their own appearance in the Super Bowl under future Hall of Fame coach Ken Perrone, were reportedly loaded with size, speed, and talent. Perrone had arrived in Salem from Maine, where he was already legendary. Like Bondy, he was an inspirational coach who knew how to generate excitement and use psychology. There were quite a number of boys participating in his program, and it seemed that he had dressed them all for the game. Spreading over Blocksidge Field to perform warm-ups, the Witches were an imposing sight.

Bondy quickly took his squad into the Fieldhouse and kept them there, explaining to Bill Bush that leaving the boys on the field would just give them more time to marvel at the sheer quantity of Salem players and worry about having to battle all of them. Before the boys again left the Fieldhouse, they heard Bondy emphasize that there could only be 11 players opposing one another during the game. That was not going to change regardless of how many opponents stood on the sideline.

An overflow crowd was on hand, including many Salem fans who were hoping to see their team avenge its 1972 opening-day loss and end the Blue's latest winning streak. Trailing 8–7 at the start of the second half, Swampscott exploded for 21 unanswered points, winning 28–8. The Witch City fans went home disappointed. However, unlike its predecessor, this Big Blue team could not rely on an overpowering ground attack. For the first time in more than two seasons, the offense accumulated more yardage passing (192) than rushing (139).

The boys continued to win convincingly, dispatching Gloucester (27–12), Saugus (33–6), and previously unbeaten Danvers (31–8) on successive weekends. In the victory over Danvers, Michael Jauron scored 19 points, running for two touchdowns while kicking all four PATs and a 28-yard field goal. Among other playmakers were Ralph Boyce, who picked off a pass in the end zone, and gritty Captain David Faulkner, who recovered a fumble. Faulkner was in the mold of Carl "Mad Dog" Kester. At 160 pounds, he was undersized for a lineman/linebacker, but totally fearless.

The running backs were good athletes who executed well. Over the first four games, Bane, Boyce, Beatrice, Bessom, and DiLisio all found the end zone, while ends MacCallum and Dedrick hauled in multiple passes. SHS had passed for 674 yards and run for 582. Coupling the balanced attack with a tough, stingy defense, the Big Blue had outscored its first four opponents 119–34.

In his October 10, 1973, *Danvers Herald* article about Swampscott's one-sided victory over the Falcons, reporter Ted St. Pierre, like so many others, attempted to explain the Big Blue's incredible run of football success, citing, "super organization, the attitude of the boys, the loyalty of the town, the psyched-out opposition, and the creator of the whole show—Stan Bondelevitch." Describing the community's involvement, he wrote that "Football in Swampscott is more than just a way of life. It's a fashion show, a church gathering, a social event and a fiesta all rolled up into one...."

St. Pierre touched upon numerous other factors but suggested that perhaps most important was Bondy's "ability to instill in the boys the feeling that they can't, and won't be beaten and the teaching of his teams to handle the incredible pressure of a long winning streak." Noting that it was impossible to say how long the streak could continue, St. Pierre observed that the 1973 team had made some mistakes, but that opponents had not yet been able to capitalize on them.

With Danvers safely dispatched, the team focused on Bob DeFelice's Winthrop Vikings. Games against Winthrop were frequently characterized by hard hits and tough defense. Such was the case when the teams met on October 13. Winthrop planned to pressure Swampscott's quarterback as much as possible and hopefully disrupt the passing attack. According to DeFelice, "We felt we had to get to Jauron. We knew that if we sat back and waited for him, he'd pick us apart."

The Vikings did a masterful job executing the plan, blitzing and otherwise breaking through to harass the quarterback. The only significant completion all day was a 20-yard option pass from Beatrice to MacCallum near the end of the first half that moved Swampscott to the Vikings' 16. With only two seconds remaining, Michael Jauron booted a 33-yard field goal.

The Big Blue arrived in Winthrop averaging 30 points per game but never scored after Jauron's field goal, finishing with only three points. It was the first time in over seven years that Swampscott failed to score at least one touchdown. Yet when the contest ended, the team had notched a 3–0 win and remained atop the conference standings, its streak intact. It was Mike's second critical game-winning field goal, the first having been the last-second winner against Lynn English in 1972. Michael Jauron never worried about following in the footsteps of his famous brother Dick. Good-natured and confident in his abilities, he was comfortable being himself and leaving his own footprints.

Despite the victory, the dearth of points was troubling. The Vikings had nearly shut out what had been a highly productive offense. Ralph Boyce was also lost for the rest of the season with a knee injury. His absence would be keenly felt, especially in the defensive backfield. Major challenges loomed because the Big Blue would face all three Lynn schools in succession before finishing against strong Marblehead. Those teams had undoubtedly scouted the Winthrop game and were aware of the defensive scheme that had been so effective for the Vikings.

The first of the three Lynn opponents was 5–0 Technical Training High School or "Tech" as it had come to be known. This was the same school that SHS had met in Bondy's coaching debut in 1953 when it had been known as "Trade". Although the vocational school played in a lower-rated division, this particular squad posed a greater challenge than either English or Classical. Coach Mike Carr's unbeaten Tech Tigers were primarily seniors who had been playing regularly on the varsity for more than two years.

Speaking with the *Item*, Carr emphasized that Tech was a mature club that had not yet played up to its potential. He knew that there would be no problem motivating his team. Every opponent had extra incentive to knock off the Big Blue and end the team's long winning streak. Moreover, Tech was focused on achieving its own undefeated season and a possible division championship. In addition, a victory over Swampscott would earn the program considerable recognition and help to alter a general perception that Tech teams were inferior to those of the other Lynn schools. Carr said that it was simply the biggest game ever for his players.

Over the years, attendance at Manning Bowl had fallen to a point where it sometimes seemed that only friends and relatives of the participants were on hand. George Tracy, Lynn's ticket supervisor, was lamenting the situation but was promised by the *Item's* J. F. Williams that there would be a big crowd when Swampscott met Tech. Tracy said that he would believe it when he saw it. But Williams knew that at this point Swampscott always attracted crowds, even without the added interest generated by a battle of unbeaten teams. On Friday night, Tracy became a believer. With the possible exception of the English v. Classical Thanksgiving game, it was the largest, most energized Manning Bowl crowd in years.

Tech players gave their fans something to cheer about when star halfback Mike Wolfe galloped 36 yards for a touchdown. The conversion attempt failed. Strong defense by both teams thwarted further threats until late in the game when Tommy Beatrice ran in from the 7 to even the score. The visitors had an opportunity to take the lead and possibly win with the conversion, but the snap from center was high and the kick was blocked. The contest ended with the teams knotted at six apiece. It was the first time in 28 games that the Blue had not emerged victorious.

While the teams played to a tie, the reactions told a different story. On the Tech side, players and fans celebrated. They had ended Swampscott's long winning streak while preserving their own undefeated season. The Tigers had made an emphatic statement, showing that they could compete with the top teams from the higher-rated conference. For the Big Blue, it felt more like a loss. There would be no return to the Super Bowl or repeat Division II championship, and the winning streak was over. Nonetheless, if the team could win its final three games, it could still claim the conference title outright and extend the undefeated streak to 31 straight.

The first remaining obstacle was Lynn English at Blocksidge Field. The 2–3 Bulldogs came to town intent on avenging their last-second 1972 loss. They were not successful, falling once more to Swampscott, this time by a score of 13–7. While the home team's offense generated a fairly modest 214 yards, the defense held English to less than 100. Beatrice was a standout, intercepting two passes and running for a touchdown. DiLisio registered the other score, while Dedrick and Faulkner were singled out for strong performances.

The following weekend, SHS revisited Manning Bowl for another Friday night encounter; this time against old adversary Classical. The 1–4–1 Rams seemed to find extra motivation against Swampscott, playing inspired ball and seizing an 8–0 lead in the second quarter. Defensively, Classical held the visitors to just 26 yards through the first half. Classical still led 8–0 when the third quarter ended. As the final quarter wore on, the Big Blue's unbeaten streak was in jeopardy, especially when the offense came up six yards short on third down and prepared to punt from its own 48.

However, punter Tom Kelliher faked the kick and handed off behind his back to Beatrice, who, aided by great blocks, made it to the end zone. The two-point conversion attempt failed, but when Swampscott regained possession following a Rams punt, the team put together a drive highlighted by Don DiLisio's running and receiving. After scoring the go-ahead touchdown, DiLisio again carried for the two-point conversion, extending the lead to 14–8. Then, after a Kevin Donelan fumble recovery, DiLisio scored again and Swampscott secured its seventh win of the season, 20–8 and remained unbeaten.

Due to an open date, the team had almost three weeks to prepare for its Thanksgiving contest at Marblehead. The only blemish on the Blue's record was the tie against non-conference Tech. Swampscott remained unbeaten over its past 30 games and had won 48 straight in the Northeastern Conference.

The talented Headers were led by Brian Buckley, a gifted junior quarterback. With a strong, accurate arm, the southpaw was capable of picking defenses apart. He had done so throughout the season, particularly in his last two games, when the Whips had soundly beaten both Bishop Fenwick and English, each by a score of 35–0. They entered Thanksgiving with a 6–2 record, having lost only to Salem and Winthrop.

Since the 7–0–1 Blue had beaten both of those squads, some considered Swampscott the favorite. Yet a comparison of the rivals' recent performances told a different story. While the Magicians were routing two opponents by a combined 70–0, Swampscott had barely beaten English, a team that the Whips humiliated. The Blue then trailed 1–4–1 Classical until rallying in the final quarter to pull out a victory. The offense, which had averaged 30 points per game over its first four outings, had averaged only 10 since then. During the season, the Magicians scored more points than had Swampscott and surrendered fewer. Their recent one-sided victories suggested that they were peaking at the right moment.

As in most years, there was much at stake for the rivals when they met in Marblehead on Thanksgiving. Bondy, always capable of firing up the troops with his season-ending, pregame speech, did so with another masterpiece. However, one of the less level-headed seniors may have over-reacted to his coach's exhortations. Once the game got underway, the kid lost his composure and was ejected after being flagged for two personal fouls. At halftime, Bondy urged game officials to allow the boy to play the last two quarters of what would be his final high school game. Header coach Alex Kulevich graciously consented and the ejected player returned to the fray.

Playing on a soggy field, SHS clung to a 12–6 halftime lead. While the Headers advanced through the air late in the second quarter, Swampscott managed to keep them from scoring. If the boys could hold on to that lead, they could complete a third consecutive undefeated season, extend the unbeaten streak to 31, and remain perfect in the conference for the seventh consecutive year.

However, with their first possession of the second half, the Headers resumed the aerial assault, driving all the way to the Blue end zone. Swampscott ultimately succumbed, losing 20–12. Pass defense had traditionally been a hallmark of Big Blue football, but Brian Buckley completed 21 of 30 passes for 256 yards. Overall, the Headers gained 368 yards compared to 153 for the visitors. In his postgame comments, the Swampscott coach said that the long layoff following the Classical game had hurt his team. However, in typical fashion Bondy lauded the

Marblehead coaches and players, noting, among other things, "Their pass protection was outstanding and their passing cut us to pieces."

While the boys fell short of their goal, they were still champions, sharing the conference crown with Marblehead. All things considered, the team had done very well. With only two returning starters and just a few others who had seen prior regular action, 7–1–1 Swampscott exceeded expectations. This, however, would prove to be the last championship of any kind for a Bondelevitch-coached team.

The *Item's* prophetic sports headline read, "Reign Ended By Magicians, 20–12." Thanksgiving Day 1973 marked more than a season-ending loss at Marblehead. It marked the end of the incredible reign of Stan Bondelevitch. While he would continue to coach for a number of years and field some strong teams, they would never again achieve lengthy winning streaks or undefeated seasons.

In 1974, the regular season schedule expanded to 10 games, and the Big Blue finished with a 5–5 record. The 1975 club, featuring star Tommy Beatrice and a number of other experienced seniors, improved to a respectable 7–3, beating Marblehead in the season finale. But Dot had been battling cancer and passed away in September. Shortly after her death, Bondy gave notice that he intended to retire. On May 14, 1976, he made it official, ending what the *Item* described as "The greatest coaching era in the history of New England schoolboy football."

He explained his resignation by insisting that, as a single parent, he needed to devote more time to his children. However, other factors played a role. Since at least 1973, Bondy had been claiming that townspeople were not giving his team the credit it deserved. He felt strongly that the town had failed to properly honor him and his players for their recent accomplishments, particularly the 1972 Super Bowl win.

While some would not have given such things much thought, for Stan, being ignored may have been worse than being criticized. For example, Dick Lynch recalled sitting next to Bondy on the team bus, riding to a game. Rolling through town past the Tedesco Country Club they saw a number of men playing golf. Obviously annoyed, Stan grumbled, "Just look at those selfish bastards!" In his view, it was hugely disloyal for Swampscott residents to play golf instead of attending the football game to cheer for the Big Blue.

For several years, he had also been expressing concern that the incredible success of Big Blue football could not continue, at least if Swampscott remained in the Northeastern Conference. A November 8, 1973, article in the weekly *Swampscott Reporter* predicted that SHS might soon leave the conference because the increasing enrollments of most other conference members, combined with the addition of larger schools like Salem and Beverly, made the Big Blue's athletic success unsustainable. Swampscott's male enrollment had always been smaller than practically all of the other conference schools throughout Stan's tenure. According to the article, the numbers gap was widening. In Bondy's words:

> Nobody gives even a bat of an eyelash to this growing problem. Very little credit is given where deserved and people take the problem for granted because we've won 62 out of our last 63 contests.
>
> Sure, fine for now, but wait until we lose 40 or so ball games in a row. And in the process, many of our players will really get smashed around on the field....
>
> When these things suddenly begin to occur, you'll see how fast everyone will want us to get the hell out of the league.

Stan foresaw that the tougher competition, combined with low enrollment, changing times, and enhanced opportunities to opt for different sports or activities made it practically impossible for SHS to continue its remarkable streak of wins and championships. The advent of soccer as another fall sport was both a literal and figurative sign that football would no longer be the only game in town.

Stan also continued to describe Swampscotters as spoiled by all of the winning. After his retirement announcement, he told the *Item's* Red Hoffman, "I'd have to win 11 games out of 10 now to get any recognition." In short, Stan believed that people in the town had unrealistic expectations. He was a victim of his own success.

There were also problems with the school committee, where some members were not in his corner and rumored to be looking for ways to force him out. Many factors could have contributed, including unhappiness of some parents or other relatives over his actual or perceived treatment of their boys. Certainly, not every player left the program with warm and fuzzy feelings for the head coach. It seemed that there were always a few who, rightly or wrongly, ended up in Bondy's dog house.

Some folks also had issues with Bondy's performance as athletic director where, among other things, he had always prioritized football. His tendency to focus on football and occasionally make dismissive comments about other sports rubbed some people the wrong way. He was, without question, a football coach first and an athletic director second.

Bondy, a coaching legend and man of no small ego, did not appreciate the criticism. He also resented changes that had been made by the school committee, such as eliminating the faculty manager position following Frank Coletti's retirement, and requiring all coaches, including Stan, to annually re-apply for their jobs and interview with the committee. He told the *Item's* Hoffman, "I was of the opinion that my position and my accomplishments within the town deserved more respect."

Whatever role such factors played in Stan's decision, he concluded that it was time to move on. Following his resignation announcement, he said a number of things in a rambling interview with the *Item*. He mentioned the death of David Coughlin as one of the saddest experiences of his life. He said that he might coach again but that he would never coach against Swampscott. He talked about his 1953 squad and the upset win over Amesbury. And he lauded his various championship teams.

Responding to a question about the type of coach he would like to see as his successor, Bondy said that he would want someone as dedicated to the kids as he had been. What followed, as reported by Hoffman, may have been his most insightful message on high school coaching:

> "DIGNITY," he fairly shouted. "You have to leave a young man his dignity at all times. You can't abuse him, torment him, or degrade him. Whenever I've been on a boy for any length of time, I always manage to end it by telling him he's done something well or that he's improving … something to lift him up."

For the vast majority who played football during Bondy's reign, it had indeed been an uplifting experience—one that left deep and lasting marks on the players, their families, and the Swampscott community.

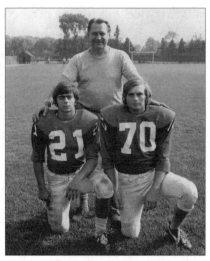

1970 team quarterback Mike Lynch (5) and captain Jim Carone (44) with Coaches (l-r) DeFelice, Bondelevitch, and Lynch. 1971 *Seagull*

Bondy with Danny Losano (21) and 1971 captain Bobby Murray (70). 1972 *Seagull*

1971 coaching staff, (l-r) Ron Corcoran, Dick Lynch, Stan Bondelevitch, Fran York, George Pleau. Bob Crosby photo, courtesy *Daily Item*

Bobby Murray explodes through the Big Blue hoop in 1971.

Captain Jeff Hegan rambling in 1972.

1972 Super Bowl MVP Donny Page scores against Catholic Memorial.

1972—Left halfback Ray DiPietro adds to his team-leading rushing yards.

Bondy with quarterback Mike Jauron at 1972 Super Bowl game.

Michael Jauron passing against Danvers in 1973. George MacNaughton photo, courtesy *Danvers Herald*

Epilogue

The word that best describes Stan Bondelevitch is *motivator*. As former assistant, Fran York said, "He motivates people; he motivates players; he motivates coaches; he motivates everyone." His pregame talks were masterful. Bill Adams, who heard numerous such talks from many coaches over his long athletic career, said, "He made the best pregame speeches of any coach I've ever had for any sport I've ever played—at any level." But Stan's talent went far beyond a mere ability to fire up his players for a football game. He excelled in motivating boys to attain the confidence and perseverance that were essential to success in life. And he excelled in organizing and motivating the greater community to support, and take pride in, the accomplishments of its high school team.

He did it, not through fear and intimidation, but through contagious passion, spirit, and frequent recognition of players' accomplishments. He also did it through humor. Whenever I think of Bondy, I see the wide, beaming smile and hear the deep, oft-amused voice. There was little doubt that he loved coaching high school kids. Players inevitably caught the positive vibes.

After David Coughlin's death, Stan famously said that he decided to remain in coaching because of "smiles"; adding that there was "nothing like a boy's smile." The head coach was frequently the reason for such smiles. It is not likely that many high school football players in other programs could describe practices as enjoyable. Yet, preaching that football was fun, Bondy often injected humor and laughter into practice sessions that were tough and physically demanding. "I had so much fun playing for him," recalled Bill Adams. Hundreds, from stars to benchwarmers, could say the same.

While some truly extraordinary athletes played for the Big Blue during the Bondelevitch era, a number of others were not physically gifted or blessed with much talent. Participation in Bondy's program helped them gain confidence in themselves and hone their skills. They may not have wanted, or been able, to play in some other places but, inspired by the Big Blue culture, they yearned to play in Swampscott. Many ultimately played well, as Bondy built them up while Dick Lynch and other fine assistants coached them up, teaching techniques that compensated for what they lacked in natural ability. As a result, in the words of 1961 co-captain Richard Fuller, "Bondy took young men of average talent and made them winners."

Stan Bondelevitch believed that playing football bred confidence, saying, "Once you've played football, you can tackle anything." Indeed, confidence, self-esteem, and perseverance were the life lessons so many former players mention when discussing their Big Blue football experience. Sandy Tennant, speaking at Stan's 1976 testimonial dinner, put it this way:

> Stan, you make people feel they're worth something. You demanded hard work and excellence, but when we walked away we believed in ourselves. And that is how I would explain it when people ask me how we won so consistently; how Stan was able to motivate us. Stan Bondelevitch made me believe in myself.

Of course, playing for Stan never guaranteed future success. Yet it was a gateway for many players to college and productive careers. Some followed in his footsteps to become legendary high school coaches. Norman Walker, Ron Corcoran, Bruce Jordan, and Bill Adams are in the Massachusetts High School Football Coaches Association Hall of Fame. Dick Gowen was inducted into the Massachusetts Basketball Coaches Association Hall of Fame.

Tom Toner, like his high school teammates Bill Adams and Dick Jauron, built a career in sports, becoming an agent after his Green Bay playing days ended. He spoke glowingly of his Swampscott experience, describing it to the *Boston Herald American's* David Cataneo as "almost a Utopia." He raved about how vibrant and alive the community was on game days. In trying to further express the euphoric feelings he'd experienced playing for the Big Blue, he contrasted it to his time with the Packers, saying, "I started my first Monday night football game and, who knows, maybe 50 million people were watching. But that didn't give me the same feeling I had at Swampscott." Tragically, he succumbed to cancer in 1990, leaving behind his wife and two children. Collectively, brothers Tommy, Billy, and John played on five SHS championship teams. The legacy continued with the next generation. Tom's nephew, Ed Toner Jr., attended SHS and Boston College, and then followed in the footsteps of his father and uncle, playing for a number of seasons in the NFL.

For Tom's teammate Andy Rose, growing up in Swampscott and playing for the Big Blue was a memorable, treasured experience. It was, as Bondy liked to say, a special time in a special place. When Andy's youngest daughter Nicole, a gifted soccer player, reached high school age, he and his wife discussed sending her to private school. But Andy did not want her to miss the same kind of special opportunity that he had been given—that of attending the local public school and playing sports for the Big Blue. His daughter had that opportunity, playing for the SHS soccer team and serving as one of its co-captains during her senior year. Her father, of course, never missed a game.

My brother Dick has always cherished his Swampscott experience, crediting his coaches and teammates for much of his success in sports. The most acclaimed athlete in the Big Blue's storied history; he was a high school and college All-American. He set countless records at SHS and then at Yale, where, among other things, he won the Bushnell Cup as the Ivy League's best football player and the Bulger Lowe Award as the most outstanding college football player in New England. He was named one of the top 10 Massachusetts schoolboy football players of the twentieth century, and he has been inducted into the National Football Foundation's College Football Hall of Fame. He also captained Yale's baseball team and was drafted by the Saint Louis Cardinals, as well as the NFL's Detroit Lions. Dick chose football. As a professional player, he was a member of the NFL's All-Rookie Team and a participant in the Pro Bowl. After a lengthy and accomplished playing career, Dick joined the coaching ranks, ultimately serving five-year stints as the head coach of both the Chicago Bears and the Buffalo Bills. In 2001 Dick was named NFL Coach of the Year.

Notwithstanding all of his athletic and professional honors and accomplishments, Dick would most treasure being recognized as a loyal and supportive friend, brother, son, father, and husband. It is a tribute earned and richly deserved. He has lived his life guided by the words and actions of our mother, who liked to say that the best gift is a good example.

Harvard Professor and Dean W. Carl Kester has always remembered how Bondy was able to motivate him with just a few simple words of recognition and has made such positive reinforcement a staple of his own teaching and management style. While his academic and professional achievements have been extraordinary, Carl says that he may be proudest of having played as a rather small but hard-hitting lineman on two Big Blue championship teams. Dick Jauron says that he has never played with, or against, anyone more fearless than his old high school teammate, Carl "Mad Dog" Kester.

Frank DeFelice, having experienced success during his five seasons at Xaverian Brothers, returned to Swampscott and served as the Big Blue's head football coach from 1976 through 1981. It can be difficult to follow a legend, and Frank's Swampscott teams struggled, with none able to finish with a winning record. However, Frank ultimately also became legendary in Swampscott, coaching the SHS baseball team for a total of 35 years. One of the most successful high school baseball coaches in state history, he was voted into the Massachusetts Baseball Coaches Association Hall of Fame in 2002. In 2011, Francis DeFelice, the man who had originally wanted nothing to do with the Big Blue, was also inducted into the SHS Hall of Fame. He recalls his five years working with Bondy and Dick Lynch as a young assistant on the Swampscott football staff as the most instructive and, in many ways, happiest and rewarding, in his long coaching career, echoing so many others in describing it as a special time in a special place.

My youngest brother Michael spent a postgraduate year at Maine's Berwick Academy where he was an All-American quarterback for the football team. After attending Boston University and working with our dad in the sporting goods business, Michael embarked on a long career as a commercial real estate appraiser. He and his wife Kathy, the sister of Mike's Big Blue teammates Richard and Billy Dedrick, spend much of their free time enjoying the golf links with their many friends at Lynn's Gannon Golf Course.

As for our dad, he ultimately became a member of the Nashua High School, Peoria, Illinois, and Saint Joseph's College athletic halls of fame. As a football coach, he combined a brilliant understanding of the game with an innate ability to teach fundamentals. Demanding and sometimes short-tempered, he would not have won popularity contests with many of the boys when they played for him. But decades later they called or wrote, expressing gratitude, respect, and, yes, love. They explained how the lessons he taught had helped them throughout their lives. With different personalities, styles, and approaches, he and Bondy were both remarkable teachers.

Dad's final coaching job, performed for 16 years during retirement, was mentoring the SHS golf team. While he mellowed over time, he never lost his passion for coaching and excelled in the role, regardless of the sport. He was an outstanding young athlete and then perhaps an even more outstanding coach, winning multiple championships and honors. However, I believe his most impressive accomplishment was facing and overcoming his personal problems in the mid-sixties, rebuilding his life and staying sober for the remainder of his days, which were many. He passed away in 2010 at the age of 91.

Dick Lynch retired as Danvers Athletic Director in 1988. At age 90, he resides with his wife in the Swampscott home they purchased in 1954. SHS basketball teams play in the Richard Lynch Gymnasium. While at Harvard, Coach Lynch's son Michael again kicked a winning field goal in the last minutes of a season-ending game, thereby helping to beat Yale in 1975. For many years, Mike Lynch has been a highly acclaimed television sports anchor in Boston. He is undoubtedly far better known throughout Massachusetts than is his father. But Dick Lynch will always be "the man" in Swampscott. And he remains quick with one-liners. When a former player returned after a long absence and saw the "Bondelevitch Way" sign near the Fieldhouse, he asked when it was that Bondy had gotten his Way. Coach Lynch immediately replied, "Bondelevitch *always* got his way!"

But Bondy did not quite always get his way. Shortly after tendering his resignation in 1976, he became the head football coach at Bishop Fenwick High School in Peabody, Massachusetts. After a few years, his Fenwick team fell just short of an undefeated, championship season. In 1982, he returned to coach Swampscott. During his six-year absence, the team posted an overall record of 17–40–3.

After a 7–13 start in his first two years back in Swampscott, Bondy coached the Blue to three consecutive winning seasons, including an 8–2 finish by the 1984 squad quarterbacked by Roger Baldacci, son of Stan's old assistant. The 1986 team finished with a strong 7–3 record and beat favored Marblehead on Thanksgiving, preventing the Headers from winning the conference crown. Bondy coached while on crutches, having broken his leg in a fall at the Fieldhouse. The big upset victory seemed like a fitting conclusion to a remarkable career, and in early February of 1987, Stan Bondelevitch announced his retirement, leaving the coaching ranks forever.

While Stan insisted he was retiring due to continuing pain and disability from the leg fracture, there was, unfortunately, widespread speculation that he had been forced out. Reportedly, three of the five school committee members were opposed to rehiring the 68-year-old coach, although only one publicly confirmed such opposition, saying that Stan's "time had come." Unspecified complaints from a number of unidentified parents, and concern over circumstances of a mid-season suspension of players for drinking were mentioned, and there was also talk that one starter would be attending private school if Stan remained as coach.

Yet there was a good deal of support for the coach throughout the community. Athletic Director Richard Baker stated that he would have strongly recommended that the coach be rehired. SHS Principal Peter Sack and two school committee members voiced their backing, crediting Bondy with having done a fine job. Tom Corcoran, president of the Swampscott Gridiron Club, announced that he was resigning in protest over what he felt was mistreatment of the coach, saying,

> I feel I have to do something out of respect for the guy.... We wanted a tradition, not necessarily a winner, and we got both. This breaks everything I've ever strived for. He's a legend. And whatever he's done, he's done not only for himself, but for the kids too.

Regardless of the views of those who wished him gone, the highly publicized controversy was regrettable. As observed by the *Item's* Rich Fahey, "The ending should have been storybook. Instead, it's sad." In retrospect, it might have been better for Bondy if he had not returned to coach in Swampscott, a sentiment he eventually expressed.

Yet, Stan lifted the program out of the doldrums. Thirty-six players reported for football in 1981. With Bondy's return in 1982, 80 students signed up to play. The teams in his final three years all enjoyed successful seasons, winning 21 of 30 games. Following Stan's departure, his assistant

Bill Bush became the head coach. Continuing many of his mentor's organizational and motivational approaches, he impressively directed the program for 11 years. In only his second season, Bush went 9–1. In 1996 and 1997, his Swampscott squads played in consecutive Division III Super Bowls.

Bush was succeeded by his, and Bondy's, former player, 1988 co-captain Steve Dembowski. The bright, innovative Dembowski left after the 2014 season. Like Bush, Dembowski was considered one of the top football coaches on the North Shore. He changed the offensive scheme, jettisoning anything resembling Bondy's old wing-T and installing a wide-open, pass-heavy, spread attack. As a quarterback in that offense, Peter Beatrice's son Kyle threw a record-shattering 73 touchdown passes over two seasons. Dembowski's teams played in three more Super Bowls, winning the final one in 2007. His successor is another member of the Big Blue family, former SHS player and assistant coach, Bob Serino.

Thus, despite the concerns expressed by Bondy in 1973, future SHS teams experienced considerable success and, more often than not, were strongly competitive. Yet one Bondelevitch prediction has proven accurate over the past 30 years. Stan told Bill Bush that SHS would never again enjoy multi-year winning streaks or undefeated seasons. In over a century of Swampscott football, there have been eight undefeated teams. All eight played for Stan Bondelevitch and Dick Lynch during the 16 years from 1957 through 1972.

As Tom Corcoran observed, Bondy built a winning tradition. A number of players since his departure were brothers, sons, nephews, and grandsons of men who played on his teams, but a boy named Alex Stone was not. Nonetheless, he was another Big Blue legacy. Alex was the grandson of Myron and Roz Stone, owners of the house where our family lived while my younger siblings and I attended school in Swampscott. We were in one unit of the duplex, while the Stones resided in the other. Alex's father Sam played high school baseball with my brother Dick and served as the student manager of the football squad.

By the time Alex arrived at SHS, his grandfather Myron had been an active member of the Boosters for many decades, enthusiastically supporting the football program despite the fact that none of his three sons played. Myron got his reward when he was able to watch grandson Alex perform as the star running back on Steve Dembowski's 2003 Super Bowl squad. After graduating, Alex followed in his proud grandfather's footsteps by enlisting in the United States Marine Corps. Myron Stone, now in his ninth decade, remains a stalwart Big Blue Booster and rarely misses a game.

S wampscott High School girls have their own tradition of playing and winning. Flora McLearn, who did so much to help build that tradition, was inducted into the SHS Hall of Fame in 1994. Four of her outstanding players, trailblazers Faith Shoer, Suzanne Sarra, Barbara Segel Yozell, and Janice Maselbas Sundell have also been inducted. And in 2011, the Hall of Fame Committee specially recognized the entire group of girls who participated in Mrs. McLearn's programs over the decades. Barb Yozell spoke at the event, noting that the Floradora Girls had "soared to unbelievable win-loss records in field hockey, basketball, softball, and reaped the character-building and fitness derived from athletic competition." She added:

> Tonight is a tremendous and well-deserved honor for these hundreds of gals who practiced long hours with commitment and dedication, who developed skills and were competing long before Title 9 and organized leagues, conferences, All-Star teams, and college scholarships for women. □

Stan Bondelevitch was, of course, inducted into the SHS Hall of Fame, as well as the Anselmian Athletic Club Hall of Fame (Saint Anselm College) and the Massachusetts Football Coaches Association Hall of Fame. The man who said that he would never last long enough to win 200 games concluded a 41-year coaching career that included 251 victories, 125 losses, and 11 ties. His name always comes up in discussions of the greatest high school coaches in Massachusetts history.

On September 7, 1991, Barry Gallup was in upstate New York, about to coach his first game for Northeastern against Colgate. Shortly before the game started, he learned that Bondy had made the five-hour drive from Swampscott and was outside the locker room. Excited, Gallup rushed to find his old coach. After thanking Bondy for making the long trip, Barry asked him to say a few words to the team. He led Bondy into the locker room and introduced him to the squad, telling the players to listen carefully. Standing on a chair, Bondy spoke for only a moment and basically said the following,

> Boys, football has not changed. It is still the same simple game. All that you need to do is hit them harder than they hit you. If most of you can do that and beat the guy on the other side of the line your team will win.

His message was brief, unadorned, and effective. Northeastern won, 35–10.

Following Dot's death, Bondy remarried. As he had done with Dot, he teased his new wife, the former Mary Patricia Donovan, with his litany of Irish jokes. In 1993, Bondy and Pat moved to New Hampshire where he could be closer to daughters Nancy and Sally and his two grandchildren. Not surprisingly, his daughters were school teachers.

Bondy lived a quiet retirement life. Having been raised on a farm, he never lost his love for gardening. He spent his days reading history, preparing meals containing fruits and vegetables grown in his garden, and watching documentaries and sports on television.

But he never got to watch his son play high school football. David Bondelevitch served as a Big Blue waterboy and played for the Pop Warner team. Recognizing that he was small and non-athletic, he chose not to continue. Bondy was forced to face the fact that David would never be a gridiron star. While disappointed, he accepted his son's decision.

David was, and remains, an accomplished musician, a skill he seemed to have come by naturally. He played the trumpet in the school band and thereafter attended both Boston's acclaimed Berklee College of Music and the Massachusetts Institute of Technology. He was the first person to earn a Bachelor of Arts Degree in Music from Berklee and concurrent Bachelor of Science Degree in Art and Design from MIT. He also received a Master of Fine Arts Degree in Film Production from the University of Southern California and embarked on a noteworthy and award-winning career combining expertise in music and film.

While Bondy joked that his son had three degrees and no job, he respected David's accomplishments and was proud of his success. When

David called to inform his dad that he had won an Emmy for Sound Editing, Bondy seemed as pleased as his son could ever recall. David ultimately became an Associate Professor and Department Chair at the University of Colorado, Denver.

Bondy sometimes spoke to his players about opportunities and the American dream. His own family story was a perfect example. Walter and Mary Bandalewicz had been illiterate immigrants from Eastern Europe. Their son earned college and advanced degrees and became a high school teacher, administrator, and legendary football coach. Today, their grandson holds three degrees from esteemed academic institutions and is a college professor and department chair.

Lloyd Benson still sings the praises of the gregarious Polish-American who motivated him to become a varsity football player. He last saw Bondy when the old coach returned for one of the annual Swampscott-Marblehead football dinners held on the Monday before Thanksgiving. The years had by then taken their toll. Bondy was sitting at a table when Benson approached. Though not sure that Stan would remember him, Lloyd wanted to say hello to the man who had inspired him so long ago.

Benson walked over, leaned down and told his former coach that it was good to see him. They shook hands as Bondy continued to gaze up at Lloyd. It was obvious that he could not recall Lloyd's name and was struggling to place him among all those who had played back in the day. A few seconds passed as he stared intently. Suddenly, there was a spark of recognition and his face lit up. "Number 63!" he boomed. "Smart Jewish kid!"

Stanley Walter Bondelevitch died on March 17, 2002, which was exactly 49 years from the day that he resigned as Hudson coach to take the job in Swampscott. Having in mind his two Irish-American wives, he surely would have seen the irony in having died on Saint Patrick's Day.

On September 10, 2011, the road that leads from Humphrey Street to the parking lot behind Blocksidge Field was dedicated as "Bondelevitch Way," in honor of the "Father of Big Blue Football." Stan's daughter Sally DeCost, an elementary school teacher, wrote the following comment in her educational blog after returning from that dedication ceremony:

It's hard to believe that I could have a lot in common with a man who coached football. Me, with zilch athletic ability. Me, who prefers to sing or tap dance or teach small children. But we both have a common theme. We both do everything within our power to get young people to be the best that they can be. We are both motivators. We are both passionate people who care about kids being successful. The man has been gone for 9 years, and yet he is with me every day. He is my hero.

It was not the only time that Sally posted thoughts about coaches as educators. In a piece titled, "What Does a Non-Athletic Girl Learn From a Football Coach?" she briefly discussed how football provided lessons in optimism, empathy, creativity, grit, self-control, and resilience, and then pointed out that mastering such traits was, of course, important for all kids.

I suspect that none of us as high school players fully understood that football fields were classrooms where coaches taught important life lessons, often in a straightforward and highly effective way. My most vivid recollection from high school football is of a moment at the end of a seemingly insignificant play. I had been chasing an opposing quarterback toward our sideline when one of his teammates blindsided me at the knees. I was momentarily airborne before hitting the ground hard. As I lay there, shaken, I heard a command shouted by a nearby familiar voice. I looked and there was Bondy, crouching on the sideline just a few feet away. He had been following the action and was fully engaged in the moment. His face was flushed and his eyes, as large as saucers, were riveted on me. He yelled the words a second time. Just two short words: "Get Up!"

As was true for many players, Bondy may have provided me with more help during high school than anyone outside my immediate family. In my case, it was much needed. I was married and the father of a child before graduating. Stan Bondelevitch was there for me, offering support and encouragement, including assistance with part-time job opportunities and college planning. Thanks to my parents and many others, including Stan and people associated with Brown University, I was able to attend and graduate from college. I started on the freshman football team but, after struggling as a sophomore, I stopped playing, choosing to focus on family, work, and academics.

After college, I worked as a legislative assistant in the Massachusetts Senate while attending Boston's Suffolk Law School at night. Thereafter, I practiced law for 37 years, retiring in 2014. My wife and I have been married for over 50 years and have three daughters and six grandchildren, all now living in Swampscott.

When I played, I was never able to celebrate a football victory over Marblehead. However, in 2015, I stood smiling in the rain after watching my oldest grandchild Megan score the winning goal for the SHS girls' soccer team in a victory over Marblehead that secured a share of the conference championship. I can't imagine that a Thanksgiving win over the Headers back in the day could have made me any happier. I think of my good fortune in having received so much help, guidance, and encouragement when I was younger. I owe debts that I'll never be able to repay.

Of all the stories I've heard about Bondy's influence on young people, Winslow Shaw's is the most memorable. An All-Star end and co-captain of Bondy's 1954 Swampscott squad, the Norwich graduate served in the U.S. Army for 29 years, retiring in 1990 as a highly decorated colonel. After his discharge, he embarked on a second career as an executive with Gulfstream Corporation. I contacted Colonel Shaw in May of 2015 and asked if he would be willing to speak with me about SHS and Stan Bondelevitch.

He talked about growing up in Swampscott and how Bondy had arrived and transformed what had been a losing football culture and how he instilled in the boys a confidence essential to winning. We discussed the games during Shaw's junior and senior years, including the enormous win over Amesbury and his last game as a senior when Swampscott defeated Marblehead for the first time in seven years. I finally asked if he could talk about how he may have benefited educationally from playing football at SHS.

Shaw thoughtfully replied that playing for Bondy, he learned lessons that guided the rest of his life; lessons about discipline, loyalty, fair play, trust and belief in teammates. The experience, he told me, provided a cornerstone on which his leadership traits were built.

He then said that lessons from Bondy had served him well in dealing with certain combat experiences. He hesitated and explained that those were not matters that he had ever discussed with anyone, not even his wife of more than 52 years. But he wanted to relate something that was important in explaining what his coach meant to him. He paused again and when he resumed it was obvious that he was struggling to control his emotions.

He explained that in late 1964, he had been stationed in South Vietnam as a military advisor assisting the South Vietnamese army in its fight against the Viet Cong and the army of North Vietnam. He was assigned to an elite brigade that operated with tracked vehicles in highland areas. An enemy tactic was to put a village under siege as a means of inducing a relief mission by a South Vietnamese army unit. While the villagers often suffered horribly, the enemy's main purpose was to inflict as many casualties as possible on the military units that attempted to provide relief.

In responding to one such attack, Shaw's unit encountered a sizable hostile force. A fierce, extended firefight ensued, with heavy casualties on both sides. Ultimately the defensive line of Shaw's unit was breached and they faced the prospect of being overrun and massacred. Shaw radioed an urgent request for air support as he and the other men dug in and struggled for hours into the night to fend off the assault. Finally, gunships flew in and helped turn the tide.

Speaking some 50 years after that battle, Shaw relived with me his thoughts and emotions. He told me that while they were under siege, he had begun to fear he might never be able to return to America, reunite with his family, and see his wife whom he had married just two years earlier.

But he recalled that his thoughts had then oddly turned to a day during preseason of his senior year in Swampscott. It had been a long, grueling practice on a brutally hot afternoon. Bondy finally called a break and the boys gathered in a shaded corner of the field, removed their helmets, knelt down, and relaxed.

The coach held forth for a while on matters relating to the team's performance, but then turned and gazed up at the roof of the New Ocean House Hotel, visible in the distance. Pointing to a large American flag that waved from a pole atop that roof, Bondy told the boys that there were three priorities that they should hold dear throughout their lives: family, religious belief, and that flag in the distance. He explained that they lived in a great country where they would be free to vote and pursue their dreams, and he continued for some time with his talk about the flag and what it meant to live in the United States.

Shaw did not pay much attention to Bondy's message on that afternoon in 1954. The 17-year-old was more focused on how much longer the practice might last, and his plans for the rest of the day. Yet, 10 years later, as he lay surrounded by enemies in a distant land wondering whether he would survive, Bondy's talk about the blessings of liberty somehow came back to him. The flag represented those blessings and the service and sacrifice of the people who made them possible. On that dark night in South Vietnam, Winslow Shaw found strength and reassurance in remembered words of his old high school coach.

On Thanksgiving morning, November 28, 2002, Swampscott paid tribute to the memory of Coach Bondelevitch at Blocksidge Field before the start of the Marblehead game. Tom Gorman, the star of Bondy's inaugural team, spoke. Gorman attended Amherst College where, as a quarterback, he was named a Little College All-American. He then served as a U.S. Marine officer before commencing a highly successful business career. His description of Stan included the following:

> He was a man of great warmth ... and of great understanding. And by his strong work ethic, by his infectious enthusiasm, and by his can-do attitude, he taught the youth of this town how to win, first on this very field and later, more importantly, in life.... Today, let us acknowledge the obvious—that Stan Bondelevitch lives on in the minds and in the hearts and in the memories of thousands who were guided by him at a critical time in their lives.

Much has changed in Swampscott over the years. Many of those who played or coached between 1953 and 1973 have passed away, including Jim Ryan, Bob Mansfield, Peter Cassidy Sr., Fred Bogardus, Al Owens, Tom Lyons, Norman Walker, Billy Nelson, Jim Rothwell, Fred Marino, Chuck Lynch, Terry Lyons, Ray Mansfield, Billy Carlyn, Billy Wood, Bill Ring, George Pleau, Richard Coe, Tim Nevils, Dick Maitland, Jimmy Lyons, Bruce Jordan, Pete Gnaedinger, Arthur Palleschi, Tom Santanello, Bob Arnold, Henry Legere, Steven Santanello, Bill Hinch, Bill Herlihy, Paul Legere, Barry Ryan, Rick Jacobs, Tony Benevento, Phil Berkeley, Brian Bates, Alan Gardner, Mark Bogardus, Gerry McGettrick, Tom Toner, Lou DeFelice, Don Page, Terry Fitzgerald, Jeff Hegan, Bobby

Lippa, Bob Andersen, Brock Maher, Fran Chiary, Harold Foster, Doc
Marden, Dick Stevenson, and Stan Bondelevitch. Others have suffered
tragic and staggering personal losses.

Condominiums or private homes have replaced the Ionic Club, the
New Ocean House Hotel, the Preston Beach Inn, the Willey House,
Cap'n Jack's Inn, and the Surf Theatre. By the time this book is in print,
the silent old high school building with its landmark cupola may also be
gone, felled by a developer's wrecking ball.

High school football is still played at Blocksidge Field, but that too
has changed. Attendance dwindled in recent years. There is no drill team
and fewer students play in the school's band. The days when Blocksidge
was reserved for exclusive use by the football players have long passed.
Many of the athletes elect to play other sports like soccer. The Big Blue
is classified as a Division V team, the result of continued growth of other
communities, combined with Swampscott's relatively small enrollment.
Bondy would not recognize the spread offenses run by the Dembowski/
Serino squads.

Attending some games during the past few seasons and gazing at the
half-empty stands and the small group of dedicated boys wearing the
blue and white, I could not help but think of another time. A time when
synchronized drill teams and 80-piece bands performed before standing-
room-only crowds; when elated students and Boosters flooded Humphrey
Street and paraded to the Fieldhouse to cheer the returning victorious
team; when fired-up players burst through the "Big Blue Hoop" and raced
along a gauntlet of cheerleaders and spirit squad members, confident that
the team would win again; and when the husky, broad-faced man in the
Swampscott cap paced the sidelines—the master of his domain.

It will never be quite the same again, and that's alright. Life is about
change. Nostalgia can and should be more than pining for what is past.
Recalling what was special and memorable can help us learn from, and
build upon, the positives in our history. The Big Blue football players
soldier on and there is cause for much excitement and optimism. Since
the advent of the 2017 season, SHS has been playing at a sparkling,
updated Blocksidge Field, equipped with new bleachers, and press box,
and a state-of-the-art turf surface. The modern facility can herald an era
of renewed energy, spirit, and pride.

It has been more than 30 years since Stan Bondelevitch coached in Swampscott. Yet, his legacy remains. In June of 2015, Massachusetts Governor Charlie Baker spoke at the SHS graduation ceremony at Blocksidge Field. He told the 155 graduates that they had been brought up in one of the greatest towns on earth and would forever be members of "the Big Blue family."

Appendix A

The Record

Swampscott High School Football Record (1953–1973)

1953	5–3	**1960**	6–3	**1967**	9–0
1954	5–3	**1961**	6–1	**1968**	9–0
1955	7–2	**1962**	5–4	**1969**	9–0
1956	6–3	**1963**	8–0	**1970**	8–1
1957	9–0	**1964**	5–2–2	**1971**	9–0
1958	8–0	**1965**	2–7	**1972**	10–0
1959	5–3–1	**1966**	7–2	**1973**	7–1–1

Won: **145**

Lost: **35**

Tied: **4**

Appendix B
Undefeated Teams

1957 (9–0)

Woburn **25–6**

Cambridge Latin **44–7**

Danvers **31–6**

Winthrop **19–12**

Amesbury **27–0**

Saugus **19–6**

Revere **32–0**

Rindge Tech **27–6**

Marblehead **27–0**

Points Scored: **251**

Points Allowed: **43**

Average Points Scored: **27.9**

Average Points Allowed: **4.8**

Average Margin of Victory: **23.1**

1957 Big Blue team. *Front row:* Matt Faino, Dick Gowen, Ed Cohen, Dick Owens, Peter Karalekas, Frank Parsons, Dave Frary, Bill Carlyn (co-captain), Jim Gorman (co-captain), Chuck Lynch, Eliot Rothwell, Bill Ring, Dick Winick, Bill Wood. *Back row:* Coach Foster, Coach Stevenson, Tom Lindsey, Jack Milo, Bob Andrews, Dick Coe, Ed Loveday, Phil Somerby, John Flanagan, George Blais, Ken Stein, Dick Maitland, Dan Vousboukis, Bob Browning, Phil Cudmore, Frank Cahoon, Tim Nevils, Coach Bondelevitch. 1958 *Seagull*

1958 (8–0)

Andover	(Rained Out)	Saugus	**38–12**
Woburn	**46–12**	Malden Catholic	**58–0**
Danvers	**41–0**	Newburyport	**16–0**
Winthrop	**22–0**	Marblehead	**41–6**
Amesbury	**38–6**		

Points Scored: **300**

Points Allowed: **36**

Average Points Scored: **37.5**

Average Points Allowed: **4.0**

Average Margin of Victory: **33**

1958 Big Blue Team. *Front row:* Steven Schawbel (manager), Paul Bartram, Phil Cudmore, Richard Maitland, Bob Browning, Jack Milo, John Flanagan, tri-captains George Blais, Frank Cahoon, and Bob Andrews; Richard Shulman, Tim Nevils, Ken Stein, Richard Coe, Ed Loveday, Phil Somerby, Peter Corcoran, George Pleau. *Second row:* Paul Wilson (manager), Tom Santanello, Paul Pagnotti, Bob Arnold, Paul Langevin, David Hapgood, John Hayden, Larry Milo, John Engstrom, Stuart Bass, Randy Browning, Mike Powers, Jim Lyons, Peter Gnaedinger, Charles Easterbrooks, Bruce Jordan, Phil Janvrin, Sam Kessell, Alan Manganaro. *Third row:* Gino Spelta (manager), Tom Peters, Arthur Palleschi, Ed Nelson, Ray Hennessey, Bill Palmquist, Bill Loveday, James Dexter, Philip McTague, Lloyd Spain, Mike Janvrin, Steven Brown, Jerry Garfield, Jim Levesque, Richard Spence, Mike Martin, Neal Kline, Richard Leger, Peter Smith, David Corbett. *Back row:* Dennis Caron, Fred Johnson, Jim Randell, Bill McGettrick, Tobey Moore, Dana Bagnell, Steve Waldman, John DiLisio. Bob Crosby photo, courtesy *Daily Item*

1963(8–0)

Andover **38–22**	Saugus **24–6**
Woburn **28–12**	Classical (Rained Out)
Danvers **26–6**	Newburyport **26–12**
Winthrop **8–6**	Marblehead **34–14**
Amesbury **16–8**	

Points Scored: **200**

Points Allowed: **86**

Average Points Scored: **25**

Average Points Allowed: **10.8**

Average Margin of Victory: **14.3**

1963 Big Blue team. *Front Row :* P. Smith, W. Costello, T. Tamborini, D. Bokozanska, Co-captains W. Herlihy and P. Legere; M. McKenney, S. Buswell, N. Rossman, W. Peckham, W. Rose, W. Strauss. *Second Row:* N. DeRobertis, A. Poltrino, N. Jacobs, W. Conigliaro, D. Andersen, P. Cohen, R. Frizzell, N. Green, D. Lyons, R. Tilden, B. Gallup, R. Lappin. *Back Row:* S. Roderick, P. Gapinski, B. Sogoloff, P. Cullen, A. Clippinger, B. Corcoran, M. Maselbas, W. Hayes, C. Picariello, D. DiPietro, L. Mangini, S. Soutter. 1964 *Seagull*

1967(9–0)

Gloucester **25–16**

Woburn **40–24**

Danvers **28–0**

Winthrop **20–6**

Amesbury **47–7**

Saugus **28–0**

Classical **7–6**

Newburyport **28–27**

Marblehead **24–6**

Points Scored: **247**

Points Allowed: **86**

Average Points Scored: **27.4**

Average Points Allowed: **9.6**

Average Margin of Victory: **17.9**

1967 Big Blue Team. *Front Row:* Charles Brigham, Francis Mayo, Roger Bruley, Michael Vernava, Richard Polisson, Ben Williams, John Carden, Mike Hoffman, Billy Adams (captain), Dan Videtta, Alan Gottfried, Mark Bogardus, Gerry McGettrick. *Second Row:* Dick Jauron, Andy Rose, Tom Toner, Bob Cropley, Phil Abram, Carl Kester, Paul Bartlett, Doug Greeley, Lloyd Benson, John Squires, Bob Rebholz, Ed Clippinger, Chris Riser, Ricky Anderson. *Back Row:* Sam Stone (manager), Sandy Tennant, Jay Coughlin, Greg Brand, Ray MacCallum, Peter Murray, Peter Beatrice, Louis DeFelice, Steve Dushan, Tom O'Shea, David Caras, Ralph Floria, Bob Brand, Buddy Porter, John Clayman (manager), Fred Duratti. 1968 *Seagull*

1968 (9–0)

Gloucester	**34–12**	Saugus	**56–32**
Woburn	**40–12**	Classical	**21–0**
Danvers	**41–20**	Newburyport	**24–6**
Winthrop	**35–8**	Marblehead	**40–0**
Amesbury	**33–6**		

Points Scored: **324**

Points Allowed: **96**

Average Points Scored: **36**

Average Points Allowed: **10.7**

Average Margin of Victory: **25.3**

1968 Big Blue Team. *Front Row:* Andy Rose, Bob Brand, Paul Hayes, Phil Abram, Erik Fredrickson, Dick Jauron (captain), Al Duratti, Carl Kester, Lloyd Benson, John Squires, Tom Toner, Ray MacCallum, Buddy Porter. *Second Row:* Bob Cropley, Ralph Floria, Dennis Popp, Barton Hyte, Tom O'Shea, Roger Carroll, David Caras, Louis DeFelice, Jay Coughlin, Mark Adelson, Steven Dushan, Bob Merrow, Bill Toner. *Back Row:* Managers Richard Brady and John Clayman, Charles Houghton, Randy Gibbs, Jim Carone, Jerry Mangini, Mike DiPrisco, Billy Goade, Mike Lynch, Randy Werner, David Callahan, Bob Goodman, Peter Murray, Peter Beatrice, Greg Brand, Sandy Tennant and Manager Cookie Guilford. Photo courtesy *Daily Item*

1969 (9–0)

Gloucester **42–8**   Saugus **27–6**

English **26–6**   Classical **55–14**

Danvers **31–22**   Newburyport **34–22**

Winthrop **14–6**   Marblehead **15–14**

Amesbury **36–8**

Points Scored: **280**

Points Allowed: **106**

Average Points Scored: **31.1**

Average Points Allowed: **11.8**

Average Margin of Victory: **19.3**

1969 Big Blue Team. *Front Row:* Bill Toner, Dave Caras, Jerry Mangini, Ben Mosho, Mark Adelson, Richie Conigliaro, Sandy Tennant (captain), Peter Beatrice, Steve Dushan, Greg Brand, Randy Gibbs. Middle Row: Coach DeFelice, Richard Brody (manager), Danny Losano, Charlie Cardillo, Lou DeFelice, Bob Goodman, Stephen Rowe, Marty Orloff, Ronnie Tamborini, Randy Kline, Jeff Gassman, Mike Donahue, Coach Bondelevitch. *Back Row:* Coach Lynch, John Clayman (manager), Richard Gibbs, Kevin Riley, Gil Baker, Mike DiPrisco, Randy Werner, Mike Lynch, Stu Greely, Peter Bartolik, Jim Carone, Dan Moreau, Bill Goade, Don Ribicanti, John Cawley, Bill Leone, Barton Hyte. Photo courtesy *Daily Item*

1971 (9–0)

Gloucester **29–0**	St. John's Prep **35–6**
Saugus **38–14**	Classical **20–0**
Danvers **20–6**	Newburyport **28–0**
Winthrop **26–12**	Marblehead **20–0**
English **41–14**	

Points Scored: **257**

Points Allowed: **52**

Average Points Scored: **28.6**

Average Points Allowed: **5.8**

Average margin of Victory: **22.8**

1971 Big Blue Team. *Front Row:* Steve Zuchero, Ray DiPietro, Terry Fitzgerald, Mike Kassoy, Ronnie Shadoff, Paul Palleschi, Brian Cousin, Jimmy Feldmen, Danny Giant, Timmy Barrett, John Bedard, Rusty Walker, Bill Vousboukis, Larry Moran. *Second Row:* Marc Weiss, Howie Rogosa, Ken Carpenzano, Rick Young, Bruce Savatsky, Jim Morash, Bob Moses, Dan Losano, Charlie Cardillo, Billy Leone, Richard Fromer, Kevin Riley, Steve Kruger, Maury Maniff, Gary Gladstone (manager). *Back Row:* Marvin Cohen (manager), Gary Orloff, Wayne Smith, Fred Keach, John Toner, Don Page, Pete Cassidy, Roy Ostrovitz, Bobby Murray (captain), Billy Wharff, Greg Beatrice, Jeff Hegan, Alan Barbanel, John Hoffman, Richard Dedrick, Arthur Herbert, Billy Borek, Steve Corben (manager). Bob Crosby photo, courtesy *Daily Item*

1972 (10–0)

Salem **19–7**

Gloucester **42–9**

Saugus **33–6**

Danvers **35–6**

Winthrop **27–6**

English **15–12**

Classical **27–0**

Newburyport **35–7**

Marblehead **29–0**

Catholic Memorial **28–21**
(Division II Super Bowl)

Points Scored: **262**

Points Allowed: **53**

Average Points Scored: **29.1**

Average Points Allowed: **5.9**

Average margin of Victory: **23.22***
[*above are based on regular season results)

1972 Big Blue Team. *Front row:* Fred Keach, Bill Vousboukis, Rusty Walker, Al Barbanel, Don Page, Jeff Hegan (captain), Peter Cassidy, Roy Ostrovitz, Marc Weiss, Terry Fitzgerald, and Peter Kain. *Middle row:* Tom Kelliher, Bill Dedrick, Steve Zuchero, Greg Beatrice, Bill Wharff, Richard Dedrick, Paul Losano, Mike Tumulty, John Toner, John Hoffman, and Ray DiPietro. *Back row:* Ralph Boyce, Robert Lippa, John McKenney, Wayne Smith, Gary Orloff, David Faulkner, Kevin Donelan, Reid Cassidy, Scott MacCallum, Mike Jauron, Mike Curtis, Ken Bane, Bill Palleschi. Jack L. Paster photo, courtesy *Swampscott Reporter*

Appendix C

All-Stars (1953–1973)

Swampscott Players Named *Daily Evening Item* First Team All-Stars (1953–1973):

1953   Jim Ryan, Winslow Shaw

1954   Al Owens

1955   Bobby Carlin*

1956   Terry Lyons, Fred Marino

1957   Billy Carlyn, David Frary

1958   George Blais, Bob Browning, John Flanagan, Jackie Milo*

1959   Bruce Jordan

1960   Jim Randell*

1961   Ronny Corcoran, Richard Fuller

1962   Billy Hinch, Bill Sjogren*

1963   Barry Gallup, Bill Herlihy

1964   Billy Conigliaro

1966   Robert Jauron, Tom Murray, Gary Savatsky, Mark Stevenson

1967   Bill Adams, Richard Polisson*

1968   Bob Brand, Dick Jauron*, Andy Rose

1969   Peter Beatrice, Greg Brand, Sandy Tennant*

1970   Jim Carone, Mike DiPrisco, Stu Greeley, Michael Lynch

1971   Steve Kruger, Dan Losano*, Bill Leone, Bruce Savatsky

1972   Greg Beatrice, Ray DiPietro, Jeff Hegan, John Hoffman, John Toner

1973   Billy Dedrick, David Faulkner, Michael Jauron

        *Thom McAn Shoe Award Winners

Notes

Preface

"the greatest coaching era": Red Hoffman, <u>Bondelevitch retires after 23 seasons</u>, *Daily Evening Item* ("*Item*"), May 14, 1976.

Time for a Change

"a crippled Methuen team": Harvey L. Southward, <u>Sculpins With New Coach Hope For Better Things</u>, *Item*, August 29, 1953.

"the former wizard": Ibid.

"Playing at end": November 23, 1940, Game Program—St. Anselm v. American International College (Saint Anselm College Archives).

"Why should I work": Rosenberg and Goldman, <u>The Coach</u>, a recorded interview of Stan Bondelevitch (part of an undated video documentary about Swampscott)

"Where the hell is Swampscott, Benny?": Matt Rillovick, <u>A Healthy Legend A Sporting Legacy</u>, Stan Bondelevitch Testimonial Program (March 8, 1969).

A Breath of Fresh Air

Note: Sources consulted concerning Swampscott facts and history included: The Swampscott Historical Commission, *Swampscott, Massachusetts Celebrating 150 Years, 1852–2002*; Dorothy M. Anderson, *The Era of the Summer Estates —Swampscott, Massachusetts 1870/1940*; Sue Ellen Woodcock, *Then & Now Swampscott*; Town of Swampscott, Massachusetts Website, <u>About Swampscott</u>.

He could not recall ever having told his wife: Rosenberg, and Goldman, <u>The Coach</u>, a recorded interview of Stan Bondelevitch (part of an undated video documentary about Swampscott)

1953—Giant Killers

"You could float a toy duck": <u>Swampscott Coach Goes Lightly In Hot Weather</u>, *Item*, September 3, 1953.

"You've got to have music": Grove Potter, <u>Bondelevitch returns to scene of former glory</u>, *Swampscott Reporter*, August 26, 1982.

"For Swampscott grid followers": <u>Sculpins Open With 34–0 Victory Over Lynn Trade</u>, *Item*, September 28, 1953.

"big, powerful and dangerous": <u>Sculpins Go Fishing For Biggest Catch Of Season</u>, *Item*, October 22, 1953.

"undoubtedly prove Swampscott's crucial game of the season": Ibid.

"There's small consolation for Swampscott": Ed Cahill, <u>The Cracker Barrel</u>, *Item*, October 23, 1953.

"nobody but ourselves": Cahill, <u>The Cracker Barrel</u>, *Item*, October 27, 1953.

"They're touting Stan Bondelevitch": Ibid.

"a profoundly indecent swear word": Mr. W.H.I.P. (William Hooper Ireson Peach), <u>Twenty Things Every Marblehead[er] Should Know</u>, *Marblehead Magazine*, Spring 1980.

"When Stan came around": Greg Walsh, <u>Friends Lament end of an era as Bondy retires</u>, *Swampscott Reporter*, February 12, 1987.

1954—Sculpins No More

"It's fortunate for us that our rivals over the years haven't uncovered the true meaning of the word": Cahill, <u>The Cracker Barrel</u>, *Item* September 22, 1954.

"With this program we hope to wipe out all traces of parental objection": Cahill, <u>The Cracker Barrel</u>, *Item,* September 15, 1954.

"showed all the spark and dash that marked their successful season a year ago": Cahill, <u>Swampscott, Saugus and English All Triumph In '54 Grid Debuts</u>, *Item,* September 20, 1954.

"still sporting a limp and used only in spots": <u>Swampscott Surprises Amesbury High, 26–14</u>, *Item*, October 25, 1954.

"This step was taken upon the advice of the team physician": <u>Swampscott Grid Game Is Canceled</u>, *Item*, November 9, 1954.

He replied that he was just praying that the flu did not break out: <u>Sachems Hoping To Snap Big Blue's Win Streak</u>, *Item*, November 1, 1957.

1955—You Couldn't Hit Him with a Handful of Raisins

"smart-looking, aggressive Swampscott team": Cahill, <u>English, Swampscott, Haverhill, Newburyport And Wakefield Win</u>, *Item*, September 14, 1955.

"If I were running an ice cream parlor": <u>Big Blue Hosts Winthrop In Saturday Morning Tilt</u>, *Item*, October 13, 1955.

"twisting, squirming, hard-running, 165-pound halfback": <u>Bobby Carlin Sparks Swampscott Win</u>, *Item*, October 18, 1955.

"the Comet": <u>State's Top Scorer Helps Blue Belt Stoneham 31–6</u>, *Item*, November 12, 1955.

"[i]n a spontaneous, unprecedented move": <u>Merchants Offer Awards To Swampscott Gridders</u>, *Item*, November 23, 1955.

"In a ding-dong battle": Don Flynn, <u>Lead Changes Hands Five Times; Carlyn Gets All-Important Point</u>, *Item*, November 25, 1955.

"the best defensive man on our team": <u>Carlin, Ball Win Thom McAn Awards</u>, *Item*, December 1, 1955.

"The finest boy I've ever coached": Ibid.

1956—A Cure for Fumbleitis

"Doug is loyal, a high character, respectful": Letter from Stan Bondelevitch to Mrs. Grace Haley, December 6, 1955.

"Every buck is a boost!": Cahill, The Cracker Barrel, Item, September 26, 1956.

"would take the pressure off of a 16-year-old quarterback": Cahill, Swampscott Tinkers With Short-Wave Radio, Item, October 2, 1956.

"fumbleitis": Blue's Win Streak Halted By Winthrop Eleven, 12–6, Item, October 13, 1956.

"Coach Stan Bondelevitch whose Swampscott High Team dropped its first decision in eight successive starts yesterday": Bondelevitch Pup Gets New Name, Item, October 13, 1956.

"well pleased with the results": All Three Swampscott Teams Defeat Concord, Item, October 25, 1956.

"Give me 11 boys like these two": Cahill, Swampscott Boosts Courageous Pair, Item, October 31, 1956.

1957—The Fairytale Season

"The Health of Your Boy": Swampscott Grid Squad Plans Clinic For Parents, Item, September 19, 1957.

"Booster Clubs are not exactly a new device": Cahill, The Cracker Barrel, Item, September 26, 1957.

"first string talent two deep": Swampscott Gridders Battle For Starting Jobs, Item, September 17, 1957.

"We're just praying that the flu bug doesn't break out": Saugus Confident On Eve Of Swampscott Duel, Item, November 1, 1957.

"The locker room grew hush": Jim Gorman, The Fairytale of 1957, Swampscott High School Football Website.

"definitely a team victory": Big Blue Blasts Saugus For Sixth Straight Win, Item, November 4, 1957.

"as far as the money lasted out": Lions Club Spearheads Own Drive For Funds, Item, November 6, 1957.

"smiled with approval": Swampscott Baby Blues Win 26th, Item, November 7, 1957.

The idea of a football game with Miami Edison had been shelved: Possibility of Miami Game Fades, Swampscott Plans Educational Trip, Item, November 12, 1957.

"lacking the drive exhibited in previous games": Swampscott Tips Rindge Tech 27–6, Item, November 18, 1957.

"So well behaved were our youngsters": Cahill, The Cracker Barrel, Item, January 7, 1959.

1958—Anything You Can Do, We Can Do Better

"on the part of the line to hold off the opposition": High School Mentors Unhappy At Point Values Conversions, *Item*, September 24, 1958.

"Swampscott again looked like the class of the party": Cahill, Swampscott's 16-0 Win Steals Bowl Grid Show, *Item*, September 22, 1958.

"The football setup at Swampscott with its big squad of eager beavers": Swampscott Expecting Rugged Test At Woburn, *Item*, October 2, 1958.

"All we need is a dry day": Ibid.

"[Y]ou can quote me": Rival Coaches Agreed On Shifting Site of Struggle, *Item*, October 7, 1958.

"We'll be lucky to survive": Swampscott Will Meet Old Rival At Winthrop, *Item*, October 16, 1958.

it would take "a real good football team" to defeat his club: Three Changes Possible In Swampscott Lineup, *Item*, October 23, 1958.

"The honeymoon is over": Stan Bondelevitch Says Big Blue Faces Danger, *Item*, October 30, 1958.

Playing before 7,000 fans: Swampscott Clobbers Saugus, *Item*, November 3, 1958.

"scared to death": George Blais May Be Out Of Swampscott Lineup, *Item*, November 7, 1958.

"an awfully good offer to get me out of Swampscott": Bondelevitch Declines Comment On Reports Of Several Coaching Bids, *Item*, November 24, 1958.

"potentially one of the greatest All-Star squads in history": Swampscott, Beverly Stars To Clash, *Item*, December 1, 1958.

"whoever will be coaching in Swampscott next year will have a real tough job": Ralph Pearson, Big Blue Seeking Second Unbeaten Season In Row, *Item*, November 26, 1958.

1959—Tough as Nails

"a well-coached, well-drilled football team to beat this stubborn and spirited group": Swampscott Prepares To Defend Grid Crown, *Item*, September 1, 1959.

"the best I've ever coached": Ibid.

"tough, stable, punctual always at the practice sessions": Stan Bondelevitch Tells Why Big Blue Succeeds, *Item*, September 2, 1959.

"The most important part of life in our high school": Game Program— Swampscott v. Newburyport, November 14, 1959.

Swampscott Has Three Blind Mice: *Item*, October 5, 1959.

"No coach ever worked with a finer or more loyal bunch": Not Boys' Fault,- Bondelevitch, *Item*, October 12, 1959.

"very well drilled and well coached": Sachems Favored Over Swampscott, *Item*, October 30, 1959.

"the best conditioned group": <u>Swampscott Lions Club Banquet Football Team</u>, *Item*, November 24, 1959.

1960—The Woburn World Series

"Promoting football interest at Swampscott High": Cahill, <u>The Cracker Barrel</u>, *Item*, September 15, 1960.

"Coach Bondelevitch and his new Hi-Fi offense": <u>1960 Joyce Jamboree Program</u>.

"the best tackle in the country": Ernest Dalton, <u>Swampscott Has Best Tackle In the World, Coach Claims</u>, *Boston Globe*, September 27, 1960.

"It will be a one-game affair": <u>"Series Not In Pittsburg, In Woburn," Bondelevitch</u>, *Item*, September 26, 1960.

"With Saturday's 22–16 win over Woburn safely on the record books": <u>Big Blue Dumps Woburn With 70-Yard Pass Play</u>, *Item*, October 3, 1960.

"We were outplayed completely": <u>Big Blue Fans Staggered By 34–6 Loss To Danvers</u>, *Item*, October 10, 1960.

"goofing off, slipping, bobbling the ball": <u>Coach Janusas Prepares To Face Swampscott Foe</u>, *Item*, October 27, 1960.

"Just imagine us taking on this big Class A power": <u>Big Blue To Seek Revenge On Rams</u>, *Item*, November 2, 1960.

"We certainly don't intend to be taken": Ibid.

"Swampscott is the toughest opponent we will face": <u>Conference Title On Line In Traditional Meeting</u>, *Item*, November 23, 1960.

"But for numerous penalties": Fred Goddard, <u>Marblehead Wins, 12–6, Big Blue Is Frustrated By Penalties</u>, *Item*, November 25, 1960.

"We need a commissioner": Cahill, <u>The Cracker Barrel</u>, *Item,* November 29, 1960.

1961—The Sad Season

"This is just the beginning": Cahill, <u>The Cracker Barrel</u>, *Item*, September 14, 1961.

"We haven't a championship team": J.F. Williams, <u>As I See It</u>, *Item*, September 15, 1961.

"It's a shattering thing. I'll see that boy's face": Cahill, <u>The Cracker Barrel</u>, *Item*, September 26, 1961.

"It's hard for us to think of football": <u>Swampscott-Woburn Tilt Called Off</u>, *Item*, September 27, 1961.

"We are not eager to play a game the Saturday before Thanksgiving": Cahill, <u>The Cracker Barrel</u>, *Item*, October 17, 1961.

"This isn't a great football team": Cahill, <u>The Cracker Barrel</u>, *Item*, October 19, 1961.

"As for the present it appears that": Williams, <u>As I See It</u>, *Item*, October 27, 1961.

In the November 1 *Item*: Williams, <u>As I See It</u>, *Item*, November 1, 1961.

"If I had my life to live over again": Cahill, <u>The Cracker Barrel</u>, *Item*, November 2, 1961.

if the Big Blue could beat its three remaining opponents: <u>Wage Scorching Battles For Class A-B Gonfalons</u>, *Item*, October 31, 1961.

"a generally improved ball club": <u>Big Blue Seeks Class B Crown</u>, *Item*, November 22, 1961.

"up and ready": Ibid.

"We were going into the game undefeated": Douglas Black, <u>On The Gridiron, Thanksgiving was his day</u>, *Swampscott Reporter*, November 25, 1981.

1962—Our Tiny Country School

"But do you know what changed my mind?": Will McDonough, <u>Tragedy Tightens Swampscott Boys' Bonds</u>, *Boston Globe*, October 20, 1961.

"going with the kids": Swampscott High School Football Website—1962 Swampscott Football Season.

"You're Not Ready, Sonny!": *Item*, September 20, 1962.

Seven Big Blue players were unavailable: <u>Outweighed Blue Team Awaits Woburn Invasion</u>, *Item,* September 29, 1972.

Sports Editor Ed Cahill responded: Cahill, <u>The Cracker Barrel</u>, *Item*, September 27, 1962.

a "mediocre" Danvers team: <u>Big Blue Lineup Shuffled For Saturday's Contest</u>, *Item*, October 8, 1962.

"he throws pretty good": <u>Swampscott Polishing Offense For Winthrop</u>, *Item*, October 11, 1962.

The *Item* predicted that Amesbury would romp: <u>Underdog Swampscott Entertains Amesbury</u>, *Item*, October 19, 1962.

Coach Jauron expressed concern …: Cahill, <u>Classical Smothers Newburyport, 43–13</u>, *Item,* October 29, 1962.

"We're in for a battle": Hoffman, <u>Both Camps Engage In Psychological Warfare</u>, *Item*, October 31, 1962.

"We're facing a Class A power with our tiny country school": Ibid.

"He wanted this game": Cahill, <u>Pregame Rivalry Building Steam As Big Blue Awaits Visit By Rams</u>, *Item,* November 2, 1962.

"So any talk about this being a mismatch": Ibid.

"We can't play the game in the newspapers": Ibid.

"next year when it's their home game": Cahill, <u>The Cracker Barrel</u>, *Item*, November 1, 1962.

"There weren't a thousand fans at Blocksidge Park": Hoffman, <u>Soggy Swampscott Upsets Rain-Soaked Rams</u>, *Item*, November 5, 1962,

"much less of a test": <u>Newburyport High Next For Swampscott Eleven</u>, *Item*, November 9, 1962.

"It would have taken the New York Giants": Goddard, <u>81-Yard Kickoff Return Beats Blue</u>, *Item*, November 23, 1962.

1963—The Gritty Champs

the *Item's* Red Hoffman provided brief assessments: Hoffman, <u>Red-Hot Items</u>, *Item*, October 19, 1963.

"highly regarded as the dark-horse": <u>Blue Treks To Andover For Conference Debut</u>, *Item*, September 26, 1963.

"I saw Newburyport beat Woburn": Williams, <u>As I see It</u>, *Item*, September 30, 1963.

"Parents Day": <u>Big Blue Hosts Vikings In Conference Collision</u>, *Item*, October 18, 1962.

Bondy rewarded players with blue star: Hoffman, <u>Red-Hot Items</u>, *Item*, October 29, 1963.

"Newburyport, after that trouncing by Marblehead": <u>Porters Could be Tough Says Swampscott Coach</u>, *Item*, November 14, 1963.

"Game of the Year": <u>Wins Set Up Title Clash For Conference Foes</u>, *Item*, November 18, 1963.

"as polished a performance as these tired old eyes": Cahill, <u>The Cracker Barrel</u>, *Item*, November 19, 1963.

On November 20, Swampscott got more publicity: Ibid.

"The more people see this game the better it is": Hoffman, <u>Red-Hot Items</u>, *Item*, November 21, 1963.

"It was a great team effort": Bill Rolfe, <u>Conigliaro, Herlihy Star As Blue Nails 'B' Crown</u>, *Item*, November 29, 1963.

1964—Harvard and Yale can move over—this is THE GAME!

"We must keep every boy who wants to play football active": Williams, <u>As I See It</u>, *Item*, September 18, 1964.

"blessed with size, great speed, and versatility": <u>The Swampscott Story</u>, *Item*, September 1, 1964.

"If we're going to lose this season …": <u>Need Win Over Winthrop To Retain Class B Title</u>, *Item*, October 15, 1964.

"a great Classical team": Williams, <u>As I See It</u>, *Item*, October 23, 1964.

"We're going to throw and keep throwing": <u>Swampscott May Unveil New passer Tomorrow</u>, *Item*, October 23, 1964.

"They'll be sky high for us": Williams, <u>As I See It</u>, *Item*, November 2, 1964.

"tossup": Williams, <u>As I See It</u>, *Item*, November 6, 1964.

"Harvard and Yale can move over—": Hoffman, <u>Cohen v. Brown In Pitching Duel</u>, *Item*, November 25, 1964.

"GO BIG BLUE": Ibid.

the biggest sports thrill: Bob Keaney, A Bowl Full of Memories, City of Lynn Municipal Website.

1965—The Aberrant Season

"There will be a lot of new faces": Beaton, Quarterback, Linemen Bondy's Key Problems, *Item*, September 7, 1965.

"We knew we had our hands full": Hoffman, Red-Hot Items, *Item*, September 29, 1965.

"Our entire defense fell apart": Bondelevitch Shuffles Swampscott Defenses, *Item*, October 8, 1965.

"no Revere": Ibid.

"You could cut the gloom with a knife": Hoffman, Red-Hot Items, *Item*, October 13, 1965.

"nice guys seldom win.": Bondy Plans 'New Look' For Big Blue Gridders, *Item*, October 14, 1965.

"rock em and knock em player": Ibid.

"A couple of bad breaks hurt us": Winthrop Hands Big Blue Fourth Straight Defeat, *Item*, October 18, 1965.

"Swampscott may be in the throes of a losing grid season": Cahill, The Cracker Barrel, *Item*, October 21, 1965.

"Dickie Jauron was all over the field": Dick Jauron Shines For Baby Blues, *Item*, October 15, 1965.

1966—The Bandito Resurgence

"a good player": Rosenberg and Goldman, The Coach, a recorded interview of Stan Bondelevitch (part of an undated video documentary about Swampscott)

"We'll be hearing quite a bit from this boy": Beaton, Big Blue Grid Team Should Bounce Back This Fall, *Item*, September 13, 1966.

"surprisingly Swampscott": Swampscott Also Rates Among Teams To Watch, *Item*, September 21, 1966.

The *Item's* Red Hoffman predicted: Hoffman, Red-Hot Items, *Item*, October 28, 1966.

an estimated 11,000 fans: Jauron Runs Wild To Settle Battle Of Unbeatens, 13–12, *Item*, October 31, 1966.

"When his pass crossed the field": *Ibid.*

Headers Coach Noel Reebenacker described Newburyport as the best high school machine: Hoffman, Red-Hot Items, *Item*, November 9, 1966

"We just couldn't come up with anything": Hoffman, Red-Hot Items, *Item*, November 16, 1966

"The thing about the game is": Black, "On The Gridiron, Thanksgiving was his day," *Swampscott Reporter,* November 25, 1981

1967—Dickie, Speed, and the Harpooned Whale

"**football, food and fun**": Cahill, Football, Food, and Fun At Big Blue Grid Camp, *Item*, September 1, 1967.

"**speed and Dickie Jauron**": Ibid.

"**When you have a valuable commodity**": Appearance Of Jauron Big Boost For Jamboree, *Item*, September 4, 1968.

When Bondy and Marblehead's Reebenacker were asked by the *Item* for their assessments: Conference Elevens Open Saturday, *Item*, September 21, 1967.

"**Swampscott's star halfback, Dick Jauron, completely demoralized Woburn**": John Shapiro, Jauron Bags Four TD's In Swampscott Debacle, *Item*, October 2, 1967.

Mentioning that, aside from Adams, his squad should have the advantage: Bill Beaton, Rams Must Stop Jauron—Moriarty, *Item*, November 2, 1967.

"**When you think of post-World War II great ones**": Hoffman, Red Hot Items, *Item*, November 1, 1967.

"**Six of the boys in our starting lineup**": Beaton, Rams Must Stop Jauron – Moriarty, *Item*, November 2, 1967.

"**We didn't have any Dick Jauron to kick it for us**": Hoffman, Red-Hot Items, *Item*, November 8, 1967.

"**People sometimes overlook the fact**": Cahill, Classical Falls In 7–6 Thriller, *Item*, November 6, 1967.

"**Everybody has heard about the football star who could do everything**": Cahill, Big Blue Football Star Real All-Around Boy, *Item*, November 6, 1967.

"**the best schoolboy football team in the state**": Hoffman, 'Facing Best Schoolboy Team In The State' … Reebenacker, *Item*, November 3, 1967.

"**Ed is the finest running back I've had the privilege of coaching**": Beaton, Jauron, O'Bara Collide In Conference Struggle, *Item*, November 9, 1967.

"**Beat Newburyport!**": Hoffman, Red-Hot Items, *Item*, November 8, 1967.

Some 25 buses: Beaton, Jauron, O'Bara Collide In Conference Struggle, *Item*, November 9, 1967.

"**Dick stole it from the grasp**": Hoffman, Big Blue Nips Clippers In Cliff-Hanger, 28–27, *Item*, November 13, 1967.

"**I've always figured that if we lost**": Ibid.

1968—Juggernaut

"**experience, depth and speed**": Swampscott Eleven Highly Regarded This Fall, *Item*, September 20, 1968.

Bondy generated an early season sports page headline: Cahill, Swampscott To Elect Starting Eleven, *Item*, September 13, 1968.

"**Dick Jauron is terrific**": Hoffman, Red-Hot Items, *Item*, September 25, 1968.

As an example of the growing regional interest: Bondelevitch On Channel 56 With Big Blue Films, *Item*, October 4, 1968.

"a good club": Local Gridirons Busy This Week, *Item*, October 4, 1968.

The Item reported that Scholastic Roto, a national publication based in New York, had named the Big Blue the fifth best high school football team in the United States: Tab Swampscott 5th In National Rankings, *Item*, October 10, 1968.

According to the *Item*, Kester: Beaton, Swampscott Star Impresses New 'Grid Mothers' Group, *Item*, October 10, 1968.

"Teenage Athlete of the Month": Cahill, The Cracker Barrel, *Item*, October 16, 1968.

"In my 24 years of coaching I've never seen anything like him": Ibid.

"the Jauron era": Williams, As I See It, *Item*, December 2, 1968.

"Compliments don't go to his head. They go to his heart": Hoffman, Coach: Jauron Is Superman! , *Item*, November 27, 1972.

Ed Cahill devoted an entire column to the possibility: Cahill, Bondy Rumored For H.C. Berth, *Item*, December 13, 1968.

1969—Determined To Do Well

"Big Blue's 18-Game Streak In Danger This Fall": Beaton, *Item*, September 16, 1969.

"Tennant is the finest linebacker in the state": Ibid.

"We're going to lean on our sophomores": Ibid.

"Swampscott is still the Class B champion": Ibid.

telling the *Item* that, according to his reports, Salem was better then Swampscott: Muddy Gridirons Face Schoolboys, *Item*, October 3, 1969.

"I must say these kids have surprised me": Hoffman, Blue Makes Bulldogs No. 20 On Hit Parade, *Item*, October 6, 1969.

Despite the Big Blue's 20 consecutive victories: Blue-Falcon Struggle Tops Schoolboy Card, *Item*, October 9, 1969.

"Tennant Dies!": Hoffman, Red Hot Items, *Item*, October 10, 1969.

Bondy explained that the coaching staff had pulled the old 38 Hurricane out of moth balls: Hoffman, Hurricane Blows Danvers Aside As Big Blue Train Rolls On, *Item*, October 14, 1969.

"We have no excuses": Ibid.

According to Marblehead coach Reebenacker: Grid Coaches Comment On Past, Future, *Item*, October 22, 1969.

According to their coach Doug Wood: Blue Frightened, But Storms To 'Easy' Win, *Item*, October 27, 1969.

"Amesbury was a town with a dream": Ibid.

"We were in man-to-man": Ibid.

"*TO WHOM IT MAY CONCERN:*": Cahill, The Cracker Barrel, *Item*, October 23, 1969.

Yet, according to the *Item*, North Shore football experts: <u>Big Blue-Sachem Showdown Tops Weekend School Card</u>, *Item*, October 28, 1969.

"And I mean just that": Hoffman, <u>Coaches Foresee Scoring Binge For Dream Game On Saturday</u>, *Item*, October 30, 1969.

"Coach, if you lose this game": Hoffman, <u>Red Hot Items</u>, *Item*, October 29, 1969.

According to Bondy, Osgood: Hoffman, <u>Coaches Foresee Scoring Binge For Dream Game On Saturday</u>, *Item*, October 30, 1969.

"I must say we were simply out-played": Hoffman, <u>Big Blue 'Wagon' Rolls Past Indians' Ambush</u>, *Item*, November 3, 1969.

"The most important thing about any football program": Williams, <u>As I See It</u>, *Item*, November 4, 1969.

"The 200-pound senior tackle": Hoffman, <u>Blue Preps For Headers</u>, *Item*, November 17, 1969.

"The line did it": Ibid.

"quite a team": <u>Grid Coaches Comment On Past, Future</u>, *Item*, October 22, 1969.

"One of the finest backs I've ever seen": Ibid.

"absolutely fantastic": Hoffman, <u>61st Go-Round At Marblehead,</u> *Item*, November 26, 1969.

"They can do the job": Ibid.

The Headers were 26-point underdogs: Hoffman, <u>Lynch's Field-Goal Tips Scales, 15–14</u>, *Item*, November 28, 1969.

"It is doubtful whether any winning or losing team": Ibid.

1970—Homegrown Heartbreaker

he would be relying on a *"Kosher Defense"*: Beaton, <u>Big Blue Eleven Will Field 'Kosher' Defense This Fall</u>, *Item*, September 2, 1970.

"I think the Jamboree is the greatest thing": <u>Big Blue Injury Fails To Dampen Enthusiasm</u>, *Item*, September 24, 1969.

"When we go into the Jamboree": Beaton, <u>Coaches Disagree Over Jamboree</u>, *Item*, September 23, 1970.

Swampscott football players were "taught to respect their parents": Cahill, <u>The Cracker Barrel</u>, *Item*, September 24, 1970.

"Sometimes I think some people": Ibid.

"It's not fair": <u>Many Big Games On Saturday Card</u>, *Item*, October 2, 1970.

"'We Think We'll Win': Bondelevitch": *Item*, October 10, 1970.

"awesome offense": Hoffman, <u>Flying Danvers Falcons Brought Down Hard, 35–22</u>, *Item*, October 13, 1970.

"Kool Kat Defense": Ibid.

"They beat us right up front": Hoffman, <u>St. John's Savoring Upset Victory Over Swampscott</u>, *Item*, November 2, 1970.

Red Hoffman expressed great respect for Swampscott's fans: Hoffman, Red-Hot Items, *Item*, November 4, 1970.

"absolutely incredible win streak": Dave Shribman, "Big Blue Week" Given Priority In Swampscott, *Salem Evening News*, November 5, 1970.

1971—I Wonder Who Will Beat This Team

Ray ran wild in that game: Ray-Ray Runs Rampant; Little Blue Wins Title, *Item*, November 17, 1970.

"an experienced team with good size": Beaton, Swampscott, Winthrop Tops In Conference, *Item*, September 21, 1971.

"a real battle": Big Blue Rolls over Gloucester, *Item*, September 27, 1971.

"Swampscott always rises to the occasion": Careening Blue Eases Past Vikings, *Item*, October 18, 1971.

"rejuvenated" and "powerful": Williams, As I See It, *Item*, October 18, 1971.

"put it all together": Ibid.

"fastest, biggest and best": Passing Key For Bulldogs vs. Blue, *Item*, October 19, 1971.

"They out-hit us from the beginning": Hoffman, Blue, Tech, Magicians Win; Saugus, Lynnfield Beaten, *Item*, October 26, 1971.

"I wonder who will beat this team": Ibid.

"We're determined": Big Blue Favored, *Item*, November 23, 1971.

The story of the game according to Bondy: Hoffman, Swampscott Unbeaten Again, 20–0! *Item*, November 29, 1971.

1972—Super Champs

"But you don't win football games with size": Line-Shifts Key To Blue's Hopes, *Item*, September 7, 1972.

"definitely awesome": Hoffman, Big Blue Trails, Rolls Over Danvers, *Item*, October 10, 1972.

"described by opposing coaches as certainly better": Ibid.

"with enough authority": Hoffman, Bulldog Vs. Blue … The Run Vs. The Pass … It All Happens Friday Night, *Item*, October 17, 1972.

such a result would be "ridiculous": Cahill, Un-Un Blue Could Miss 'Super Bowl', *Item*, November 9, 1972.

"the best I've ever had": Hoffman, Blue Wins 29–0, Super-Bowl Bound, *Item*, November 24, 1972.

"the finest two-way player in the state": Hoffman, 'Super' Rival To Present Powerful Problem To Blue, *Item*, November 28, 1972.

"accurate both long and short": Ibid.

"It certainly was one of the best practices": Hoffman, Blue Tries BU Astro-Turf, *Item*, November 30, 1972.

"flawless": Hoffman, <u>This Was A Game They Had To Win</u>, *Item*, December 4, 1972.

"The two coaches, in tandem harness": Hoffman, <u>Rumor: Bondelevitch Retiring As Coach, Lynch Leaving Swampscott</u>, *Item*, December 5, 1972.

1973—End of the Reign

"I really don't know who'd apply": <u>Bondelevitch will coach Swampscott football</u>, *Swampscott Reporter*, February 8, 1973.

"The size, the depth": Beaton, <u>Soph-Studded Big Blue In Trouble?</u> *Item*, September 5, 1973.

"Just a matter of organization": Kevin Mannix, <u>Swampscott, Bondelevitch Reach Heights</u>, *Sunday Herald Advertiser*, November 18, 1973.

"super organization, the attitude of the boys": Ted St. Pierre, <u>Big Blue clobbers Falcons</u>, *Danvers Herald*, October 10, 1973.

"Football in Swampscott is more than just a way of life": Ibid.

"ability to instill in the boys": Ibid.

"We felt we had to get to Jauron": Hoffman, <u>Blue-Viking Game Peek At Future?</u>, *Item*, October 15, 1973.

Speaking with the Item, Carr emphasized: Beaton, <u>Our Biggest Game Ever" Says Tech Coach</u>, *Item*, October 18, 1973.

Over the years, attendance at Manning Bowl had fallen: Williams, *Item*, October 23, 1971.

"Their pass protection": Hoffman, <u>Reign Ended By Magicians, 20–12</u>, *Item*, November 23, 1973.

"The greatest coaching era": Hoffman, <u>Bondelevitch retires after 23 seasons</u>, *Item*, May 14, 1976.

"Nobody gives even a bat of an eyelash": Jeff Yoffa, <u>Thoughts are high that Big Blue will leave Northeastern conference</u>, *Swampscott Reporter*, November 8, 1973.

"I'd have to win 11 games": Hoffman, <u>Bondelevitch retires after 23 seasons</u>, *Item*, May 14, 1976.

"I was of the opinion": Rich Fahey, <u>Bondelevitch retires—Problems with school board are indicated</u>, *Item*, February 5, 1987.

"'DIGNITY', he fairly shouted": Ibid.

Epilogue

"He motivates people": <u>Swampscott pays tribute to Coach Bondelevitch</u>, *Swampscott Reporter*, July 29, 1976.

"He made the best pregame speeches": Mike Grenier, <u>The 11 Greatest Football Coaches in North Shore History</u>, *The Salem News*, September 3, 2010.

"I had so much fun playing for him": Ibid.

"Bondy took young men": <u>Swampscott pays tribute to Coach Bondelevitch</u>, *Swampscott Reporter,* July 29, 1976.

"Once you've played football": Potter, <u>Bondelevitch returns to scene of former glory</u>, *Swampscott Reporter,* August 26, 1982.

"Stan, you make people feel": <u>Swampscott pays tribute to Coach Bondelevitch</u>, *Swampscott Reporter*, July 29, 1976.

"almost a Utopia": David Cataneo, <u>Swampscott Memories</u>, *Boston Herald American*, October 31, 1980.

"I started my first Monday night football game": Ibid.

his "time had come": Lynn Sears, <u>School board was divided; coach says it was not a factor</u>, *Swampscott Reporter*, February 12, 1987.

But strong support for Bondy remained: Ibid.

"I feel I have to do something": Paul Halloran, <u>Swampscott bitter over Bondy</u>, *Item*, February 7, 1987.

"The ending should have been storybook": Rich Fahey, <u>Bondelevitch retires</u>, *Item*, February 5, 1987.

With Bondy's return in 1982, 80 students signed up to play: Potter, <u>Bondelevitch returns to scene of former glory</u>, *Swampscott Reporter*, August 26, 1982.

"It's hard to believe that I could have a lot in common": *Elementary Matters* (Sally DeCost Blog) "Speaking of Heroes," September 10, 2011.

"What Does a Non-Athletic Girl Learn From a Football Coach?": *Elementary Matters* (Sally DeCost Blog), March 29, 2015.

"I feel I have to do something out of respect for the guy": Paul Halloran, <u>Swampscott bitter over Bondy</u>, *Item*, February 7, 1987.

"the Big Blue family": Will Broaddus, <u>Gov. Baker addresses Swampscott graduation</u>, *Salem News*, June 8, 2015.

Index

Page numbers in italics indicate photographs.

A

Abbott Park, 9, 90–91, 115, 239

Abernathy, Walter, 169

Abram, Phil
  academic achievement of, 238
  football team (1967), 214, 219–220, 222, 226, 230, 232–233, *273, 357*
  football team (1968), 235, 237–238, 252, *358*

Adams, Lola, 185

Adams, William "Billy"
  All-Stars (1967), 233, 362
  anger and, 204, 211–213, 219, 226
  athletic ability of, 186
  basketball and, 234
  "battlefield promotion" of, 184–185
  coaching career, 338
  early years of, 185–186
  football team (1965), 184–185
  football team (1966), 189–190, 195, 198, 204–207
  football team (1967), 211–213, 216, 219–222, 224–227, 233–234, *273, 357*
  Frank DeFelice and, 189–190, 198, 292
  at Holy Cross, 234, 253
  injustice and, 213
  Lloyd Benson and, 213
  on pregame speeches, 337
  professional career of, 234, 338
  Tom Toner and, 237
  white socks speech and, 264

Adamson, Steve "Tank," 166

Adelson, Mark, 257, *358–359*

Agganis, Aristotle George "Harry," 40–41, 185, 224, 236, 252

Agganis Memorial All-Star games, 73, 77, 86, 210

Alice Shaw Junior High School, 119, 131, 186

All-Stars history (1953–1973), 362

Amesbury High School
  games v. SHS: 1953, 18–23; 1954, 34; 1955, 43; 1956, 56; 1957, 66; 1958, 82; 1959, 97; 1960, 116; 1961, 125–126; 1962, 138; 1963, 154; 1964, 166–167; 1965, 182; 1966, 200; 1967, 222; 1968, 247; 1969, 260–261

Andersen, Bob, 323, 351

Andersen, Dean, 165, *356*

Anderson, Ricky, 213, 216, 219–220, *357*

Andover High School
  games v. SHS: 1958, 80; 1959, 94; 1960, 111; 1961, 121; 1962, 134–35; 1963, 152; 1964, 165

Andrews, Bob, 60, 79–80, *106, 354–355*

Anselmian Athletic Club Hall of Fame, 344

Arnold, Bob, 99, 110, 350, *355*

B

Bagnell, Dana, *355*

Baker, Charlie, 352

Baker, Gil, *359*

Baker, Richard, 342

Baldacci, Dick, 125, 176

Baldacci, Roger, 341

Bandalewicz, Mary Kasparowicz, 2–3, 346

Bandalewicz, Stanley Walter. *See* Bondelevitch, Stanley W.

Bandalewicz, Walter, 2–3, 346

"Banditos" defensive unit, 200, 203, *272*

Bane, Ken, 325–326, *361*

Barbanel, Al, 304, 318–319, *360–361*

Barrett, Timmy, *360*

Bartlett, Paul, *357*

Bartolik, Peter, *359*

Bartram, David, 41, 48–49

Bartram, Paul, *355*

Bass, Stuart, 101, *355*

Bates, Brian, 170, 175, 193–194, 200, 350

Beaton, Bill, 192, 256, 322

Beatrice, Greg
   All-Stars (1972), 362
   football team (1970), 277, 289
   football team (1971), 294, *360*
   football team (1972), *274*, 304–305, 310, 313, *361*

Beatrice, Kyle, 343

Beatrice, Peter
   All-Stars (1969), 362
   football team (1967), *357*
   football team (1968), 235, 247, 251, *358*
   football team (1969), 256, 259, 261, 267–268, 275–276, *359*

Beatrice, Tommy, 325–329, 331

Bedard, John, *360*

Benedetto, Elmo, 6–7, 27, 41, 111, 236

Benevento, Tony, 175, 350

Benson, Lloyd
   academic achievement of, 238
   Billy Adams and, 213
   Coach Bondelevitch and, 241–245, 346
   college and career of, 253
   football team (1967), 213–214, *357*
   football team (1968), 235, 238, 241–246, 250–252, *358*

   Frank DeFelice and, 243–246, 250–251, 253

Berkeley, Philip "Bimbo," 175–176, 194–195, 350

Bertram Field, 157

Bessette, Ernie "Butch," 134, 138

Bessom, Ricky, 325–326

Bessom, Robert, 63, 121–122, 302

Beverly High School, 67, 82, 85–86, 182, 297, 332
   games v. SHS: 1960 (scrimmage), 110; 1961 (scrimmage), 120; 1964 (Jamboree), 165

Big Blue Bulletin, 93

Big Blue football
   name change to, 28–29, *104*
   teams in, 40
   . *See also* Swampscott High School football; Swampscott Sculpins

Big Blue Notes, 93, 301–303

Big Blue Week, 289

"Big Stud." *See* Bates, Brian

Bishop Bradley High School
   game v. SHS: 1967 (scrimmage), 214

Bishop Fenwick High School, 341

Blais, George
   All-Stars (1958), 362
   college and career of, 87
   football team (1956), 48–49, 54
   football team (1957), 61, 65–66, 68–70, 73, *354*
   football team (1958), 78–84, 86–87, *106–107*, *355*
   impact of, 115, 223

Blocksidge, John Enos, 9

Blocksidge Field, 1–2, 9, 50, *108*

Blood, Bobby, 183, 205, 207, 232–233

Blood, Tony
   football team (1964), 165–171
   football team (1965), 175–176, 180
   football team (1966), 187, 193, 206, *272*

Blue Devils. *See* Winthrop High School

Bogardus, Fred, 350

Bogardus, Mark, 213, 216, 220, 350, *357*

Bokozanska, D., *356*

Bondelevitch, David, 150, 345–346

Bondelevitch, Dorothy "Dot" Tierney, 5–6, 10, 15, 150, 331

Bondelevitch, Mary Patricia "Pat" Donovan, 345

Bondelevitch, Nancy, 345

Bondelevitch, Sally DeCost, 345–347.

Bondelevitch, Stanley W., *104, 106–107, 270–273, 334, 336, 354–355, 359*

    on American liberty, 349–350

    as athletic director, 15, 57, 111, 130, 162, 242, 333

    "battlefield promotions," 185

    Big Blue name change, 28–29

    Big Blue Notes and, 301–303

    biography: at Boston University, 6; children, 10, 150, 345–346; death of, 346, 351; Dot and, 5–6, 10, 15, 150, 331; early years of, 3; marriage to Dot Tierney, 6; marriage to Mary Patricia Donovan, 345; military service, 4–5; move to Swampscott, 10; parents of, 2–3, 346; Providence Steamrollers and, 4; retirement (1976), 331–333; retirement (1987), 342; retirement life of, 345; at St. Anselm College, 3–4; as Swampscott summer parks director, 38–39; teaching position, 5

    Camp Columbus and, 16, 27

    Camp Fun and, 38–39, 114, 137

    on character, 302–303

    coaching assistants and, 176–177, 188–191, 196–197, 211, 234, 247–248, 322

    coaching career: 100th high school victory, 126–127; 100th Swampscott victory, 249–250; as 1968 coach of the year, 252; as 1969 coach of the year, 268; Bishop Fenwick High School, 341; conference titles, 252,

268, 290–291, 300, 312; Division II championship, 319; Greater Lynn/Swampscott All-Stars, 86; Hall of Fame inductions, 344; Hudson High School, 6, 10, 18, 23; lessons of, 347–350; Maynard High School, 5–6, 254; North Shore All-Star team, 73, 77; resignation from Swampscott (1976), 331–333; resignation from Swampscott (1987), 342; return to Swampscott (1982), 341–342; SHS Hall of Fame and, 344; Swampscott High School (1953) position, 10; testimonial dinner for, 254. *See also* Swampscott High School football (1953–1973, 1982–1987)

    coaching record of, xiii, xiv, 18, 25, 160–161, 183, 233, 303, 331

    coaching relationships: development of, 338; Dick Lynch and, 27–28, 43, 83–84, 92, 162–163, 184, 188, 200, 214, 317, 321; Dick Stevenson and, 31; Flora McLearn and, 162–163; Fran York and, 293; Frank DeFelice and, 191, 196–198, 200, 244–245, 247–248, 292

    coaching style of, 12–16, 19–20, 22, 42–43, 53–56, 66, 83–84, 93, 111, 118, 151, 166–167, 190, 195, 197–198, 204, 278–279, 330–331

    college coaches and, 41, 250, 301, 347

    criticism of, 332–333, 342

    death of David Coughlin and, 131, 196, 333, 337

    disciplinary style of, 101–102, 212, 215

    ego of, 333

    enthusiasm of, 11–12, 16–17, 25

    game field and, 155

    grass drills and, 198

    "Great Neck Spread" formation, 194

    Gridiron Girls and, 238, 247–248

    helmet sticker incentives, 143, 154

    on hockey, 205

    humor and, 12, 177–179, 197, 205–206, 220–221, 225, 277, 281 hurricane offense formation, 19–20, 259, 314–315

hydration and, 196

impact of, 5, 15, 25, 337–342, 346–350, 352

importance of schooling to, 93–94, 174

locker room talks, 20–21, 53, 65–67, 71–72, 85, 89, 221, 337, 345

math team and, 324

media commentary: on community support, 331–333; on death of David Coughlin, 123, 131, 333, 337; on Dick Jauron, 241; on Joyce Jamboree, 277; on Sandy Tennant, 256

media coverage of, 17, 52–53, 62, 71, 89, 112, 121, 126–127, 142–144, 157, 236–238, 249–250, 262–264, 279–281, 295, 332–333

motivational skills of, 20–22, 25, 66–68, 71–72, 78, 82, 85, 89, 95, 97, 99, 101–102, 111, 114, 143, 153–154, 181, 196, 205–206, 249, 254, 258, 281, 323–326, 330, 337–340, 345

offensive philosophy of, 14–15, 83–84, 151–152

parent relations and, 92, 153, 238, 302–303

Parents Clinics, 29–31, 40–41, 63, 110

player nicknames by, 194, 277

player relationships: Andy Rose and, 218; Arthur Palleschi and, 100–101, 164; Barry Gallup and, 150, 160; Bill Sjogren and, 132; Bobby Carlin and, 41, 46–47; Carl Kester and, 238, 240–241; confidence-building, 337–338, 347–348; development of, 15, 326; Doug Haley and, 50–51; expectations of conduct and, 101; Frank Challant and, 137, 148–149; Italian-American players, 277, 294; Jaurons and, 174, 195; Jewish players, 136, 152, 199, 225, 251, 277, 294; Jimmy Lyons and, 91–92, 96; Lloyd Benson and, 241–245; Mark

Stevenson and, 195; Marvin Cohen and, 300–301; Mike Powers and, 91–92, 96, 98; praise for, 238, 301–302; Randy Werner and, 281–282, 284, 286; Ray DiPietro and, 306; recognition of, 288–289, 306, 312; Richard Fuller and, 114–115; Ronny Corcoran and, 97, 114; support of, 347; Walter Costello and, 132–133, 160

on postseason Miami trip, 74–75

on post-touchdown conversion points, 77

praise for school and community support, 16, 93, 181, 250, 264, 301–303, 324

promotional efforts of, 31, 52–53, 62–64, 93, 111–112, 134, 236, 238, 250, 262, 301–303, 326

recruitment efforts of, 29–30, 132–133, 164, 223, 242

reserve players and, 56, 164

respect for parents by, 93, 100–101, 264, 278

St. Anselm College training camp and, 211–213, 217

temper and, 176–177

on Thanksgiving Day games, 71, 85, 99, 124–125, 129, 209, 299, 330

theatrics of, 56, 66, 177–178, 184–185

tower, 187, *274*

tribute to, 350

white socks speech, 264

wind sprints and, 197

wing-T offense, 14, 62, 151, 195, 279

winning tradition of, 343, 348

youth sports programs and, 57, 59, 78, 114, 119, 323

Bondelevitch Way, 1, 341, 346

Bondy, Coach. *See* Bondelevitch, Stanley W.

Booma, Rollie, 250

Boosters Club

Coach Bondelevitch and, 25, 63

David Coughlin Memorial Trophy, 123

fundraising and, 31, 63

Pop Warner teams and, 78

postseason awards of, 73, 150

support of, 23, 32, 52, 64, 94–95, 250, 343

transportation and, 17

whirlpool tub and, 31

Boosters Club dances, 182, 195

Borek, Billy, *360*

Boston Steamrollers, 188

Boyce, Ralph, 325–327, *361*

Boyce, Tommy, 166, 169, 175, 177, 180–183

Brady, Richard, *358*

Brand, Bob, 214, 235, 237, 245, 252, *357–358*

    All-Stars (1967), 362

Brand, Greg

    All-Stars (1969), 362

    football team (1967), *357*

    football team (1968), 245–246, *358*

    football team (1969), 256, 259, 263, 265, 269, *359*

Brennan, Walter, 99–100

Brigham, Charles, *357*

Brine Sporting Goods, 30

Brody, Richard, *359*

Brown, Paul, 53

Brown, Peter, 171, 205

Brown, Steven, *355*

Browning, Bob, 66, 79–81, 87, *354–355*

    All-Stars (1958), 362

Browning, Randy, 81, *355*

Bruley, Roger, *357*

Buckley, Brian, 329–330

Buckley, Ed, 77

Bufalino, Billy, 92, 98, 101

Bufalino, Tom, 125, 131–132, 134–135

Bulldogs. *See* Lynn English High School

Burk, Fred, 35, 42, 49

Bush, Bill, 322–323, 343

Bush, Lou, 322

Buswell, Steve, 134, 151, *356*

C

Cahill, Ed

    on Boosters Club, 63–64

    on Coach Bondelevitch, 23, 253, 278

    on death of David Coughlin, 123

    on Dick Jauron, 227

    on drill team performance, 157

    on game officials, 118

    on mouth guards, 135

    on Parents Clinics, 29, 111

    on player behavior, 75

    promotion of Swampscott team, 52

    on Swampscott media coverage, 261–262

    on Swampscott v. Amesbury, 18, 125

    on Swampscott v. Lynn Classical, 142–143

    on walkie-talkie experiment, 53–54

Cahoon, Don "Toot," 205, 207–208

Cahoon, Frank "Truck"

    football team (1957), 61, 66, *354*

    football team (1958), 78–81, 84, *106*, *355*

Callahan, David, *358*

Cambridge Latin School

    games v. SHS: 1956, 53; 1957, 65

Camp Columbus, 16, 27

Camp Fun, 38–39, 97, 114, 137

Cape Ann League, 311

Cap'n Jack's , 8, 351

Caras, David

    football team (1967), 219–220, 222–223, 231, 233, *357*

    football team (1968), 235, 237, *358*

    football team (1969), 256–261, 263, 266–269, *359*

Carden, John, 214, 229, 231, *273, 357*

Cardillo, Charlie
football team (1969), 256, 258, 261, 268, *359*
football team (1970), 275, 277, 280–281
football team (1971), 293, 295–296, 299, 306, *360*

Cardillo, Joseph "Jo-Jo," 281

Carey, Ed, 71

Carlin, Bill, 10

Carlin, Robert "Bobby"
All-Stars (1955), 362
athletic ability of, 10–11
as Camp Fun counselor, 114
as coach, 282
Coach Bondelevitch and, 11–12, 46
Coach Bondelevitch testimonial and, 254
college and career of, 47
Dick Lynch and, 43
football team (1953), 20, 22, 24
football team (1954), 32, 34, 36
football team (1955), 41–44, 46, 69, *105*
impact of, 97
scoring titles of, 87
Thom McAn Shoe Trophy (1955), 46

Carlin, Virginia Friberg, 11

Carlyn, Bud, 41

Carlyn, Charles "Billy," 350
All-Stars (1957), 362
athletic ability of, 48, 77
college and career of, 73
county scoring title, 73, 87
football team (1955), 41, 44, *105*
football team (1956), 48–49, 51, 54
football team (1957), 59, 61, 65–66, 68–70, 73, *106, 354*
"good cop-bad cop" act, 65–66
impact of, 115, 193

Indiana University and, 78, 87
Northeastern Oklahoma A&M College and, 87
personality of, 48, 237

Caron, Dennis, *355*

Carone, Jim
All-Stars (1970), 362
football team (1968), 235, 238, *358*
football team (1969), 256–257, *359*
football team (1970), 275–277, 279–280, 289–290, *334*

Carpenzano, Ken, 294, *360*

Carr, Mike, 327–328

Carriagemakers. *See* Amesbury High School

Carroll, Roger, *358*

Cashman, Bill, 203

Cassidy, Peter "Hopalong" (father), 12, 17, 19, 24–25, 320, 350

Cassidy, Peter (son)
football team (1971), 294–295, 299, *360*
football team (1972), 304, 307, 309–310, 314–317, 320, *361*

Cassidy, Reid, 323, *361*

Castiglione, Joe, 33, 42, 51, 53

Cataneo, David, 338

Catholic League, 313

Catholic Memorial High School
game v. SHS: 1972 (Division II Super Bowl), 312–320

Cawley, John, *359*

Cerone, Alfie, 78, 90

Chaisson, George, 203

Challant, Frank, 134, 136–137, 148–149

Challant, Nate, 137

cheerleaders, 16, 67, 71, 73, 80, 93, 99, 141, 153, 181, 206, *271*

Chesnulevich, Pete, 139

Chiary, Fran, 115, 323, 351

Ciarlante, Nick, 169

Clayman, John, *357–359*

Clippers. *See* Newburyport High School

Clippinger, Arthur, 165, 175, *356*

Clippinger, Ed, 214, *273, 357*

Coe, Richard "Dick," 350
    football team (1957), 61, 65–66, *354*
    football team (1958), 79–81, 84–87, *355*

Coe, Roger, 20, 22, 32–35, 37–38, 65, 84–85, 97

Cohen, Ed, 61, 65, *354*

Cohen, Marvin, 300–301, *360*

Cohen, Peter
    football team (1962), 134, 136, 138, 144–145, 147
    football team (1963), 151–156, 159–160, *356*
    football team (1964), 165–167, 169–171
    SHS Hall of Fame and, 172
    Tufts University and, 171

Coletti, Frank, 71, 248, 333

Collier, Jeff, 195, 202, 205–206, 209

Collins, Mike, 165, 175

Collins, Tom, 250

Conigliaro, Billy
    All-Stars (1964), 362
    baseball career of, 172
    football team (1962), 134–135, 137–138, 145
    football team (1963), 151–153, 155–156, 159, *356*
    football team (1964), 165, 167–168, 170–172
    SHS Hall of Fame and, 172

Conigliaro, Richie
    football team (1967), 219
    football team (1969), 256–257, 259–260, 263, 267–269, *359*

Conigliaro, Tony, 120–121

Conn, Ronnie, 45–46, 51, 70

Connors, Dick, 174, 323

Coolidge, Calvin, 8

Corben, Steve, *360*

Corbett, Dave, 99, 110–111, *355*

Corcoran, B., *356*

Corcoran, David, 170, 175

Corcoran, Peter, *355*

Corcoran, Ronny
    All-Stars (1961), 362
    as backfield coach, 322
    as Big Blue waterboy, 97, 114, 275
    as coaching assistant, *273, 334*
    coaching career, 338
    early years of, 97
    football team (1959), 96–98
    football team (1960), 110–114, 116–117
    football team (1961), 119, 124–126, 128–129, 131, 133, *270*
    as JV coach, 211, 292

Corcoran, Tom, 342–343

Cordette, Gary "Stumpy," 194

Costello, Walter, Jr.
    as Big Blue waterboy, 132
    Coach Bondelevitch and, 132–133
    coaching and, 179
    college and career of, 161
    Denver Broncos linemen and, 134, *270*
    football team (1962), 133–134, 136–138, 143, 145
    football team (1963), 151–153, 155–156, 159–160, *271, 356*
    Taft School and, 160
    track and, 133

Cotton, Terry, 61

Coughlin, Dana
    football team (1960), 110–112, 115–117
    football team (1961), 119, 123, 125, 128, *270*
    football team (1962), 131, 133

Coughlin, David "Red"

Coach Bondelevitch and death of, 131, 196, 333, 337
  death of, 121–125
  Dick Lynch and death of, 121–122
  Dick Stevenson and death of, 131
  football team (1958), 85
  football team (1959), 97
  football team (1960), 110, 116
  football team (1961), 119–121, *270*
  memorializing, 123, 125, 150
  Philip A. Jenkin on, 129–130
Coughlin, Jay, 263, *357–358*
Coughlin, Oliver, 123, 125, 130
Coughlin, Richard, 123
Cousin, Brian, *360*
Cousy, Bob, 26, 161
Cozza, Carmen, 252
Cronin, Kevin, 202–203
Cropley, Bob, *357–358*
Crowley, Clark, 308
Cudmore, Phil, 61, 82, *354–355*
Cullen, Paige, 151, 165, *356*
Curry, Jack, 290
Curtis, Mike, *361*

D

Dalton, Ernie, 111
Dancewicz, John, 200
Danvers High School
  games v. SHS: 1953, 23; 1954, 34; 1955, 42; 1956, 53; 1957, 65; 1958, 81; 1959, 95; 1960, 113; 1961, 124–125; 1962, 136; 1963, 152–153; 1964, 166; 1965, 180–181; 1966, 199–200;1967, 220; 1968, 241, 244–245; 1969, 258–259; 1970, 280–281; 1971, 295–296; 1972, 306–307; 1973, 326
David Coughlin Memorial Trophy, 123
Davie, Jim, 296
DeCost, Sally. *See* Bondelevitch, Sally DeCost

Dedrick, Billy, 311, 315, 320, 325–326, 329, 340, *361*
  All-Stars (1973), 362
Dedrick, Richard, *274*, 294, 298–299, 301, 304, 318, 340, *360–361*
DeFelice, Bobby, 188, 198, 281, 295, 297, 327
DeFelice, Frank, *273*, *334*, *359*
  Andy Rose and, 219, 251–252
  as baseball coach, 209, 340
  as basketball coach, 190, 283
  Billy Adams and, 189–190, 198, 292
  Boston College and, 188
  Coach Bondelevitch and, 191, 196–198, 200, 244–245, 247–248, 292
  as football coach, 191, 195–200, 208, 214–215, 218–219, 237, 240, 242–244, 250–252, 259, 265, 276, 282, 340
  Lloyd Benson and, 242–246, 250–251, 253
  military service and, 188
  Randy Werner and, 281–286, 290
  SHS Hall of Fame and, 340
  as Swampscott gym teacher, 188–190
  as Swampscott head coach (1976–1981), 340
  Winthrop football team and, 55
  as Xaverian Brothers High School coach, 292, 314, 340
DeFelice, Lou, 350
  football team (1967), *357*
  football team (1968), *358*
  football team (1969), 256–257, 259–260, 267–269, *359*
DeFelice, Susan Mahegan, 246
DeMarco, Mike, 296, 307
Dembowski, Steve, 343
Dempsey, Dave, 227
DePaolo, George, 325
DePaolo, Mickey, 165, 167
DeRobertis, Norm, 132, 151, *356*

Dexter, James, *355*

DiGregorio, Mark, 296, 307

DiGregorio, Pat, 296

DiLisio, Don, 325–326, 329

DiLisio, John, 110–112, 117, *355*

DiPietro, Dennis, 165, *356*

DiPietro, Ray
  All-Stars (1972), 362
  football team (1970), 289
  football team (1971), 293–294,
    296–297, 299, *360*
  football team (1972), 304–307, 309,
    311–313, 317–320, *335*, *361*

DiPietro, Steve "Link," 175, 180, 182,
  293

DiPrisco, Mike
  All-Stars (1970), 362
  football team (1968), *358*
  football team (1969), 257, 263, 269,
    359
  football team (1970), 276, 280, 288
  Randy Werner and, 282, 284
  Sandy Tennant and, 215

Dobie, "Gloomy Gil," 139

Donahue, Mike, *359*

Donelan, Kevin, 324, 329, *361*

drill team, 16, 73, 80, 93, 99, *105*, 141,
  153, 157, 181

Driscoll, Bill, 30

Dunn, James, 27–28

Duratti, Al, 78, *358*

Duratti, Fred, *357*

Dushan, Steven, 256–259, 267–268,
  357–359

E

Eagles. *See* Saint John's Preparatory School

Earle, Gary, 165, 175

Easterbrooks, Charles, *355*

Easterbrooks, Vinny, 31, 66, 98, 164, 227

Eastern Massachusetts Super Bowl games,
  312–320, 343

Eickelberger, Tom, 53

Eldridge, Ken, 148

Engstrom, John, *355*

F

Fahey, Rich, 342

Faino, Matt, 60–61, 73, *354*

Falcons. *See* Danvers High School

Farland, Jackie, 306

Farren, Mike, 32, 34, 36

Farrer, Mike, 175

Farrer, Steve, 175

Faulkner, David, 324, 326, 329, *361*
  All-Stars (1973), 362

Faulkner, Mr., 275

Feldmen, Jimmy, *360*

female athletes, 90–91, 228, 344

field hockey team, 57, 64, 73–74, 90, 124,
  157, 228, 344

Fishermen. *See* Gloucester High School

Fitzgerald, Terry, 304, 316, 319, 350,
  360–361

Flanagan, John
  All-Stars (1958), 362
  Barbara Segel and, 90
  foot disability and, 57, 79, 148
  football team (1956), 57
  football team (1957), 60, *354*
  football team (1958), 79–80, 84,
    86–87, 101, *355*

Flint, Chuck, 258

Floradora Girls, 228, 344

Floria, Ralph, 214, 235, *357–358*

Foley, Ed, 112, 121

football
  4-3 defense, 190
  formations for, 151
  Happy Jack Pass, 208
  Hi-Fi offense, 111
  hook and lateral play, 169

hurricane offense formation, 19,
    314–315
lessons of, 347–349
mouth guards in, 135, 218
placekicking in, 196
post-touchdown conversion scoring, 77
pro-T formation, 151
tackle-fumble, 50, 114
wing-T offense formation, 14, 62, 151,
    195, 279
. *See also* Swampscott High School
    football
Forbes, George, 109, 115, 117, 120, 125,
    131
Foster, Harold "Hal," 351
    as coaching assistant, 13, 25, *104*
    death of son, 33–34, 37
    football team (1957), *354*
    Saint Mary's High School coaching,
        79, 120
    team game ball for, 34
Francis, Ralph, 42, 49
Frary, Dave, 49, 60, 68, 73, *354*
    All-Stars (1957), 362
Fravel, Russ, 258–259, 264, 307
Frederickson, Erik, *358*
Friberg, Bernie, 10–11
Friberg, Robert, 10
Frizzell, Bob, 165, 170, *356*
Fromer, Richard, 280, 287, 294–298, *360*
Fuller, Richard "Bronco"
    All-Stars (1961), 362
    as Big Blue waterboy, 114
    Coach Bondelevitch and, 114–115,
        338
    Coach Chiary and, 115
    college and career of, 129
    early years of, 114–115
    football team (1959), 97
    football team (1960), 109, 113–116,
        118

football team (1961), 120–122,
    124–125, 129, *270*
impact of, 275
Jimmy Lyons and, 115
Mike Powers and, 115

G

Gallo, Louis, 324
Gallup, Barry
    All-Stars (1963), 362
    athletic ability of, 120, 149, 160
    at Boston College, 161, 174, 211
    at Northeastern University, 161, 344
    career of, 161
    Coach Bondelevitch testimonial and,
        254
    football coaching of, 161, 344–345
    football team (1961), 120–121, 125
    football team (1962), 131–132,
        135–138, 145, 147, 149
    football team (1963), 150–156, 160,
        271, 356
    postseason honors of, 160
    SHS Hall of Fame and, 161
    strength and conditioning program of,
        211, 214, 217, 235, 283
    team captain selection and, 150
    year at Deerfield, 161
Gallup, Earl, 120, 150, 161
Gamble, Willard, 18–20, 22
Gapinski, Phil, 151, 153, 165–167, *356*
Gardner, Alan "Rugs," 175, 194–195,
    272, 350
Garfield, Jerry, *355*
Gassman, Jeff, *359*
Giant, Danny, *360*
Giarla, Dave, 142–143, 145
Gibbs, Henry, 250
Gibbs, Paul, 250
Gibbs, Randy, 256–257, *358–359*
Gibbs, Richard, *359*
Gilligan, Charlie, 45

Gillis, Billy, 131, 176–177, *271–272*
girls' sports teams
    basketball, 90, 162–163, 228, 344
    field hockey, 57, 64, 74–75, 90, 228, 344
    fitness programs, 119
    Flora McLearn and, 73–74, 90, 157, 162–163, 228, 344
    gym time for, 162–163
    soccer, 348
    softball, 90, 228, 344
    . *See also* cheerleaders; drill team
Gladstone, Gary, *360*
Gloucester High School, 46, 68,128,152
    games v. SHS: 1953, 18; 1954, 33; 1962 (Jamboree), 134; 1966, 199; 1967, 216; 1968, 237; 1969, 257; 1970, 278–279; 1971, 295; 1972, 306; 1973, 326
Gnaedinger, Pete, 99, 350, *355*
Goade, Billy, 256, *358–359*
"Golden Palomino." *See* Bates, Brian
Goldman, Marty, 250, 284
Gonsalves, Danny, 24, 35
Goodman, Bob, *358–359*
Goodwin, Danny "Mumbles," 110, 117, 119, 121, 125, 129, 131
Gorman, Jimmy
    on Amherst-Williams game, 70
    Coach Bondelevitch and, 56, 67
    college and career of, 75–76
    Dick Lynch and, 72
    early years of, 11
    football team (1956), 56
    football team (1957), 59–60, 65–69, 72–73, *106, 354*
    "good cop-bad cop" act, 65–66
    Mike Powers and, 103
Gorman, Tom, 11–12, 15, 17, 20, 46, 68, 70, 97, 350
Gottfried, Alan, *357*
Gowen, Dick, 60–61, 90, 338, *354*

grass drills, 198
"Great Neck Spread" formation, 194
Greater Lynn/Swampscott All-Stars team, 86
Greater Salem/Beverly All-Stars team, 86
Greeley, Doug, *357*
Greeley, Stu, 257, 276, 289, *359*
    All-Stars (1970), 362
Greeley, Tim, 175
Green, N., *356*
Gridiron Girls, 238, 247–248
Gridiron Grits, 93
Guilford, Cookie, *358*

H
Haley, Doug, 45, 49–52, 58, *106*
Hall, Billy, 177, 297–298, 300, 307–308, 310
Hammond, Don, 80, 240
Handy, Dave, 287
Hapgood, David, *355*
Happy Jack Pass, 208
Harris, Jimmy, 325
Harvard Club, 254
Hatch, Mark, 175
Hayden, Bill, 42, 49
Hayden, John, *355*
Hayes, Paul, 214, *358*
Hayes, W., *356*
Headers. *See* Marblehead High School
Headmasters Association, 63, 100
Healey, Bill "Spider," 71
Healey, Dan "Jake," 128–129
heat stroke, 122
Hegan, Jeff, 350
    All-Stars (1972), 362
    college and career of, 320
    football team (1970), 289
    football team (1971), 293–294, 297–299, 301, *360*

football team (1972), 304, 306–309, 311, 313–315, 319, *335*, *361*

Hegan, Jim, 293

helmet sticker incentives, 143, 154

Hennessey, Ray, *355*

Henshaw, Walter, 90

Herbert, Arthur, *360*

Herlihy, Bill, 350
  All-Stars (1963), 362
  college and career of, 160
  football team (1962), 134, 138
  football team (1963), 150–152, 154–155, 159–160, *356*

Hi-Fi offense, 111

Hinch, Billy, 350
  All-Stars (1962), 362
  college and career of, 149
  football team (1961), 120, 125, 128
  football team (1962), 131–132, 137–138, 145–147, 149

Hoffman, John
  All-Stars (1972), 362
  football team (1971), 294, 296, 298, *360*
  football team (1972), *274*, 304–305, 313, 319, *361*

Hoffman, Mike, 214, 243, *273*, *357*

Hoffman, Red
  on Danvers game, 280–281
  on Dick Jauron, 224, 236
  on Dick Lynch departure, 320
  on Lynn Classical game, 145
  on Lynn English game, 308
  on recognition of Coach Bondelevitch, 332–333
  on Saugus games, 201–202, 263
  on Swampscott fans, 288
  on Swampscott player age and size, 143
  on Swampscott v. Knights of Catholic Memorial game, 320
  team assessments of, 151

on Thanksgiving Day games, 157–158, 171, 266

Holmes, Andy, 90

hook and lateral play, 169

Hopkins, Bobby, *272*
  Coach Bondelevitch and, 193
  college and career of, 209–210
  early years of, 192–193
  football team (1965), 175, 180–181
  football team (1966), 192–193, 200, 204, 207–209
  JV team and, 193
  touchdown pass record of, 209, 290

Hotel Bellevue, 8

Houghton, Charles, *358*

Hudson High School, 6, 10, 12, 18, 23, 41, 58, 346

Hughes, Dana, 287–289

Hughes, Jim, 65, 131, 253

Humphrey, John, 7

Hurley, Bob, 42

hurricane offense formation, 19, 314–315

Hussey, Herm, 37, 44, 99

hydration, 196

Hyte, Barton, *358–359*

I

Indiana Collegiate Conference (ICC), 140

Indians. *See* Amesbury High School

Ingalls, John, 123, 195

Ionic Social Club, 63, 182, 351

J

J. M. Fields Department Store, 100

Jackson Park, 9

Jacobs, Norman, 151–152, 165, *356*

Jacobs, Ricky, 165, 175, 350

Janusas, John, 67, 81–82, 97, 116

Janvrin, Mike, 94, 102, *107*, 109–110, 113, 118, *355*

Janvrin, Phil, 80, 89, 110, *355*

Jardine, Frank, 35

Jauron, Dick
  academic achievement of, 238
  as All-American, 233, 252
  All-Stars (1968), 362
  athletic ability of, 191–192, 236–237, 339
  baseball and, 339
  basketball and, 234
  on Carl Kester, 340
  character of, 227, 252
  Coach Bondelevitch and, *272*
  Coach Bondelevitch testimonial and, 254
  early years of, 146, 174–175
  football team (1966), 195–196, 198–203, 206–208, 210, *272*
  football team (1967), 213–214, 216, 219–222, 224–227, 229–233, *273, 357*
  football team (1968), 235–237, 241, 244–245, 247, 251, *358*
  freshman team (1965), 182, 192, 228
  friendships of, 244
  as halfback, 193
  love for football, 191–192
  Massachusetts scoring record of, 251–252
  naming of, 191
  national attention and, 241
  professional career of, 252, 338–339
  records and honors of, 339
  as teammate, 210, 241
  at Yale University, 252
Jauron, Katherine Strain, 140, 191, 339
Jauron, Kathy Dedrick, 340
Jauron, Michael, *336*
  as All-American, 340
  All-Stars (1973), 362
  as Big Blue waterboy, 175, 305
  at Boston University, 340
  Coach Hall and, 308, 310

football team (1972), 305–311, 313, 316–318, 320–321, *336, 361*
football team (1973), 323, 325–327, *336*
Jauron, Robert E., *272*
  All-Stars (1966), 362
  Coach Bondelevitch and, 174, 196, 205–206, 347
  college and career of, 347–348
  early years of, 168, 173
  family and, 347–348
  father and, 168–169
  football team (1965), 175–176, 183–185
  football team (1966), 200, 205–210
  move to Swampscott, 173–174
Jauron, Robert Thomas (Coach)
  at Boston College, 139, 144
  characteristics of, 192
  Coach Bondelevitch and, 191, 314
  coaching career of, 140–141, 191
  drinking problems and, 168–169
  early years of, 138–139
  as football coach, 340–341
  as golf team mentor, 341
  as 1956 Little All-American Coach of the Year, 141
  at Saint Joseph's College, 140–141
  hall of fame honors of, 340
  impact of, 341
  loss of Lynn position, 168, 173
  as Lynn coach, 141–142, 146
  Manchester Memorial teaching and coaching, 308
  media coverage of, 143–144
  military service of, 140
  move to Swampscott, 173–174
  Nashua, 138–139, 340
  parents of, 139
  sporting goods business of, 173
  sports and, 139

on Swampscott v. Classical game, 143–144
Jauron, Susan, 175
Jauron, Wayne, 146, 168
Jeffers, Dick, 12
Jenkin, Philip A., 129
Jermyn, Don, 147
Johnson, Bill, 146
Johnson, Fred, *355*
Johnson, Lyndon, 158
Johnson, Murray, 138
Johnson, Tippy, 224
Jordan, Bruce, 350
    All-Stars (1959), 362
    coaching career, 338
    college and career of, 102
    football team (1958), 79–80, *355*
    football team (1959), 91, 93–94, 98, 100, 102, *107*
    personality of, 79–80, 181
Joyce, Bill, 31
Joyce Jamboree, 31, 41, 64, 80, 111, 134, 152, 165, 199, 236–237, 257, 277

K

Kain, Peter, *361*
Karalekas, Peter, *354*
Kassoy, Mike, *360*
Keach, Fred, 294, 304–305, 307, 320, *360–361*
Keiver, Bobby, 123
Keiver, Ozzie, Jr., 123
Kelliher, Tom, 312, 329, *361*
Kennedy, John F., 158
Kessell, Sam, *355*
Kester, Carl "Mad Dog," *273*
    academic achievement of, 238
    academic career of, 253, 340
    at Amherst College, 253
    early years, 239–240
    Coach Bondelevitch and, 240, 340

Dick Jauron on, 340
    football team (1967), 214, 225, 233, *357*
    football team (1968), 235, 237–241, 243, 250, 252, *358*
    love for football, 239–240
Kester, Waldemar "Cowboy," 250, *273*, 283, 285–286
Kimball, Charley, 212
Kimball, Mike, 200
Kinsey, Ken, 167, 170, 175, 182–183
Kline, Neal, *355*
Kline, Randy, 276, 280, *359*
Knight, Dick, 169
Knights of Catholic Memorial High School
    game v. SHS, 1972, 312–320
Kruger, Steve, 276, 294, 297, 301, *360*
    All-Stars (1971), 362
Kulevich, Alex, 289, 312, 330

L

Ladd, Pat, 229–231
Ladik, John, 134
Lancers. *See* Lawrence High School
Landry, Dave, 109
Langevin, Paul, 91, *355*
Lappin, R., *356*
Lawrence High School, 75, 77, 141, 297
    games v. SHS: 1957 (Jamboree), 64; 1958 (Jamboree), 80–81; 1960 (Jamboree), 111
Leahy, Frank, 139
Leger, Dick, 97–99, 110, *355*
Legere, Henry, 120, 131, 350
Legere, Paul, 134, 150–151, *271*, 350, *356*
Legro, Frankie, 266–268
Lehman, Harry, 2
Leone, Billy
    All-Stars (1971), 362
    Coach Bondelevitch on, 301
    college and career of, 300

football team (1969), 256, 268, *359*

football team (1970), 275, 277, 287, 289

football team (1971), 293–294, 296–298, 300–301, *360*

Levesque, Jim, *355*

Lindsey, Tom, *354*

Lincoln House Hotel, 8

Lions Club, 68, 71

Lippa, Bobby, 324, 351, *361*

Little, Arthur, 8

Livingston, Tom, 205

Losano, Danny
   All-Scholastic team and, 300
   All-Stars (1971), 362
   college and career of, 300, 320
   football team (1969), 256, 263, 268, *359*
   football team (1970), 275, 277–280, 287, 289–290
   football team (1971), 293–300, 306, *334, 360*
   Thom McAn Shoe Trophy (1971), 300

Losano, Paul, *361*

Loveday, Billy, 110–112, 115–116, *355*

Loveday, Eddie
   coaching assistance of, 132
   football team (1957), 61, 66, 68–69, 72–73, *354*
   football team (1958), 78–79, 82–84, 86–87, *355*

Loveday, Elizabeth "Betsy," 124

Lowell High School, 297

Lucy, Kevin, 203

Lynch, Chuck, 53–54, 58, 61, 350, *354*

Lynch, Joanne, 27

Lynch, Mike
   All-Scholastic team and, 290
   All-Stars (1970), 362
   college and career of, 290, 341
   football team (1968), 251, *358*

football team (1969), 257–258, 260–261, 263, 267–269, *359*

football team (1970), 275–276, 278–280, 282, 286–290, *334*

Lynch, Richard "Dick," *271, 273, 334, 359*
   as baseball scout, 49
   basketball coaching of, 28, 92, 162–163, 234
   on Bobby Carlin, 47
   Camp Columbus and, 27
   Coach Bondelevitch and, 317, 331
   Coach Bondelevitch testimonial and, 254
   coaching assistants and, 176
   coaching style of, 43, 72
   as Danvers athletic director, 320, 341
   death of Agganis and, 40
   death of David Coughlin and, 121–122
   disciplinary style of, 27
   on Don Page as safety, 306
   early years of, 26
   football coaching of, 27–28, 31, 33, 37, 45, 53, 61, 79, 83–84, 92–93, 96, 103, 119, 121–122, 150–151, 160–162, 188, 193, 200, 214–215, 217, 240, 261, 265, 292, 309–310, 317, 320–321
   as gym teacher, 27–28, 79
   Jimmy Lyons and, 92–93
   on Mickey DePaolo, 167
   Mike Powers and, 92–93, 103
   at Milford (NH) High School, 26–27
   parent relations and, 92
   player development and, 321
   player nicknames by, 61
   on postseason Miami trip, 74–75
   Randy Werner and, 282–284
   recruitment efforts of, 79
   on Ronny Corcoran as safety, 119
   surgery leave and, 179, 184, 188, 190
   as track coach, 133

wit of, 26, 43, 45, 47, 49, 61, 215, 217, 341

Lynch, Terry, 275

Lynn, Mass.
athletes in, 10–11, 26, 40
Joyce Jamboree in, 31
as a manufacturing center, 7–8
merged teams in, 141–142

Lynn Classical High School, 17, 157, 327–328
combined teams and, 141
games v. SHS: 1959, 97–98; 1960, 116; 1962, 138, 142–146, 148; 1963, 155; 1964, 168–170; 1965, 183; 1966, 203; 1967, 223–227; 1968, 247; 1969, 265; 1970, 289; 1971, 298; 1972, 311; 1973, 329–330

Lynn English High School, 17, 157, 327–328
combined teams and, 141
games v. SHS: 1963 (Jamboree), 152; 1968 (Jamboree), 236–237; 1969, 258; 1970, 286; 1971, 297–298; 1972, 307–310; 1973, 329

Lynn Lions, 141–142

Lynn Technical Training High School (PKA "Lynn Trade High School")
combined teams and, 141
games v. SHS, 1953, 17; 1973, 327–328

Lynn Trade High School. See Lynn Technical Training High School

Lyons, D., 356

Lyons, Jimmy "Gangsta," 350
Boston Steamrollers and, 188
Coach Bondelevitch and, 91–92, 96
college and career of, 102
combativeness of, 80, 91–93, 95–96, 103
Dick Lynch and, 92–93
football team (1958), 79–80, 355
football team (1959), 91–98, 100–101
Mike Powers and, 91–93, 95–98

Richie Fuller and, 115
Ronny Corcoran and, 97–98

Lyons, Terry "T-Butts," 49, 91, 102, 350
All-Stars (1956), 362

Lyons, Tommy "Mash," 35–36, 91, 350

M

MacCallum, Ray, 214, 229–231, 235, 273, 357–358

MacCallum, Scottie, 318, 320, 323, 325–327, 361

MacConachie, Pete, 42

Madden, Bruce, 258

Magicians. See Marblehead High School

Maguire, Ed, 200, 202

Maguire, Paul, 223, 263–264, 266

Mahegan, Robert "Shorty," 246

Maher, Brock, 174, 323, 351

Mahoney, Billy, 169

Maitland, Dick, 60, 79, 350, 354–355

Malden Catholic High School, 313
games v. SHS: 1958, 82–84; 1963 (scrimmage), 152

Manchester Central High School, 297
game v. Manchester Memorial: 1960, 308
game v. SHS: 1965 (scrimmage), 177

Manchester Memorial High School, 295
game v Manchester Central: 1960, 308
game v. SHS: 1971 (scrimmage), 295

Manchester West High School, 308

Manganaro, Alan, 355

Mangini, Jerry, 256, 263, 267–269, 358–359

Mangini, Larry, 165, 356

Maniff, Maury, 360

Manning, Tom "Bucket," 117–118

Manning Bowl, 31, 73, 77, 81–82, 86, 97–98, 155, 157, 183, 328

Mannix, Kevin, 323

Mansfield, Bob "Bun," 12, 20, 22, 48, 87, 350

Mansfield, Ray "Buzzy," 41, 48–49, 350

Marblehead, 1, 24

Marblehead High School
  games v. SHS: 1943, 10; 1953, 24–25; 1954, 37; 1955, 44–46, 51; 1956, 57–58; 1957, 71–73; 1958, 85–86; 1959, 99, 102; 1960, 117–118; 1961, 128–129; 1962, 147–148; 1963, 156–159; 1964, 171; 1965, 183; 1966, xiii, 205–209; 1967, 232–233; 1968, 250–251; 1969, 265–268; 1970, 289–290; 1971, 299–300; 1972, 312; 1973, 329–331; 1975, 331; 1986, 341–342
  rivalry with Swampscott, 24, 35, 37, 44, 71, 85, 99, 128, 156–157, 171

Marden, Leon "Doc"
  as assistant coach, 25, 33, 65, *104*, 157, 160, *271*, 323, 351
  Coach Bondelevitch on, 161
  coaching style of, 161
  freshman team and, 19, 50, 59
  JV team and, 131
  scouting by, 19, 35

Marino, Bob, 134–136, 138, 145

Marino, Freddy, 41, 48–49, 56, 58, 350
  All-Stars (1956), 362

Martin, Harold, 2, 10, 162, 194, 239

Martin, Mike, *355*

Maselbas, Mike, 151, 165–172, *356*

Massachusetts High School Baseball Coaches Association Hall of Fame, 340

Massachusetts High School Basketball Coaches Association Hall of Fame, 338

Massachusetts High School Football Coaches Association Hall of Fame, 338, 344

Massey, Dick, 45

Massidda, Joe, 34, 42, 60

math team, 324

Matignon High School, game v. SHS: 1955, 42

Maynard High School, 5–6, 254

Mayo, Fran, 214, 231, *357*

Mazareas, Peter, 224

McDonough, Will, 131

McGettrick, Bill, *355*

McGettrick, Gerry, 214, 226, 238, *273*, 350, *357*

McGinn, Bill, 36

McKenney, John, 324, *361*

McKenney, Marty, 151, 153–155, *356*

McLaughlin, John I., 130

McLaughry, Tuss, 41

McLean, Ray "Scooter," 4

McLearn, Flora, *271*
  Barbara Segel and, 90
  Dick Lynch and, 162–163
  drill team and, 157
  as field hockey coach, 73–74
  girls' basketball team and, 162–163
  girls' sports teams and, 228, 344
  retirement of, 228
  SHS Hall of Fame and, 344

McTague, Philip, *355*

Melrose High School, 224
  game v. SHS: 1966 (scrimmage), 196

Merrimack Valley All-Star team, 77

Merrow, Bob, *358*

Methuen High School
  games v. SHS: 1952, 2; 1953, 23; 1954, 35; 1955, 44, 51–52

Mezquita, Dick, 45

Miami Edison Senior High School, 68–70, 75

Miles, John, 166

Milo, Jackie
  All-Stars (1958), 362
  Barbara Segel and, 90
  on Big Blue football, 87
  college and career of, 87
  football team (1956), 48–49, 56
  football team (1957), 61, 65–66, 68, *354*

football team (1958), 78, 80–81, 84, 86–87, *355*
 impact of, 115
 SHS Hall of Fame and, 87
 Thom McAn Shoe Trophy (1958), 87
Milo, Larry, *355*
Moore, Brad, 250
Moore, Brian, 214
Moore, Tobey, 109, 117, *355*
Moran, Larry
 football team (1970), 275, 277, 287, 289
 football team (1971), 293, 295–299, *360*
Morash, Jim, 294, 298, 320, *360*
Moreau, Dan, *359*
Moriarty, George, 116, 169, 224, 226
Moriarty, Richie, 169–170
Moses, Bob, 294, *360*
Mosho, Ben, 257, *359*
Mosho, Steve, 195
mouth guards, 135, 218
Murphy, Mike, 298
Murray, Bobby, 276, 294–295, 297–299, 301, *334, 360*
Murray, Greg, 180, 194
Murray, Peter, *357–358*
Murray, Richard, 194
Murray, Tommy "Rabbit," 170, 193–194, 200, 207, 209
 All-Stars (1966), 362

N

Nash, Bobby, 142–145, 160
Naumkeag Indians, 7
Nelson, Billy, 32–33, 41–42, 44, 282, 350
Nelson, Ed, *355*
Nevils, Tim, 65, 79, 350, *354–355*
New Ocean House Hotel, 1, 7, 9, 255, 349, 351
Newburyport High School

games v. SHS: 1958, 84; 1959, 98–99; 1960, 116–117; 1961, 128; 1962, 146–147; 1963, 156; 1964, 170; 1965, 183; 1966, 203–204; 1967, 228–231; 1968, 248–249; 1969, 265; 1970, 289; 1971, 298–299; 1972, 311
Norden, Roy, 120
Northeastern Conference, 9, 63, 160, 289, 304, 332

O

O'Bara, Ed, 203, 229–231, 248
O'Brien, Joey, 313, 316, 318–319
O'Brien, Mark, 325
Ocean House, 7
 . *See also* New Ocean House Hotel
O'Connor, Jim, 315
Olsson, Bill, 166
Olsson, Ron, 166
Oniontowners. *See* Danvers High School
Orlando, Ambrose, 278
Orloff, Gary, 294, 304–305, 307, 312, 319, *360–361*
Orloff, Marty, 263, *359*
Ormiston, John, 205, 207
Osgood, Bob, 263
O'Shea, Tom, *357–358*
Ostrovitz, Roy
 football team (1970), 289
 football team (1971), 294, 299, 301, *360*
 football team (1972), *274*, 304, 313, 318–319, *361*
Oswald, Lee Harvey, 158
Owens, Al, 32, 34, 350
 All-Stars (1954), 362
Owens, Dick, *354*

P

Page, Donnie, 350
 as 1972 Super Bowl MVP, 319, *335*

college and career of, 320

football team (1971), 294, 296–297, *360*

football team (1972), 304–307, 311, 313, 316–319, *335, 361*

Pagnotti, Mike "Skip," 250, *273*

Pagnotti, Paul, *355*

Palleschi, Arthur, 100–101, 164, 350, *355*

Palleschi, Bill, 325, *361*

Palleschi, Paul, *360*

Palmquist, Bill, *355*

Panthers. *See* Beverly High School

Paolini, Jim, 200, 202

Paradise Dairy Bar, 93

Parents Clinics, 29–31, 40–41, 63, 110

Parents Day, 1963, 153

Parker, Jack, 208

Parsons, Frank, 60–61, 65–66, 73, *354*

Parsons, William, 235–236

Patrinos, Dr., 302

Patriots. *See* Revere High School

Peabody High School, 141, 297

game v. SHS: 1970 (Jamboree), 277

Peckham, W., *356*

Pedro, Pete, 224

Perrone, Ken, 325

Perry, Ron, 313

Peters, Tom, *355*

Petersen, Donny, 175

Phillips High School, 9

. *See also* Swampscott High School (SHS)

Phillips Park, 1, 9, 13, 62, 134, 211

Picariello, C., *356*

Pierre, Tony, 250

placekickers, 196

Pleau, George, 81–82, 292–293, *334*, 350, *355*

Polio Bowl Game, 77, 86

Polisson, Dick, 213, 229–231, 233, *273, 357*

All-Stars (1967), 362

Poltrino, A., *356*

Pop Warner football teams, 78, 323

Popp, Dennis, *358*

Porter, Billy, 175

Porter, Buddy, *357–358*

Powers, Billy, 91

Powers, Mike

Coach Bondelevitch and, 96

combativeness of, 91–93, 95–96

Dick Lynch and, 92–93, 103

early years of, 91

football and, 102–103

football team (1958), 79–81, *355*

football team (1959), 91–101, *107*, 110

Jim Gorman on, 103

Jimmy Lyons and, 91–93, 95–98

Richie Fuller and, 115

Ronny Corcoran and, 97–98

Preston Beach Inn, 8, 351

Prince, Daynor, 147, 159

pro-T formation, 151

Providence Steamrollers, 4, 47, 188

R

Radcliffe, Bob, 117–118

Rafter, Ted, 97, 109, 120, 125, 131

Ragucci, Paul, 313, 315–316, 320

Rams. *See* Lynn Classical High School

Randell, Jim, 109, 111, 118, *355*

All-Stars (1960), 362

Reading High School

games v. SHS: 1953, 17; 1954, 32

Reardon, Carl, 178, 324

Rebholz, Bobby, 214, 232–233, *357*

Reebenacker, Noel, 99, 117, 128, 147, 157, 171, 203, 220, 222, 228, 232, 260, 266

Repetto, Andy, 125, 131

Revere High School

games v. SHS: 1954 (Jamboree), 32;
1956, 57; 1957, 69; 1965, 179; 1966
(scrimmage), 196; 1969 (Jamboree),
257

Ribicanti, Don, *359*

Richard Lynch Gymnasium, 341

Riley, Kevin, 276, 289, 294, 298, *359–360*

Rillovick, Matt, 249–250

Rindge Tech School
games v. SHS: 1956, 57; 1957, 70

Ring, Bill, 350, *354*

Riser, Chris, *357*

Rizzo, Charlie, 175

Robarts, Jack, 71

Roderick, S., *356*

Roger, Bertrand, 289, 302

Rogosa, Howie, *360*

Rose, Andy
All-Stars (1968), 362
Big Blue sports and, 339
Billy Adams and, 219
Coach Bondelevitch and, 218
college and career of, 253
football team (1967), 214, 217–220,
233, *273*, *357*
football team (1968), 235, 237–238,
244, 251–253, *358*
Frank DeFelice and, 219, 244, 251

Rose, Nicole, 339

Rose, W., *356*

Rossman, Jeff, 195, 200, 204

Rossman, Neil, 195, *356*

Rothwell, Bill "Rocky," 134, 138

Rothwell, Eliot, 60–61, 69, 73, *354*

Rothwell, Jim, 42, 350

Rousseau, George, *104*

Rowe, Stephen, *359*

Ruby, Jack, 158

Ruddock, Charlie, 258

Rundle, Randy, 266, 289–290, 299–300

Russell, Larry, 183, 203–204

Ryan, Barry, 175, 181, 350

Ryan, Jim, 12, 350
All-Stars (1953), 362

S

Sachems. *See* Saugus High School

Sack, Peter, 342

Saint John the Evangelist Elementary
School, 8, 11

Saint John's Preparatory School
games v. SHS: 1970, 286–288; 1971,
298

Saint Joseph's College, 140, 191

Saint Mary's High School
games v. SHS: 1955, 44; 1956, 56–57;
1961 (Jamboree), 120–121

Salem, 7

Salem/Beverly All-Star Teams, 86

Salem High School, 159, 232, 258, 332
games v. SHS: 1955 (Jamboree), 41;
1967 (scrimmage and Jamboree),
216; 1972, 305–306; 1973, 325–326

Santanello, Steven, 350
football team (1961), 120, 125–126,
128
football team (1962), 131, 133–138,
145

Santanello, Tom, 95–96, 110, 350, *355*

Santangelo, Fred, 185

Sapira, Sam, 142–143

Sarno, Moody, 10

Sarra, Suzanne, 344

Saugus High School
games v. SHS: 1957, 66–68; 1958,
81–82; 1959, 97; 1960, 116; 1961,
126; 1962, 138; 1963, 154–155;
1964, 167–168; 1965, 182–183;
1966, 200–202; 1967, 223; 1968,
247; 1969, 262–264; 1970, 279–280;
1971, 295; 1972, 306; 1973, 326

Saunders, Wayne, 278

Savatsky, Bruce, 294, 298, 300–301, *360*
All-Stars (1971), 362

Savatsky, Gary
  All-Stars (1966), 362
  college and career of, 209
  football team (1965), 175–176
  football team (1966), 193–194, 200,
    207, 209
Savino, Tony, 48–49, 53, 58
Schawbel, Steven, *355*
Scholastic Roto Magazine, 238
Segel, Barbara, 90–91, 344
Segel, Linda, 90
Sentner, Billy, 57, 79
Sentner, George, 124
Serino, Al, 175–176, 195
Serino, Bob, 343
Serino, Chris, 200, 202
Serino, Vinny, 175–176, 195, *272*
Shadoff, Ronnie, *360*
Shapiro, Steve "Silky," 175
Shaw, Winslow
  All-Stars (1953), 362
  on Coach Bondelevitch, 348–350
  Coach Bondelevitch testimonial and,
    254
  college and career of, 38, 348
  football team (1954), 32, 34, 36, 38
Sheehan, Fran, 217
Sheperd, Steve, 175–176, 195, *272*
Sheridan, Brad, 190
Sheridan, Walter, 86, 167, 182, 200, 202,
  223
Shoer, Faith, 344
SHS. *See* Swampscott High School (SHS)
S.H.S. Teams of Yesterday exhibit, 250
Shub, Ed, 250
Shulman, Richard, *355*
Shumrak, Mike, 195
Silvonic, Jimmy, 224, 226, 247
Silvonic, Joey, 142, 145
Singleton, Dave, 313, 316, 318–319
Sjogren, Billy

All-Stars (1962), 362
baseball and, 132
college and career of, 148
early years of, 131–132
football team (1961), 120–121, 125
football team (1962), 131–132, 134,
  136–137, 143, 148
Thom McAn Shoe Trophy (1962), 148
Smith, Bob, 175
Smith, Peter, 132, 134, *355–356*
Smith, Wayne
  college and career of, 320
  football team (1971), 294, 298–299,
    301, *360*
  football team (1972), *274*, 304–306,
    309, 312–313, 319–320, *361*
Snyder, Mike, 325
Sogoloff, B., *356*
Somerby, Phil, *354–355*
Soutter, S., *356*
Spain, Lloyd, *355*
Spediacci, Bob, 134, 148
Spelta, Gino, *355*
Spence, Richard, *355*
spirit squad, 93, 99, 141
Squires, Jack, 223
Squires, John "Squirrel"
  as Big Blue waterboy, 223
  college and career of, 253
  early years of, 223
  football team (1967), 214, 220,
    222–223, *357*
  football team (1968), 235, 237, *358*
St. Anselm College
  Anselmian Athletic Club Hall of Fame,
    344
  Coach Bondelevitch at, 3–4
  training camp at, 211–213, 217, 229,
    235, 240, 295
St. Pierre, Ken, 258–259
St. Pierre, Ted, 326

Stehlin, Jim, 203, 216, 229, 231, 265
Stein, Ken, 79, *354–355*
Stevenson, Dick, 351
   on Big Blue name, 28
   as coaching assistant, 13, 25, 31, 33, 53, 60, *104*, 115, 131
   coaching style of, 198–199
   death of David Coughlin and, 131
   football team (1957), *354*
   as teacher and administrator, 13
Stevenson, Mark
   as All-American, 209
   All-Stars (1966), 362
   college and career of, 209
   football team (1965), 175–176, 180
   football team (1966), 194–195, 205–206, 209, 242, *272*
   Frank DeFelice and, 292
Stinson, George, 12
Stone, Alex, 343–344
Stone, Myron, 174, 250, 343–344
Stone, Roz, 174, 343
Stone, Sam, 343, *357*
Stoneham High School, game v. SHS: 1955, 44
Stoughton High School
   games v. SHS: 1953, 24; 1954, 35
Strain, Katherine. *See* Jauron, Katherine Strain
Strauss, W., *356*
Sullivan, Dan, 203
Sullivan, Mike, 229
Sundell, Janice Maselbas, 344
Surf Theatre, 351
Swampscott, Mass.
   early history of, 7–8
   football enthusiasm of, 23, 25, 59, 68, 141, 181–182, 238, 250, 326
   recreation in, 8–9, 114
   schools in, 8
   as a summer resort, 7–8
   youth sports program in, 57, 59, 78, 119
Swampscott fight song, 99
Swampscott Gridiron Club, 342
Swampscott High School football
   All-Stars (1953–1973), 362
   coaching of, 2, 10, 340–343. *See also* Baldacci, Dick; Bondelevitch, Stanley W.; Bush, Bill; Corcoran, Ron; DeFelice, Frank; Dembowski, Steve; Foster, Harold "Hal"; Gillis, Billy; Hughes, Jim; Lynch, Richard "Dick"; Lehman, Harry; Marden, Leon "Doc"; Martin, Harold; Parsons, Bill; Serino, Bob; Stevenson, Dick; York, Fran
   coaching staff, *104*
   community involvement in, 23, 59, 63, 68, 141, 174–175, 181–182, 326, 351
   competition with, 332
   freshman team, 20, 50, 69, 71, 73, 85, 87, 110, 182, 276, 279
   game plans for, 19
   hurricane offense formation, 19
   JV team, 30, 40, 45, 57, 60–61, 73, 87, 110, 133, 164, 184, 276, 279
   Lions Club support, 68, 71
   Marblehead rivalry and, 24, 35, 37, 44, 71, 85, 99, 128, 156–157, 171
   media coverage of, 261–262
   national attention and, 238
   play terminology, 14
   player size and speed, 33–34
   resentment of, 261–262
   season records (1953–1973), 353
   spirit and pride in, 16, 23–24, 93–94, 206
   St. Anselm College training camp and, 211–213, 217, 229, 235, 240, 295
   strength and conditioning program, 211, 214, 217, 235, 257, 283
   success of, 331–332, 342–343, 348

titles, xiii, xiv, 75, 86, 160, 252, 268, 291, 300, 312, 319, 331, 343

wing-T offense formation, 14, 62, 151, 195, 279

youth feeder program for, 40, 57, 59, 78, 323

Swampscott High School Athletic Hall of Fame, 87, 120, 161, 172, 340, 344

Swampscott High School (SHS), *104*

appreciation for support by, 16, 93, 181–182, 324

athletic conference, 9

early history of, 9

S.H.S. Teams of Yesterday exhibit, 250

Swampscott Little League, 90

Swampscott school band, 16, 73, 93, 99, *105*, 141, 153, 157, 181

Swampscott Sculpins

coaching of, 10–11

losing seasons of, 2

name change of, 28

rivalry with Marblehead Magicians, 24

success of, 10, 17–18, 22–23

. *See also* Swampscott High School football

T

tackle-fumble football, 50, 114

Tamborini, Ron, 257, *359*

Tamborini, T., *356*

Tanners. *See* Woburn High School

Tassinari, Tony, 18, 34, 43

Tech Tigers. *See* Lynn Technical Training High School

Tennant, Alexander "Sandy"

All-Stars (1969), 362

Coach Bondelevitch on, 256

Coach Bondelevitch testimonial and, 338

early years of, 215

football team (1967), 215–216, 219–220, 229, 231, 233, *357*

football team (1968), 235, 237, 247, 252, *358*

football team (1969), 255–260, 268–269, *359*

Thom McAn Shoe Trophy, 46, 87, 118, 148, 233, 252, 269, 300, 362

Tierney, Dorothy "Dot." *See* Bondelevitch, Dorothy Tierney

Tilden, R., *356*

Tomeo, Mike, 86

Toner, Billy, 214, 257, 339, *358–359*

Toner, Ed, 214

Toner, Ed, Jr., 339

Toner, John, 214, 339

All-Stars (1972), 362

college and career of, 320

football team (1971), 294, 297–298, *360*

football team (1972), *274*, 304–307, 311–312, 314, 316–317, 319–320, *361*

Toner, Mark, 214

Toner, Paul, 214

Toner, Tommy, 350

college and career of, 252–253, 338

death of, 339

football team (1967), 214–216, 225, 230–233, *273, 357*

football team (1968), 235, 237, 246, 252, *358*

personality, 237

on Swampscott football, 338

Tracy, George, 328

Tumulty, Mike, 325, *361*

V

Vernava, Michael, *357*

Veterans Memorial Fieldhouse, 1, 9, 258, 303

Videtta, Dan

football team (1967), 214, 216, 220–221, 226, 229–233, *273, 357*

Vikings. *See* Winthrop High School

Viola, Al, 254

Vousboukis, Bill, *360–361*

Vousboukis, Dan, *354*

W

Wakefield High School, game v. SHS:
1966 (Jamboree), 199

Waldman, Steve, *355*

Walker, Norman, 17, 32, 34, 38, 350

Walker, Rusty, 305, 308, 310, 318, 338,
360–361

Waltham High School, 73, 75, 80,
games v SHS: 1957 (scrimmage),
62–63; 1963 (scrimmage), 152

Weiss, Marc, 311, *360–361*

Werner, Randi, 290–291

Werner, Randy "Hawk"

Coach Bondelevitch and, 286

college and career of, 290–291

Dick Lynch and, 282–284

family life of, 281–282, 284, 290

football team (1968), 238, *358*

football team (1969), 257, *359*

football team (1970), 276, 281,
284–285, 290–291

Frank DeFelice and, 281–286

JV basketball and, 283

marriage to Randi, 290–291

Waldemar Kester and, 283, 285–286

Wharff, Bill

Coach Bondelevitch on, 301

college and career of, 320

football team (1971), 294, 297, 299,
301, *360*

football team (1972), 304–307,
312–313, 320, *361*

Whips. *See* Marblehead High School

White Court, 8

White, Walter, 112, 124

white socks speech, 264

Willey House, 8, 351

Williams, Ben, 214, *273, 357*

Williams, J. F., 126, 143, 252, 297, 328

Wilson, Paul, *355*

wing-T offense formation, 14, 62, 151,
195, 279

Winick, Dick, 61, 65–66, 68, *354*

Winthrop, 54

Winthrop High School

games v. SHS: 1953, 18; 1954, 34;
1955, 42–43; 1956, 54–56; 1957,
65–66; 1958, 82; 1959, 96; 1960,
113, 115; 1961, 125; 1962, 136–137;
1963, 153–154; 1964, 166; 1965,
181; 1966, 200; 1967, 220–222;
1968, 246; 1969, 259–260; 1970,
281; 1971, 296–297; 1972, 307;
1973, 327

Witches. *See* Salem High School

Woburn High School

conference titles, 33

games v. SHS: 1954, 32; 1955, 42;
1956, 53; 1957, 65; 1958, 80–81;
1959, 94; 1960, 112; 1962, 135;
1963, 152; 1964, 165; 1965,
179–180; 1966, 199; 1967, 219–220;
1968, 237–238

Wolfe, Mike, 328

Wood, Billy, 60, 350, *354*

Wood, Doug, 260–261

Y

York, Fran "Rudy," 293, 322, *334, 337*

York, Phyllis, 293

Young, Rick, 294, *360*

Yozell, Barbara Segel. *See* Segel, Barbara

Z

Zagaeski, Paul, 266

Zeno, Joe, 73

Zuchero, Steve, *274,* 294, 304–305, 319,
360–361